Hands-On Software Architecture with Golang

Design and architect highly scalable and robust applications using Go

Jyotiswarup Raiturkar

Hands-On Software Architecture with Golang

Commissioning Editor: Merint Mathew
Acquisition Editor: Chaitanya Nair
Content Development Editor: Rohit Kumar Singh
Technical Editor: Ketan Kamble
Copy Editor: Safis Editing
Project Coordinator: Vaidehi Sawant
Proofreader: Safis Editing
Indexer: Tejal Daruwale Soni
Graphics: Alishon Mendonsa
Production Coordinator: Arvindkumar Gupta

First published: December 2018

Production reference: 1071218

Published by Packt Publishing Ltd.
Livery Place
35 Livery Street
Birmingham
B3 2PB, UK.

ISBN 978-1-78862-259-2

www.packtpub.com

`mapt.io`

Mapt is an online digital library that gives you full access to over 5,000 books and videos, as well as industry leading tools to help you plan your personal development and advance your career. For more information, please visit our website.

Why subscribe?

- Spend less time learning and more time coding with practical ebooks and videos from over 4,000 industry professionals

- Improve your learning with Skill Plans built especially for you

- Get a free ebook or video every month

- Mapt is fully searchable

- Copy and paste, print, and bookmark content

Packt.com

Did you know that Packt offers ebook versions of every book published, with PDF and ePub files available? You can upgrade to the ebook version at `www.packt.com` and as a print book customer, you are entitled to a discount on the ebook copy. Get in touch with us at `customercare@packtpub.com` for more details.

At `www.packt.com`, you can also read a collection of free technical articles, sign up for a range of free newsletters, and receive exclusive discounts and offers on Packt books and ebooks.

Contributors

About the author

Jyotiswarup Raiturkar has architected products ranging from high-volume e-commerce sites to core infrastructure products. Notable products include the Walmart Labs Ecommerce Fulfillment Platform, Intuit Mint, SellerApp, Goibibo, Microsoft Virtual Server, and ShiftPixy, to name a few. Nowadays, he codes in Golang, Python, and Java.

About the reviewer

Peter Malina is a CTO at a Brno-based software agency called FlowUp. He is a cloud lover, a bleeding-edge technology pioneer, and a Golang and Angular specialist. He also is a speaker at local events and is an enthusiastic Kubernetes and GCP solution architect.

Packt is searching for authors like you

If you're interested in becoming an author for Packt, please visit `authors.packtpub.com` and apply today. We have worked with thousands of developers and tech professionals, just like you, to help them share their insight with the global tech community. You can make a general application, apply for a specific hot topic that we are recruiting an author for, or submit your own idea.

Table of Contents

Preface

Golang was conceived and built at Google around 2007 by Robert Griesemer, Rob Pike, and Ken Thompson. The objective was to build a pragmatic programming language to handle large code bases, complex multi-threading scenarios, and multi-core processors. Version 1.0 went out in March 2012, and since then, the language has grown in leaps and bounds in terms of popularity. Developers like me love its simplicity, expressiveness, explicit nature, and awesome community.

Having built a few production-grade applications in Go over the past few years, I have tried to distill my learning from a hands-on architect perspective in this book. Primarily, the book is a broad overview of the Go ecosystem, but at a few junctures, we deep dive and write code to demonstrate the theory. Finally, we build a non-trivial e-commerce application using the learned constructs!

Who this book is for

Today, the majority of backend software is still in languages such as Java, C++, and C#. Companies have invested a lot in these technologies and they are sometimes apprehensive about newer tech, including Go. This book is for software developers, architects, and CTOs, in similar situations, looking to use Go in their software architecture to build production-grade applications and migrating from other platforms.

What this book covers

Chapter 1, *Building Big with Go*, takes a broad view of what considerations are needed when setting out to build mission-critical software. It gives an overview of microservices and how Go is a good fit for this architectural paradigm. We end the chapter with a quick tour of Go, for the sake of those who are new to the language.

Chapter 2, *Packaging Code*, delves into ways of organizing code at various levels in Go. It looks at project organization, packages, object orientation, and structuring tests. Many first timers get the encapsulation wrong, leading to unmanageable code or cyclic dependencies later on. This chapter provides pointers on how to avoid these and structure code for feature velocity.

Chapter 3, *Design Patterns*, takes us through various design patterns, such as the creational, structural, and behavioral design patterns, looking at descriptions of each pattern and examining the Go code for each implementation. We also look at the general principles of class (struct/interface) design.

Chapter 4, *Scaling Applications*, explores what scalability means, and how to quantify systems in terms of scalability. We describe how to scale algorithms and data structures, and how to identify bottlenecks and alleviate them. Then we'll look at ways of running multiple application instances and what mechanisms work best for different use cases.

Chapter 5, *Going Distributed*, looks at building distributed systems in Go, as your application is not going to run on a single machine. The chapter starts by listing common fallacies when it comes to distributed systems. It goes into detail on the common problems, such as consensus and consistency, and the patterns and protocols for solving them. We then go deep into various distributed architectures.

Chapter 6, *Messaging*, covers some messaging theory and then dives into Apache Kafka and NSQ—a brokerless messaging platform. Messaging systems are described in detail, and illustrated with code. This chapter also describes various messaging patterns, such as request-reply, fan-out, and pipes-and-filters.

Chapter 7, *Building APIs*, shows how to build REST and GraphQL services in Go. APIs are the *lingua franca* of the microservices world. At the end, the chapter takes a deep dive into Go-Kit, a collection of packages that together give a slightly opinionated framework for quickly building a service-oriented architecture.

Chapter 8, *Modeling Data*, starts off by introducing the entity-relationship way of modeling data. It then describes various persistence stores (such as relational databases, key-value stores, and column-oriented stores). This chapter takes a deep dive into MySQL, Redis, and Cassandra, the most commonly used storage technologies. This chapter outlines the architecture of the stores and showcases the Go code for interacting with them.

Chapter 9, *Anti-Fragile Systems*, explores various facets of building resilient systems, from *ruggedizing* individual services to achieving high availability. Each of these facets need to work together to enable systems that thrive under stress. We describe common patterns such as Hystrix and explain how to implement them in Go. The chapter also briefly covers disaster recovery and business continuity.

Chapter 10, *Case Study – Travel Website*, details some high-level architecture, low-level design, and key code constructs. Having a sense of the various building blocks, we will build an e-commerce app – a travel website, to be exact. Essentially, we will use everything we will have learned so far to build a non-trivial system.

Chapter 11, *Planning for Deployment*, discusses deployment considerations for Go programs. These includes things such as **Continuous Integration and Continuous Deployment (CICD)** pipelines, as well as application monitoring using tools such as New Relic. We build a robust CICD pipeline for a sample program using Jenkins and tools such as `fmt` and `lint` to ensure code quality before the push to production.

Chapter 12, *Migrating Applications*, describes a migration strategy that systematically moves relevant/critical parts of your applications to Go and showcases the business value of doing so at every stage. In this final chapter of the book, I also describe my experience with hiring and staffing a team for Go development—a common concern for many companies.

To get the most out of this book

You will need to install all the tools that are required to run Go programs on your computer; this includes the following:

- Go (preferably v 0.9).
- An editor. Nothing fancy needed; Sublime Text will do just fine.
- Also, a few chapters deal with Cassandra, Kafka, Redis, and NSQ. All of these can be installed on a regular laptop. On a Mac, all of them are available via Homebrew. The latest stable version should be fine for all of them.

As you read a chapter, be sure to consider what you are learning and try to play around with the code. These moments will help you distill and crystallize the concepts you encounter.

Download the example code files

You can download the example code files for this book from your account at www.packt.com. If you purchased this book elsewhere, you can visit www.packt.com/support and register to have the files emailed directly to you.

You can download the code files by following these steps:

1. Log in or register at www.packt.com.
2. Select the **SUPPORT** tab.
3. Click on **Code Downloads & Errata**.
4. Enter the name of the book in the **Search** box and follow the onscreen instructions.

Once the file is downloaded, please make sure that you unzip or extract the folder using the latest version of:

- WinRAR/7-Zip for Windows
- Zipeg/iZip/UnRarX for Mac
- 7-Zip/PeaZip for Linux

The code bundle for the book is also hosted on GitHub at `https://github.com/PacktPublishing/Hands-On-Software-Architecture-with-Golang`. In case there's an update to the code, it will be updated on the existing GitHub repository.

We also have other code bundles from our rich catalog of books and videos available at `https://github.com/PacktPublishing/`. Check them out!

Download the color images

We also provide a PDF file that has color images of the screenshots/diagrams used in this book. You can download it here: `http://www.packtpub.com/sites/default/files/downloads/9781788622592_ColorImages.pdf`.

Conventions used

There are a number of text conventions used throughout this book.

`CodeInText`: Indicates code words in text, database table names, folder names, filenames, file extensions, pathnames, dummy URLs, user input, and Twitter handles. Here is an example: "Then you can enable it for remote invocation using the `rpc` package."

A block of code is set as follows:

```
type Args struct {
    A, B int
}

type MuliplyService struct{}

func (t *Arith) Do(args *Args, reply *int) error {
    *reply = args.A * args.B
    return nil
}
```

When we wish to draw your attention to a particular part of a code block, the relevant lines or items are set in bold:

```
type Args struct {
    A, B int
}

type MuliplyService struct{}

func (t *Arith) Do(args *Args, reply *int) error {
    *reply = args.A * args.B
    return nil
}
```

Bold: Indicates a new term, an important word, or words that you see onscreen. For example, words in menus or dialog boxes appear in the text like this. Here is an example: "Select **System info** from the **Administration** panel."

Warnings or important notes appear like this.

Tips and tricks appear like this.

Get in touch

Feedback from our readers is always welcome.

General feedback: If you have questions about any aspect of this book, mention the book title in the subject of your message and email us at customercare@packtpub.com.

Errata: Although we have taken every care to ensure the accuracy of our content, mistakes do happen. If you have found a mistake in this book, we would be grateful if you would report this to us. Please visit www.packt.com/submit-errata, selecting your book, clicking on the Errata Submission Form link, and entering the details.

Piracy: If you come across any illegal copies of our works in any form on the Internet, we would be grateful if you would provide us with the location address or website name. Please contact us at copyright@packt.com with a link to the material.

If you are interested in becoming an author: If there is a topic that you have expertise in and you are interested in either writing or contributing to a book, please visit authors.packtpub.com.

Reviews

Please leave a review. Once you have read and used this book, why not leave a review on the site that you purchased it from? Potential readers can then see and use your unbiased opinion to make purchase decisions, we at Packt can understand what you think about our products, and our authors can see your feedback on their book. Thank you!

For more information about Packt, please visit packt.com.

Building Big with Go

1

It's easy to solve small confined problems with limited constraints. It's also easy to comprehend and mentally model requirements and build a solution. However, as problems become more complex or constraints add up, problem-solving without a plan more often than not ends in failure. On the other hand, sometimes we overdo planning and are left with little room to react to new situations as they crop up. Architecture is the fine act of balancing the long versus the short.

This chapter asks the question: *Why engineer software?*. It outlines the elements needed for making and executing a blueprint for a successful software product. The topics covered in this chapter include the following:

- Problem solving for the big picture and the role that the architect is supposed to play in this
- The basic tenets of software architecture
- A deep dive into microservices
- Introduction to Golang

Problem solving for the big picture

Suppose you're planning a trip from New York to Los Angeles. There are two major aspects that you need to keep in mind:

- What do you need to do before starting the trip?
- What do you need to do during the trip to ensure that you stay on the right track?

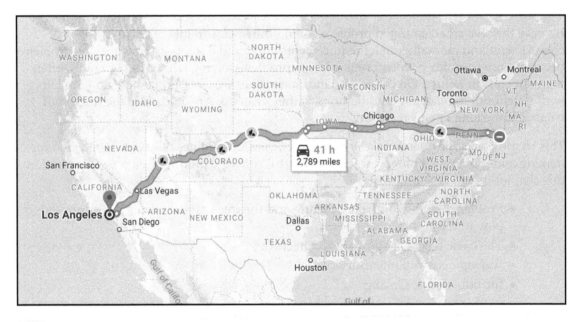

Generally, there are two extreme options in planning for such a trip:

- Take your car and start driving. Figure things out along the way.
- Make a very detailed plan—figure out the route, note down the directions at every junction, plan for contingencies such as a flat tire, plan where you're going to stop, and so on.

The first scenario allows you to execute fast. The problem is that, more likely than not, your trip will be very adventurous. Most likely, your route will not be optimal. If you want to update your friend in LA on when you'll be reaching the destination, your estimates will vary wildly based on your current situation. Without a long-term plan, planning for an outcome in the future is best effort.

But the other extreme is also fraught with pitfalls. Every objective has time constraints, and spending time over-analyzing something might mean that you miss the bus (or car). More frequently, if you give these directions to someone else and, at a juncture, reality turns out not to be what you predicted, then the driver is left with little room to improvise.

Extending the analogy, the architecture of a software product is the plan for the journey of building a product that meets the requirements of the customers and other stakeholders, including the developers themselves!

 Writing code for computers to understand and use to solve a problem has become easy. Modern tools do all of the heavy lifting for us. They suggest syntax, they optimize instructions, and they even correct some of our mistakes. But writing code that can be understood by other developers, works within multiple constraints, and evolves with changing requirements is an extremely hard thing to do.

Architecture is the shape given to a system by those who build it. Shape essentially means the constituent components, the arrangement of those components, and the ways in which those components communicate with each other. The purpose of that shape is to facilitate the development, deployment, operation, and maintenance of the software system contained within it. In today's world of ever changing requirements, building a platform on which we can execute quickly and effectively is the key to success.

The role of the architect

An architect is not a title or a rank; it's a role. The primary responsibility of the architect is to define a blueprint for what needs to be built and ensure that the rest of the team has sufficient details to get the job done. The architect guides the rest of the team toward this design during execution, while managing constant dialogues with all of the stakeholders.

The architect is also a sounding board for both developers and non-technical stakeholders, in terms of what is possible, what is not, and the cost implications (in terms of effort, trade-offs, technical debt, and so on) of various options.

It's possible to do the architect's job without coding. But in my personal opinion, this leads to stunted design. It's not possible to come up with a great design unless we understand the low-level details, constraints, and complexity. Many organizations dismiss the architect's role because of their negative experiences of architects that dictate from ivory towers and aren't engaged with the actual task of building working software. But, on the other hand, not having a blueprint can lead to a wild west code base, with small changes causing non-intuitive effects, in terms of effort and the quality of the product.

This book is not a theoretical study in software engineering. This book is meant for architects who want to build awesome, reliable, and high-performance products, while being in the kitchen as the product is getting built!

So what are the guidance systems or guard rails that the architect is expected to deliver on? Essentially, the team needs the following things from an architect.

Requirements clarification

Clarifying and distilling the top-level functional and nonfunctional requirements of the software is a key prerequisite for success. If you don't know what to build, your chances of building something that customers want are pretty slim. Product managers often get caught up on features, but rarely ask what non-functional requirements (or system qualities) the customers need. Sometimes, stakeholders will tell us that the system must be fast, but that's far too subjective. Non-functional requirements need to be specific, measurable, achievable, and testable if we are going to satisfy them. The architect needs to work with all stakeholders and ensure that functional and nonfunctional requirements are well crystallized and consumable for development.

In today's agile world, requirement analysis is an almost ongoing activity. But the architect helps the team navigate the requirements and take decisions on what to do (which may not always be so obvious).

True North

Besides the requirements, we need to define key engineering principles for the system. These principles include the following:

- **High-level design**: This is the decomposition of the system into high-level components. This serves as the blueprint that the product and code need to follow at every stage of the product development life cycle. For example, once we have a layered architecture (see the following section), then we can easily identify for any new requirement to which layer each new component should go to.
- **Quality attributes**: We want high quality code, and this means no code checking would be allowed without unit tests and 90% code coverage.

- **Product velocity**: The product has a bounded value in time and, to ensure that there is high developer productivity, the team should build **Continuous Integration / Continuous Deployment** (**CICD**) pipelines from the start.
- **A/B testing**: Every feature should have a flag, so that it can be shown only to an x percentage of users.

These generic guidelines or principles, along with the high-level design, help the team to make decisions at every stage.

Technology selection

Once we have an architecture, we need to define things, such as the programming languages and frameworks, and make source-versus-build choices for individual constructs. This can include database selection, vendor selection, technology strategy, deployment environment, upgrade policies, and so on. The sum of these factors can often make a straightforward task of choosing something simple into a complete nightmare. And then, finally, all of these technologies have to actually work well together.

Leadership in the kitchen

Once the team starts executing, the architect needs to provide technical leadership to the team. This does not mean taking every technical decision, but implies having ownership and ensuring that the individual components being built add up to the blueprint made. The architect sells the vision to the team at every design review meeting. Sometimes, steering needs to happen, in the form of tough questions asked to the developers in the design review (rather than prescribing solutions).

Coaching and mentoring

The developers working on such a product often need, and seek out, coaching and mentoring outside of their immediate deliverables. One of their core objectives is to learn, discuss tough problems, and improve their skills. Not having an environment where such interactions are facilitated leads to frustrations and developer churn.

While managing the technical stewardship of the product, many times, the architect needs to play the coach and mentor role for the developers. This could involve things ranging from technical feedback sessions to career counseling.

Target state versus current state

When architects and developers are given requirements, they often come up with beautiful and elegant designs. But generally, once the project kicks off, there is pressure on the team to deliver quickly. The business stakeholders want something out fast (a *Minimum Viable Product*), rather than wait for the *Grand Final Product* to be released. This makes sense in terms of de-risking the product and provides key feedback to the team, in terms of whether the product is fulfilling business requirements or not.

But this mode of operation also has a significant cost. Developers cut corners while building the project in order to meet the deadlines. Hence, even though we have a clean, beautiful *target state* in terms of architecture, the reality will not match this.

Having this mismatch is not wrong; rather, it's natural. But it is important for the team to have the target state in mind and define the next set of bite-sized chunks to take the product to the target state during each sprint. This means the architect needs to get involved in sprint planning for the team, along with the product and engineering managers.

Software architecture

This section briefly explores the tenants of software architecture, its relationship with design, and various architectural lenses or paradigms that are used to analyze and solve a problem.

Architecture versus design

The word is often used to refer to something at a high level that is distinct from the lower-level details, whereas design more often refers to structures and decisions at a lower level. But the two are intrinsically linked, and we cannot have a good product without synergy between the two. The low-level details and high-level structure are all part of the same whole. They form a continuous fabric that defines the shape of the system. You can't have one without the other; there is a continuum of decisions from the highest to the lowest levels.

Working separately on architecture and design, without a central theme and principles guiding both, leads to developers perceiving the code base in the same way that the blind men perceived the elephant in the famous parable.

On the other hand, it is not practical (or desirable) for the architect to document every aspect of low-level design. The key is to build a vision and guiding principles for the code, which can be used as guard rails by the developers when making decisions at each level.

What does architecture look like?

There have been multiple architectural paradigms over the year, but all of them have one key goal: managing complexity. How can we package code into *components* and work with these components as abstract entities to infer about and build chunks of behavior?

These components divide the system into partitions, so that each partition has a specific concern and role. Each component has well defined interfaces and responsibilities and is segregated from the rest of the components. Having this abstraction allows us to not worry about the inner workings of the components.

System decomposition needs to be a well thought-out activity. There are two key metrics for assessing how good your components are, named **cohesion** and **coupling**:

- **High cohesion** means a component performs a single related task.
- **Low coupling** means components should have less dependency between themselves.

A component can easily be extended to add more functionality or data to it. And, if needed, it should be completely replaceable, without that affecting the rest of the system.

Robert Cecil Martin (more commonly known as Uncle Bob) is a software engineer and author. He paints a beautiful picture through his clean architecture blog, describing the component/layering idea:

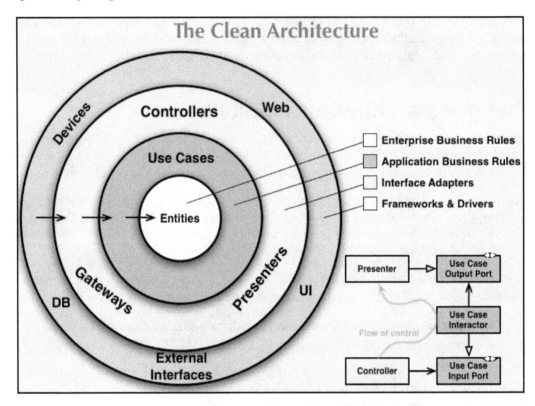

The concentric circles represent different layers (that is, different sets of components or higher-order components) of software.

In general, the inner circles are more abstract, and deal with things such as business rules and policies. They are the least likely to change when something external changes. For example, you would not expect your employee entity to change just because you want to show employee details on a mobile application, in addition to an existing web product.

The outer circles are mechanisms. They define how the inner circles are fulfilled using the mechanisms available. They are composed of things such as the database and web framework. This is generally code that you re-use, rather than write fresh.

The **Controllers** (or **Interface Adaptors**) layer converts data from the formats available in the mechanisms to what is most convenient for the business logic.

The rule that is key to making this architecture successful is the **dependency rule**. This rule says that source code dependencies can only point inward. Nothing in an inner circle (variables, classes, data, and private functions) can know anything at all about something in an outer circle. The interfaces between the layers and the data that crosses these boundaries are well defined and versioned. If a software system follows this rule, then any layer can be replaced or changed easily, without affecting the rest of the system.

 These four layers are just indicative—different architectures will bring out different numbers and sets of layers (circles). The key is to have a logical separation of the system so that, as new code needs to be written, developers have crisp ideas on what goes where.

Here is a quick summary of main architectural paradigms that are commonly used:

Package-based	The system is broken down into packages (here, the component is the package), where each package has a well-defined purpose and interface. There is clear separation of concerns in terms of the components. However, the level of independence and enforcement of segregation between modules is variable: in some contexts, the parts have only logical separation, and a change in one component might require another component to be re-built or re-deployed.
Layering/N-tier/3-tier	This segregates functionality into separate layers, where components are hosted in a specific layer. Generally, layers only interact with the layer below, thereby reducing complexity and enabling reusability. Layers might be packages or services. The most famous example of layered architecture is the networking stack (7 layer OSI or the TCP/IP stack).

Async / message-bus / actor model / Communicating Sequential Processes (CSP)	Here, the key idea is that systems communicate with each other through messages (or events). This allows for clean decoupling: the system producing the event does not need to know about the consumers. This allows allows for *1-n* communication. In Unix, this paradigm is employed via pipes: simple tools, such as `cat` and `grep`, are coupled through pipes to enable more complex functionality such as `search for cat in words.txt`. In a distributed system, the messages exist over the network. We shall look at distributed systems in detail in a later chapter. If you're wondering what the actor model or CSP is, these paradigms are explained later in this chapter.
Object-oriented	This is an architectural style where components are modeled as objects that encapsulate attributes and expose methods. The methods operate on the data within the object. This approach is discussed in detail in `Chapter 3`, *Design Patterns*.
Model-View-Controller (MVC) / separated presentation	Here, the logic for handling user interaction is placed into a view component, and the data that powers the interaction goes into a model component. The controller component orchestrates the interactions between them. We shall look at this in more detail in `Chapter 6`, *Messaging*.
Mircoservices / service-oriented architecture (SOA)	Here, the system is designed as a set of independent services that collaborate with each other to provide the necessary system behavior. Each service encapsulates its own data and has a specific purpose. The key difference here from the other paradigms is the existence of independently running and deployable services. There is a deep dive on this style further on in this chapter.

Microservices

While the theoretical concepts discussed previously have been with us for decades now, a few things have recently been changing very rapidly. There is an ever increasing amount of complexity in software products. For example, in object-oriented programming, we might start off with a clean interface between two classes, but during a sprint, under extra time pressure, a developer might cut corners and introduce a coupling between classes. Such a technical debt is rarely paid back on its own; it starts to accumulate until our initial design objective is no longer perceivable at all!

Another thing that's changing is that products are rarely built in isolation now; they make heavy use of services provided by external entities. A vivid example of this is found in managed services in cloud environments, such as **Amazon Web Services** (**AWS**). In AWS, there is a service for everything, from a database to one that enables building a chatbot.

It has become imperative that we try to enforce separation of concerns. Interactions and contracts between components are becoming increasingly **Application Programming Interface** (**API**)-driven. Components don't share memory, hence they can only communicate via network calls. Such components are called as **services**. A service takes requests from clients and fulfills them. Clients don't care about the internals of the service. A service can be a client for another service.

A typical initial architecture of a system is shown here:

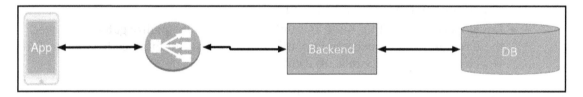

The system can be broken into three distinct layers:

- **Frontend (a mobile application or a web page)**: This is what the users interact with and makes network classes go to the backend to get data and enable behavior.
- **Backend piece**: This layer has the business logic for handling specific requests. This code is generally supposed to be ignorant of the frontend specifics (such as whether it is an application or a web page making the call).
- **A data store**: This is the repository for persistent data.

In the early stages, when the team (or company) is young, and people start developing with a greenfield environment and the number of developers is small, things work wonderfully and there is good development velocity and quality. Developers pitch in to help other developers whenever there are any issues, since everyone knows the system components at some level, even if they're not the developer responsible for the component. However, as the company grows, the product features start to multiply, and as the team gets bigger, four significant things happen:

- The code complexity increases exponentially and the quality starts to drop. A lot of dependencies spurt up between the current code and new features being developed, while bug fixes are made to current code. New developers don't have context into the tribal knowledge of the team and the cohesive structure of the code base starts to break.
- Operational work (running and maintaining the application) starts taking a significant amount time for the team. This usually leads to the hiring of operational engineers (DevOps engineers) who can independently take over operations work and be on call for any issues. However, this leads to developers losing touch with production, and we often see classic issues, such as *it works on my setup but fails in production*.
- The third thing that happens is the product hitting scalability limits. For example, the database may not meet the latency requirements under increased traffic. We might discover that an algorithm that was chosen for a key business rule is getting very latent. Things that were working well earlier suddenly start to fail, just because of the increased amount of data and requests.
- Developers start writing huge amounts of tests to have quality gates. However, these regression tests become very brittle with more and more code being added. Developer productivity falls off a cliff.

Applications that are in this state are called **monoliths**. Sometimes, being a monolith is not bad (for example, if there are stringent performance/latency requirements), but generally, the costs of being in this state impact the product very negatively. One key idea, which has become prevalent to enable software to scale, has been microservices, and the paradigm is more generally called **service-oriented architecture (SOA)**.

The basic concept of a microservice is simple—it's a simple, standalone application that does one thing only and does that one thing well. The objective is to retain the simplicity, isolation, and productivity of the early app. A microservice cannot live alone; no microservice is an island—it is part of a larger system, running and working alongside other microservices to accomplish what would normally be handled by one large standalone application.

Each microservice is autonomous, independent, self-contained, and individually deployable and scalable. The goal of microservice architecture is to build a system composed of such microservices.

The core difference between a monolithic application and microservices is that a monolithic application will contain all features and functions within one application (code base) deployed at the same time, with each server hosting a complete copy of the entire application, while a microservice contains only one function or feature, and lives in a microservice ecosystem along with other microservices:

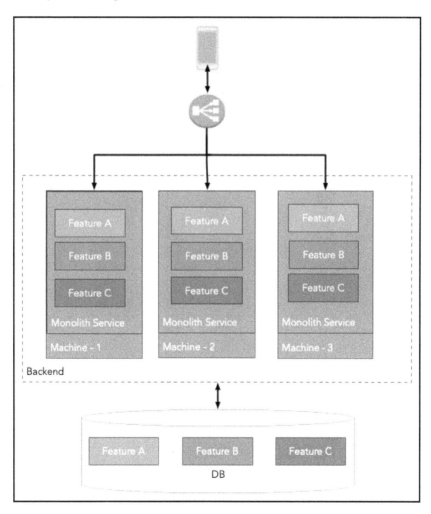

Monolithic architecture

Here, there is one deployable artifact, made from one application code base that contains all of the features. Every machine runs a copy of the same code base. The database is shared and usually leads to non-explicit dependencies (**Feature A** requires **Feature B** to maintain a Table X using a specific schema, but nobody told the **Feature B** team!)

Contrast this with a microservices application:

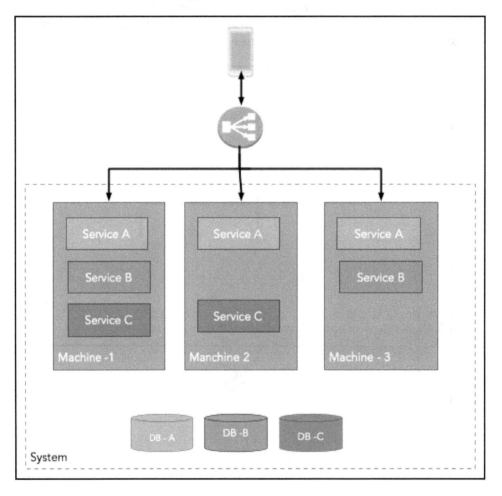

Microservices-based architecture

Here, in it's canonical form, every feature is itself packaged as a **service**, or a microservice, to be specific. Each microservice is individually deployable and scalable and has its own separate database.

To summarize, microservices bring a lot to the table:

- They allow us to use the componentization strategy (that is, *divide and rule*) more effectively, with clear boundaries between components.
- There's the ability to create the right tool for each job in a microservice.
- It ensures easier testability.
- There's improved developer productivity and feature velocity.

The challenges for microservices – efficiency

A non-trivial product with microservices will have tens (if not hundreds) of microservices, all of which need to co-operate to provide higher levels of value. A challenge for this architecture is deployment—*How many machines do we need?*

Moore's law refers to an observation made by Intel co-founder Gordon Moore in 1965. He famously noticed that the number of transistors per square inch on integrated circuits had doubled every year since their invention, and hence, should continue to do so.

This law has more or less held true for more than 40 years now, which means that high-performance hardware has become a commodity. For many problems, throwing hardware at the problem has been an efficient solution for many companies. With cloud environments such as AWS, this is even more so the case; one can literally get more horsepower just by pressing a button:

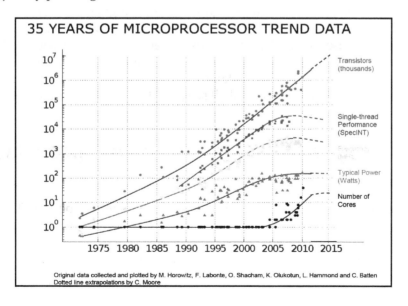

However with the microservices paradigm, it is no longer possible to remain ignorant of efficiency or cost. Microservices would be in their tens or hundreds, with each service having multiple instances.

Besides deployment, another efficiency challenge is the developer setup—a developer needs to be able to run multiple services on their laptop in order to work on a feature. While they may be making changes in only one, they still need to run mocks/sprint-branch version of others so that one can exercise the code.

A solution that immediately comes to mind is, *Can we co-host microservices on the same machine?* To answer this, one of the first things to consider is the language runtime. For example, in Java, each microservice needs a separate JVM process to run, in order to enable the segregation of code. However, the JVM tends to be pretty heavy in terms of resource requirements, and worse, the resource requirements can spike, leading to one JVM process to cause others to fail due to resource hogging.

Another thing to consider about the language is the concurrency primitives. Microservices are often I/O-bound and spend a lot of time communicating with each other. Often, these interactions are parallel. If we were to use Java, then almost everything parallel needs a thread (albeit in a thread pool). Threads in Java are not lean, and typically use about 1 MB of the heap (for the stack, housekeeping data, and so on). Hence, efficient thread usage becomes an additional constraint when writing parallel code in Java. Other things to worry about include the sizing of thread pools, which degenerates into a trial-and-error exercise in many situations.

Thus, though microservices are language-agnostic, some languages are better suited and/or have better support for microservices than others. One language that stands out in terms of friendliness with microservices is Golang. It's extremely frugal with resources, lightweight, very fast, and has a fantastic support for concurrency, which is a powerful capability when running across several cores. Go also contains a very powerful standard library for writing web services for communication (as we shall see ourselves, slightly further down the line).

The challenges for microservices – programming complexity

When working in a large code base, local reasoning is extremely important. This refers to the ability of a developer to understand the behavior of a routine by examining the routine itself, rather than examining the entire system. This is an extension of what we saw previously, compartmentalization is key to managing complexity.

In a single-threaded system, when you're looking at a function that manipulates some state, you only need to read the code and understand the initial state. Isolated threads are of little use. However, when threads need to talk to each other, very risky things can happen! But by contrast, in a multi-threaded system, any arbitrary thread can possibly interfere with the execution of the function (including deep inside a library you don't even know you're using!). Hence, understanding a function means not just understanding the code in the function, but also an exhaustive cognition of all possible interactions in which the function's state can be mutated.

It's a well known fact that human beings can juggle about seven things at one time. In a big system, where there might be millions of functions and billions of possible interactions, not having local reasoning can be disastrous.

Synchronization primitives, such as mutexes and semaphores, do help, but they do come with their own baggage, including the following issues:

- **Deadlocks**: Two threads requesting resources in a slightly different pattern causes both to block:

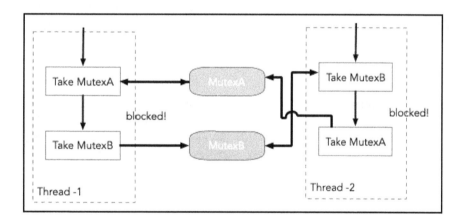

- **Priority inversion**: A high priority process wait on a low-priority slow process
- **Starvation**: A process occupies a resource for much more time than another equally important process

In the next section, we will see how Golang helps us to overcome these challenges and adopt microservices in the true spirit of the idea, without worrying about efficiency constraints or increased code complexity.

Go

The level of scale at Google is unprecedented. There are millions of lines of code and thousands of engineers working on it. In such an environment where there are a lot of changes done by different people, a lot of software engineering challenges will crop up—in particular, the following:

- Code becomes hard to read and poorly documented. Contracts between components cannot be easily inferred.
- Builds are slow. The development cycles of code-compile-test grow in difficulty, with inefficiency in modeling concurrent systems, as writing efficient code with synchronization primitives is tough.
- Manual memory management often leads to bugs.
- There are uncontrolled dependencies.
- There is a variety of programming styles due to multiple ways of doing something, leading to difficulty in code reviews, among other things.

The Go programming language was conceived in late 2007 by Robert Griesemer, Rob Pike, and Ken Thompson, as an open source programming language that aims to simplify programming and make it fun again. It's sponsored by Google, but is a true open source project—it commits from Google first, to the open source projects, and then the public repository is imported internally.

The language was designed by and for people who write, read, debug, and maintain large software systems. It's a statically-typed, compiled language with built-in concurrency and garbage collection as first-class citizens. Some developers, including myself, find beauty in its minimalistic and expressive design. Others cringe at things such as a lack of generics.

Since its inception, Go has been in constant development, and already has a considerable amount of industry support. It's used in real systems in multiple web-scale applications (image source: `https://madnight.github.io/githut/`):

# Ranking	Programming Language	Percentage (Change)	Trend
1	JavaScript	22.525% (-5.733%)	
2	Python	15.861% (+0.943%)	
3	Java	10.197% (+0.270%)	
4	Ruby	7.041% (-0.088%)	^
5	Go	6.941% (+1.967%)	^
6	PHP	6.717% (-0.730%)	v
7	C++	6.373% (+1.089%)	v
8	C	3.519% (+0.150%)	
9	TypeScript	3.381% (+1.241%)	^
10	C#	3.309% (-0.042%)	v
11	Shell	2.291% (+0.209%)	
12	Scala	1.558% (+0.187%)	^
13	Swift	1.094% (-0.324%)	v
14	Rust	1.074% (+0.208%)	^
15	DM	0.873% (+0.532%)	»
16	Objective-C	0.831% (-0.176%)	v

For a quick summary of what has made Go popular, you can refer to the *WHY GO?* section at `https://smartbear.com/blog/develop/an-introduction-to-the-go-language-boldly-going-wh/`.

We will now quickly recap the individual features of the language, before we start looking at how to utilize them to architect and engineer software in the rest of this book.

The following sections do not cover Go's syntax exhaustively; they are just meant as a recap. If you're very new to Go, you can take a tour of Go, available at `https://tour.golang.org/welcome/1`, while reading the following sections.

Hello World!

No introduction to any language is complete without the canonical Hello World program (http://en.wikipedia.org/wiki/Hello_world). This programs starts off by defining a package called `main`, then imports the standard Go input/output formatting package (`fmt`), and lastly, defines the `main` function, which is the standard entry point for every Go program. The `main` function here just outputs `Hello World!`:

```
package main

import "fmt"

func main() {
    fmt.Println("Hello World!")
}
```

Go was designed with the explicit object of having clean, minimal code. Hence, compared to other languages in the C family, its grammar is modest in size, with about 25 keywords.

"Less is EXPONENTIALLY more."

- Robert Pike

Go statements are generally C-like, and most of the primitives should feel familiar to programmers accustomed to languages such as C and Java. This makes it easy for non-Go developers to pick up things quickly. That said, Go makes many changes to C semantics, mostly to avoid the reliability pitfalls associated with low-level resource management (that is, memory allocation, pointer arithmetic, and implicit conversions), with the aim of increasing robustness. Also, despite syntactical similarity, Go introduces many modern constructs, including concurrency and garbage collection.

Data types and structures

Go supports many elementary data types, including `int`, `bool`, `int32`, and `float64`. One of the most obvious points where the language specification diverges from the familiar C/Java syntax is where, in the declaration syntax, the declared name appears before the type. For example, consider the following snippet:

```
var count int
```

It declares a `count` variable of the integer type (`int`). When the type of a variable is unambiguous from the initial value, then Go offers a shorted variable declaration syntax `pi := 3.14`.

It's important to note the language is strongly typed, so the following code, for example, would not compile:

```
var a int = 10

var b int32 = 20

c := a + b
```

One unique data type in Go is the `error` type. It's used to store errors, and there is a helpful package called errors for working with the variables of this type:

```
err := errors.New("Some Error")
if err != nil {
    fmt.Print(err)
}
```

Go, like C, gives the programmer control over pointers. For example, the following code denotes the layout of a point structure and a pointer to a `Point Struct`:

```
type Point Struct {
    X, Y int
}
```

Go also supports compound data structures, such as `string`, `map`, `array`, and `slice` natively. The language runtime handles the details of memory management and provides the programmer with native types to work with:

```
var a[10]int  // an array of type [10]int

a[0] = 1       // array is 0-based

a[1] = 2       // assign value to element

var aSlice []int // slice is like an array, but without upfront sizing

var ranks map[string]int = make(map[string]int) // make allocates the map
ranks["Joe"] = 1  // set
ranks["Jane"] = 2
rankOfJoe := ranks["Joe"] // get

string s = "something"
suff := "new"
```

```
fullString := s + suff // + is concatenation for string
```

Go has two operators, make() and new(), which can be confusing. new() just allocates memory, whereas make() initializes structures such as map. make() hence needs to be used with maps, slices, or channels. Slices are internally handled as struct, with fields defining the current start of the memory extent, the current length, and the extent.

Functions and methods

As in the C/C++ world, there are code blocks called functions. They are defined by the func keyword. They have a name, some parameters, the main body of code, and optionally, a list of results. The following code block defines a function to calculate the area of a circle:

```
func area(radius int) float64 {
    var pi float64 = 3.14
    return pi*radius*radius
}
```

It accepts a single variable, radius, of the int type, and returns a single float64 value. Within the function, a variable called pi of the float64 type is declared.

Functions in Go can return multiple values. A common case is to return the function result and an error value as a pair, as seen in the following example:

```
func GetX() (x X, err error)

myX, err := GetX()
if err != nil {
    ...
}
```

Go is an object-oriented language and has concepts of structures and methods. A struct is analogous to a class and encapsulates data and related operations. For example, consider the following snippet:

```
type Circle struct {
    Radius int
    color String
}
```

It defines a `Circle` structure with two members and fields:

- `Radius`, which is of the `int` type and is public
- `color`, which is of the `String` type and is private

 We shall look at class design and public/private visibility in more detail in `Chapter 3`, *Design Patterns*.

A method is a function with a special parameter (called a **receiver**), which can be passed to the function using the standard dot notation. This receiver is analogous to the `self` or `this` keyword in other languages.

Method declaration syntax places the receiver in parentheses before the function name. Here is the preceding `Area` function declared as a method:

```
func (c Circle) Area() float64 {
    var pi float64 = 3.14
    return pi*c.radius*c.radius
}
```

 Receivers can either be pointers (reference) or non-pointers (value). Pointer references are useful in the same way as normal pass-by-reference variables, should you want to modify `struct`, or if the size of `struct` is large, and so on. In the previous example of `Area()`, the `c Circle` receiver is passed by value. If we passed it as `c * Circle`, it would be pass by reference.

Finally, on the subject of functions, it's important to note that Go has first-class functions and closures:

```
areaSquared := func(radius int) float64 {
    return area*area
}
```

There is one design decision in the function syntax that points to one of my favorite design idioms in Go—keep things explicit. With default arguments, it becomes easy to patch API contracts and overload functions. This allows for easy wins in the short term, but leads to complicated, entangled code in the long run. Go encourages developers to use separate functions, with clear names, for each such requirement. This makes the code a lot more readable. If we really need such overloading and a single function that accepts a varied number of arguments, then we can utilize Go's type-safe variadic functions.

Flow control

The main stay of flow control in code is the familiar `if` statement. Go has the `if` statement, but does not mandate parentheses for conditions. Consider the following example:

```
if val > 100 {
    fmt.Println("val is greater than 100")
} else {
    fmt.Println("val is less than or equal to 100")
}
```

To define loops, there is only one iteration keyword, `for`. There are no `while` or `do...while` keywords that we see in other languages, such as C or Java. This is in line with the Golang design principles of minimalism and simplicity—whatever we can do with a `while` loop, the same can be achieved with a `for` loop, so why have two constructs? The syntax is as follows:

```
func naiveSum(n Int)  (int){
    sum := 0;
    for i:=0; i < n ; i++ {
        sum += index
    }
    return sum
}
```

As you can see, again, there are no parentheses around the loop conditions. Also, the `i` variable is defined for the scope of the loop (with `i := 0`). This syntax will be familiar to C++ or Java programmers.

Note that the `for` loop need not strictly follow the three-tuple initial version (declaration, check, increment). It can simply be a check, as with a `while` loop in other languages:

```
i:= 0
for i <= 2 {
    fmt.Println(i)
    i = i + 1
}
```

And finally, a `while(true)` statement looks like this:

```
for {
    // forever
}
```

There is a `range` operator that allows iterations of arrays and maps. The operator is seen in action for maps here:

```
// range over the keys (k) and values (v) of myMAp
for k,v := range myMap {
    fmt.Println("key:",k)
    fmt.Println("val:",v)
}

// just range over keys
for key := range myMap {
    fmt.Println("Got Key :", key)
}
```

The same operator works in an intuitive fashion for arrays:

```
input := []int{100, 200, 300}
// iterate the array and get both the index and the element
for i, n := range input {
    if n == 200 {
        fmt.Println("200 is at index : ", i)
    }
}

sum := 0
// in this iteration, the index is skipped, it's not needed
for _, n := range input {
    sum += n
}
fmt.Println("sum:", sum)
```

Packaging

In Go, code is binned into packages. These packages provide a namespaces for code. Every Go source file, for instance, `encoding/json/json.go`, starts with a package clause, like this:

```
package json
```

Here, `json` is the package name, a simple identifier. Package names are usually concise.

Packages are rarely in isolation; they have dependencies. If code in one package wants to use something from a different package, then the dependency needs to be called out explicitly. The dependent packages can be other packages from the same project, a Golang standard package, or from a third-party package on GitHub. To declare dependent packages, after the package clause, each source file may have one or more `import` statements, comprising the `import` keyword and the package identifier:

```
import "encoding/json"
```

One important design decision in Go, dependency-wise, is that the language specification requires unused dependencies to be declared as a compile-time error (not a warning, like most other build systems). If the source file imports a package it doesn't use, the program will not compile. This was done to speed up build times by making the compiler work on only those packages that are needed. For programmers, it also means that code tends to be cleaner, with less unused imports piling up. The flip side is that, if you're experimenting with different packages while coding, you may find the compiler errors irritating!

Once a package has been imported, the package name qualifies items from the package in the source file being imported:

```
var dec = json.NewDecoder(reader)
```

Go takes an unusual approach to defining the visibility of identifiers (functions/variables) inside a package. Unlike private and public keywords, in Go, the name itself carries the visibility definition. The case of the initial letter of the identifier determines the visibility. If the initial character is an uppercase letter, then the identifier is public and is exported out of the package. Such identifiers can be used outside of the package. All other identifiers are not visible (and hence not usable) outside of the host package. Consider the following snippet:

```
package circles

func AreaOf(c Circle) float64 {
}

func colorOf(c Circle) string {
}
```

In the preceding code block, the `AreaOf` function is exported and visible outside of the circles package, but `colorOf` is visible only within the package.

We shall look at packing Go code in greater detail in `Chapter 3`, *Design Patterns*.

Concurrency

Real life is concurrent. With API-driven interactions and multi-core machines, any non-trivial program written today needs to be able to schedule multiple operations in parallel, and these need to happen concurrently using the available cores. Languages such as C++ or Java did not have language-level support for concurrency for a long time. Recently, Java 8 has added support for parallelism with stream processing, but it still follows an inefficient fork-join process, and communication between parallel streams is difficult to engineer.

Communicating Sequential Processes (CSP) is a formal language for describing patterns of interaction in concurrent systems. It was first described in a 1978 paper by Tony Hoare. The key concept in CSP is that of a process. Essentially, code inside a process is sequential. At some point in time, this code can start another process. Many times, these processes need to communicate. CSP promotes the message-passing paradigm of communication, as compared to the shared memory and locks paradigm for communication. Shared memory models, like the one depicted in the following diagram, are fraught with risks:

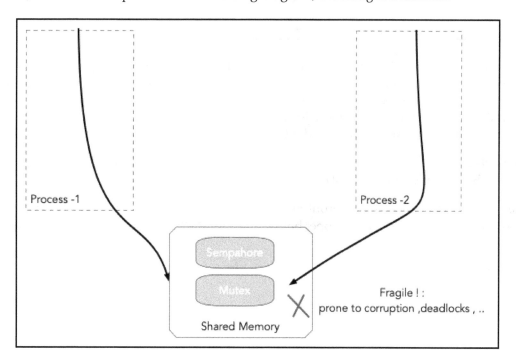

It's easy to get deadlock and corruption if a process misbehaves or crashes inside a critical section. Such systems also experience difficulty in recovering from failure.

In contrast, CSP promotes messages passing using the concept of channels, which are essentially queues with a simple logical interface of send() and recv(). These operations can be blocking. This model is described in this following:

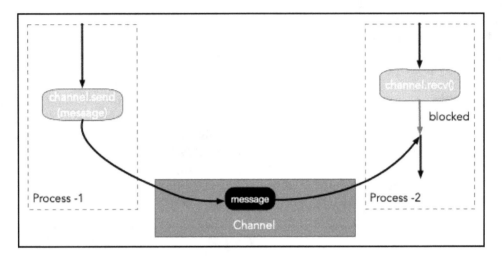

Go uses a variant of CSP with first-class channels. Procedures are called goroutines. Go enables code, which is mostly regular procedural code, but allows concurrent composition using independently executing functions (goroutines). In procedural programming, we can just call a function inline; however, with Go, we can also spawn a goroutine out of the function and have it execute independently.

Channels are also first-class Go primitives. Sharing is legal and passing a pointer over a channel is idiomatic (and efficient).

The main() function itself is a goroutine, and a new goroutine can be spawned using the go keyword. For example, the snippet below modifies the Hello World program to spawn a goroutine:

```go
package main

import (
    "fmt"
    "time"
)

func say(what string){
    fmt.Println(what)
}

func main() {
```

```
    message := "Hello world!"
    go say(message)
    time.Sleep(5*time.Second)
}
```

Note that, after the `go say(message)` statement is executed, the `main()` goroutine immediately proceeds to the next statement. The `time.Sleep()` function is important here to prevent the program from exiting! An illustration of goroutines is shown in the following diagram:

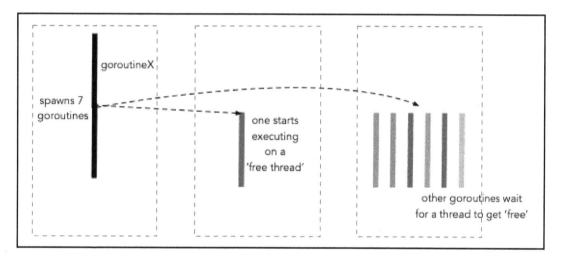

We shall look at channels and more concurrency constructs in `Chapter 4`, *Scaling Applications*.

Garbage collection

Go has no explicit memory-freeing operation: the only way allocated memory can be returned to the pools is via garbage collection. In a concurrent system, this is an must-have feature, because the ownership of an object might change (with multiple references) in non-obvious ways. This allows programmers to concentrate on modeling and coding the concurrent aspects of the system, without having to bother about pesky resource management details. Of course, garbage collection brings in implementation complexity and latency. Nonetheless, ultimately, the language is much easier to use because of garbage collection.

Not everything thing is freed on the programmer's behalf. Sometimes, the programmer has to make explicit calls to enable the freeing of an object's memory.

Object-orientation

The Go authors felt that the normal type-hierarchy model of software development is easy to abuse. For example, consider the following class and the related description:

---

org.springframework.aop.framework
Class AbstractSingletonProxyFactoryBean

java.lang.Object
    └─ org.springframework.aop.framework.ProxyConfig
        └─ org.springframework.aop.framework.AbstractSingletonProxyFactoryBean

All Implemented Interfaces:
    Serializable, BeanClassLoaderAware, FactoryBean, InitializingBean

Direct Known Subclasses:
    TransactionProxyFactoryBean

```
public abstract class AbstractSingletonProxyFactoryBean
extends ProxyConfig
implements FactoryBean, BeanClassLoaderAware, InitializingBean
```

Convenient proxy factory bean superclass for proxy factory beans that create only singletons.

Coding in such large class hierarchies usually generates brittle code. Early decisions become very hard to change, and base class changes can have devastating consequences further down the line. However, the irony is that, early on, all of the requirements might not be clear, nor the system well understood enough, to allow for great base class design.

The Go way of object-orientation is : *composition over inheritance*.

For polymorphic behavior, Go uses interfaces and duck typing:

> *"If it looks like a duck and quacks like a duck, it's a duck."*

Duck typing implies that any class that has all of the methods that an interfaces advertises can be said to implement the said interface.

We shall look at more detail on object-orientation in Go later on in Chapter 3, *Design Patterns*.

Summary

In this chapter, we looked at why having a plan is important when building big. We reviewed various design paradigms and key aspects of Golang. The discussion of these topics here was focused and very condensed. For more insights, I strongly recommend reading *Clean Architecture: A Craftsman's Guide to Software Structure and Design* by Robert C. Martin and *A tour of Go* (https://tour.golang.org/welcome/1).

In the next chapter, we will look at the problem statement of the case study that we will be working on for the rest of this book. At the end of each section of the book, we will apply whatever we learned in the section's chapters to build solutions for specific aspects of the case study.

2
Packaging Code

When Mihai Budiu interviewed Brian Kernighan in 2000 (http://www.cs.cmu.edu/
~mihaib/kernighan-interview/index.html), Brian Kernighan was asked the following
question:

> *"Can you tell us about the worst features of C, from your point of view?"*

He responded with the following:

> *"I think that the real problem with C is that it doesn't give you enough mechanisms for
> structuring really big programs, for creating firewalls within programs so you can keep
> the various pieces apart. It's not that you can't do all of these things, that you can't
> simulate object-oriented programming or other methodology you want in C. You can
> simulate it, but the compiler, the language itself, isn't giving you any help."*

Developers should be warned when they feel that code is being pushed into arbitrary
places. This generally implies that the code base does not have a coherence or a sense of
purpose distilled from the architecture. This is not just aesthetics or traceability; good
packaging is the first step to a maintainable code base.

As we saw in Chapter 1, *Building Big with Go*, managing complexity is one of the main
objectives of architecture. One way of doing this is **encapsulation**—packaging code into a
higher level of abstractions, which create the firewalls that Kernighan described earlier.

This chapter delves into ways of organizing code at two levels:

- Object-orientation in Go
- Code layout of packages, dependencies, and so on

But before we go there, we need to define crisply a key aspect of module design—**contracts**.

Contracts

A software contract is a formalized documentation of an interaction with a software component. It can be an interface (in the object-oriented sense), an API, or a protocol (for example, TCP). Contracts allow diverse unconnected components of a system to work together. Having clear, crisp contracts is a prerequisite to enabling successful distributed software development. Here, *distributed* means not just in the normal distributed systems sense (software with independent components), but also distributed teams.

All libraries and products implement contracts, explicit or implicit. Contracts may be documented (using formal prose such as RFCs, ideally), or embedded in code (less than ideal unless clearly called out).

Contracts do change. The key task of the architect is to ensure the following:

- Contracts are durable and not reactive, and there is no change amplification, such that small requirement changes cause churn in the contract.
- Contracts are versioned. You can never know what the state is of the clients interacting with your component. Hence, it is important that contracts have a version associated with them. Generally, contracts should be backward compatible (for example, version 2.2 of the component should interact reliably with a client assuming version 1.1 of the contract). Sometimes, the burden of backward compatibility can be substantial. In this case, you can make an informed decision to make a breaking change. Even then, interactions with earlier clients should gracefully fail, and communicate a clear error message that the version of the contract is no longer supported.
- Contracts should include non-functional requirements, typically called **service-level agreements** (**SLAs**). These help clients in figuring out how to calculate things such as timeouts.

Within this context, let's look at how object orientation plays out in Go.

Object orientation

In object-oriented programming, the key idea is to split code into several small, manageable parts or objects. Each object has its own identity, data (or attributes), and logic (or behavior). For example, consider modeling an elephant in software.

Attributes are the properties of the object. For example, in the case of the elephant, things such as these:

- Weight
- Color
- Type
- Location

The collection of all these attributes describes the current state of an object. The state of one object is generally independent of another. Behavior is things that the object can do; in the case of an elephant, it can trumpet. Behavior is the object's interface with the outside world. The individual constructs (or functions) by which you can invoke behavior on the object are called **methods**.

A class is a blueprint, or a template for objects that share the same behavior and properties. Being a template, it can be used as a specification to create objects. It is usually correct to say that objects instantiated from a class are of the same type. So, our `Elephant` class can be something such as the following:

Encapsulation is the key guiding principle for class design. It implies exposing a contract for the behavior of objects and hiding volatile implementation details. The `private` attributes and methods are hidden inside a capsule according to a need-to-know basis.

Instead of having a long procedural program, the design paradigm is to decompose behavior into small manageable (and ideally reusable) components (objects), each with a well-defined contract (interface). Doing this effectively allows me, as the class developer, to change implementation while not affecting my clients. Also, we can ensure safer behavior in the system, as we don't need to worry about the clients misusing implementation constructs, thereby reducing complexity of the overall system.

Many times, we come across a set of objects/classes that are very similar, and it helps to reason about these classes as a group. For example, let's say we are designing a zoo, where there are multiple animals. There is some behavior that we expect from all animals, and it simplifies code immensely if we use the abstract interface of the animal, rather than worry about specific animals. This type of relationship is normally modeled as inheritance, as shown in the following diagram:

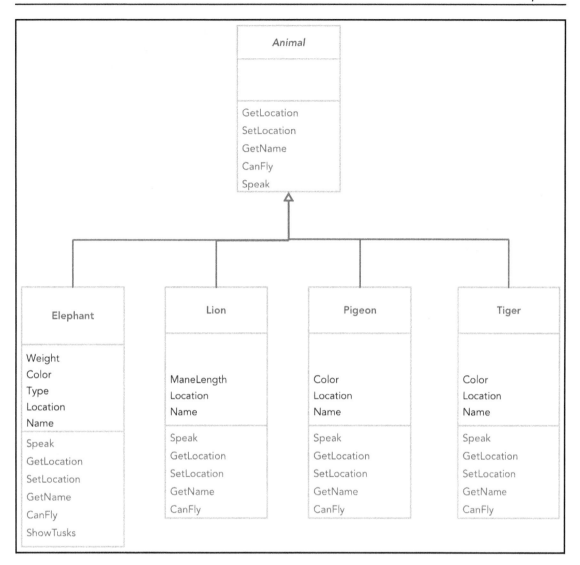

Here, we have an animal interface and multiple animal classes implementing the contract defined by the interface. The child classes can have extra attributes or methods, but they cannot omit methods specified by the parent. This inheritance modeling implies an *is a* relationship (for example, a tiger *is an* animal). Now a feature such as zoo roll call, where we want to find names of all the animals in the zoo, can be built without worrying about individual animals, and will work even as new animals enter the zoo or some types of animals move out.

You might notice that each animal has a unique sound—tigers roar, elephants trumpet, and so on and so forth. During the roll call, however, we don't care what the sound is as long as we can prompt the animal to speak. The how of speaking can be different for each animal and is not relevant to the feature in question. We can implement this using a `Speak` method on the `Animal` interface, and depending on the `Animal`, what `Speak` does will be different. This ability of an interface method to behave differently based on the actual object is called **polymorphism** and is key to many design patterns:

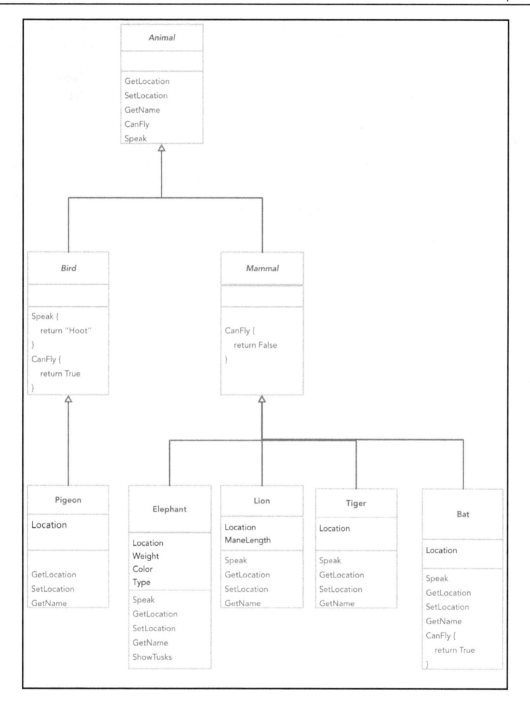

Inheritance, though useful, has its pitfalls. It often leads to a hierarchy of classes, and sometimes the behavior of the final object is spread across the hierarchy. In an inheritance hierarchy, super classes can often be fragile, because one little change to a superclass can ripple out and affect many other places in the application's code. One of the better things that can happen is a compile time error (compiled languages), but the really tricky situations are those where there are no compile time errors, but, subtle behavior changes leading to errors/bugs in fringe scenarios. Such things can be really hard to debug; after all, nothing changed in your code! There is no easy way to catch this in processes such as code review, since, by design, the base class (and the developers who maintain that) don't care (or know) about the derived classes.

An alternative to inheritance is to delegate behavior, also called **composition**. Instead of an *is a*, this is a *has a* relationship. It refers to combining simple types to make more complex ones. The preceding `Animal` relationship is modeled as the following:

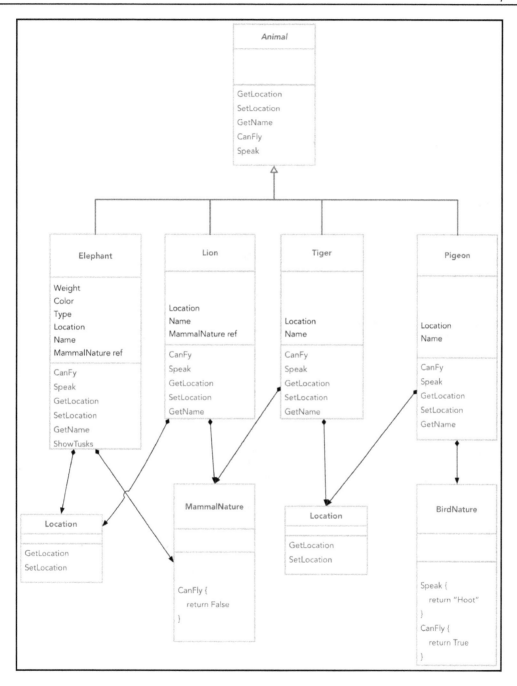

Here, instead of a *hierarchy*, there are only two constructs:

- Classes implement an interface—which is the contract the base class offers.
- Functionality reuse happens through having references to objects, rather than deriving from classes.

This is why many people, including people who code in Go, have the **Composition Over Inheritance** principle.

Before closing this topic, there is another key advantage of composition that needs to be called out. Building objects and references through compositions allows you to delay the creation of objects until and unless they are needed, thereby improving the memory footprint of the program. Objects can also mutate the state of the referenced objects dynamically, allowing you to express complex behavior through simple constructs. One example is the state design pattern as detailed in Chapter 4, *Scaling Applications*. When efficiency and dynamism is a requirement, composition is super-key!

Object orientation in Go – the struct

In Go, instead of Java and C++ classes, the equivalent container for encapsulation is called a struct. It describes the attributes of the objects for this class. A struct looks like this:

```
type Animal struct {
    Name string
    canFly bool
}
```

This defines a new type with the collection of fields mentioned.

Once you have defined struct, you can instantiate it as follows:

```
anAnimal := Animal{Name: "Lion", canFly: false}
```

This creates a new object, anAnimal of type Animal. Once you have an object such as anAnimal, we can use it to access fields using the dot notation as shown here:

```
fmt.Println(anAnimal.Name)
```

You can also use dots with pointers to objects (rather than the actual object). The pointers are automatically dereferenced. So, in the next example, aLionPtr.age works in both cases: aLionPtr being a pointer to an object, as well as being a reference to the object itself:

```
aLionPtr := &anAnimal
fmt.Println(aLionPtr.age)
```

Methods are functions that operate on particular `struct`. They have a receiver clause that mandates what type they operate on. For example, consider the following `struct` and method:

```
// This `Person` struct again
type Person struct {
    name string
    age int
}
func (p Person) canVote() bool {
    return p.Age > 18
}
```

In the preceding example, the language construct between the `func` keyword and the method name is the **receiver**:

```
( p Person )
```

This is analogous to the *self* or *this* construct of other object-oriented languages. You can view receiver parameters analogous to this or self-identifiers in other languages. There can be only one receiver, and you can define methods using pointer receivers:

```
func (t * type) doSomething(param1 int)
```

And you can use non-pointer method receivers:

```
func (t type) doSomething(param1 int)
```

A pointer receiver method makes for **Pass-By-Reference** semantics, while a non-pointer one is a **Pass-By-Value**. Generally, pointer receiver methods are used if either of the following apply:

- You want to actually modify the receiver (read/write, as opposed to just read).
- The `struct` is very large and a deep copy is expensive.

Slices and maps act as references, so even passing them as value will allow mutation of the objects. It should be noted that a pointer receiver method can work with a non-pointer type and vice-versa. For example, the following code will print "11 11", as the `DoesNotGrow()` is working on a non-pointer receiver, and thus the increment there won't affect the actual value in `struct`:

```
package main
import (
    "fmt"
)
type Person struct {
```

```
    Name string
    Age int
}
func (p *Person) Grow() {
    p.Age++
}
func (p Person) DoesNotGrow() {
    p.Age++
}
func main() {
    p := Person{"JY", 10}
    p.Grow()
    fmt.Println(p.Age)
    ptr := &p
    ptr.DoesNotGrow()
    fmt.Println(p.Age)
}
```

This can be confusing for people, but it is clarified in the Go Spec (reference: `https://golang.org/ref/spec#Method_sets`).

> *"A method call* `x.m()` *is valid if the method set of (the type of)* x *contains* m *and the argument list can be assigned to the parameter list of* m. *If* x *is addressable and* `&x` *value's method set contains* m, `x.m()` *is shorthand for* `(&x).m():."*

And if you are wondering what a method set is, the spec defines this as follows:

> *"The method set of any other type T consists of all methods declared with receiver type T. The method set of the corresponding pointer type *T is the set of all methods with receiver *T or T (that is, it also contains the method set of T)."*

Object orientation in Go – visibility

Managing visibility is key to good class design and, in turn, to the ruggedness of the system. Unlike other object-oriented languages, there are no public or private keywords in Go. A `struct` field with a lowercase starting letter is private, while if it is in uppercase, then it's public. For example, consider a `Pigeon` package:

```
package pigeon

type Pigeon struct {
    Name string
    featherLength int
}
```

```
func (p *Pigeon) GetFeatherLength() int {
    return p.featherLength
}
func (p *Pigeon) SetFeatherLength(length int)  {
    p.featherLength = length
}
```

Here, inside `struct` we have the following:

- `Name` is a public attribute, and the code outside of the package can reference it.
- `featherLength` is a private attribute, and the code outside of the package cannot reference it.

The implications of this packaging mean that the following code will not compile (assuming the code is outside of the `Pigeon` package):

```
func main() {
    p := pigeon.Pigeon{"Tweety", 10} //This will not compile
}
```

`featherLength` is not exposed from the `Pigeon` package. The right way to instantiate an object of this `struct` would be to use the setter function provided:

```
func main() {
    p := pigeon.Pigeon{Name :"Tweety", }
    p.SetFeatherLength(10)
    fmt.Println(p.Name)
    fmt.Println(p.GetFeatherLength())
    //fmt.Println(p.featherLength) - This will not compile
}
```

The capitalization-of-initial-letter convention also extends for methods too. Public methods have the first letter capitalized, whereas private ones start with a lowercase character

Object oriented in Go – the interface

As we saw in `Chapter 1`, *Building Big with Go*, the interface construct is key to polymorphism in Go—abstracting out details from a set of related objects so that we can simplify code. The interface defines a contract that can be assumed by clients, without knowledge (and thus coupling) of the actual class that implements the interface. **Interfaces** are types that declare sets of methods. Similar to interfaces in other languages, they have no implementation. Interfaces are at the core of Go's object-oriented support.

Many object-oriented languages define explicit implementations of an interface; however, Go is different. Here, the implementation is implicit through duck typing (as we saw in Chapter 1, *Building Big with Go*). Objects that implement all the interface methods automatically implement the interface. There is no inheritance or subclassing or implements keyword.

Duck typing is found in other languages such as Python, but one advantage of Go is the ability of the compiler to catch obvious mistakes, such as passing an int where a string was expected or calling with the wrong number of arguments.

To use interfaces, first define the interface type like so:

```
type LatLong stuct {
    Lat  float64
    Long float64
}
type Animal interface {
    GetLocation() LatLong
    SetLocation(LatLong)
    CanFly() bool
    Speak()
}
```

In Golang, all implementations are implicit. If the method set of a type T is a super set of the method set declared by an interface type I, then the type T implements the interface type I, implicitly. Here, T can also be an interface type. If T is a named non-interface type, then *T must also implement I, for the method set of *T is a super set of the method set of T.

So, for example, for the animal interface, we can define Lion and Pigeon classes that both implement the interface, as follows:

```
// The Lion Family
//
type Lion struct {
    name       string
    maneLength int
    location   LatLong
}

func (lion *Lion) GetLocation() LatLong {
    return lion.location
}
func (lion *Lion) SetLocation(loc LatLong) {
    lion.location = loc
}
func (lion *Lion) CanFly() bool {
```

```
      return false
  }
  func (lion *Lion) Speak() string {
      return "roar"
  }
  func (lion *Lion) GetManeLength() int {
      return lion.maneLength
  }
  func (lion *Lion) GetName() string {
      return lion.name
  }
```

Here is the code for the Pigeon class:

```
  // The Pigeon Family
  //
  type Pigeon struct {
      name     string
      location LatLong
  }
  func (p *Pigeon) GetLocation() LatLong {
      return p.location
  }
  func (p *Pigeon) SetLocation(loc LatLong) {
      p.location = loc
  }
  func (p *Pigeon) CanFly() bool {
      return false
  }
  func (p *Pigeon) Speak() string {
      return "hoot"
  }
  func (p *Pigeon) GetName() string {
      return p.name
  }
```

The whole point of this is, of course, polymorphism—Lion and Pigeon can be used in any place where the animal interface is expected.

As described in Chapter 1, *Building Big with Go*, this is also called duck typing—*"If it quacks like a duck, it must be a duck."* Specifically, if a type T implements an interface type I, then values of T can be assigned to values of I. Calling a method of an interface value will call the corresponding method of the dynamic value of the interface value. The polymorphism is demonstrated by this code:

```
// The symphony
func makeThemSing(animals []Animal) {
    for _, animal := range animals {
    fmt.Println(animal.GetName() + " says " + animal.Speak())
  }
}
func main() {
    var myZoo []Animal
    Leo := Lion{
        "Leo",
        10,
        LatLong{10.40, 11.5},
    }
    myZoo = append(myZoo, &Leo)
    Tweety := Pigeon{
        "Tweety",
        LatLong{10.40, 11.5},
    }
    myZoo = append(myZoo, &Tweety)
    makeThemSing(myZoo) // do some work with the collection
}
```

A note on the implementation: polymorphism is typically implemented as either of the following:

- Tables for all the method calls prepared statically (as in C++ and Java)
- A method lookup at each call (JavaScript and Python)

Go has slightly different method tables but computes them at runtime. Essentially, interfaces are represented as a pointer-pair: one pointer to information about the type and method tables (called **i-table**), and the other pointer references the associated data. For example, take a look at the following assignment:

```
var aAnimal Animal
aAnimal =   &Lion{
    "Leo",
    10,
    LatLong{10.40, 11.5},
  }
```

It can be pictorially visualized as follows:

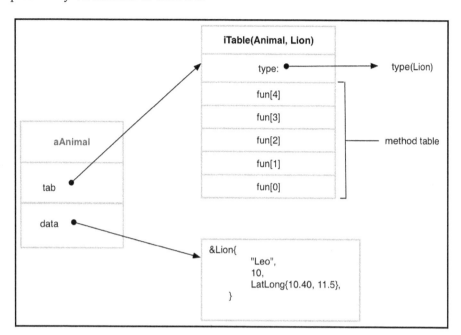

This diagram can help us visualize how the language runtime implements interfaces and polymorphism.

Object oriented in Go – embedding

Embedding is a mechanism to allow the ability to borrow pieces from different classes. It is the equivalent of multiple inheritance with non-virtual members.

Let's call `Base`, `struct` embedded into a `Derived` struct. Like normal (public/protected) subclassing, the fields and methods of the `Base` class are directly available in the `Derived` struct. Internally, a hidden/anonymous field is created with the name of the base struct. The following code sample demonstrates the behavior:

```
type Bird struct {
    featherLength  int
    classification string
}
type Pigeon struct {
    Bird
    Name       string
```

```
    }

    func main() {
        p := Pigeon{Name :"Tweety", }
        p.featherLength = 10
        fmt.Println(p)
    }
```

Base fields and methods can be shadowed, if redefined in the derived class. Once shadowed, the only way to access the base member is to use the hidden field named as the base-struct-name:

```
    type Bird struct {
        featherLength  int
        classification string
    }

    type Pigeon struct {
        Bird
        featherLength  float64
        Name         string
    }

    func main() {
        p := Pigeon{Name :"Tweety", }
        p.featherLength = 3.14
        // featherLength refers to the member of  the Pigeon struct NOT Bird
        fmt.Println(p)
    }
```

This may feel like inheritance, but embedding does not provide polymorphism. Embedding differs from subclassing in an important way: when a type is embedded, the methods of that type are available as methods of the outer type; however, for invocation of the embedded struct methods, the receiver of the method must be the inner (embedded) type, not the outer one.

Embedding can also be done on interfaces. A famous example of this is the ReaderWriter interface in the Golang stdlib, which combines both the Reader and Writer interface:

```
    type ReadWriter interface {
        Reader
        Writer
    }
```

Golang allows multiple structures to be embedded inside one. This gives the ability to borrow behavior from multiple classes. This is similar to multiple inheritance. However, a note of caution: there is a reason why languages such as Java avoid multiple inheritance. It's called the **deadly diamond of death** problem. This problem refers to the ambiguity that arises when two classes, B and C, inherit from A, and a third class, D, inherits from both B and C. Here, if there is a method in A that B and C have overridden but D has not, then it is ambiguous on what exact method version is advertised by D:

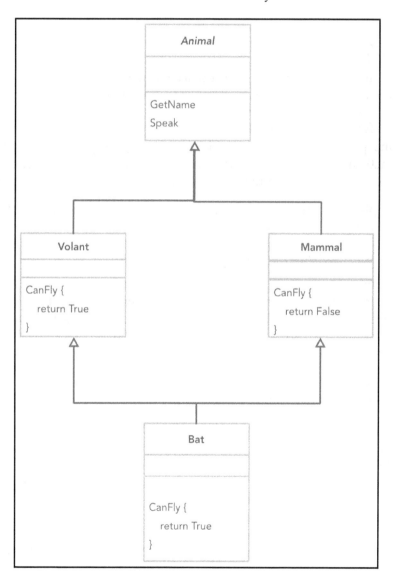

That said, in Golang, since embedding essentially means that inherited fields remain in the inheriting `struct` namespace (`struct`), the compiler catches any ambiguities.

 To know more about method overriding, visit `https://en.wikipedia.org/wiki/Method_overriding`.

Modules

Eventually, any interesting software project will come to depend on another project, library, or framework. Packages provide a namespace or a firewall for your code. By *firewall* I mean, insulate the code in the package from changes in other parts or packages. Entities inside a package (types, functions, variables, and so on) can be exported (public—visible outside the package) or unexported (private—not visible outside the package). The way to control visibility is exactly like the mechanism described for classes: if the identifier name starts with a capital letter, and it is exported from the package, otherwise, it's unexported.

This is an example of a *convention over configuration* paradigm and is one of the key enablers of encapsulation in Go. The rule of thumb is this:

> *All code of the package should be private, unless explicitly needed by other client packages.*

Go's standard library comes with a lot of useful packages that can be used for building real-world applications. For example, the standard library provides a `net/http` package that can be used for building web applications and web services. Besides the standard packages, it is idiomatic in Go to use third-party packages. You can literally pick any third-party package on GitHub and use it in your code, after a simple `go get` command.

While this flexibility is good, it is important to have a packing philosophy and guidelines so that developers know exactly where to put and find code.

Code layout

Go mandates code to be organized on the filesystem in a certain way—the organization has to be at the highest level in terms of a workspace. While there are general recommendations to have one workspace for all projects, in practical situations, I have found it much more scalable to have one workspace per project; for example, consider the situation of two projects using a common dependency, with a different version (more on that in the next section, *third-party dependencies*.

Here is the recommended high-level structure for the code:

- `bin`: This directory contains the executables; that is, the output of the compiler.
- `pkg`: This folder is for the package objects.
- `<package>`: A folder for each of the top-level packages that make the components of the project.
- `vendor`: This folder hosts third-party dependencies. There will be more on this in the following section, *third-party libraries*.
- `Makefile`: This makes it easier to organize various tasks such as compilation, linting, tests, and also stage code. This again is described in more detail in the next section, *third- party libraries*.
- `scripts`: Various scripts including DB provisioning/migrations.
- `Main driver`: The main file(s) that drive the components and control the life cycle of top-level objects.

This is how a typical Golang workspace looks:

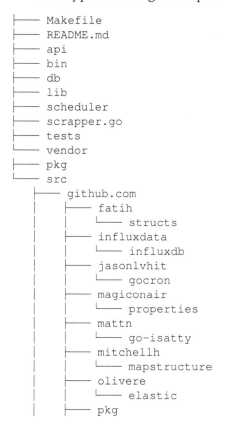

```
├─── Makefile
├─── README.md
├─── api
├─── bin
├─── db
├─── lib
├─── scheduler
├─── scrapper.go
├─── tests
└─── vendor
├─── pkg
└─── src
    ├─── github.com
    │   ├─── fatih
    │   │   └─── structs
    │   ├─── influxdata
    │   │   └─── influxdb
    │   ├─── jasonlvhit
    │   │   └─── gocron
    │   ├─── magiconair
    │   │   └─── properties
    │   ├─── mattn
    │   │   └─── go-isatty
    │   ├─── mitchellh
    │   │   └─── mapstructure
    │   ├─── olivere
    │   │   └─── elastic
    │   ├─── pkg
```

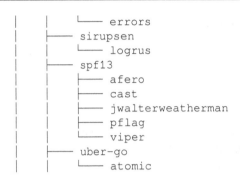

```
|     |       └──── errors
|     ├──── sirupsen
|     |       └──── logrus
|     ├──── spf13
|     |       ├──── afero
|     |       ├──── cast
|     |       ├──── jwalterweatherman
|     |       ├──── pflag
|     |       └──── viper
|     ├──── uber-go
|     |       └──── atomic
```

The GOPATH environment variable specifies the location of your workspace. It defaults to a directory named go inside your home directory. If you would like to work in a different location, you will need to set GOPATH to the path to that directory with a fallback to the Go home directory. The following section shows you how to do this in detail.

Third-party dependencies

While using third-party libraries allows rapid development, it also brings some challenges. Consider what happened in 2016 in the JavaScript/NPM word—11 lines of JavaScript broke big projects such as Node and Babel. Here's what happened:

Azer Koçulu got unhappy with NPM because a brand-infringement inquiry on an lib called **Kik** went against him. In retaliation, he unpublished around 250 of his modules from NPM, one of which was left-pad. This library was used to pad out the left-hand side of strings with zeros or spaces. It so happened that thousands of projects (including Node and Babel) relied on this library. Without the dependency being available in NPM, these widely-used applications failed (for reference, visit http://www.informit.com/articles/article.aspx?p=1941206).

In professional software development, we need to insulate ourselves from such impact. That is why I'm an ardent supporter of managing your dependencies in your own version control, with clear versioning. Even here, there are two options:

- Have a company-wide/cross-project dependency repository.
- Have per-project dependencies.

A common issue with the first approach is versioning—not all projects in your team may want to use the same version all the time. With a common Go Workspace, this becomes tough to manage. To circumvent such issues, and to retain control of dependencies, I usually advocate the following:

- Checking in the dependencies in the the same source tree as the main code under a `vendor` folder.
- Using a unique `GOPATH` (and workspace) for each project, effectively using `GOPATH` as follows:

   $ (PWD) /vendor:$ (PWD)

- `$ (PWD)` is the source root.
- Using a `Makefile`, as shown here, to help stage vendor code before checking into the parent repository:

```
.PHONY: build doc fmt lint run test clean vet

TAGS = -tags 'newrelic_enabled'

default: build

build: fmt clean
  go build -v -o ./myBin

doc:
  godoc -http=:6060 -index

# https://github.com/golang/lint
# go get github.com/golang/lint/golint
lint:
  golint ./src

clean:
  rm -rf `find ./vendor/src -type d -name .git` \
  && rm -rf `find ./vendor/src -type d -name .hg` \
  && rm -rf `find ./vendor/src -type d -name .bzr` \
  && rm -rf `find ./vendor/src -type d -name .svn`
  rm -rf ./bin/*
  rm -rf ./pkg/*
  rm -rf ./vendor/bin/*
  rm -rf ./vendor/pkg/*


# http://godoc.org/code.google.com/p/go.tools/cmd/vet
```

```
# go get code.google.com/p/go.tools/cmd/vet
vet:
# go vet ./src/...
```

This mechanism takes a snapshot of the dependencies, with actual code, and checks it into the vendor folder. Thus, everything required to build the project is contained in the Git repository.

A few people who have interacted with me have expressed reservations about managing dependencies inside the parent repository; they suggested things such as git submodules as alternatives.

Submodules are *pseudo* git repositories stored within the parent repository. The parent just stores the SHA (hash ID) of a specific commit for each submodule inside a directory for each dependency. While this looks convenient and clean in terms of isolation, it can lead to lot of subtle issues:

- **Easy overwrite of submodules**: You need to run an explicit `git submodule update` command to pull the latest version of the dependencies. Without this command, even with a normal `git pull`, the submodules don't get updated. If the submodule update is not done, then the submodule repository reference will still be pointing to an older version. If someone else updates the submodule, the update will not be available for your checkout. Also, it's quite easy to commit the old submodule version in your next parent commit—thus effectively reverting the submodule update for all others! Submodule maintenance needs a strict process to be used properly.
- **Merge difficulty**: If you are rebasing, and there is a conflict in the dependency, all that shows up are different SHAs. There is no way to figure out the difference.
- **Detached head**: When you invoke git submodule update, each submodule gets a checkout of the corresponding SHA, and this puts the submodule into a detached `HEAD` state. Any changes you commit will still leave the submodule in a detached `HEAD` state. In this situation, an action such as `rebase` (which merges other changes) won't show up as conflicts, and your changes will be overwritten by what is being merged.

While there are other tools, such as **Git subtree**, considering simplicity, I still recommend checking in the vendor folder (with source) in the parent repository.

Framework

Once your company/team starts writing Go code, you will notice that people are building lots of similar code. You would ideally want to re-factor such code into a `framework` package that can be used by multiple projects in the company. Typical areas of re-use include authentication, logging, configuration, helper classes, and so on.

This can be thought of as an `internal third-party` package under the vendor and maintained as mentioned.

While common code is good, it is also tougher to engineer right. We need to ensure that there are clear guidelines for writing such code. Some of these are as follows:

- The configuration for the code should be externalized. For example, it should not expect a configuration file at `/etc/config/my_lib`.
- This logger inside the code should get context from the environment.
- This code should as far as possible, not handle errors on its own. It should translate library events into something meaningful related to the contract and emit them.

Testing

There are two critical aspects that affect the testability of a good application:

- Writing code that can be tested easily
- Having self-contained, easily reproducible tests

The first part is about structuring code so that the code business logic is isolated from dependencies such as external services, and so on. This allows mocking the dependencies about these boundaries to allow the test cases to exercise the execution flow along various interesting paths. For example, consider you are writing the flight search feature on a travel marketplace. There are two aspects to this:

- Obtaining prices for a sector from various providers
- Running some business logic to filter and sort the results

Now, it may not be possible to get various error scenarios reliably reproduced by making direct calls to the provider. Also, it might be expensive (and insecure) to give API keys to each developer. This will affect the testability of our overall code. To overcome this, you might cleanly segregate the two parts as follows:

- The `Seller` package(s) that implements the logic to interact with the seller, using the API and getting the prices (among other things).
- The `Search` package that implements the business logic of aggregating results and sorting them.

These two packages can be built and tested independently.

For testing the `leaf` package Seller, you need simple Golang test driver code, which exercises the code along interesting paths and validates output. Examples of how we can structure this using tables is given next.

For testing the interior `Search` package, you can mock the `Seller` package to return mock data. Mocking can be done at the interface level (using tools such as **GoMock.** For more details, visit `https://github.com/golang/mock`), or at the package level using build tags. The latter is a neat way of mocking—essentially, you can selectively compile parts of a package based on a tag. So, for example, we can have a single file that implements mocks for all the exported methods of the package:

```
// +build AirlineAMock
// Mock for the Airline A Seller
package airlineA
func NewClient() *airlineA {
return makeAMockClient()
}
func (a *airlineA )  getPrices( srcDate, dstDate TravelDate, src, dst
Places) {
        return getPricesFromLocalFile(srcDate, dstDate, srcDate,
dstDate)
}
```

The other files in the package can be prefixed with the `// +build !AirlineAMock` string. With this, when the package is built using the following, a mocked version of the package is built:

```
go build airlineA -tags 'AirlineAMock'
```

Structuring tests

Many times when writing tests, you will find yourself copying and pasting code. Experienced programmers know that this is never an ideal scenario. To remain **DRY** (**Don't Repeat Yourself**), one excellent solution is table-driven tests. Here, the test cases are written as (`<complete inputs>`, expected output) tuples in a table with a common driver code. Each table entry can sometimes have additional information such as a test name to make the test output easily readable. Here is a good example from the testing code for the `fmt` package (http://golang.org/pkg/fmt/):

```
var flagtests = []struct {
in  string
out string
}{
{"%a", "[%a]"},
{"%-a", "[%-a]"},
{"%+a", "[%+a]"},
{"%#a", "[%#a]"},
{"% a", "[% a]"},
{"%0a", "[%0a]"},
{"%1.2a", "[%1.2a]"},
{"%-1.2a", "[%-1.2a]"},
{"%+1.2a", "[%+1.2a]"},
{"%-+1.2a", "[%+-1.2a]"},
{"%-+1.2abc", "[%+-1.2a]bc"},
{"%-1.2abc", "[%-1.2a]bc"},
}

func TestFlagParser(t *testing.T) {
    var flagprinter flagPrinter
        for _, tt := range flagtests {
                s := Sprintf(tt.in, &flagprinter)
                if s != tt.out {
                t.Errorf("Sprintf(%q, &flagprinter) => %q, want %q", tt.in,
s, tt.out)
                }
            }
        }
```

Given a table of test cases, the actual test simply iterates through all table entries and, for each entry, performs the necessary tests. The test code can be written well once (good error messages, and so on) and reused across tests. This structure makes adding new tests a very low-overhead task.

With Go 1.7, the testing package supports sub-tests that can be run in parallel, thereby reducing the total test execution time. For example, the following code runs through in one second, not four:

```
func TestParallel(t *testing.T) {
        tests := []struct {
        dur time.Duration
    }{
            {time.Second},
            {time.Second},
            {time.Second},
            {time.Second},
        }
    for _, tc := range tests {
        t.Run("", func(subtest *testing.T) {
            subtest.Parallel()
            time.Sleep(tc.dur)
    })
    }
    }
```

A final word of caution on unit tests. While automated unit tests provide the insurance/guardrails to move fast in terms of development, on many occasions, the very frameworks that we choose to make our lives easier sometimes get in the way. As Daniel Lebrero aptly summarized in his blog (`http://labs.ig.com/code-coverage-100-percent-tragedy`), one common anti-pattern is writing a huge amount of test harness code for something that is straightforward. This results in code being fragile and tough-to-iterate-on. Every technique/recommendation has a context, and when the recommendation is applied blindly, it can lead to developer frustration and, ultimately, lack of quality.

Summary

To summarize, good packaging is important because it enables changes to code to happen faster with less risk (it is easy to grasp what to change and where due to the clear separation of concerns within the modules). This also leads to fewer bugs in production.

Good packaging also helps the non-technical aspects of engineering: there is a clear quanta of ownership for teams, and so there are fewer conflicts/communication and more of a sense of ownership.

In the next chapter, we will begin to look at design patterns. These are blueprints for solutions to various well-known scenarios that we encounter in software engineering.

3
Design Patterns

Design patterns are solutions to recurring problems in software engineering. Rather than a comprehensive solution, a design pattern is a description of a problem and a template of how to solve it. This template then becomes usable in many different contexts.

The idea is to study both the problem and the applicable solutions. The motivation is that once you have done this, it is easy to recognize patterns among the product requirements and architecture and bring ruggedized, pre-conceived solutions to the problem. Another key advantage is that once your design is composed of well-known patterns, it is easy to communicate and discuss the design with other colleagues/stakeholders.

Design patterns can be roughly categorized into three areas:

- Creational
- Structural
- Behavioral

We shall look at these patterns in detail in the following sections. However, we will begin the discussion with the basic design principles that form the guidelines for all the patterns.

Design principles

There are two key aspects to be taken care of in low-level design:

- **Responsibility assignment**: What is the responsibility of each class?
- **Dependency management**: What other classes should this class depend on, and what is the contract between these classes?

Robert C Martin (Uncle Bob) has very nicely laid out five principles of good class design to guide us when doing low-level object-oriented design in his book *Agile Software Development, Principles, Patterns, and Practices*. Though the book and the languages used there are old, the principles are still true and extensible to Go. A mnemonic to remember these principles has been called SOLID (each letter corresponding to a specific principle), as shown here:

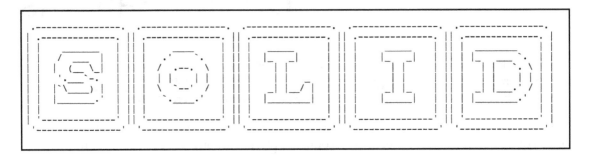

Single Responsibility Principle (S)

The principle states the following:

> *"One class should have one, and only one, responsibility."*

While this seems obvious, it is important to have discipline to maintain this principle in the face of the ever-increasing complexity of product requirements. For example, on our travel website, let's say we model a ticket using an entity struct (entity classes are a representation of persistent objects in memory; they present the *data*). Initially, the company did only airline reservations and the ticket was modeled as such. However, after some time, the product had requirements for hotel reservations or bus tickets. With the knowledge of the new requirements, our previous design might not be the best one possible. When such new requirements arise, it is important to refactor code to stay true to the guidelines mentioned here.

So, in this specific example, instead of clubbing the ticket semantics of all business verticals, it is important to build a hierarchy with say `reservation` as the base class and `AirlineTicket`, `BusTicket`, and `HotelReservations` as all the derived classes. Patterns to build such a hierarchy are described later in the chapter. An example of the reservation interface is shown here:

```
type Reservation interface {
    GetReservationDate() string
    CalculateCancellationFee() float64
```

```
        Cancel()
        GetCustomerDetails() []Customer
        GetSellerDetails() Seller
    }
```

Of course, this is a very minimal set of methods for illustrative purposes only. When the client code does not care about the type of the reservation, extraneous coupling is not introduced.

Besides classes, this principle is more important in package design. For example, packages named `utils` become a dumping ground of miscellaneous functions. Such a name and collection should be avoided. On the other hand, some examples of good package names from the Go standard library, which clearly indicate the purpose, are as follows:

- `net/http`: this provides `http` clients and servers.
- `encoding/json`: this implements JSON serialization/deserialization.

Open/Closed Principle (O)

The original text of the principle is this:

> *"You should be able to extend a class's behavior without modifying it."*

This essentially means that classes should be open for extension but closed for modification, so it should be possible to extend or override class behavior without having to modify code. Behavior change should be pluggable into the class, either through overriding some methods or injecting some configuration. One excellent example of a framework exhibiting this principle is the Spring Framework.

One common place to use this principle is for algorithms or business logic. In our travel website, let's say we have two requirements:

- We should be able to bundle airline and hotel reservations into a `Trip` object.
- We should be able to calculate the cancellation fee for a trip.

Thus, we can model `Trips` as a `struct` with a collection (repository) of reservations, and for the cancellation, have each derived type of reservation compute the cancellation fee, as shown here:

```
        type Trip struct {
            reservations []Reservation
        }
```

```
func (t *Trip) CalculateCancellationFee() float64 {
    total:= 0.0

    for _, r:= range(t.reservations) {
        total += r.CalculateCancellationFee()
    }

    return total
}

func (t *Trip) AddReservation (r Reservation) {
    t.reservations = append(t.reservations, r)
}
```

In the future, if we have a new type of reservation, as long as it implements the `CalculateCancellationFee()` method of the reservation interface, the `CalculateCancellationFee()` method should be calculating the cancellation fee.

Liskov Substitution Principle (L)

This is a slight variation of the **Open/Closed Principle**, and Uncle Bob states it as follows:

"Derived types must be substitutable for their base types."

This principle is called **Liskov** because it was first written by Barbara Liskov:

"What is wanted here is something like the following substitution property: If for each object o1 of type S there is an object o2 of type T such that for all programs P defined in terms of T, the behavior of P is unchanged when o1 is substituted for o2—then S is a subtype of T.

The crux of the principle is that derived classes must be usable through the base class interface without the need for the client to know the specific derived class.

As we have seen earlier, in Go, object orientation is enabled by composition (prototype pattern), rather than class hierarchies. So, though this principle does not imply as strongly as other languages, it does give us guidance to interface design: the interface should be able to suffice for all structs that implement that interface.

A good example for application of this principle is the previous example of cancellation fee calculation. This enables a clear separation of concerns:

- The client who wants to compute the cancellation fee for a trip does not care about the specific type of reservations in the trip.
- The trip's code does not know how each reservation computes the cancellation fee.

If, however, the client code tries to check the type of derived class (through `Reflection` for example) to explicitly call the `cancellation-fee` method on each (concrete) type of reservation, then the abstraction breaks down. The **Liskov Substitution Principle** (**LSP**) precisely advises against doing this type of thing.

Interface Segregation Principle (I)

This principle states this:

"Many client-specific interfaces are better than one general-purpose interface."

As our code evolves, it is a common symptom for base classes to be a *collect-all* for behavior. However, this makes the whole code brittle: derived classes have to implement methods that don't make sense to them. Clients also can get confused by this variable nature of derived classes. To avoid this, this principle recommends having an interface for each type of client.

For example, in the preceding reservation example, let's say we have a *fat* reservation base class for all airline, hotel, bus tickets, and so on. Now suppose airline reservations have a special method; say, `AddExtraLuggageAllowance()`, which allows the ticket holder to carry extra luggage. With a hotel reservation, we need the ability to change the room type—`ChangeType()`. With a naive design, all these methods would be stuffed in the base reservation class, with derived classes having to implement unrelated methods. A better design is to have the base reservation class just deal with the common behavior and have specific interfaces for airline, bus, and hotel reservations:

```
type Reservation interface {
    GetReservationDate() string
    CalculateCancellationFee() float64
}

type HotelReservation interface {
    Reservation
    ChangeType()
}
```

```
type FlightReservation interface {
    Reservation
    AddExtraLuggageAllowance(peices int)
}

type HotelReservationImpl struct{
    reservationDate string
}

func (r HotelReservationImpl) GetReservationDate() string {
    return r.reservationDate
}

func (r HotelReservationImpl) CalculateCancellationFee() float64 {
    return 1.0 // flat:P
}

type FlightReservationImpl struct{
    reservationDate string
    luggageAllowed int
}

func (r FlightReservationImpl) AddExtraLuggageAllowance(peices int)   {
    r.luggageAllowed = peices
}


func (r FlightReservationImpl) CalculateCancellationFee() float64 {
    return 2.0 // flat but slight more than hotels:P
}


func (r FlightReservationImpl) GetReservationDate() string {
    // this might look repetitive, but the idea is to provide freedom for
the
    // derived classes to flux independently of each other
    return r.reservationDate
}
```

Dependency Inversion Principle (D)

The final principle is the **Dependency Inversion Principle**, which states the following:

"Depend on abstractions, not on concretions."

This means that higher-level modules should depend only on interfaces and not on concrete implementations. In Java, huge frameworks such as Spring have come up as *dependency injection* capabilities so that beans (objects) can be injected into the application at runtime, while the rest of the code just works with interfaces of the beans (rather than the concrete implementations).

In Go, this principle boils down to two recommendations:

- Every package should have interfaces that advertise functionality without the implementation specifics.
- When a package needs a dependency, it should take that dependency as a parameter.

To illustrate the second point, let's say we have built two packages (layers) for the search microservice of our travel website:

- **Service layer**: This layer has a lot of the business logic for the searching and sorting.
- **Communication layer**: This layer is just responsible for getting data from different sellers. Each seller has its own API, and thus this layer has a lot of different implementations of a `SellerCommunication` interface.

According to this principle, we should be able to *inject* a specific instantiation of the communication layer to the service layer. The injection of the concrete implementation of the communication layer can be done through the driver's main function. This allows the service layer to function just knowing (depending on) on the `SellerCommunication` interface and not on a specific implementation. One way to immediately exploit this is mocking—the `SellerDAO` interface can be mocked for test cases of the service layer components.

With these principles in mind, let's look at specific design patterns, beginning with **creational design patterns**.

Creational design patterns

Creational design patterns are design patterns that deal with object creation mechanisms in a safe and efficient manner and decouple clients from implementation specifics. With these patterns, the code using an object need not know details about how the object is created, or even the specific type of object, as long as the object adheres to the interface expected.

Factory method

A **factory** is an object that is used to create other objects. We looked at the preceding reservation interface. Essentially, it is an association between an item for sale and a user who bought it, along with some metadata such as dates and so on, and there will be multiple types of reservation. So, how does the client code create a reservation without knowing about implementation classes such as `HotelReservationImpl`?

In a factory method pattern, a helper method (or function) is defined, to enable object creation without knowing the implementation class details. For example, in the case of reservation, the simple factory can be this:

```
func NewReservation(vertical, reservationDate string) Reservation {
    switch(vertical) {
        case "flight":
            return FlightReservationImpl{reservationDate,}
        case "hotel":
            return HotelReservationImpl{reservationDate,}
        default:
            return nil
    }
}
```

It can be used as follows:

```
hotelReservation:= NewReservation("hotel","20180101")
```

Builder

Sometimes, object creation is not so straightforward. For example:

- It might be necessary to have business rules to validate some parameters or derive some added attributes. For example, in a reservation, we might derive a `nonCancellable` attribute based on the vertical, seller, and travel date details.
- We might need some code to bring in efficiency—for example, retrieving an object from the cache rather than reading from the DB.
- It might be necessary to have idempotency and thread safety in object creation. That is, multiple requests for object creation with the same parameters should give the same object.
- The objects might have multiple constructor arguments (typically called **telescopic constructors**), and it is difficult to remember the order of parameters for the clients. Some of these parameters might be optional. Such constructors frequently lead to bugs in client code.

The builder pattern allows you to create different flavors of an object while enforcing the constraints mentioned previously. For our reservation example, the builder will look like this:

```
type ReservationBuilder interface {
    Vertical(string) ReservationBuilder
    ReservationDate(string) ReservationBuilder
    Build() Reservation
}

type reservationBuilder struct {
    vertical string
    rdate string
}

func (r *reservationBuilder) Vertical(v string) ReservationBuilder {
    r.vertical = v
    return r
}

func (r *reservationBuilder) ReservationDate(date string)
ReservationBuilder {
    r.rdate = date
    return r
}

func (r *reservationBuilder) Build() Reservation {
    var builtReservation Reservation

    switch r.vertical {
        case "flight":
            builtReservation = FlightReservationImpl{r.rdate}
        case "hotel":
            builtReservation = HotelReservationImpl{r.rdate}
    }

    return builtReservation
}

func NewReservationBuilder() ReservationBuilder {
    return &reservationBuilder{}
}
```

As you can see, our object creation is much more powerful. The lazy creation (after we have all the arguments) also helps us exploit efficiency goals; for example, loading an expensive-to-create object from the cache.

Abstract factory

With real-life problems, there are many *related* (family of) objects that need to be created together. For example, if our travel website decides to give away invoices for reservations, then with our two verticals we essentially have the following:

- Two types of entities: reservation and invoice
- Two verticals/types of products: hotel and flight

When the client code is creating such related products, how do we ensure that clients don't make mistakes (for example, associating a flight invoice to a hotel reservation)? The simple factory method does not cut it here, since the client would need to figure out all the right factories needed for each type of entity/object.

The abstract factory pattern attempts to solve this issue with a *factory of factories* construct: a factory that groups the different related/dependent factories together without specifying their concrete classes:

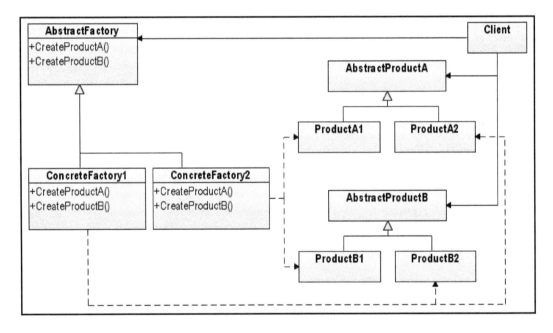

An implementation of an abstract factory with the reservation/invoice:

```go
// We have Reservation and Invoice as two generic products
type Reservation interface{}
type Invoice interface{}
```

```go
type AbstractFactory interface {
    CreateReservation() Reservation
    CreateInvoice() Invoice
}

type HotelFactory struct{}

func (f HotelFactory) CreateReservation() Reservation {
    return new(HotelReservation)
}

func (f HotelFactory) CreateInvoice() Invoice {
    return new(HotelInvoice)
}

type FlightFactory struct{}

func (f FlightFactory) CreateReservation() Reservation {
    return new(FlightReservation)
}

func (f FlightFactory) CreateInvoice() Invoice {
    return new(FlightReservation)
}


type HotelReservation struct{}
type HotelInvoice struct{}
type FlightReservation struct{}
type FlightInvoice struct{}

func GetFactory(vertical string) AbstractFactory {
    var factory AbstractFactory
    switch vertical {
        case "flight":
            factory = FlightFactory{}
        case "hotel":
        factory = HotelFactory{}
    }

    return factory
}
```

The client can use the abstract factory as follows:

```go
hotelFactory:= GetFactory("hotel")
reservation:= hotelFactory.CreateReservation()
invoice:= hotelFactory.CreateInvoice()
```

Singleton

Sometimes, you may come across a need to restrict the number of objects of a specific time in the system. **Singleton** is the design pattern that restricts the creation of objects to a single one. This might be useful, for example, when you want a single *coordinator* object across in multiple places of the code.

The following code snippet shows how to implement the singleton pattern in Go. Note that we have used the `sync.Do()` method: if `once.Do(f)` is called multiple times, only the first call will invoke the function *f*, even in the face of multiple threads calling this simultaneously:

```go
type MyClass struct {
    attrib string
}

func (c* MyClass ) SetAttrib(val string) {
    c.attrib = val
}

func (c* MyClass ) GetAttrib() string {
    return c.attrib
}

var (
    once sync.Once
    instance *MyClass
)

func GetMyClass() *MyClass {
    once.Do(func() {
        instance = &MyClass{"first"}
    })

    return instance
}
```

It can be used as follows:

```go
a:= GetMyClass()
a.SetAttrib("second")
fmt.Println(a.GetAttrib()) // will print second
b:= GetMyClass()
fmt.Println(b.GetAttrib()) // will also print second
```

It should be noted that the singleton pattern is actually considered an anti-pattern because of the introduction of a global state. This causes a *hidden* coupling between components and can lead to difficult-to-debug situations. It should not be overused.

Structural design patterns

In software engineering, structural design patterns help delineate clean relationships between objects and simplify design. Unlike creational patterns that we saw previously, these patterns are quite varied and represent a bouquet of recipes for various situations.

Adaptor

Many times when you code, you come across situations where you have a new requirement, and a component that almost meets that requirement. A non-software example of this situation is the power adapter: a three-legged plug from India can't be connected to a two-pronged outlet in the US. You need to use a power adapter to enable compatibility and use both entities.

In the pattern, there is an adaptor class that proxies what is required and delegates the work to the **Adaptee** (the incompatible class), using a method expected by the **Adaptee**. This is shown in the following diagram:

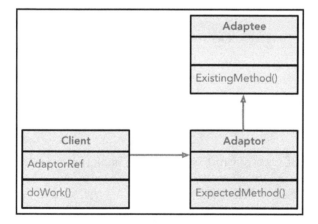

In theory, there are two ways of implementing this pattern:

- Object **Adaptor**: Here, the adaptor class has an instance of the **Adaptee** class and the adaptor method delegates the work to the wrapped instance.
- Class **Adaptor**: Here, the adaptor is a *mix-in* (a class with multiple inheritance) and inherits from both places:
    - The interface that is expected
    - The **Adaptee** interface

In Golang, the object `Adaptor` is much more amenable. A sample is given here:

```
type Adaptee struct{}
    func (a *Adaptee) ExistingMethod() {
    fmt.Println("using existing method")
}

type Adapter struct {
    adaptee *Adaptee
}

func NewAdapter() *Adapter {
    return &Adapter{new(Adaptee)}
}

func (a *Adapter) ExpectedMethod() {
    fmt.Println("doing some work")
    a.adaptee.ExistingMethod()
}
```

And the client `doWork()` will look as simple as this:

```
adaptor:= NewAdapter()
adaptor.ExpectedMethod()
```

Bridge

Consider a use case in our travel product where we have two types of reservations:

- **Premium reservations**: special benefits such as free cancellation, better cashback, and so on.
- **Normal reservation**: normal restrictions.

Also, recall from `Chapter 2`, *Packaging Code*, that we have two types of sellers:

- **Institutional**: those who can give us an API to pull data off and do our bookings.
- **Small scale**: those who will use a platform we build as a part of this product to onboard inventory.

The reservations are finally fulfilled by the sellers. The naive implementation will have a matrix of the reservation type for each type of seller. However, very soon, the code will become unmaintainable. As the code grows in complexity, we might find hard-to-engineer binding between interface and implementation.

The *is a* relationships between the interfaces start getting mixed up with the implementation details. The abstraction and implementation cannot both be independently extended.

The bridge pattern aims to solve this as follows:

- Decoupling the abstraction from the implementation so that both can vary independently
- Segregating the interface hierarchy and the implementation hierarchy into two separate trees

This pattern is described here:

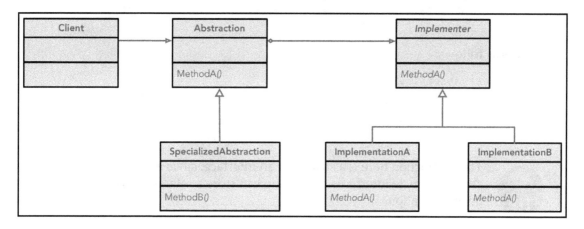

The dummy implementation for the use case mentioned previously is given here:

```
type Reservation struct {
    sellerRef Seller // this is the implementer reference
}
```

```go
func (r Reservation) Cancel() {
    r.sellerRef.CancelReservation(10) // charge $10 as cancellation feed
}

type PremiumReservation struct {
    Reservation
}

func (r PremiumReservation) Cancel() {
    r.sellerRef.CancelReservation(0) // no charges
}

// This is the interface for all Sellers
type Seller interface {
    CancelReservation(charge float64)
}

type InstitutionSeller struct {}

func (s InstitutionSeller) CancelReservation(charge float64) {
    fmt.Println("InstitutionSeller CancelReservation charge =", charge)
}

type SmallScaleSeller struct {}

func (s SmallScaleSeller) CancelReservation(charge float64) {
    fmt.Println("SmallScaleSeller CancelReservation charge =", charge)
}
```

Its usage is as follows:

```go
res := Reservation{InstitutionSeller{}}
res.Cancel()                // will print 10 as the cancellation charge

premiumRes := PremiumReservation{Reservation{SmallScaleSeller{}}}
premiumRes.Cancel()   // will print 0 as the cancellation charge
```

The abstraction here is a struct not an interface, since in Go you can't have abstract structs/interfaces where you can store a reference to the seller implementation.

Composite

Many times, we come across structures that are comprised of leaf elements. However, the clients don't really care about this nature and want to behave with single (leaf) and composite structures in the same way. The expectation is that composites delegate the behavior to each constituent leaf.

The pattern can be visualized by this figure:

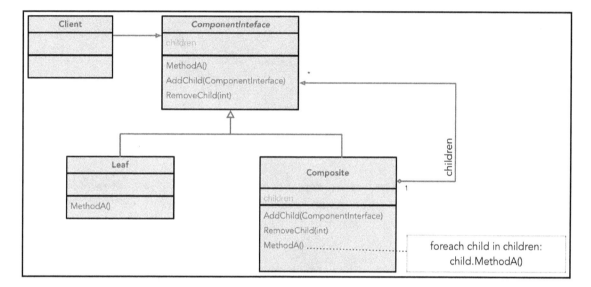

Here is some sample code in Golang:

```go
type InterfaceX interface {
    MethodA()
    AddChild(InterfaceX)
}

type Composite struct{
    children []InterfaceX
}

func (c *Composite) MethodA() {
    if len(c.children) == 0 {
        fmt.Println("I'm a leaf ")
        return
    }

    fmt.Println("I'm a composite ")
```

```
        for _, child:= range c.children {
            child.MethodA()
        }
    }

    func (c *Composite) AddChild(child InterfaceX) {
        c.children = append(c.children, child)
    }
```

The usage is shown as follows:

```
    func test() {
    var parent InterfaceX

    parent = &Composite{}
    parent.MethodA() // only  a leaf and the print will confirm!

    var child Composite
    parent.AddChild(&child)
    parent.MethodA() // one composite, one  leaf
    }
```

 The code for composite implements the interface using pointer receivers because the AddChild method needs to mutate the struct.

Decorator

The **decorator** pattern allows the extension of a function of an existing object dynamically without the need to alter the original object. This is achieved by wrapping the original object and function into a new function.

The decorator pattern is illustrated by the following code, which can be used to profile how much time another function takes to execute.

A toy profiler that just works with a function taking and returning float is shown here:

```
    type Function func(float64) float64

    // the decorator function
    func ProfileDecorator(fn Function) Function {
        return func(params float64) float64 {
            start:= time.Now()
            result:= fn(params)
            elapsed:= time.Now().Sub(start)
```

```
        fmt.Println("Function completed with time: ", elapsed)
        return result
    }
}


func client(){
    decoratedSquqreRoot:= ProfileDecorator(SquareRoot)
    fmt.Println(decoratedSquqreRoot(16))
}
```

Like the tracing example, logging and other types of middleware are common places where the decorator pattern is employed.

Facade

When a package has multiple interfaces, it can get difficult for clients to use it. Though the individual interfaces may be exciting for a power user, most clients will get confused with the complicated details they don't care about.

The facade design pattern solves this, with advertising an alternative/simplified interface to other parts of the code. This is shown by this figure:

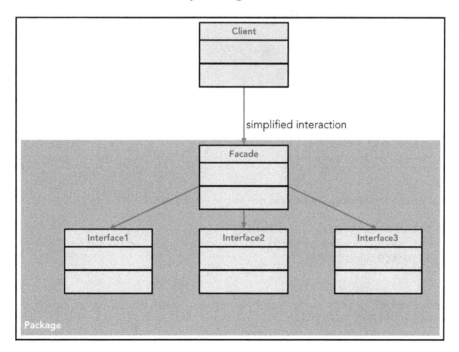

In Golang, a facade can be implemented using an interface and struct, which offers a simplified interaction model over the rest of the interfaces.

Proxy

In our product, the fulfilment is done by external sellers. For institutional sellers, there is an external API that needs to be called to perform actions such as booking. Suppose an institutional seller, say HotelBoutique, gives a REST API (more on API types in a follow-up chapter); how should the system interact with this external agent? Obviously, the first thought that comes to our mind is to encapsulate and isolate the HotelBoutique specifics in one place.

A proxy is essentially a class functioning as an interface to something else. It is an object that delegates the work to the subject (that which is being proxied) and abstracts clients from the subject specifics. The specifics include the location, so this allows cool design where the client and the subject may or may not be in the same compiled binary, but the rest of the code works without any change.

The proxy delegation can simply be forwarding, or it can provide additional logic (for example, caching).

For the HotelBoutique example, the proxy pattern, with a dummy class instead of the API call, is given here:

```
// Proxy
type HotelBoutiqueProxy struct {
    subject *HotelBoutique
}

func (p *HotelBoutiqueProxy) Book() {
    if p.subject == nil {
        p.subject = new(HotelBoutique)
    }

    fmt.Println("Proxy Delegating Booking call")

    // The API call will happen here
    // For example sake a simple delegation  is implemented
    p.subject.Book()
}

// Dummy Subject
type HotelBoutique struct{}
```

```
func (s *HotelBoutique) Book() {
    fmt.Println("Booking done on external site")
}
```

Behavioral design patterns

Behavioral design patterns are design patterns that identify communication patterns among objects and provide solution templates for specific situations. In doing so, these patterns increase the extensibility of the interactions.

Some of the patterns are concerned with reducing the coupling of sending and receivers, while others describe how the internal state (and any change notifications) of an object's state can be made available to other interested objects. So, as you can imagine, this is a pretty diverse bunch of patterns.

Command

The command pattern is a behavioral design pattern in which an object is used to represent a request (or actions) and encapsulate all information needed to process the same. This information includes the method name, the object that owns the method, and values for the method parameters.

Many times, the command needs to be persisted. This can happen if the command is going to be a long-running one or when you need to remember the commands to support features such as **undo** in a word processor (here, each change to the document will be a command).

The players in the command pattern are as follows:

- A command interface that encapsulates various actions to be done. It generally has a single `execute()` method to actually perform the requested command. There are many common interface declared for all concrete commands.
- Concrete commands implement the actual operations. Some commands can be self-contained. Others require a receiver, an external object that actually does the work. In the latter case, the concrete command's `execute()` method delegates to the receiver.
- An invoker object knows how to execute a command, and optionally does book keeping about the command execution. The invoker is only dependent on the command interface and not the concrete commands. It usually has a repository of commands. In case of long-running background jobs, the invoker also plays the role of a scheduler for these commands.

- The last is the client that has references to all the invoker objects, command objects, and receiver objects and orchestrates the flow:

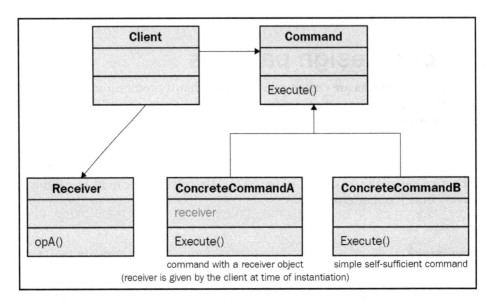

command with a receiver object   simple self-sufficient command
(receiver is given by the client at time of instantiation)

A key requirement to the travel marketplace was business insights gleaned from reports. These could vary from user insights on various features to top-performing sellers in a specific category.

As we have seen in the introductory chapter, all such functionality is split into frontend (the client side code mostly responsible for rendering elements) and the backend (an API server that does the actual computation). We have a dedicated chapter on API design later on, but a common method of modeling such APIs is called **Representational State Transfer (REST)**. Here, we have a resource analogous to an object, and the APIs are essentially methods that get/set on this resource.

We can model this analytics API as a report API, where clients can request a report by doing POST on a */reports* URL. The backed will turn this request to a command and schedule it to be done by background workers. The following code snippet shows the command pattern in action in this scenario. Here, report is the command interface and client is the web layer of the API handler:

```
// The Command
type Report interface {
    Execute()
}
```

```go
// The Concrete Commands
type ConcreteReportA struct {
    receiver *Receiver
}

func (c *ConcreteReportA) Execute() {
    c.receiver.Action("ReportA")
}

type ConcreteReportB struct {
    receiver *Receiver
}

func (c *ConcreteReportB) Execute() {
    c.receiver.Action("ReportB")
}


// The Receiver
type Receiver struct{}

func (r *Receiver) Action(msg string) {
    fmt.Println(msg)
}

// Invoker
type Invoker struct {
    repository []Report
}

func (i *Invoker) Schedule(cmd Report) {
    i.repository = append(i.repository, cmd)
}

func (i *Invoker) Run() {
    for _, cmd:= range i.repository {
        cmd.Execute()
    }
}
```

The client code will look as follows:

```go
func client() {
    receiver:= new(Receiver)
    ReportA:= &ConcreteReportA{receiver}
    ReportB:= &ConcreteReportB{receiver}

    invoker:= new(Invoker)
```

```
    invoker.Schedule(ReportA)
    invoker.Run()
    invoker.Schedule(ReportB)
    invoker.Run()
}
```

Chain of Responsibility

Many times, the commands described previously might need handling such that we want a receiver to do work only when it is able to, and it's not then hand off the command to someone else next in the *chain*. For example, for the reports use case, we might want to handle authenticated and unauthenticated users differently.

The Chain of Responsibility pattern enables this by chaining a set of receiver objects. The receiver at the head of the chain tries to handle the command first, and if it's not able to handle it, delegates it to the next.

The sample code is given here:

```go
type ChainedReceiver struct {
    canHandle string
    next *ChainedReceiver
}

func (r *ChainedReceiver) SetNext(next *ChainedReceiver) {
    r.next = next
}

func (r *ChainedReceiver) Finish() error   {
    fmt.Println(r.canHandle, " Receiver Finishing")
    return nil
}

func (r *ChainedReceiver) Handle(what string) error {
    // Check if this receiver can handle the command
    if what==r.canHandle {
        // handle the command here
        return r.Finish()
    } else if r.next != nil {
        // delegate to the next guy
        return r.next.Handle(what)
    } else {
        fmt.Println("No Receiver could handle the request!")
        return errors.New("No Receiver to Handle")
    }
}
```

Mediator

The mediator pattern adds a third-party object (called a *mediator*) to control the interaction between two objects (colleagues). By virtue of the mediator object, the communicating classes don't get coupled to each other's implementation .

It helps reduce the coupling between the classes communicating with each other, because now they don't need to have the knowledge of each other's implementation.

Sample code is given here:

```go
// The Mediator interface
type Mediator interface {
    AddColleague(colleague Colleague)
}


// The Colleague interface
type Colleague interface {
    setMediator(mediator Mediator)
}


// Concrete Colleague 1 - uses state as string
type Colleague1 struct {
    mediator Mediator
    state string
}

func (c *Colleague1)  SetMediator(mediator Mediator) {
    c.mediator = mediator
}

func (c *Colleague1)  SetState(state string) {
    fmt.Println("Colleague1: setting state: ", state)
    c.state = state
}

func (c *Colleague1)  GetState()  string {
    return c.state
}


// Concrete Colleague 2 - uses state as int
type Colleague2 struct {
    mediator Mediator
    state int
```

```
    }

    func (c *Colleague2)  SetState(state int) {
        fmt.Println("Colleague2: setting state: ", state)
        c.state = state
    }

    func (c *Colleague2)  GetState()  int {
        return c.state
    }

    func (c *Colleague2)  SetMediator(mediator Mediator) {
        c.mediator = mediator
    }


    // Concrete Mediator
    type ConcreteMediator struct {
        c1 Colleague1
        c2 Colleague2
    }

    func (m *ConcreteMediator)  SetColleagueC1(c1 Colleague1) {
        m.c1 = c1
    }

    func (m *ConcreteMediator)  SetColleagueC2(c2 Colleague2) {
        m.c2 = c2
    }

    func (m *ConcreteMediator)  SetState(s string) {
        m.c1.SetState(s)
        stateAsString, err:= strconv.Atoi(s)
        if err == nil {
            m.c2.SetState(stateAsString)
            fmt.Println("Mediator set status for both colleagues")
        }
    }
```

Client code is given here:

```
    c1:= Colleague1{}
    c2:= Colleague2{}

    // initialize mediator with colleagues
    mediator:= ConcreteMediator{}
    mediator.SetColleagueC1(c1)
    mediator.SetColleagueC2(c2)
```

```
// mediator keeps colleagues in sync
mediator.SetState("10")
```

Memento

The memento pattern is about capturing and storing the current state of an object so that it can be restored later on in a smooth manner. This pattern has three players:

- The originator is an object that has an internal state.
- The caretaker is planning to do something that might change the originator state. But in case of any problems, it wants to be able to undo (or rollback) the change.
- To accomplish this, the caretaker starts off by asking the originator for a memento object. After this, the caretaker performs the mutation/operations. If some trouble ensues, it returns the memento object to the originator.

The important thing in this pattern is that the memento object is opaque, and thus encapsulation of the originator object is not broken.

The code for the pattern is given here:

```
// Originator
type Originator struct {
    state string
}

func (o *Originator) GetState()   string {
    return o.state
}

func (o *Originator) SetState(state string) {
    fmt.Println("Setting state to " + state)
    o.state = state
}

func (o *Originator) GetMemento() Memento {
    // externalize state to Momemto objct
    return Memento{o.state}
}


func (o *Originator) Restore(memento Memento) {
    // restore state
    o.state = memento.GetState()
}
```

```go
// Momento
type Memento struct {
    serializedState string
}

func (m *Memento) GetState() string {
    return m.serializedState
}


// caretaker

func Caretaker() {
    // assume that A is the original state of the Orginator
    theOriginator:= Originator{"A"}
    theOriginator.SetState("A")
    fmt.Println("theOriginator state = ", theOriginator.GetState() )

    // before mutating, get an momemto
    theMomemto:= theOriginator.GetMemento()

    // mutate to unclean
    theOriginator.SetState("unclean")
    fmt.Println("theOriginator state = ", theOriginator.GetState() )

    // rollback
    theOriginator.Restore(theMomemto)
    fmt.Println("RESTORED: theOriginator state = ",
theOriginator.GetState() )
}
```

Observer

In many situations, there is one entity (subject) with state and several others (observers) that are interested in that state. The observer pattern is a software design pattern that defines the interaction between the subject and the observer. Essentially, the subject maintains a list of observers and notifies them of any state changes. The pattern is shown in this figure:

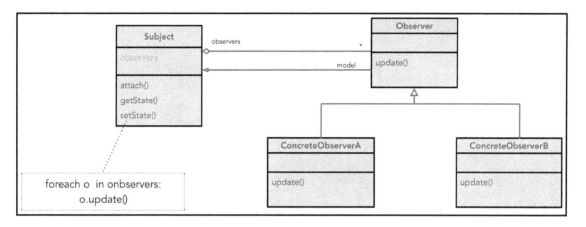

Here is the implementation in Go:

```go
// The Subject

type Subject struct {
    observers []Observer
    state string
}

func (s *Subject) Attach(observer Observer) {
    s.observers = append(s.observers, observer)
}


func (s *Subject) SetState(newState string) {
    s.state = newState
    for _,o:= range(s.observers) {
        o.Update()
    }
}

func (s *Subject) GetState()   string {
    return s.state
}

// The Observer Inteface

type Observer interface {
    Update()
}

// Concrete Observer A
```

```
type ConcreteObserverA struct {
    model *Subject
    viewState string
}

func (ca *ConcreteObserverA) Update()    {
    ca.viewState = ca.model.GetState()
    fmt.Println("ConcreteObserverA: updated view state to ", ca.viewState)
}

func (ca *ConcreteObserverA) SetModel(s *Subject)    {
    ca.model = s
}
```

And the client will call as follows:

```
func client() {
    // create Subject
    s:= Subject{}

    // create concrete observer
    ca:= &ConcreteObserverA{}
    ca.SetModel(&s) // set Model

    // Attach the observer
    s.Attach(ca)

    s.SetState("s1")
}
```

 Note that in the textbook form of the object pattern (shown in the figure), the model reference is in the observer interface (as in, an abstract base class in Java). However, since in Go interfaces can't have data and there is no inheritance, the model reference gets pushed down to the concrete observers.

Visitor

Many times, we want to do different things with elements (nodes) of an aggregate (array, tree, list, and so on). The naive approach is, of course, to add methods on the nodes for each functionality. If there are different type of nodes then the concrete nodes all have to implement each *processing function*. As you can see, this approach is not ideal and defeats the segregation principles and introduces a lot of coupling between the nodes and the different types of processing.

The objective of the visitor design pattern is to encapsulate and isolate processing that needs be done to each element (node) of an aggregate. This avoids the method pollution that we described in the earlier paragraph.

The key elements of the pattern are these:

- **Visitor**: This class defines the interfaces for various processing and has a single method, `visit()`, which takes a node object as an argument. Concrete visitor classes describe the actual node processing in their implementation `visit()` method.
- **Node**: This is the element of the aggregate on which we want to do the visiting. It has an `accept()` method that takes visitor as argument and starts the processing by calling the visitor's `visit()` method. Each concrete node can add more functionality to this as needed.

In most design patterns, polymorphism is implemented through single dispatch; that is to say, the operation being executed depends on the type of the called object. In visitor, we see the *double dispatch* variation: the operation to be executed finally depends both on the called object (the concrete node object), as well as the caller object (the concrete visitor):

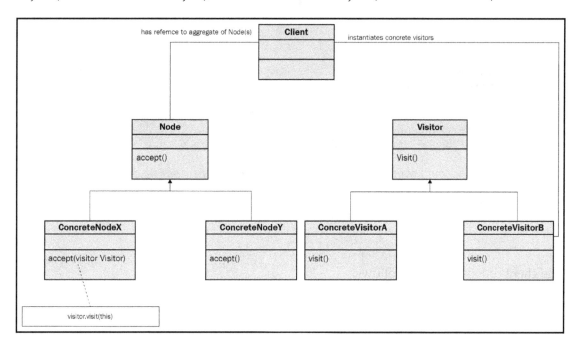

New processing can easily be added by just subclassing to the original inheritance hierarchy by creating a new visitor subclass. Here is some sample code in Go:

```go
// the Node interface
type Node interface {
    Accept(Visitor)
}

type ConcreteNodeX struct{}
func (n ConcreteNodeX) Accept(visitor Visitor) {
    visitor.Visit(n)
}

type ConcreteNodeY struct{}
func (n ConcreteNodeY) Accept(visitor Visitor) {
    // do something NodeY-specific before visiting
    fmt.Println("ConcreteNodeY being visited !")
    visitor.Visit(n)
}


// the Vistor interface
type Visitor interface {
    Visit(Node)
}

// and an implementation
type ConcreteVisitor struct{}
func (v ConcreteVisitor) Visit(node Node) {
    fmt.Println("doing something concrete")
    // since there is no function overloading..
    // this is one way of checking the concrete node type
    switch node.(type) {
        case ConcreteNodeX:
            fmt.Println("on Node ")
        case ConcreteNodeY:
            fmt.Println("on Node Y")
    }
}
```

The client code will look as follows:

```go
func main() {
    // a simple aggregate
    aggregate:= []Node {ConcreteNodeX{}, ConcreteNodeY{},}
    // a vistor
    visitor:= new(ConcreteVisitor)
```

```
    // iterate and visit
    for _, node:= range(aggregate){
        node.Accept(visitor)
    }

}
```

Strategy

The goal of the strategy pattern is simple: allow the user to change the algorithm used without changing the rest of the code. Here, the developer focuses on the inputs and outputs of a *generic algorithm* and implements this as a method for an interface. Then each specific algorithm implementation implements the interface. The client code is only coupled to the interface, not to the specific implementation. This allows the user to plug-out and plug-in new algorithms on the fly.

Sample code for an algorithm that finds the *breadth* (difference between the smallest and largest number in an array) is given here:

```
type Strategy interface {
    FindBreadth([]int) int // the algorithm
}

// A O(nlgn) implementation
type NaiveAlgo struct {}
func (n *NaiveAlgo) FindBreadth(set []int) int {
    sort.Ints(set)
    return  set[len(set)-1] - set[0]
}

// A O(n) implementation
type FastAlgo struct {}
func (n *FastAlgo) FindBreadth(set []int) int {
    min:= math.MaxInt32
    max:= math.MinInt64

    for _,x:= range(set) {
        if x < min {
            min = x
        }
        if x > max {
            max =x
        }
    }
```

```
        return max - min
    }


    // The client is ignorant of the algorithm
    func client(s Strategy) int {
        a:= []int { -1, 10, 3, 1}
        return s.FindBreadth(a)
    }
```

A variation of this pattern is called the template method. Here, an algorithm is broken down into parts: the main class defines the *master algorithm* and uses some methods (steps), which are defined in specific concrete classes that subtly change the master algorithm by implementing the steps differently.

Here is the code:

```
    // The 'abstract' MasterAlgorithm
    type MasterAlgorithm struct {
        template Template
    }

    func (c *MasterAlgorithm) TemplateMethod() {
        // orchestrate the steps
        c.template.Step1()
        c.template.Step2()
    }


    // The steps which can be specialized
    type Template interface {
        Step1()
        Step2()
    }


    // Variant A
    type VariantA struct{}
    func (c *VariantA) Step1() {
        fmt.Println("VariantA step 1")
    }
    func (c *VariantA) Step2() {
        fmt.Println("VariantA step 2")
    }
```

The instantiation can be as follows:

```
func client() {
    masterAlgorithm:= MasterAlgorithm{new(VariantA)}
    masterAlgorithm.TemplateMethod()
}
```

State

Most real-life objects are stateful, and they change their behavior according to the state. For example, a reservation may be in the following states, with corresponding behavior changes in the cancellation user flow:

- **INITIAL**: Here, the reservation state is very preliminary. Cancellation in this state is trivial.
- **PAID**: Here, the user has paid for the hotel/flight. But the actual booking with the seller is not yet made. Here, cancellation might mean a full refund to the customer.
- **CONFIRMED**: In this state, the booking is made, and the seller and the cancellation might incur charges.
- **FULFILLED**: The customer has used the reservation. No cancellation is possible.
- **CANCELLED**: The reservation has been cancelled. No further cancellation is possible.

The state design pattern allows us to code this elegantly with clear separation of stateful behavior, without having a big *switch* case. The main players are as follows:

- **Context**: This object has the current state of the client. It is also the interaction point for the client.
- **State**: This is the interface for the object behavior in different states. Each method in this interface needs to have polymorphic behavior, depending on the current state.

- **Concrete state(s)**: These are the actual states in which the object can be and implement the behavior methods for this state. Generally, these methods also cause state transition. New states and transitions are modeled by new subclasses of state:

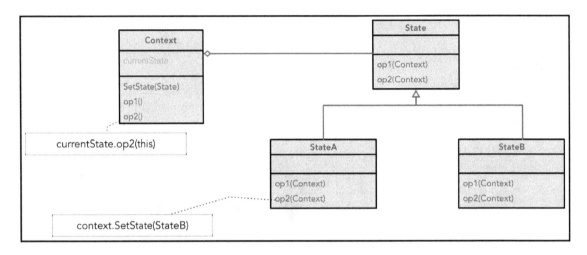

The code for the pattern is given here:

```
// The State Inteface with the polymorphic methods
type State interface {
    Op1 (*Context)
    Op2 (*Context)
}

// The Context class
type Context struct {
    state State
}

func (c *Context) Op1 () {
    c.state.Op1(c)
}

func (c *Context) Op2 () {
    c.state.Op2(c)
}

func (c *Context) SetState(state State) {
    c.state = state
}
```

```
func NewContext() *Context{
    c:= new(Context)
    c.SetState(new(StateA)) // Initial State
    return c
}
```

The client is abstracted from all the state changes as shown here:

```
func client() {
    context:= NewContext()

    // state operations
    context.Op1()
    context.Op2() // <- This changes state to State 2
    context.Op1()
    context.Op2() // <- This changes state  back to State 1
}
```

Summary

In this chapter, we looked at low-level design principles and various patterns in detail. Hopefully, this will give the reader a hands-on grasp of various low-level constructs.

In the next chapter, we will look at what scalability means for applications and the various dimensions that need to be taken care of to ensure applications meet the desired performance and reliability requirements.

4
Scaling Applications

Scalability is the attribute of a software system that allows it to handle an increased amount of work with proportionally more resources, while still maintaining the **service level agreements** (**SLAs**) that the system offered. A scalable system allows you to solve an increased amount of traffic/work by *throwing money at the problem*; that is, by adding more hardware. A non-scalable system simply cannot handle the load, even with increased resources.

For example, consider a backend software service that provides an API that is useful for an app. But it is also important that the API returns data within a guaranteed amount of time so that users don't experience latency or unresponsiveness at the app. A system not designed with scalability in mind will behave as shown here:

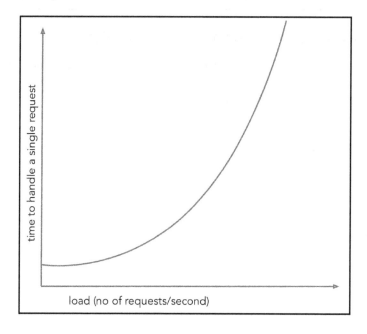

With an increase in traffic, the response times go through the roof! In contrast, with a system that is designed to be scalable, the response times will be more-or-less the same. That is, they will exhibit the characteristic shown here:

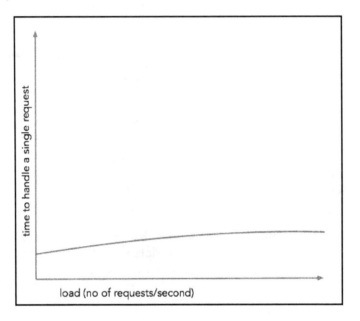

There is a key difference between performance and scalability:

- A system has a performance problem if it cannot meet the request of a single user with the needed SLA.
- A system has a scalability problem if it's good for a single user but the SLAs are compromised with an increased number of concurrent users.

In this chapter, we will look at how scalability is impacted by things such as the following:

- Algorithms
- Data structures
- Threading model
- Local state

We shall also look at the following:

- Bottlenecks
- Different options on how systems can be scaled
- Scaling deployments

Scaling algorithms

A problem can be solved in more than one way. Different algorithms have different characteristics in terms of time and space complexity. Also, some algorithms are more easier to parallelize than others. This section recaps the complexity analysis of various algorithms and demonstrates how it affects stability. It also has a section on distributed algorithms.

Algorithm complexity

Time complexity of an algorithm defines the amount of time taken by an algorithm to run as a function of the input size. Similarly, the space complexity of an algorithm gives a measure for the amount of space (memory) taken by an algorithm to run for a specific length of the input. These complexity metrics define how much time and space an algorithm takes with an increasing amount of data (inputs on which the algorithm has to work on).

For example, consider the problem of adding two numbers. Here, we will look at each digit pair in the two integers, add them, and then move to the next digit pair. If we had to denote the time taken to perform this addition, we could model it as, $T(n) = c * n$:

- Here $T(n)$ is the time taken to add two integers of n digits.
- c is time taken for the addition of a two-digit pair.

Intuitively, we can sense that the time taken will be proportional to the number of digits in the number.

Before we go into details, let's review a key mathematical notion: order of growth. For any two monotonic functions $f(n)$ and $g(n)$, we say that $f(n) = O(g(n))$ when there exist constants $c > 0$ and $n0 > 0$:

```
f(n) ≤ c * g(n), for all n ≥ n0
```

This is depicted by this graph (courtesy of Wikipedia):

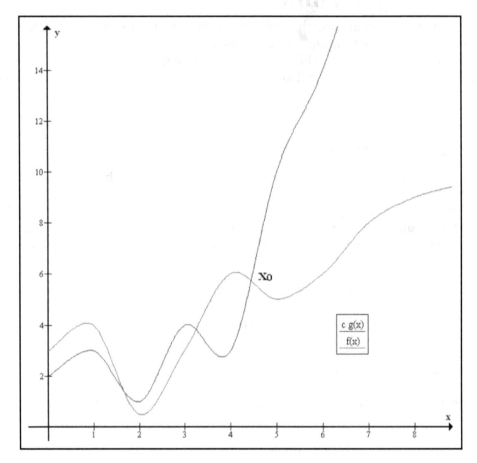

The implication is that function *f(n)* does not grow faster than *g(n)*, or that function *g(n)* is an upper bound for *f(n)*, for all sufficiently large *n*. Thus, if we can model *T(N)* in the preceding form, we get a *worst case* running time for an algorithm for any given *n*!

As a concrete example on how complexity has an impact on scalability, let's look at two ways of sorting an array of integers. Bubble sorts works by comparing adjacent elements in the array and swapping them if they are out of order. Thus, in every top-level run, the largest element *bubbles* to the end of the array. A Golang implementation is given here:

```
func bubbleSort(array []int) {
   swapped:= true;

   for swapped {
      swapped = false
```

```
    for i:= 0; i < len(array) - 1; i++ {
      if array[i + 1] < array[i] {
        array[i + 1], array[i ] = array[i], array[i + 1]
        swapped = true
      }
    }
  }
}
```

Here, as you can see, there are two `for` loops that go over the whole array. As described earlier, the top- level `for` loop always pushes the next-largest element to the end of the yet-unsorted element. Let's run this through an example input array say, [15 1 4 3 8].

First pass of the outer `for` loop:

- [15 1 4 3 8] –> [1 15 4 3 8] : swap since 15 > 1
- [1 15 4 3 8] –> [1 4 15 3 8] : swap since 15 > 4
- [1 4 15 3 8] –> [1 4 3 15 8] , swap since 15 > 3
- [1 4 3 15 8] –> [1 4 3 8 15] , swap since 15 > 8

Here is the second pass:

- [1 4 3 8 15] –>[1 4 3 8 15]
- [1 4 3 8 15] –> [1 3 4 8 15] , swap since 4 > 3

At this point, the array is already sorted, but our algorithm needs one whole pass without any swap to know it is sorted. The next pass will keep swapped as `false` and then the code will bail out. In the worst case, we will need $n * n$ comparisons; that is, $n2$ operations. Assuming each operation takes a unit time, this algorithm is thus said to have a worst case complexity of *O(n2)*, or quadratic complexity.

Quicksort is another example of solving the problem. It is a type of the divide-and-conquer strategy of algorithm design, and is based on the idea of choosing one element of the array as a pivot and partitioning the array around this so that the elements to the left of the pivot are less than the value, while those on the right are larger than the pivot. A Go implementation is shown here:

```
func quickSort(array []int) []int {
  if len(array) <= 1 {
    return array
  }
  left, right:= 0, len(array) - 1

  // Pick a pivot randomly and move it to the end
```

```
pivot:= rand.Int() % len(array)
a[pivot], a[right] = a[right], a[pivot]

// Partition
for i:= range array {
  if array[i] < array[right] {
    array[i], array[left] = array[left], array[i]
    left++
  }
}

// Put the pivot in place
array[left], array[right] = array[right], array[left]

// Recurse
quickSort(array[:left])
quickSort(array[left + 1:])

return array
}
```

As you can see from the code, at each step, the following is true:

- There is a linear scan of the data.
- The input is divided into two parts and the code recourses on it.

In a mathematical form, the time taken will be as follows:

```
T(n) = 2T(n/2) + n
```

Without going into the math details, this reduces to `nlogn`. Thus, for quicksort, the time complexity is *O(nlogn)*.

Well, the code is slightly more complicated and we have changed the complexity from *n2* to *nlogn*. Is this really worth it? To understand the difference, let's say you had to sort an array of a million elements. Bubble sort would need worst-case 1,012 operations, whereas quicksort would need just 20 * 106 operations! If each operation takes a millisecond, bubble sort would need more than 10 days, while quicksort would complete the task in around five hours! A very significant improvement in the scalability of the algorithm.

The following figure gives a graphical of the number of operations required for various **Big-O Complexity**:

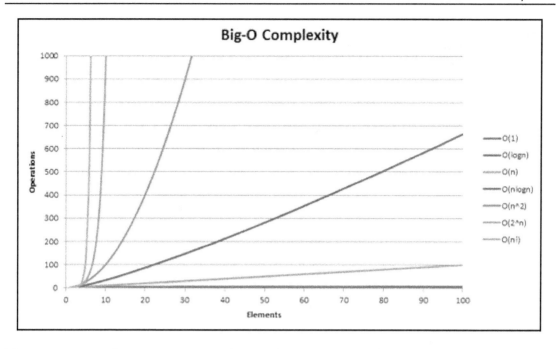

Thus, it is extremely important to analyze and profile your code and identify sub-optimal algorithms to improve the scalability of the code.

Distributed algorithms

Sometimes, systems reach a point where even the most efficient of algorithms cannot provide the answer in a reasonable amount of time by running on a single machine. Sometimes, the dataset is so large that it cannot fit into the memory or disk of a single machine. The obvious solution to this problem is to split the task across machines. However, this involves a lot of tricky low-level details, such as the following:

- Automatic parallelization
- Communication and coordination
- Distribution
- Optimization for network and disk access

Google's `MapReduce` library was the first effort to build a generic library that offered a simple programming model and could be used to solve many problems. In this, essentially programmers specify two methods:

- Map `(C) -> [(kx, vy)]`: This extracts information from a record and generates key-value tuples.
- Reduce `(k, [vx,vy...[])  ->  (k,vagg)`: The reducer takes the key-value tuples generated in the map phase, grouped by the key, and generates an aggregate result.

The `MapReduce` library takes care of the gory details described, and also does things such as the Group-Bys (shuffle and sort) for the mapper outputs to be used in the reducers.

The famous *hello world* of distributed computing is *word count*. Given a file (document), count the number of times each word is mentioned. Here, the two functions do the following:

- Map takes a chunk of the document, splits it into words, and generated KV tuples of the type: `[("this": "1"), ("is", "1"), ("good", "1")]` for a sentence, such as *This is good*.
- In the reducer phase, all the words would be grouped and the reducer function will get an array of 1 for each time that the word was counted; something such as this: `Reduce(key="this", values = "1", "1")`. The reducer in this case just needs to count the array of values to get the occurrence count of the word in the whole document!

In Golang, there are couple of libraries that offer similar distributed processing frameworks. For example, there is a project called **Glow**, which offers a master/minion framework (here, the minions are called **agents**). Code is then serialized and sent to the agents for execution. The following *word count* implementation is taken from the Glow author Chris Lu's blog on Glow (`https://blog.gopheracademy.com/advent-2015/glow-map-reduce-for-golang/`):

```go
func main() {
    flow.New().TextFile(
        "/etc/passwd", 3,
    ).Filter(func(line string) bool {
        return !strings.HasPrefix(line, "#")
    }).Map(func(line string, ch chan string) {
        for _, token:= range strings.Split(line, ":") {
            ch <- token
```

```
        }
    }).Map(func(key string) int {
        return 1
    }).Reduce(func(x int, y int) int {
        return x + y
    }).Map(func(x int) {
        fmt.println("count:", x)
    }).Run()
}
```

The author has been since working on a project called Gleam that aims to allow more flexibility in the dynamic composition of the computation flow.

Scaling data structures

The way in which we store data for an algorithm has a huge impact on the scalability for that particular algorithm. Various data structures provide different complexity for different operations. The following sections describe various data structures and the characteristics of various operations.

Profiling data structures

The algorithm scalability choices also often manifest themselves in the choice of data structures. This table gives the time and space complexity of common data structures and their operations:

Data structure	Time complexity						Space complexity
	Average			Worst			Worst case
	Search	Insert	Delete	Search	Insert	Delete	
Array	*O(n)*	*O(n)*	*O(n)*	*O(n)*	*O(n)*	*O(n)*	*O(n)*
Linked list	*O(n)*	*O(1)*	*O(1)*	*O(n)*	*O(1)*	*O(1)*	*O(n)*
Skip list	*O(logn)*	*O(logn)*	*O(logn)*	*O(n)*	*O(n)*	*O(n)*	*O(nlogn)*
Hash table	*O(1)*	*O(1)*	*O(1)*	*O(n)*	*O(n)*	*O(n)*	*O(n)*
Binary search tree	*O(logn)*	*O(logn)*	*O(logn)*	*O(n)*	*O(n)*	*O(n)*	*O(n)*
Red black tree	*O(logn)*	*O(logn)*	*O(logn)*	*O(logn)*	*O(logn)*	*O(logn)*	*O(n)*

Just as an example, to clarify the worst-case scenario performance, consider inserting the following numbers:

```
3, 4, 5, 6, 7, 8, 9
```

For an empty **Binary Search Tree (BST)** and a Red-Black Tree.

In the case of a BST, this is the worst case, and it would degenerate to a linked list as shown:

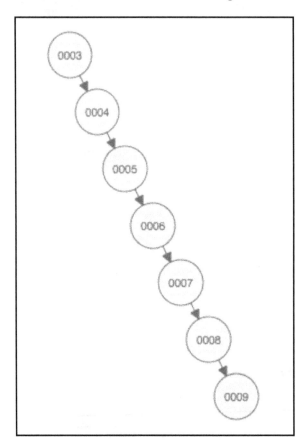

This is because there is no re-balancing in the plain BST. However, for a Red-Black Tree, there are periodic rotations to keep the invariant.

Red-Black Tree is a self-balancing BST, where the following invariants have to be maintained at every stage at every node:

- Every node has a color; either red or black.
- The root of tree is always black.
- There are no two adjacent red nodes (a red node cannot have a red parent or a red child).
- Every path from the root to the leaves has same number of black nodes.

At every insertion, the initial procedure for insertion is the same as the BST, but if the invariants change, there is rotation so that the self-balancing occurs. For example, for the same insertion, the Red-Black Tree looks like this:

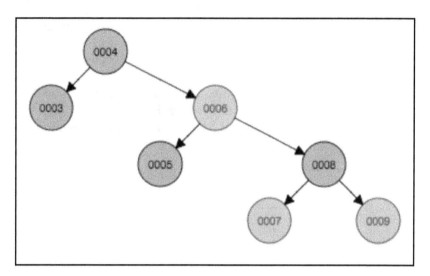

To summarize, based on what operation you want to do, how often, with a data structure, you can choose the right one for a job.

Another aspect to consider in data structure is how space allocation plays out with an increase in data. For example, arrays are fixed length, and thus the data structure scalability is limited to the size at the time of allocation. In contrast, linked lists need no upfront total capacity allocation, but they do not offer the O(1) access time characteristics of arrays. That said, there are some hybrid data structures such as array lists that offer the best of both worlds.

Also, for a large amount of data, it is useful to think about how efficiently we can store the information. For example, if we have to store a Boolean flag for all users on a website, then there are two options:

- Boolean array: one byte per flag/user
- Bitset: a bit for each user/flag

The first option is slightly easier to code, but 50 M users will need 47 MB for the first option verses about 6 MB for the second. If there are multiple such flags for different use cases, you can imagine that bit sets will allow us to store more data in RAM, leading to better performance.

Probabilistic data structures

Sometimes, the scalability problem is just the sheer number of elements that the data structure has to handle. This can be solved by probabilistic data structures. Consider the problem of finding the top-K frequent elements in a set, where the number of different values is very large. A straightforward solution might be to use a hash table to count frequencies and a min-heap of elements ordered by frequencies of the elements. However, this requires space proportional to the number of elements in the set. An alternative data structure is called count-min sketch. Internally, this consists of a two-dimensional matrix. Each element is mapped to one position at each of the d rows using d different/independent hash functions. These individual values values are then scaled by a weight vector. Each position of the matrix is a counter. This is depicted by this figure:

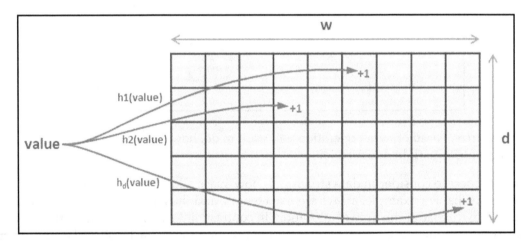

Whenever a new value is inserted, the corresponding counters are incremented and the total taken. We can then use this as an good estimate for frequency in the min-heap. If the frequency count is greater than the frequency of the element at the heap top, then the top of the heap is popped and the new element is inserted.

Another such related problem is as follows: Given a large number of elements, give a function that gives a subset of elements from the set, and the probability of the elements returned should be proportional to the total number of elements in the set. In real life, this problem manifests as things such as the following:

- Give the top 10 types of phones sold.
- Give the top 10 mobile phones in our network that make the most number of calls.

The naive way of handling this is, of course, having a large array and choosing the element randomly (without replacement) from this array. This, however, means that all the elements need to be stored, which by the problem statement would be unfeasible. We need a smarter data structure.

Reservoir sampling is an algorithm/data structure that enables these types of queries. First, we create a reservoir (array) of a size equal to the sample size required. In our case, say, 10. The first 10 elements are ingested as-in in the set. Now let's say we are processing the 11th element. Here, the new element should go into the chose set with probability 10/11. But if we do this, are we penalizing the existing elements in the set? Consider the fifth element in the set. This was chosen in the 10-member set with a probability of 100% (there were 10 slots). The probability that it will be chosen for replacement is 1/10. Thus, the probability of the element going out of the set: Probability (fifth element not being in the set):

```
=  Probability(choosing the 11 element) X  Probability(choosing the 5th
element)
= 10/11 * 1/10
= 1/11
```

Thus, the probability of the fifth element being in the set is this:

```
= 1 - Probability(5th element not being in the set)
= 1 - 1/11
= 10/11
```

This is same probability of choosing the 11th element! In fact, with this scheme, each array index has the same probability (10/11) of being in the set. Thus, if an element is present more than once, its probability gets directly proportional to the cardinality of that element in the set! This can be generalized from 11 to any n element that we are processing.

Scaling data

The way data is stored in the *database* also has a huge impact on the scalability of the system. There are essentially two ways this impact manifests:

- Like the complexity modeling of algorithms and data structures mentioned previously, having a large number of elements may make searching for a particular element inefficient. In a relational database, this typically happens when there are columns in the search query without relevant indexes.
- There are a lot of concurrent updates of the database. Typically, most databases err on the side of safety. This means some clients are *locked* while updates or reads are happening for another client.

We will look at database design and scaling in much more depth later in the book.

Scalability bottlenecks

Scalability bottlenecks are those system aspects that serialize (or choke) parallel operations. With bottlenecks, the ability of the system to do more work in parallel drops; hence, a major design objective of scalable systems is to remove these bottlenecks.

To understand system bottlenecks, let's look at a couple of very interesting problems that were encountered by architects in the recent past:

- **The C10K problem**: A web server bottleneck observed with the Apache server.
- **The Thundering Herd problem**.

The C10K problem

At the start of the 21st century, engineers ran into a scalability bottleneck: web servers were not able to handle more than 10,000 concurrent connections. For example, for the Apache server, performance was inversely proportional to the number of concurrent connections. Daniel Kegel wrote a paper (`http://www.kegel.com/c10k.html`) about this problem in detail, and included his tuning on how to get one web server to handle 10,000 connections.

Apache (until Version 2.4) could be configured to run in two main modes: pre-forked or worker **multi-process mode** (**MPM**). Either way, with each request that is currently active in the system, one thread is hogged up and competes for resources like CPU and memory with all other threads. Besides resource hogging, the increased number of threads leads to increased context switching. If the duration of each request is small, even with a high throughput (**Transactions Per Second - TPS**), the number of concurrent connections does not change much and you might not hit the concurrent-connection limit. However, if the duration for each request changes to say 10 seconds, then at the same throughput of 1,000 TPS, you'll have 10K connections open and system performance would drop off a cliff!

Another issue was the the suboptimal algorithms for different networking areas in the kernel. For example:

- Each new packet would have to iterate through all the 10K processes in the kernel to figure out which thread should handle the packet.
- The select/poll constructs needed a linear scan to figure out what file descriptors had an event.

Based on this learning, web servers based on an entirely different programming model (called the *eventing model*) got designed. Nginx is an example of this type of web server. The key architectural features are these:

- There are a static number of processes, typically one for each core.
- Each process handles a large number of concurrent connections using asynchronous I/O and without spawning separate threads. Essentially, each process manages a set of **file descriptors** (**FDs**)—one for each outstanding request and handles events on these FDs using the efficient epoll system call.

The following figure describes Nginx architecture:

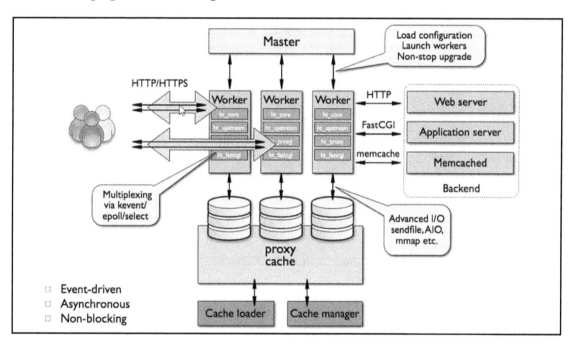

Reference: http://www.aosabook.org/en/nginx.html#fig.nginx.arch

The Thundering Herd problem

Let's say we are using a cache to avoid some heavy computations. For example, caching the seller prices in our travel website. But since the cache is transient and generally built on demand, it can cause some non-intuitive issues.

Let's say we have cached all keys with a **time-to-live** (TTL) of five seconds. For a very popular cache in the key (say NY-LA flight listings), there will be multiple requests hitting the cache simultaneously, all will not find the key and hit the *backend services* to get the data into cache. If the cache is per-server, and say there are 50 servers, then the data will be cached at 50 places at approximately the same time. Well, not so bad you think. But the insight is that all these caches will expire at the same time, resulting in 50 simultaneous requests to the backend! One way to avoid this is to slightly randomize the cache TTLs (4.8 to 5.2 seconds, instead of five seconds everywhere).

This *thundering herd* situation also happens in the case of the operating system problem of process scheduling. For example, let's say you have a number of processes that are waiting on a single event to occur. When that event happens, all the waiting process, that are eligible to handle the event are awakened. In the end, only one of those processes will actually be able to do the work, but all the others wake up and contend for CPU time before being put back to sleep. If this starts to happen many times per second, the performance impact can be significant.

Sources

The following sections describe some common bottleneck sources in various aspects of system architecture: http://highscalability.com/blog/2012/5/16/big-list-of-20-common-bottlenecks.html

Programming

We already looked at how algorithm and data structure choice can significantly impact performance and scalability. Besides this, other programming source of bottlenecks are as follows:

- **Locks**: There is no fun in having multiple threads doing something in parallel, only to take a lock and serialize themselves. Consistency is must in a thread-safe application, but you need to consider the granularity of the lock made. A common source of error is making the critical section (the part of code under the lock) too fat; not everything needs to be done with the lock taken.
- **Deadlocks**: In a multithreaded application, if threads need more than one resource to do the work, getting into deadlocks is a real possibility. Deadlocks can also happen when a thread holding a lock dies and essentially nothing else can happen in the system, without a restart. To avoid these situations, consider the following:
  - Locks need to be taken in the same order by all threads.
  - Locks need to be taken with variable amount of timeouts so that *stop-the-world* scenarios don't happen.

Databases generally offer multiversion concurrency control and timeouts retain the data in a consistent state. However, if you are using timeout locks then we need to ensure that we leave the data in a form that can be *reset* back to the consistent state. Again, lock granularity is a big factor here; for example, let's say we are updating a large object. We can compute a duplicate version of the object with the updates and just update the reference to the original object under lock. Generally, pointer updates are atomic and, thus, even under a lock, wither the object will be updated to the new version, or the old version will persist. We would not have a *half n half* object!

- **Reader/Writer locks**: Mutex and semaphores are commonly known locks. However, many times, we just want to avoid concurrent write-write or read-write scenarios. Read-read concurrency scenarios are just fine. In this case, code scalability is drastically increased by using read-write locks. With a mutex or a semaphore, the lock state is either locked or unlocked, and only one thread can lock it at a time. But with a reader-writer lock, three states are now possible:
  - **Locked for read**: Multiple threads can take the lock in this state.
  - **Locked for write mode**: The lock is only with one thread. No other thread is having the lock in any other state.
  - **Unlocked**.

These kinds of locks are highly efficient for read-more-write-less scenarios.

Context switches—too many threads or context switches can cause a drastic effect on performance, which drops off a cliff as the system spends too much time in managing context. Such systems also defeat the locality-of-reference principle on which most CPU architectures and OS constructs are based.

Operating systems

When we write application code, we tend to forget that there is a huge ecosystem of the operating system supporting the code. How we use these resources is key to how scalable the code is. Some common sources of these type of bottlenecks are as follows:

- **Disk-related**: Most disks are optimized for block access and sequential I/O and not random I/O. If your code is doing a lot of disk seeks, it will seriously slow down your code and cause non-intuitive bottlenecks. Also, multiple disks have different performance (IOPS) characteristics. As far as possible, we should use local SSD disks for high I/O use cases and reserve using networked-drives when data needs to be shipped remotely. For example, if you are writing a compiler that is supposed to write the output to a remove drive, you don't really need to store the intermediate files in the same location! The code can use different locations for the final and intermediate files (including logs), and thus achieve much better performance and scalability. Also important is how your code is using the OS cache for disk (buffer cache)— frequent unwarranted `fsync` is a sure-shot recipe for slow-downs
- **Networking**: Common source of bottlenecks are as follows:
    - **Interrupt Request handler** (**IRQ**) saturation: Soft interrupts taking up 100% CPU.

- **Non-optimal TCP buffers**: TCP uses a slow start algorithm to avoid congesting clogged/low-bandwidth links. At any point in time, it uses a *congestion window* buffer size to determine how many packets it can send at one time. The larger the congestion window size, the higher the throughput. The slow start algorithm works by starting with a modest buffer size and with each instance of not finding congestion, the buffer size is increased. On most OSes, there is a tunable for the maximum congestion window size and it defines the amount of buffer space that the kernel allocates for each socket. Though there is a default, individual programs can override this value by making a system call before opening the socket. If the buffer size is too low, the sender will be throttled. If, on the other hand, the buffer size is too large, then the sender can overrun the receiver and cause congestion control to kick in. To achieve maximum throughput, it is critical to set the buffer sizes to the right values for the network link being used. A rule of thumb for setting the buffer size is double the value for delay times bandwidth (buffer size = 2 * bandwidth * delay). The ping utility is an easy way to get the **round-trip-time** (**RTT**) or twice the delay, so you can just multiply this with the bandwidth of the link to get the buffer size.
- **Helper services such as DNS lookups**: If you are using an internal DNS server, you need to ensure that they are setup for the scale needed.

- **File descriptor limits**: in most modern systems such as Linux, nearly everything is a file descriptor. The OS caps these with some default values, and you need to ensure these are set up to the right levels to avoid process failures. In Linux, you can use the `unlimit` command to get and set the limits, as shown here:

```
$ ulimit -a
core file size          (blocks, -c) 0
data seg size           (kbytes, -d) unlimited
scheduling priority             (-e) 0
file size               (blocks, -f) unlimited
pending signals                 (-i) 32767
max locked memory       (kbytes, -l) 32max memory size
(kbytes, -m) unlimited
open files                      (-n) 1024
pipe size           (512 bytes, -p) 8
POSIX message queues     (bytes, -q) 819200
real-time priority              (-r) 0
stack size              (kbytes, -s) 10240
cpu time               (seconds, -t) unlimited
```

```
max user processes                  (-u)  50
virtual memory          (kbytes,    -v)  unlimited
file locks                          (-x)  unlimited

$ ulimit -u 100
```

Memory usage

Sometimes, our usage of memory (either from the heap or the stack) is very naive and can exceed the limits in certain scenarios, leading to **Out Of Memory** (**OOM**) crashes. For heap, the common source of errors in non-garbage collected language runtimes are *memory leaks*; that is, memory chunks allocated but no longer reference-able. For stack, memory overflow can happen if, for example, using recursion naively and the scale of the data drastically increases.

In languages where actual memory allocation is managed by the runtime, one of the key system aspects that can cause bottlenecks is the **Garbage Collector** (**GC**) pauses. Let's start with an overview of what typically happens during garbage collection:

- There are typically a few GC *roots*. These are code blocks which start off the program and could be the main driver program or static objects.
- Each of these roots has functionality that allocates memory. The GC runtime builds a graph of allocation, each graph component rooted at one of those GC roots.
- At periodic intervals, the GC runs for reclamation and does things in two phases:
    1. **Phase 1**: Runs from each of the root and marks each node as *used*.
    2. **Phase 2**: For those chunks that are not allocated, the GC reclaims the space.

In most of the initial GC algorithms, phase 1 involves a period where the application is *locked out* effectively as a *stop-the-world* activity. For low-latency applications, this is a problem, since when the stop-the-world phase runs, the application becomes unresponsive.

There have been many improvements in the GC algorithms and efforts to reduce this pause. For example, in Go v1.5, a new garbage collector (concurrent, tri-color, mark-sweep collector) was built based upon an idea first proposed by Dijkstra in 1978 (`http://dl.acm.org/citation.cfm?id=359655`). In the algorithm, every object is either white, grey, or black, and the heap is modeled as a graph of various roots. At the start of a GC cycle, all objects are white. Periodically, the GC then chooses a grey object, blackens it, and then scans it for pointers to other objects. If the scanned object is white, it turns that object grey. This process (or the GC cycle) continues until there are no more grey objects. At this point, white objects are known to be unreachable and are reclaimed. The key difference is that the mark phase does not need to stop the world. It happens concurrently with the application running. This is achieved by the runtime maintaining the invariant that no black object points to a white object. This means that there are no *dangling pointers*. Whenever a pointer on the heap is modified, the destination object is colored gray.

The result has shown to be a pause reduction of as much as 85 % (Alan Shreve's production server graphs (`https://twitter.com/inconshreveable/status/620650786662555648`)):

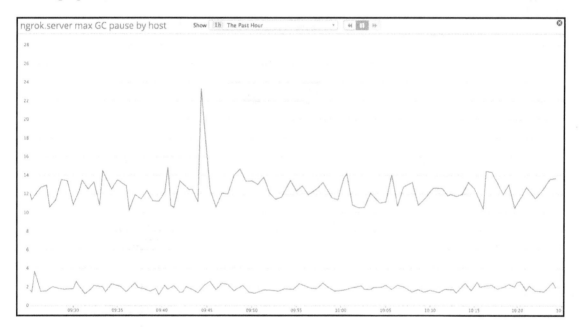

Losing state

Many websites want to give a personalized stateful experience to users. For example, they will keep users authenticated via cookies (for a limited duration), and also manage their preferences there. But, sometimes, this state tends to creep into the backend services. The system *remembers* what happened last in objects called **sessions**. These are server-side blobs of information that want to persist throughout the user's interaction with the application. The session serves as a context for further requests. With increasing requirements, a lot of state tends to be stuffed into session objects, and low-latency access to this becomes mandatory.

A common pattern for this is to keep the session state locally on servers and have the load balancer route all requests of an user to a specific server. The astute reader will notice an implication of this construct—all requests for a specific user needs to be sent to the same server so that the requests utilize the session. This can lead to hotspots, where specific users who are assigned to a server start having much more activity compared to others. This is shown here:

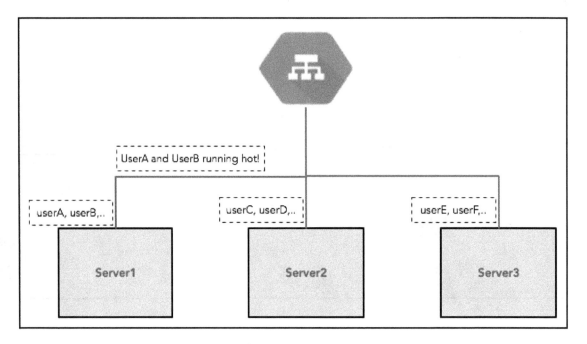

Another issue with this design is fault-tolerance: If **Server1** crashes in the deployment above, **userA** and **userB** will lose the saved state, and can even get logged out! This is clearly not ideal.

The first option to solve this that comes to mind is *Can we move the session storage to a central place?* Take a look at this diagram:

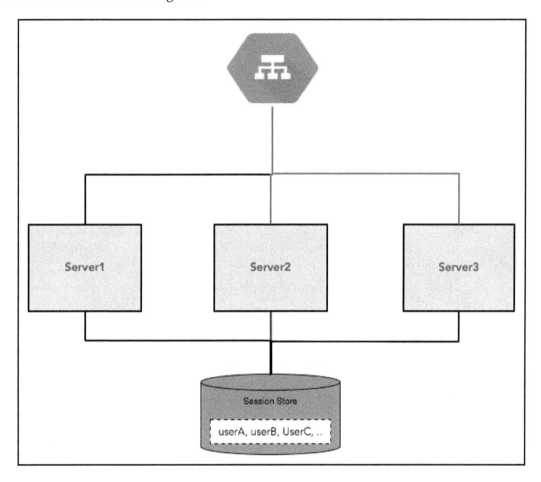

However, as the red color shows, this makes the common session store as the bottleneck. While this can be alleviated via replication of the store, it is still not a *bottleneck-free* design.

One solution that is bottleneck-free is to have all state relegated to the clients. This makes the servers all stateless:

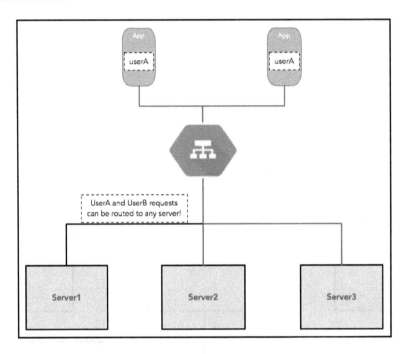

In this design, the client session is stored on the client. The server is stateless, and this means any server can service any client at any time; there is no session affinity or stickiness. The session (state) information is passed to the server as needed.

For people familiar with the **REST** (**Representational State Transfer**) paradigm, this is where the **State Transfer**, or **ST**, comes from. The state is *transferred* from the clients to the servers on the API request. We shall cover REST API in Chapter 7, *Building APIs*.

Essentially, we are delegating the session management to the client and effectively amortizing the costs. This also means the system can, at one level, *auto-scale* with new clients, since each client brings its own session management to the table.

As with most things, this design is not free:

- Clients need to retain state, so the complexity (processing and storage requirements) for them increases.
- The state needs to be sent to the servers every time; this increases the amount of traffic, and in the case of mobile apps, might mean increased traffic for your customers.

- Multiple clients (mobile app and web for example) cannot share state.

Note that this does not preclude the mixing and matching of other design patterns. For example, critical information for business objects such as the shopping cart can still be retained on the server side, while frequently changing/application state can be kept on the client.

Scaling systems

It's now time to take a slightly higher-level view of scalability. Once we have written code and deployed it, how can we scale it?

The book *The Art of Scalability* (http://theartofscalability.com/), describes a really useful, three-dimensional scalability model in the form of a scale cube:

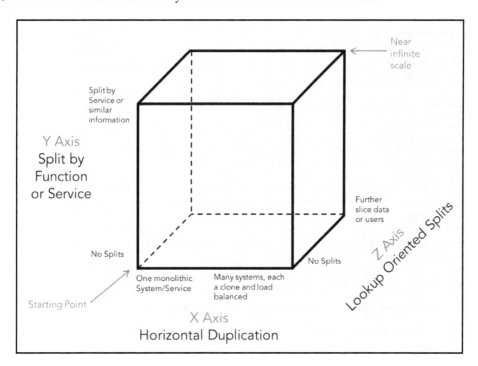

Each of the axes represents a specific way in which an application can be augmented to enable scalability in the face of increased load/traffic. They are described in the next sections.

X-axis scaling

Scaling along the *x*-axis means running multiple copies (instances) of the application behind a load balancer. If there are *n* instances, then each handles *1/n* of the load. This is the simplest way of increasing scalability, by *throwing hardware* at the problem.

However, there are drawbacks/limitations:

- The application and the distribution has to be able to scale well with the increased load. For example, if the requests take a disproportionate amount of work, then such a strategy will not work, and resources will be used inefficiently.

- If the instances need to communicate with each other, or share the same data, then this becomes a bottleneck. You will find everyone blocked of the same set of resources, and things are not able to happen in parallel.
- Lastly, and most importantly, this does not solve the problems of increasing complexity in the software architecture, which is probably the root of scalability problems.

Thus, scaling along the *x*-axis has to be done in tandem with scaling along other axes, as well as code refactoring, to be effective:

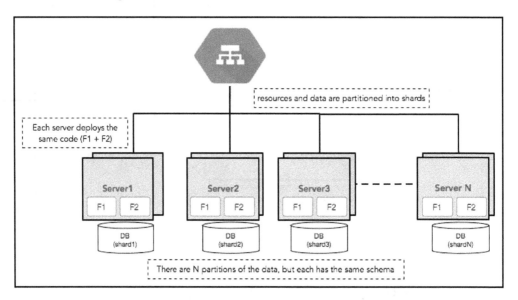

Y-axis scaling

The objective of scaling along the *y*-axis is splitting the application into multiple, different services. Each service is responsible for one or more closely related functions. This relates to our microservices discussion, and is essentially a perfect deployment strategy for a service-oriented architecture. The benefit of this type of architecture is that hardware can be efficiently used for only those areas of the application that need it. For example, on a travel website, typically *search* would have a much higher traffic than *booking* (more people search more times, compared to booking). This means that we can dedicate more machines to search versus booking. We can also choose the right set of hardware for each microservice:

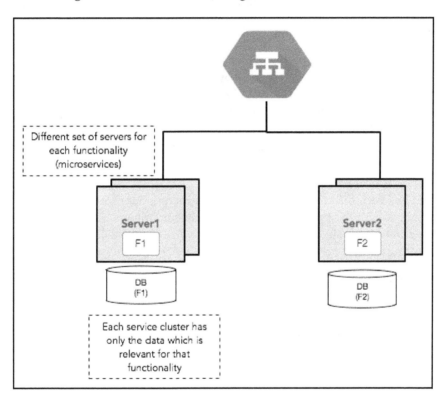

One thing to think about with this architecture is how to enable aggregated functionality. For example, on the typical Product Details pages of the travel website, the data may be served from various services such as these:

- **Product catalog**: Mostly static information about the product such as hotel name, address
- **Pricing service**: Product price
- **Availability service**: Product inventory/availability
- **Reviews and ratings**: Customer reviews, photos, and so on
- **Wallet**: Shows details about the customers' rewards points that are applicable

When a client needs to compose behavior from such varied services, does it need to make n calls? There are few things to consider here:

- The granularity of APIs provided by microservices is mostly different than what a client needs. And this granularity may change over time as the number of services (partitioning) changes. This refactoring should be hidden from clients.
- Different clients need different data. For example, the browser version of the Hotel Details page will have a different layout, and thus information needs, as compared to the mobile version.
- Network performance might be variable. A native mobile client uses a network that has very difference performance characteristics than a LAN used by a server-side web application. This difference manifests into different round-trip-times and variable latencies for the client. Based on the link, the API communication may be tuned (batched).

The solution to these issues is to implement an API gateway: an endpoint that clients calls which in turn handles the orchestration and composition of communication between services to get the clients what they need. Nginx is a popular high-performance webserver, and besides a host of configuration options, even has Lua scripting ability. All this enables a wide variety of use cases as a API gateway.

Another great example of an API gateway is the Netflix API gateway (`http://techblog.netflix.com/2013/02/rxjava-netflix-api.html`). The Netflix streaming service is used by hundreds of different kinds of devices, each with different requirements and characteristics. Initially, Netflix attempted to provide a single API for their streaming service. However, the company discovered that this does not scale because of the diversity of requests and the issues we have discussed. So, it pivoted to an API gateway that provides an API tailored for each device by running device-specific adapter code. This code does a composition over six-to-seven backend services on average. The Netflix API gateway handles billions of requests per day. For more details visit, `https://medium.com/netflix-techblog/embracing-the-differences-inside-the-netflix-api-redesign-15fd8b3dc49d`:

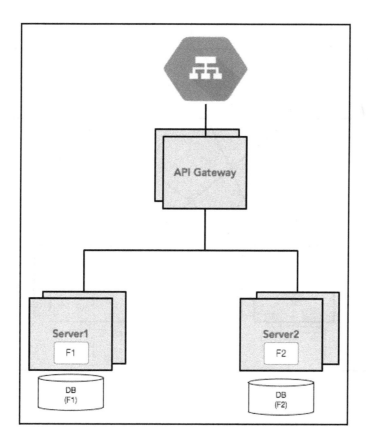

Another interesting variant of this pattern is called **Backend-For-Frontend**. Many times, the device specifics that we saw previously quickly gain complexity, and it becomes difficult to engineer this in constrained environments such as Nginx (with Lua scripting). The solution is to have a specific backend service to serve as the API gateway for each type to client. The solution is described here:

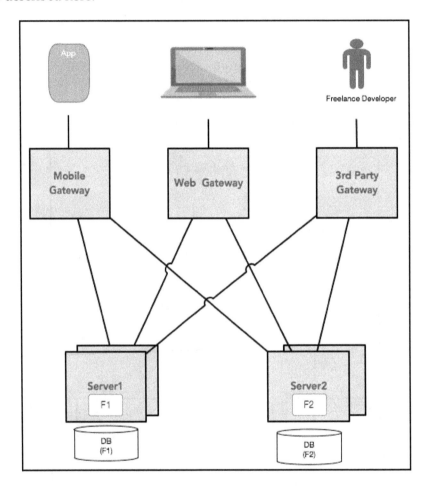

Z-axis scaling

In the z-axis scaling mode, each instance runs the same code, but with a different set of data. That is, each server is responsible for only a subset of the data. The orchestrator described previously now becomes more intelligent and has to route requests to the specific instance having the data in order for the request to complete. One commonly used routing parameter is the primary key of the attribute for which the request is being made: for example, to get bookings for a specific user, we can route the requests based on the user ID. We can route not just on specific IDs, but also on segments; for example, the travel website can provide premium customers with a better SLA than the rest by outing the requests to a specific pool of high-capacity servers.

Z-axis scaling mandates that the data (and hence the database) be split across the various set of instances. This is called **sharding**. Sharding is typically done on the primary key of the data and divides the whole data set into multiple partitions. The partitioning logic can be configurable: it can be a random distribution or something more business-specific like the premium-versus-rest distribution that we mentioned previously.

It should be noted that this type of scaling is usually done in tandem with x-axis scaling. Each shard usually runs multiple instances of the code and the connected database has a set of replicas to serve the requests:

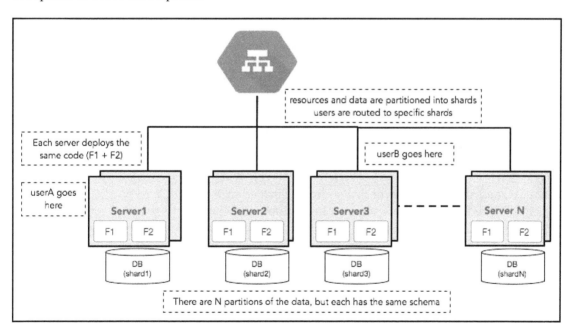

Z-axis scaling has a number of benefits:

- The irregular pattern of request workload is solved. We can use partitioning to distribute high-cost entities across the partitions.
- There is improved hardware (CPU/cache) utilization and reduction in cross-service I/O.
- There is improved fault detection and isolation. It is very apparent which part of the system is done, and it is easier to provide tolerance for the same.

Z-axis scaling has some drawbacks:

- Increased application complexity.

- We need to get the partitioning scheme right at the start. If the traffic pattern changes, our distribution will no longer be efficient. Handling such scenarios requires complicated engineering.

Scaling deployments

The place where your application is deployed and the deployment topology also plays a significant impact on the scalability of the system. For example, if you have deployed code on physical systems in a datacenter, then scalability is limited to how often can you procure hardware. The implications are as follows:

- The deployment is not elastic: you cannot scale up and scale down easily within minutes.
- You cannot scale cost easily: Hardware comes with specific quantum of capacity and cost. Also, if you want to scale down, then you cannot get back the cost of the hardware easily.

In contrast, in a cloud environment such as **Amazon Web Service** (**AWS**), you can spin up, compute, and store resources of fine-grained capacity on demand. You pay literally for the exact time you are using the resources. In addition, they have auto-scaling capabilities, which automate the launch and tear-down of resources in response to signals such as increased traffic.

We shall look at deployment considerations in much more detail in Chapter 11, *Planning for Deployment*.

Summary

In this chapter, we looked at the various tenets of building scalability in applications. It starts from the code (algorithms, data structures, and so on) and goes up to engineering scalability at a system level.

As our application is not going to run on a single machine, we need to build distributed systems in Go, which is the topic for our next chapter.

5
Going Distributed

Modern systems are rarely deployed on a single machine. With the availability of high-speed LAN interconnects, cloud-based pay-per-use environments, and microservices-based architectures, systems are increasingly composed on independent services, which are deployed on multiple computers. They work together to give a single coherent experience to the users.

Distributed architectures have two key ingredients:

- **Components**: Modular units with well-defined interfaces (such as services and databases)
- **Interconnects**: The communication links between the components (sometimes with the additional responsibility of mediation/coordination between components)

In the initial days of non-distributed computation, the components were hosted within a single process and components were essentially software modules that were orchestrated/initiated by a driver (**Main**) program. However, soon, systems began to outgrow a single machine and components that were hosted on different machines had to talk to each other. The interconnects started including network links:

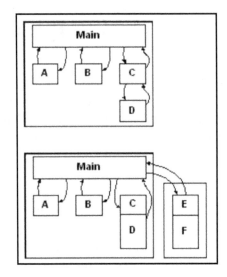

This shift meant that programs had to make use of message-passing, instead of local same-memory-based communication, as a means of communication and synchronization.

Besides fulfilling the main requirements, every distributed system has a few generic goals:

- **Scalability**: It should be easy to scale the resources allocated to the system as per demand.
- **Distributed transparency**: The system should hide the fact that it is distributed and make clients transparent to where each service or resources lies.
- **Consistency**: The clients should make the guarantees of the consistency offered by the system explicit. For example, is it guaranteed that a read after a write returns the last written value?
- **Using the right tool for a specific job**: The services and interconnect that make up the distributed system should be extensible. It should be relatively easy to add a new service to the existing milieu, even though it is on a different operating system/programming language. Having the freedom of tech-stack heterogeneity is one key advantage of distributed systems.

- **Security**: When computation happens on multiple machines and data flows through messages, it is important to consider the authentication/authorization and privacy implications of various choices.
- **Debuggability**: It should be possible to debug and localize issues or problems in the services that make up the system. We should have the ability to trace user requests as they are fulfilled by various components in the system.

This chapter discusses what happens when we go from one machine to several. In the following sections, we will cover the following topics:

- **Topology**: A top level overview of distributed systems
- **Quirks**: Unique characteristics of distributed systems
- **Consistency**: How consistency is achieved when data is distributed
- **Consensus**: How multiple independent systems agree on something
- **Architecture pattern**: Common design patterns in distributed systems

Topology

A distributed system consists of a bunch of services connected over a network. Each of the services has a specific purpose. Some of the services might be exposed for interactions with the clients (actors, in the use case parlance). Some services might just be hosting data and doing transformations for upstream services. The services communicate with each other to enable macro behavior and fulfil the requirements of the system.

The services interact with one another over the network using either of the following:

- **Application Programming Interface (API)**
- Messaging

Irrespective of the channel, the data is exchanged in a standardized format over the network.

The API paradigm is the most common. As described in `Chapter 7`, *Building APIs*, services communicate with each other over the network. They send requests and receive responses from specific endpoints. The most popular mechanism for engineering APIs is using the **Hypertext Transfer Protocol** (**HTTP**) and the **Representational State Transfer** (**REST**) standard. Multiple service instances are hosted behind a **virtual IP** (**VIP**) address by a **load balancer** (**LB**).

There are three downsides of this paradigm:

- The communication is blocking.
- The caller must know about the collie.
- The one-to-many communication paradigm is not efficiently achievable.

The second communication paradigm is messaging. Here, services communicate with each other asynchronously using messages, generally through brokers. This paradigm is much more loosely-coupled and scalable, due to the following:

- The message producers don't need to know about the consumers.
- The consumers don't need to be up when the producers are producing the message.

However, this mode has its own set of complications: brokers become critical failure points for the system, and the communication is more difficult to change/extend compared to HTTP/JSON. Messaging is covered in detail in Chapter 6, *Messaging*.

A typical distributed system is depicted here:

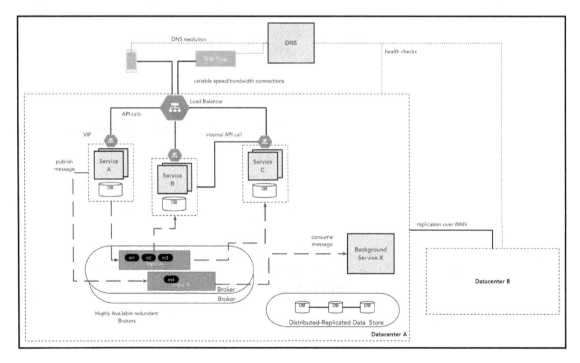

Here's how this works:

- There are four services. **Service A**, **Service B**, and **Service C** all serve requests from clients. These are behind a LB.
- Service X handles requests from other services and is responsible for background tasks (such as sending an email to a customer).
- Each service has more than one instance to enable redundancy and scalability.
- Each service has its own database. Database sharing is an anti-pattern and introduces coupling between services.
- Some of the database might be a replicated data store—so instead of one database instance to connect to, there are several.
- The services communicate with each other asynchronously using Messaging.
- The whole cluster is replicated in a remote datacenter so it enables business continuity in case of a datacenter-wide outage in the primary datacenter.

In this chapter, we will look at various aspects of building such systems. Let's start off by listing some not-so-obvious quirks of distributed systems.

Distributed system quirks

Distributed systems are more difficult to engineer and are quite error-prone, as compared to single program ones. In 1994, Peter Deutsch, who worked at Sun Microsystems, wrote about common wrong assumptions that developers/architects make, which cause things to go wrong in distributed systems. In 1997, James Gosling added to this list to create what is commonly known as the eight fallacies of distributed computing. They are described here.

The network is reliable

Things always go wrong with individual components of the networks—whether it be power failures or cable cuts. Networks are typically architected at the hardware level using a set of redundant links and software is responsible for providing an ordered, reliable message pipe between two systems. This software is typically referred to as the networking layers (TCP/IP). Even with the layers trying to achieve sanity across unreliable links, often, applications get exposed to failures and need to handle things appropriately.

This vulnerability is particularly acute for distributed data stores, and we will look at how to enable consistency in such scenarios in the *Consistency* section, later. For external calls, in `Chapter 7`, *Building APIs*, we will look at how to insulate application from network outages using a pattern called **Hystrix**.

The latency is zero

Latency is the time it takes for requests and responses to move from one place to another. Wrong assumptions about latency/distribution can cause significant performance issues in a system's otherwise elegant **object-oriented** (**OO**) designs. OO principles stress the separation of concerns, however not having a sense of distribution of the objects can cause excessive chattiness and fragility in the system. Network latency can also impact things such as the ability to back up or restore data, thus affecting uptime guarantees. This is covered in detail in Chapter 7, *Building APIs*.

The differences in latency are visualized here:

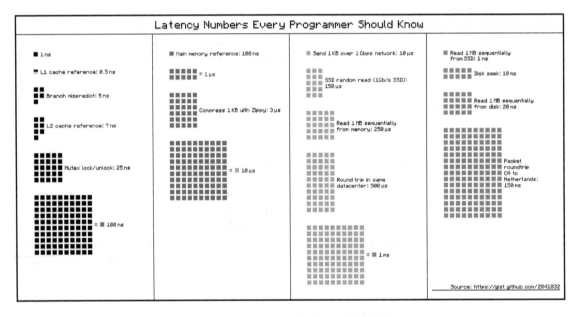

(Original source: Jeff Dean—https://gist.github.com/jboner/2841832)

Taking latency into consideration means minimizing network communication. There are a few options to solve this:

- **Co-locate chatty components**.
- **Batching**: Include multiple requests in one *meta* request payload. The server will then send a *meta* response—consisting of individual responses for each request in the batch.
- **Carry all required data in each request/response**: For example, a user profile object may be carried instead of just a user ID. This reduces the amount of calls to the profile services which would have otherwise ensued.

Once good example of solving for latency is described at `http://blogs.msdn.com/` `oldnewthing/archive/2006/04/07/570801.aspx`. Listing the contents of a folder in Windows means not just getting the filenames, but also related metadata. There was no single call that returned all required information, and these multiple roundtrips meant degraded performance for users, specially in the case of remote filesystems. The solution was to batch calls.

 Designing for minimizing latency is contradictory to other design goals, such as location transparency. While having a simpler (read: distribution unaware) architecture is always good, sometime extra constructs are needed to help with latency. This tradeoff of complexity versus solving for latency needs to be carefully considered for each use case.

The bandwidth is infinite

Bandwidth is the capacity of a network to transfer data. Even though network bandwidth capacity has been improving over the years, the sheer amount of information that needs to be transferred has also been increasing exponentially. That said, this is the weakest of all the fallacies that can be assumed (that means it's OK if this assumption was made in many situations).

Acknowledging that the bandwidth is not infinite has a balancing effect on solving for latency; that is, not going overboard with a few very large messages. The recommendation for both latency and bandwidth is to simulate production topology to figure out where one or the other needs to be optimized.

The network is secure

The only system that is completely secure is one that is not connected to any network! We need to build security into the architecture from day one. Sensitive information, such as customer names and addresses, must be encrypted at test. Data also should be encrypted in transit—which means HTTPS (and not HTTP) communication for APIs and encryption of messages for message-based communication. Authentication must be enabled for sensitive resources. These and other security-related details are covered in `Chapter 8`, *Modeling Data*.

The topology doesn't change

Topology is the definition/schematic of the components and the interconnects. With the high feature velocity in most modern systems, the topology of application deployment is rarely static. In fact, one of the reasons people opt for distributed systems and cloud deployments is the ability to change topology as needed.

What does this mean in terms of code? It means not assuming location (endpoints) for various services. We need to build in service discovery, so that clients of services can figure out how to reach a particular service. There are two ways clients can discover service endpoints:

- **Client-side discovery**: Each service instance registers itself (the connection endpoint) with a service registry when it starts up. It is removed from the service registry when the instance terminates. Clients are responsible for consulting the service registry to get an appropriate instance endpoint and *directly* talk to this endpoint. Netflix OSS has frameworks for supporting the client-side discovery pattern. Netflix Eureka is a service registry. Netflix Ribbon is an IPC client that works with Eureka to load balance requests across the available service instances.
- **Server-side discovery**: Clients are totally ignorant of the distribution of the instances for a service. The client requests go through a router (LB) that is available at a well-known URI. The LB periodically pings each instance to a service to determine the set of healthy instances for the service. When a request is received from a client, the LB uses one of multiple algorithms (such as round robin, random, or affinity) to route the request to the best possible service instance.

Server-side discovery is much simpler to code. However, it can lead to extra hops (client | router | service). Client-side service discovery also allows clients to choose a best possible instance. Thus the tradeoff is more in terms of easier scalability in server-side discovery versus more fine-grained control in client-side-discovery. In practice, the server-side discovery mechanism is more prevalent.

There is one administrator

In distributed systems, it is more likely that more than one administration domain will be involved. This means not just multiple groups within the organization, but also external companies. There might be conflicts there—for example, you might need to pass on user IDs to a third-party service for something such as user monitoring. However, this might be against the policies of the identity/profile service team—who is responsible for maintaining the customer information. The architect would then need to build glue systems that allow these multiple administration/policy domains to work together. In the case of user IDs, one possible solution could be building obfuscation logic for passing IDs to the third-party service.

The transport cost is zero

Onto fallacy number seven in the fallacy list: the transport cost is zero. There are two ways to think of cost here:

- The costs of setting and running the network infrastructure. While nothing in life is free, these costs have reduced dramatically, and in cloud-based deployments, you can actually purchase only what you need, per gigabyte or hour.
- The cost of serializing and deserializing data as it moves from memory to network and back. This is very real and needs to be accounted for in terms of latency. A optimizations are possible, for example, Google protobufs are faster to `Marshall/Unmarshall` compared to JSON. But going down this path of using a binary protocol might mean that debuggability is hampered and custom tools are needed to debug exchanges between systems; you can't just stick a service URL in a browser to what's being returned.

There are various options for serialization; it is important to consider each in the context of your application. The following table gives a brief comparison of the serialization performance of various frameworks in Go (`https://github.com/alecthomas/go_serialization_benchmarks`):

Benchmark	Time (ns/op)
BinaryMarshal-8	1,306
BinaryUnmarshal-8	1,497
BsonMarshal-8	1,415
BsonUnmarshal-8	1,996
EasyJsonMarshal-8	1,288

`EasyJsonUnmarshal-8`	1,330
`FlatBuffersMarshal-8`	389
`FlatBuffersUnmarshal-8`	252
`GencodeMarshal-8`	166
`GencodeUnmarshal-8`	181
`GencodeUnsafeMarshal-8`	104
`GencodeUnsafeUnmarshal-8`	144
`GoAvro2BinaryMarshal-8`	922
`GoAvro2BinaryUnmarshal-8`	989
`GoAvro2TextMarshal-8`	2,797
`GoAvro2TextUnmarshal-8`	2,665
`GoAvroMarshal-8`	2,403
`GoAvroUnmarshal-8`	5,876
`GobMarshal-8`	1,009
`GobUnmarshal-8`	1,032
`GogoprotobufMarshal-8`	152
`GogoprotobufUnmarshal-8`	221
`GoprotobufMarshal-8`	506
`GoprotobufUnmarshal-8`	691
`JsonMarshal-8`	2,980
`JsonUnmarshal-8`	3,120
`MsgpMarshal-8`	178
`MsgpUnmarshal-8`	338
`ProtobufMarshal-8`	901
`ProtobufUnmarshal-8`	692

The network is homogeneous

This fallacy was added to the original seven by James Gosling, the creator of Java, in 1997. The network is not one smooth pipe, rather it consists of various *legs* or *miles* with very different characteristics. For stringent requirements of performance, the application architects needs to consider this aspect to get the relevant performance characteristics.

Consistency

Consider a system that has multiple processes working against a replicated, distributed data store. The general organization of a logical data store, physically distributed and replicated across multiple processes, is shown here:

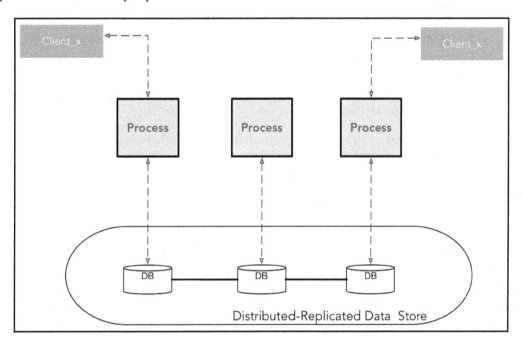

There are a few characteristics to consider:

- Each of the processes might be multiple instances of the same service, or it could be different applications trying access the data (not recommended!).
- Clients can be mobile. For example, in the preceding diagram, sometimes **Client_x** speaks to one instance, but that can change.

Considering our knowledge of the distributed system quirks, what kind of guarantees should the application code in processes expect from the data store? Rather than a single answer, a range of consistency models are possible, and these are described here.

ACID

The ACID acronym stands for:

- **Atomicity**: All operations in a transaction either succeed or all are rolled back.
- **Consistent**: The database integrity constraints are valid on completion of the transaction.
- **Isolated**: Simultaneously occurring transactions do not interfere with each other. Contentious concurrent access is moderated by the database so that transactions appear to run sequentially.
- **Durable**: Irrespective of hardware or software failures, the updates made by the transaction are permanent.

This is the most stringent of all consistency models. Most developers are familiar with and rely on the ACID properties of databases. Coding is so much easier when a data store offers this consistency, but the tradeoff is that such systems usually don't scale well (covered in Chapter 8, *Modeling Data*).

Client-centric consistency models

While ACID transactions are reliable and offer an easy programming model, they are not scalable for large datasets. For example, in the preceding diagram, if there needs to be ACID semantics, all the different nodes would need to coordinate a distributed transaction, driven by a **Transaction Manager**. A typical two-phase distributed transaction from the **XA Resource** spec is shown here:

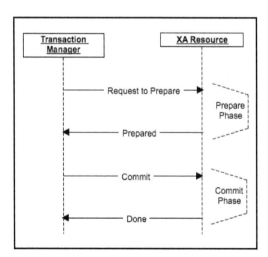

XA transactions work with two transaction IDs: a global transaction ID and local transaction ID (`xid`) for each **XA Resource**. In the first phase of the two-phase protocol (prepare), the **Transaction Manager** preps each resource participating in the transaction by calling the prepare (`xid`) method on that resource. The resource can either respond with an `OK` or `ABORT` vote. After receiving `OK` votes from each of the resources, the manager decides to execute a commit (`xid`) operation (commit phase). If an XA Resource sends ABORT, the the end (`xid`) method is called on each resource to rollback. There are multiple edge cases here—for example, a node might restart after it's responded with `OK` but before it can commit.

While many vendors claim to offer fully-resilient distributed transaction support, in my personal experience, such guarantees always come with some fine print. Such a globally coordinated locking system is also a scalability bottleneck, and hence best avoided in distributed systems.

What we need in most use cases is availability of the system and the following guarantees:

- Eventually things will be consistent for all clients
- From a single client's perspective, things should be consistent—a read after a write should return the new value

Even here, there are multiple options possible. Let's look at, options in the consistency spectrum from the client's perspective.

Strong consistency

This is the most rigid of all models. After any update, any subsequent access by any process will return the updated value.

In this model, any read on a data item, X, returns the value corresponding to the result of the most recent write of X. This is depicted in the following diagram:

Here, **P1** writes a to X, and when **P2** reads X later on, it gets a.

This is the most rigid form of consistency. Its implementation requires absolute global time and implementation of the fact that a write done on any process is simultaneously available on all processes. Building such guarantees is considered mostly impossible.

Weak consistency

This model is at the opposite end of the spectrum. The data store makes no guarantees, and the client code has to ensure consistency if needed. There are no guarantees that subsequent accesses will return the written value. The period between the update and the moment when it is guaranteed that any observer will always see the updated value is called the inconsistency window.

Eventual consistency

This is a specific form of weak consistency where the storage system guarantees that eventually all accesses will return the last updated value when writes quiesce. In the absence of failures occurring, the maximum amount of the inconsistency window can be computed (looking at things such as network delays and the load).

One example of this type of system is **Domain Name System** (**DNS**). Updates to a name are distributed according to a set pattern, thus not all nodes will have the latest information during the initial update phase. A few nodes host caches with **time-to-live** (**TTL**) and they will get the latest update after the caches expire.

For eventual consistency, there are a whole slew of models to consider when figuring out guarantees during the inconsistency window. These are described in the next section.

Sequential consistency

This model is a slightly weaker model than strict consistency. Instead of a write being available instantaneously to all processes, the order of writes to variables by different processes has to be seen as the same on all process. The operations of each individual process should appear in this sequence, as written in the program.

Leslie Lamport mentions that, *Sequential Consistency is met if the result of any execution is the same as if the operations of all the processors were executed in some sequential order, and the operations of each individual processor appear in this sequence in the order specified by its program* (reference: *how to make a multiprocessor computer that correctly executes multiprocess programs* and computers, *IEEE Transactions* by Leslie Lamport).

The diagram on the left shows a sequentially consistent system (here, all processes see *b* written before *a*). On the right, however, is a system that is not sequentially consistent (**P3** sees *b* as the value of X, while **P4** sees the value as *a*):

P1:	W(x)a				P1:	W(x)a		
P2:		W(x)b			P2:		W(x)b	
P3:			R(x)b	R(x)a	P3:			R(x)b	R(x)a
P4:			R(x)b	R(x)a	P4:			R(x)a	R(x)b

Causal consistency

This models relaxes the requirement of the sequential consistency model to enable better concurrency. If process **P1** has written a value to x and this value has been read by process **P2**, then any subsequent access by **P2** will return the updated value. Also any write by **P2** process B will supersede the earlier write. So, the behavior in the following diagram is allowed, since the b and c writes are not causal:

P1:	W(x)a			W(x)c		
P2:		R(x)a	W(x)b			
P3:		R(x)a			R(x)c	R(x)b
P4:		R(x)a			R(x)b	R(x)c

Session consistency

A important form of consistency is Read-Your-Write. Here, it is guaranteed that after a process updates the value of X to, say, *b*, all subsequent reads from that process will read *b*.

An important practical variation of this is session consistency—here, all access happens in the context of a session. For a valid session, the system guarantees Read-Your-Write semantics for any process. However, when the session is expired or deleted, there is no ordering guaranteed.

Monotonic read consistency

Here, the guarantee is that if a process, **P1**, has seen a particular value for an object, x, then all future accesses will never return values written before the time x was written last—that is, each process sees writes for an object in the order of time.

Monotonic write consistency

The storage system guarantees that a write operation by a process on a object (x) is completed before any successive write operation on x—that is, concurrent writes within the same process are serialized.

Storage system-centric consistency model

This section discusses consistency from the perspective of the storage system. Generally, the storage system has multiple replicas to allow for resilience (redundancy) and scalability. As part of accepting a write, the storage systems needs to decide how many of these replicas have to be updated before the write can be acknowledged to the client.

Let the terms be as follows:

- **N**: The number of nodes in the storage system
- **W**: The number of replicas that are updated before the write is acknowledged to the client
- **R**: The number of replicas that are contacted for a read (for a quorum, see the following)

If $W + R > N$, then it will never happen that processes see inconsistent data, thereby guaranteeing strong consistency. The problem with this configuration is that the whole write operation can fail if some nodes fail, thereby impacting the availability of the system (see the *CAP Theorem* section).

For systems needing fault-tolerance to a single machine failure, N is often an odd number greater than or equal to three. Here, both W and R can be two to give good consistency.

If the system needs to optimize for reads, then all reads should be served from local nodes. To do this, the writes should update all the replicas. Here, $W = N$ and $R - 1$.

Weak or eventual consistency arises when $W + R <= N$.

Whether the storage system can support Read-Your-Writes, Session and Monotonic consistency depends on how sticky the client it. If each process contacts the same storage node each time (unless there is failure), then such models are easier to satisfy. But this makes load balancing and fault-tolerance difficult.

All these choices are generally available as tuneables in the storage system. You need to analyze the use cases carefully to fine-tune the parameters. We will cover a few practical examples of such systems in Chapter 8, *Modeling Data*.

CAP theorem

As seen from the preceding discussion, consistency in a distributed system is a complicated subject. However, there is a theorem that cleanly summarizes the most important impacts, and it is called the CAP theorem. It was proposed by Eric Brewer in 1998, and states that it is impossible for a distributed computer system to simultaneously provide all three of the following guarantees:

- **Consistency (C)**: By consistency, we mean strict consistency. A read is guaranteed to return the most recent write, from any client.
- **Availability (A)**: The response is able to handle a request at any given point in time, and provide a legitimate response.
- **Partition-tolerance (P)**: The system remains operational, despite the loss of network connectivity or message loss between nodes.

According to the CAP theorem, only any two of the three are possible. In the face of Partition-tolerance, the system has to choose between either being available (such a system then become—AP) or Consistent (CP):

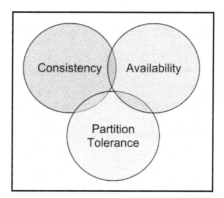

The core choice of the CAP theorem takes space when one of the data nodes want to communicate to others (maybe for replication) and there is a timeout. Here, the code must decide between two actions:

- Terminate the operation and declare the system as unavailable to the client
- Proceed with the operation locally and other reachable node, and thus compromise consistency

We can always retry communications, but the decision needs to be made at some point.

Retrying indefinitely is effectively the first choice we mentioned—choosing Consistency over Availability.

Generally, most modern systems, such as Cassandra, leave the CP or AP choice as tuneables for the user. However, understanding the tradeoff and making the application work with a soft state (the eventually consistent model) can lead to massive increase in the scalability of the application.

Consensus

Continuing with the sample system we looked at in the *Consistency* section, let's look at how these independent instances can reach an agreement. Agreements can take various forms, for example, if an email to a customer needs to be sent by a single service instance, then all the instances need to agree on which instance serves which customer.

Broadly, consensus is the process by which all nodes of a distributed system agree on some specific value for a variable. This seemingly simple problem finds large applicability in the field of distributed systems. Here are some examples:

- **Leader elections**: In a cluster of nodes, choosing one who will handle the interactions
- **Distributed lock manager**: Handling mutual exclusion between multiple machines
- **Distributed transactions**: Consistent transactions across a set of machines

For the purpose of this discussion, let's assume that there are N processes trying to reach a consensus on a value. The expectations are:

- **Agreement**: All non-faulty processes agree on the same value.
- **Validity**: The value chosen has to be one that was proposed. This rules out trivial/theoretical solutions.
- **Liveliness**: The consensus process should terminate in an bounded period of time.

In a theoretical worst-case scenario, where we cannot make assumptions of the time required for processes to finish their work for agreement or the speed of the network, we simply cannot guarantee consensus. This was proved by Fischer, Lynch, and Patterson in their paper (FLP[85]).

The two generals problem

This problem in an example of a distributed system where the processes are reliable, but the network is not. The problem is as follows:

Two divisions of an army are headed by generals **A1** and **A2.** They both want to attack another army led by general **C. A1** and **A2** can win against **C**, but only if they both attack together. **A1** and **A2** are physically separated and can communicate using a messenger—however this channel is unreliable! The messenger can be caught and killed, and so the message may not have made it to the other general! Note not just the message, but the acknowledgement of the message is also needed for generals **A1** and **A2** to be fully certain:

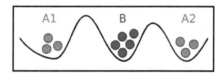

(Image: Wikipedia)

This problem cannot be reliably solved. Of course it has a solution: one message and an acknowledgement is enough for the armies to succeed. But there is no way to guarantee that scenario over an unreliable network.

The following sections describe ways in which processes (a substitute for the generals, here) can work on getting consensus over unreliable networks.

 This problem can be further complicated if we assume that one of the generals can behave in an unethical manner. This is called the Byzantine Army problem. For more on this, read Leslie Lamport's paper: http://research.microsoft.com/en-us/um/people/lamport/pubs/byz.pdf.

Consensus based on time – causality

In this model, there is no explicit blocking. Whenever a process (Px) receives a value from another process (P1), and if that value was arrived at a later point in time, then Px overwrites its own copy of the value with what P1 said it was.

Generally, it is not easy to have a common clock source for all processes. The alternatives usually used are vector clocks (designed by Leslie Lamport). Essentially, a vector clock is a vector or an array of counters, one for each Process. Every time a Process sends or receives a message, this counter is incremented. When a Process shares information (the value), it also shares the vector clock it has. The receiving Process updates each element in its own vector by the maximum of the values for each element in the received vector and its own vector.

The point of this is that if every element in the received vector is more (or equal) to the vector in the receiving process, then the receiving process can assume that it has received an updated value, after a state that it's currently in. To put in another way: the process that sent the value had seen the same point in history as the receiving process and now knows a later value. Thus, the receiving process can trust the new value.

When a vector clock, Va, has every counter with a number greater than another vector clock, Vb, Va is said to be a descendant of Vb.

If, on the other hand, this situation does not hold, then the sender process did not see everything that the receiving process did and consensus is not possible through Causality. Some other mechanism must be employed.

To illustrate this, let's look at a sample consensus problem:

Alice, Bob, Charlie, and David are planning to go to a movie together, but need to decide on a day. However, they live in different places and need to call each other to confirm (and a group call is not possible!). The sequence of events is as follows:

1. Alice meets Bob and they both decide on Wednesday.
2. David and Charlie decide on Monday.
3. David and Bob get talking and decide to stick with Wednesday.
4. Bob calls Charlie, but Charlie says he's already spoken to David and decided on Monday!
5. Dave's phone is switched off and neither Bob nor Charlie can figure out what day Dave has in mind.

The solution here would be simple if we had a sense of time. In this case, Bob and Charlie would know Dave's latest answer and reach consensus.

In the vector clock world, the ordering would look something like this (Note VC = vector clock):

1. Alice thinks of Wednesday and send a message to Bob (Day = Wednesday, VC =[Alice:1]).
2. Bob acknowledges and updates his value and vector clock. Thus, the state at Bob is as follows:

    Day = Wednesday, VC = [Alice:1, Bob:1]

3. David calls Charlie and both decide on Monday. Now, the situation for both is as follows:

David	Charlie
Day = Monday VC = [David:1]	Day = Monday VC = [David:1, Charlie:1,]

4. Bob calls David and they decide to stick to Wednesday. Now, the situation for both is as follows:

Bob	David
Day = Wednesday VC = [Alice:1, Bob:2, David:2]	Day = Wednesday VC = [Alice:1, Bob:1, David:2, Charlie:1]

5. Bob calls Charlie to propose Wednesday. The two conflicting states with Charlie are as follows:
   - Monday: VC = [David:1, Charlie:1,]
   - Wednesday: [Alice:1, Bob:2, David:2]

Charlie can see that David promised Wednesday after he said Monday and a consensus is reached!

The Labix package provides vector clock support in Go: https://labix.org/vclock.

This is a sample hello world example from the website:

```go
package main

import (
    "fmt"
    "labix.org/v1/vclock"
)

func main() {
```

```
vc1 := vclock.New()
vc1.Update("A", 1)

vc2 := vc1.Copy()
vc2.Update("B", 0)

fmt.Println(vc2.Compare(vc1, vclock.Ancestor))    // true
fmt.Println(vc1.Compare(vc2, vclock.Descendant)) // true

vc1.Update("C", 5)

fmt.Println(vc1.Compare(vc2, vclock.Descendant)) // false
fmt.Println(vc1.Compare(vc2, vclock.Concurrent)) // true

vc2.Merge(vc1)
fmt.Println(vc1.Compare(vc2, vclock.Descendant)) // true

data := vc2.Bytes()
fmt.Printf("%#v\n", string(data))

vc3, err := vclock.FromBytes(data)
if err != nil {
    panic(err)
}

fmt.Println(vc3.Compare(vc2, vclock.Equal)) // will print true
}
```

Multi-phase commit

One way to drive consensus is that a proposing Process sends the proposed value to every other process and essentially forces it to either accept or reject the proposal. The proposing process assumes that consensus is reached if it gets acceptance from all of all the processes.

There are two main versions of the distributed commit:

- Two-phase commit
- Three-phase commit

Two-phase commit

As discussed, let's assume that there is one proposing process (P0) and a bunch of other [P1...PN] processes (let's call them executors) that need to perform the value update. In the Two-Phase Commit protocol, the proposing process (P0) coordinates the consensus in two phases:

- **Prepare phase**: P0 sends a message, `Prepare Update V = x`, to the other executor processes `[P1...PN]`. Each executor process either votes `PREPARED` or `NO`, and if `PREPARED` possibly locally stages the change. A process can say `NO` if, for example, there is another concurrent transaction.
- **Commit phase**: Once all responses have been received, P0 sends either a COMMIT or ABORT message. Each of the executor processes obey this command and thus complete the transaction.

To enable easy handling of things such as restarts, each Process records its current state in durable storage before sending a message. For example, once all executors reply with PREPARED, P0 can record that it's in the Commit phase.

This algorithm is susceptible to failures in the Commit phase:

- P0 may crash after the Prepare phase. Here, all the other Executors are blocked on P0, and until P0 is up and current, the system comes to a halt in terms of consensus. P0 did know whether the crashed node wanted to go ahead or abort the transaction.
- If an executor process crashes in Phase 2, P0 does not know whether the process failed before or after committing.

To summarize, the biggest disadvantages of the two-phase commit is the blocking we just described. If one of the processes dies at a critical stage, things come to a grinding halt.

Three-phase commit

A non-blocking commit protocol is one in where the failure of a single process does not prevent the other processes from deciding whether the transaction is committed or aborted. One way of enabling this behavior is by splitting the Commit phase into two:

- **2.a – Pre-commit phase**: After receiving PREPARED messages from the executors, P0 enters a prepare-to-commit phase. P0 sends preCommit messages to all executors. During this phase, the executors stage the change (maybe get locks), but don't actually commit.
- **2.b – Commit phase**: If P0 receives YES from all executors during the prepare-to-commit phase, it then sends COMMIT messages to all executors, thereby finishing the transaction. If any executors replies with NO or fails to reply during the prepare-to-commit phase, the transaction is aborted.

This is described in the following diagram:

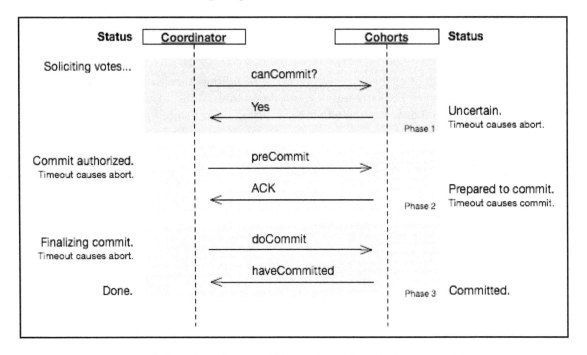

Courtesy of Wikipedia, here the Coordinator and Cohorts are other names for P0 and the Executors, respectively

The pre-commit phase helps the algorithm to recover from the cases of process failure. Processes can now have timeouts, and if the executors don't hear back from P0, they can elect a new coordinator that can drive the transaction to completion. The new coordinator can query the rest of the executors and check the current state of the transaction; if it's in state 2.b – Commit, then it knows that some failure occurred but everyone intended to Commit.

On the other hand, if an executor replies to the new coordinator that it did not receive a `Prepare-to-Commit` message, then the new coordinator can assume that P0 failed before going to the the third phase. Since no other executors have made any changes yet, the transaction can be safely aborted.

This algorithm is not perfect, and is particularly susceptible to network failures.

Paxos

Paxos is a flexible and fault-tolerant consensus protocol that was defined by Leslie Lamport in his paper *The part-time parliament*. ACM Trans. on Comp. Syst. 16 (2), 133-169 (1998).

In order to fully describe the algorithm and construct, we must generalize the assumption we made about the preceding topology. Instead of a single P0 process making the change, essentially a process (or node, in Paxos parlance) can take up one of three roles:

- **Proposer**: This is the node driving the consensus.
- **Acceptor**: These are nodes that independently accept or reject the proposal.
- **Learner**: Learners are not directly involved in the consensus building process, they learn of the accepted values from the Acceptor. Generally, Learners and Acceptors are packaged together in a single component.

The basic steps in Paxos are very similar to the two-phase commit. As in the two-phase protocol, in the standard Paxos algorithm, proposers send two types of messages to acceptors: Prepare and Accept. However, for the Prepare phase, in addition to the value being proposed, they also send a proposal number (n). These proposal numbers must be positive, monotonically increasing numbers and unique across all the processes. One way to achieve this is to construct the proposal number from two integers—one identifying the process itself and the other being a per-process counter. Whenever an Acceptor gets conflicting proposals, it chooses the one with the higher proposal number. An acceptor has to remember the highest numbered proposal that it has ever accepted and the number of the highest-numbered prepare request to which it has responded.

The various stages are described here:

- Phase 1:
    - **Prepare**: The Proposed constructs a Prepare message with the value (v) and the proposal number, N (which is greater than any previous number used by that process). This message is then sent to a Quorum of Acceptors.
    - **Promise**: When an Acceptor gets the Prepare message, it checks that the proposal's number (N) is higher than any previous proposal number that has been accepted. If so, it logs the latest accepted value and the sequence number, N. Any Prepare messages with proposal numbers less than N are ignored (even though response is not necessary, sending a NACK will help the algorithm to converge faster). If the Acceptor accepted a proposal at some point in the past, it must include the previous proposal number and previous value in its response to the Proposer.

 An acceptor can be in a state where it has accepted multiple proposals.

- Phase 2
    - **Accept Request**: Once the Proposer receives response messages from the majority of the nodes, it moves the algorithm to the Acceptance phase. The proposer essentially wants the acceptors to commit to what they accepted. Here, there are three cases:
        - If a majority of the Acceptors reply with a NACK message or fail to reply, the Proposer abandons the proposal and will go back to the initial state/phase.
        - If none of the Acceptors have accepted a proposal up to this point, the Proposer may choose the original value, v, with proposal number, N.
        - If any Acceptors had previously accepted any proposal, the value and sequence numbers will be available at the Proposer. Here, if w is the value of the accepted values with the higher sequence number (say, w), Paxos forces the Proposer to drive the acceptance of w (not v). This prevents the new Proposer who died and came back up to not diverge the system from consensus.

The Proposer sends an Accept message with the chosen value to all the Acceptors:

- **Acceptance**: When an Acceptor receives the Accept message, it checks for the following conditions:
  - The value is one from one of the previously accepted proposals.
  - The sequence number in the message is the highest proposal number the Acceptor has agreed on.
  - If both conditions are met, the Acceptor sends an `Accept` message back to Proposer. Otherwise, a `Reject` message is sent.

Paxos is more failure-tolerant than the multi-commit algorithm because of the following:

- **Proposer failure-tolerance**: If a Proposer fails in-between, another node can take up the role and issue its own proposal.
- If there are dueling Proposers, especially after an earlier Proposer recovery, then due to ordering imposed by the sequence number's only a previously accepted value can be chosen.
- Network partitioning does not affect Paxos as it does to the three-phase commit protocol, because just a majority of acceptors is needed. If a majority is there, consensus is reached, even if the other nodes are not reachable and it's not there, the round is failed.

One potential issue with Paxos is that it is possible for two dueling proposers to keep issuing proposals with increasing numbers. Acceptors might ignore messages with lower proposal numbers, which might cause Proposers to continuously try with higher and higher proposal numbers. To overcome this and ensure that progress is made, a distinguished proposer is generally selected among the Proposers. This Leader sequences the proposals and avoids this situation. Leader-election is covered in a later section.

Paxos Go implementations can be found at `https://github.com/go-distributed/epaxos` and `https://github.com/kkdai/paxos`.

Raft

Raft is a consensus algorithm, similar to Paxos, but designed to have fewer states and a much simpler algorithm.

At any given time, each Raft instance is in one of three states: leader, follower, or candidate. Every instance starts out as a follower. In this state, the instance is passive and is only supposed to respond to messages: replicate state from a Leader based on log-entry messages and answer election messages from candidates. If no messages are received for some time, the instances promote themselves to a candidate state, to kickstart an election with the objective to becoming the Leader themselves. In the candidate state, the instances request votes from other instances—their peers. If it receives a majority (quorum) of votes, it is promoted to a leader. Elections happen over a term, which is a logical unit of time. Leader-election is described in a later section.

When an instance gets promoted to Leader, it is supposed to do three things:

- Handle writes, that is, state-change requests from clients
- Replicate the state change to all the followers
- Handle reads in case stale reads are not allowed

In Raft, handling writes is essentially an append to a log. The leader does the append in durable storage and then initiates replication on the followers. The Log is a key component of the Raft architecture. The problem of consensus is essentially boiled down to a replicated log. The system is consistent if all instances have the same log entries in the same order.

A write is considered committed if the replication happens successfully for a quorum (majority) of instances. For a cluster of n instances, the quorum consists of $(n/2 + 1)$ nodes. It is a design choice to block the write for the client, until it's committed.

Once the log entry is committed, it can be applied to a finite state machine on the instances. The finite state machine hosts application-specific code, which handles the change. This code should be deterministic—since all the nodes work on the same data in the same order, the output should be the same.

Compared to Paxos, Raft is simpler and `https://ramcloud.stanford.edu/raft.pdf` offers a lot of implementation details. Hence, it's gaining popularity over Paxos. The Hashicorps implementation in Go is very comprehensive, you can refer to it at `https://github.com/hashicorp/raft`.

Leader-election

In a cluster of multiple instances, all of which are capable of doing the same job, often it is important for one instance to assume the role of Leader and coordinate actions for the rest of the instances. For example, for a set of instances representing a replicated data store, the Leader always gets the writes from clients and ensures that the write is replicated on the rest of the instances. This avoids handling issues, such as conflicting concurrent writes and resource contention/deadlock. Having a Leader coordinate actions is a common pattern of engineering consistency and consensus:

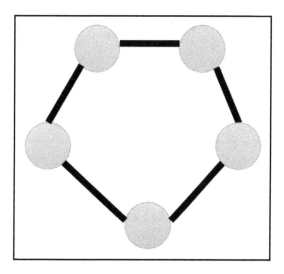

There are several well-researched strategies for electing a leader among a set of instances/nodes, including the following:

- **ID-based selection**: Each instance is given a unique ID. Whenever an election occurs, the instances exchange IDs and the one with the lowest (or highest) ID. There are both O(n2) as well as O(nlgn) algorithms for electing a leader in a ring-based topology of instances, as depicted by the preceding diagram. The Bully Algorithm is a well-known leader-election algorithm and will be described later.
- **Mutex race**: The instances race with each other to atomically lock a shared mutex/lock. The instance that gets the lock becomes the leader. This approach has issues where the Leader dies while holding onto the lock.

Generally, there is a keepalive mechanism between the Leader and the instances to ensure that in case of Leader failure, a new election takes place.

Most distributed systems divide time into units called epochs or rounds. These need not be actual units of time; a simple election-counter will do. When exchanging messages, this number is carried in the payload, which allows a node to not vote on two different leaders for the same election:

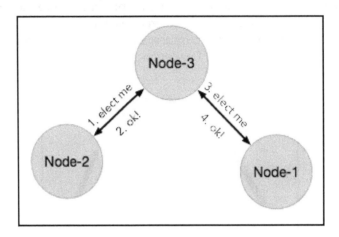

Distributed architectures

This section illustrates different patterns in building distributed architectures. These have been distilled considering the quirks described previously and arising out of the lessons learned over the years. Note that these are not mutually exclusive—rather, they can be thought of as templates for building various functionalities.

Object-based systems

The simplest (and earliest) distributed systems were composed of objects interacting with each other using Remote Procedure Calls (RPCs) or Remote Method Invocations (RMIs):

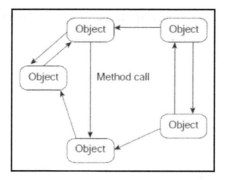

The architecture consisted of three layers on each machine:

- **The stub/skeleton layer**: These were stubs or proxies for clients and skeletons for servers. A stub is a client-held reference to a remote object and it implements the exact interface of the remote object. The stub forwards requests to the actual object on the server and the remote reference layer.
- **The remote reference layer**: Responsible for carrying out the semantics of the invocation. It delegates communication specifics to the transport layer.
- **The transport layer**: Responsible for connection management and remote object-tracking.

There were two main ecosystems for this type or architecture:

- **Common Object Request Broker Architecture (CORBA)**: Defined by a group called **Object Management Group (OMG)**, which was the RPC framework in the Java world
- **Distributed Component Object Model (DCOM)**: Sponsored by Microsoft

In Go, stdlib has an `rpc` package that allows us to export any object method through remote procedure calls.

For example, imagine you have the following Multiply service:

```go
type Args struct {
  A, B int
}

type MuliplyService struct{}

func (t *Arith) Do(args *Args, reply *int) error {
  *reply = args.A * args.B
  return nil
}
```

Then, you can enable it for remote invocation using the `rpc` package, like so:

```
func main() {
    service := new(MuliplyService)
    rpc.Register(MuliplyService)
    rpc.HandleHTTP()
    l, err := net.Listen("tcp", ":1234")
    if err != nil {
        log.Fatal("listen error:", err)
    }

    go http.Serve(l, nil)
}
```

The clients who want to make RPC calls can connect to this server and issue requests like so:

```
client, err := rpc.DialHTTP(
        "tcp",
        serverAddress + ":1234")
if err != nil {
    log.Fatal("dialing:", err)
}

// synchronous rpc
args := &server.Args{3,4}
var reply int
client.Call("Multiply.Do", args, &reply)
fmt.Printf(" %d*%d=%d", args.A, args.B, reply)
```

This style of architecture has lost popularity in recent years due to the following reasons:

- It tries to add a wrapper for remote objects and fakes a local reference to a remote object. But as we saw from the eight fallacies, remote behavior is never the same as local, and the architecture does not leave much scope for easily solving this impedance mismatch.
- The caller and collie both need to be up and running at the time of communication. Often, this is not a requirement of the application build.
- Some of the frameworks, such as CORBA, started to become horrendously complicated since they were designed by committee.

Layered architectures

As described in `Chapter 1`, *Building Big with Go*, the components are organized into tiers and communication is restricted only between adjacent layers. The layers are distributed across machines:

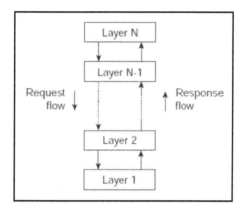

This architectural style can be thought of as an inverted pyramid of reuse, where each layer aggregates the responsibilities and abstractions of the layer directly beneath it. When the layers are on different machines, they are called tiers. The most common example of strict layering is where components in one layer can interact only with components in the same layer or with components from the layer directly below it.

The layers of an application may reside on the same physical computer (networking stack), but in distributed systems, of course, these are on different machines. In this case, they are called an n-tier architecture. For example, a typical web application design consists of the following:

- **A Presentation layer**: A UI-related functionality.
- **HTTP server layer**: This is a network server responsible for handling HTTP/HTTPS and features such as reverse caching, persistent connection handling, transparent SSL/TLS encryption, and load balancing.
- **A Business Logic layer**: Hosts the actual processing to be done as per the business rules. This is typically handled by code deployed in web containers or frameworks. In Golang, the containers tend to be much less complicated compared to other languages, such as Java (JAX-RX or Spring MVC).
- **A Data Layer**: Deals with interactions with durable data (database). This is generally built using mostly reusable code, configured with application specifics. In initial versions, this layer is co-located with the Business Logic layer.

In which tier to place which layer is an important design decision that the architect has to grapple with. There is an entire spectrum in terms of responsibility allocation:

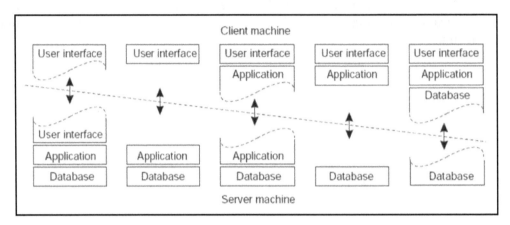

We should start by having clients as dumb as possible (left side of the preceding diagram), since this allows maximum flexibility in terms of reuse (across clients) and extensibility (generally, server code is easier to change and deploy compared with client code). However, some more layers may creep into the client to solve for things such as latency optimization.

Peer-2-peer (P2P) architecture

In the P2P architecture model, all the actors are peers and there is no central coordinator between them. Each instance takes a part of the workload or shares its resources with other peers in the network. Generally, in this architecture, the nodes or instances act as both the servers and clients.

Though traditionally this paradigm implied equally privileged peers, in practice, there can be variations of this:

- **Hybrid**: Some instances might have a specific functionality.
- **Structured P2P**: Nodes might structure themselves into some sort of overlay and processing may flow like in the layered architecture pattern described previously. However, the key difference is that the overlay is temporal and disposable.

Bit-torrent is an example of a P2P architecture. It is a file-sharing server where each node streams whatever content it has and for new content, queries a central service (web page) to figure out which nodes host what chunks of the required content:

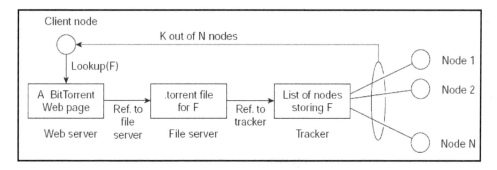

Source: http://www.bittorrent.org/

An example of a Structured P2P is a **distributed hash table (DHT)**. If you recall, a hash table is a data structure that allows for the storage of Key-Value objects. Internally, the data is stored in various buckets. A good hash function is used to map the Key to a hash value and then perform a modulo operation with a set number of buckets to get to the bucket that contains the Key. Within a bucket, Keys are stored in a format amenable to searching (such as Red-Black trees), but each bucket has to work with a much lesser scale of data than the hash table as a whole.

The DHT allows for designing a hash table that is distributed across machines. A common need for DHT is when we want to do request-specific routing—here any instance can get a request, but will consult the DHT to figure out which instance to route the instance to in order to fulfil it. So, how do we build a DHT?

An initial (naive) solution might be to hash the key and do modulo-n to get a server address. For example, with three servers, six keys could be distributed as follows:

Key	Hash	Server at (Hash- mod- 3)
Alice	3333333333	0
Bob	7733228434	1
Chris	3734343434	2
Doug	6666666666	0
Elgar	3000034135	1
Fred	6000799124	3

This scheme is simple and works fine. However, the problem is with redistribution. One of the main requirements of distributed systems is scalability—the ability to add/remove servers to scale with load. Here, if we change the number of servers to four, then the hash values, and thus the server assignments of nearly all the keys, will change! This means a lot of wasteful data movement and downtime while the cluster reconfigures.

One scheme that overcomes this limitation is called consistent hashing, and was first described by Karger et al. at MIT in an academic paper from 1997. The basic idea behind the algorithm is to hash both the servers hosting the cache and the keys using the same hash function.

The reason to do this is to map the cache to an interval, which will contain a number of object hashes. If the cache is removed, its interval is taken over by a cache with an adjacent interval. All the other caches remain unchanged.

To understand how consistent hashing works, consider a circle with values on it ranging from [0-1], that is, any point on the circle has a value between 0 and 1. Next, we pick a favorite hashing function and also scale it from [0-1]. For example, if the hash function has a range from [0-X], we use the following:

```
ringKey= hash(key) % X
```

Using this function, we can map machines (instances) and objects (using the keys) on the [0-1] range.

If we have three machines, we use the modified hash function to map each machine to a point on the circle:

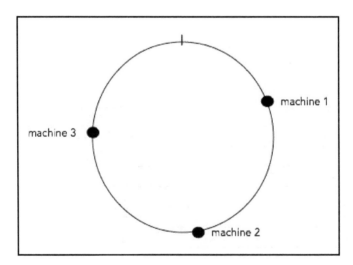

Now, we can see that the 0-1 range has been split into intervals among the machines! Suppose we have a key-value pair in the hash table, we need to do two things:

- Use the modified hash function to locate the key on the circle
- Find the first machine that appears clockwise from that point and store the key there

This is demonstrated in the following diagram: KeyX maps to a point and the machine closest from the clockwise side in machine 3. Hence KeyX is assigned to machine 3:

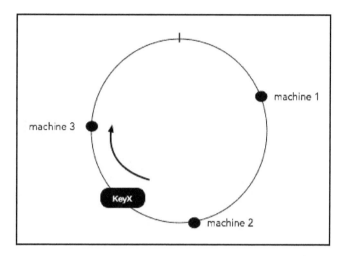

From a programming perspective, the *find closed machine clockwise* is easily achieved by storing the point values of the machines in a fashion that is easy to find "the next higher number after y." One way is to use a linked list of machine hash values in sorted order. To find the assignment, just walk this list (or use binary search) to find the first machine with a hash value greater than, or equal to, the hash of the key. We can make this a circular list so that, if no machine with "larger key" is found, the computation wraps around, and the first server in the list is assigned.

Now, let's say we add one more machine to the cluster:

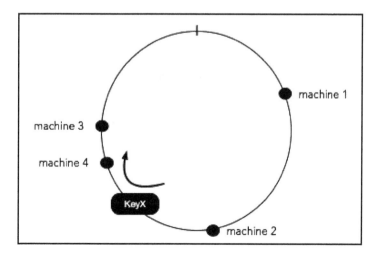

As you can see, most of the assignments are not affected by this change—in contrast to the naive hashing approach, where nearly every assignment changes. The only reassignment happens between the machine that was originally in the clockwise direction and the new one that was provisioned.

To smooth out irregularities in the distribution of the hash function, instead of one point on the ring, each machine is assigned a set of points (called vnodes). The following diagram depicts the scheme:

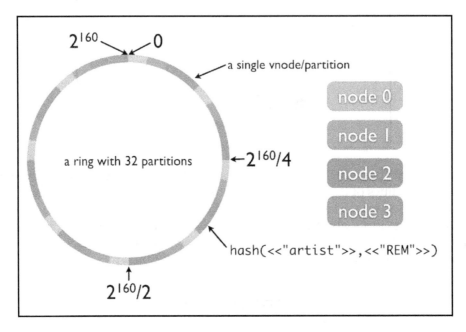

Courtesy of http://efcasado.github.io/riak-core_intro/

There have been recent improvements in consistent hashing to make it load-aware. One such algorithm is Consistent Hashing with Bounded Loads: `https://research.googleblog.com/2017/04/consistent-hashing-with-bounded-loads.html`.

It uses a uniformity parameter (ε) that is greater than 1 and controls how much imbalance there can be in terms of load (number of keys at each server). For example, if $\varepsilon = 1.5$, no server will get more than 150% of the average load. The algorithm's key modification for consistent hashing is to just *move on to the next node on the ring* if the closed node does not been the balancing factor. With large ε values, the algorithm becomes equivalent to original consistent hashing, however as it comes closer to 1, the distribution is more uniform but involves more rebalancing (fewer characteristics of consistent hashing). You can find the Go implementation of this paper at `https://github.com/lafikl/consistent`.

Sometimes, in P2P networks, the overlay can become hierarchical, with **Superpeers**:

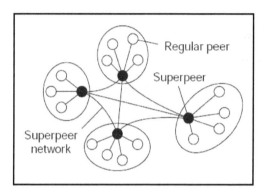

These **Superpeers** are responsible for communication between the inner cluster; they also peer with other **Superpeers** to structure interactions. One example of this type of architecture is **content-delivery networks** (**CDNs**). Each edge server here is a peer.

Distributed computations

Sometimes, your application may need to work with data that cannot be managed easily with classical databases. You might also need to perform a variety of computations/projections on the data, and maintaining an index for each column is not feasible/efficient. Google pioneered a new way of solving such computations by distributing computation—so that the same code can work with different data on a set of commodity machines. This is called MapReduce.

MapReduce defines the overall processing in two parts/functions, both of which take key/value pairs as input and give them out as output. The functions are as follows:

- **Map**: Takes an input key/value pair and generates a set of intermediate key/value pairs (which can be empty). For example, the Map function might create a histogram (mapping of word to its count) within a page of a document.
- **Reduce**: Gets the intermediate keys and a list of all associated values that were generated in the Map step—that is, all of the intermediate values that have the same key are aggregated into a list. In the word count example, each Reduce instance will get the word as the key and a list of count in each page of the document.

The flow is shown as follows:

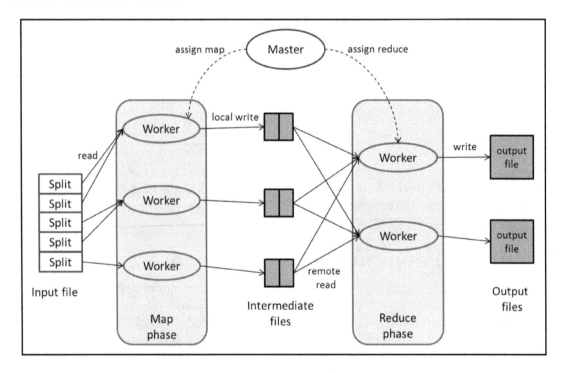

The Google framework had the **Google File System** (**GFS**) and a distributed NoSQL database, called BigTable, as supporting casts in the MapReduce framework. The distributed MapReduce computation is implemented using a master/slave architecture—a master assigns tasks and controls execution on a set of slave machines.

The preceding diagram illustrates the word count example we discussed. The input document is stored in GFS and split into chunks. The master kicks things off by sending the code of the map and reduce functions to all the workers. It then spawns Map tasks on the worker, which generate the intermediate KV pairs in files. Then, the Reduce tasks are spawned, which take the intermediate files and write the final output.

The Apache foundation has created an open source version of this paradigm, called Hadoop. It uses the **Hadoop Distributed File System** (**HDFS**), instead of GFS and YARN. **Yet Another Resource Negotiator** (**YARN**) is Hadoop's cluster execution scheduler. It spawns/allocates a number of containers (processes) on the machines in the cluster and allows one to execute arbitrary commands on them. HBase is the equivalent for BigTable. There are many higher-level projects on top of Hadoop—for example, Hive can run SQL-like queries by converting them into MapReduce functions.

Though the MapReduce framework has a simple programming model and has met its objective of crunching big data easily, it's not applicable if you have real-time response requirements. There are two reasons for this:

- Hadoop was initially designed for batch processing. Things such as scheduling, code transfers, and process (Mappers/Reducers) setup and teardown mean that even the smallest computations do not finish in less than seconds.
- The HDFS is designed for high throughput data I/O rather than high-performance. Data blocks in HDFS are very large and the IOPS are about 100 to 200 MB.

One way of optimizing on the disk IO is to store the data in memory. With a cluster of machines, the memory size of an individual machine is no longer a constraint.

In-memory computing does not mean that the entire dataset should be in memory; even caching frequently used data can significantly improve the overall job execution time. Apache Spark is built on this model. Its primary abstraction is called **Resilient Distributed Dataset** (**RDD**). This is essentially a batch of events that can be processed together. In a model similar to Hadoop, there is a main program (driver) that coordinates computation by sending tasks to executor processes running on multiple worker nodes:

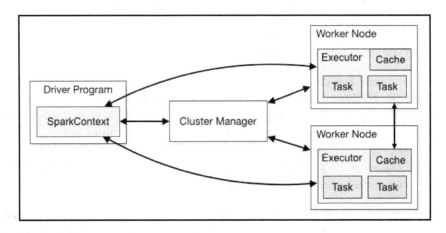

Reference: https://spark.apache.org/docs/latest/cluster-overview.html

Event-driven architecture (EDA)

A monolithic application typically has a single compute code base accessing a single relational database with **Atomicity, Consistency, Isolation, and Durability** (**ACID**) semantics. As a result, typically, multi-table updates triggered by external requests are easy to do by issuing the update statements under a transaction (Chapter 8, *Modeling Data*, covers these concepts in detail). When this monolith gets decomposed into microservices, each microservice gets its own database (to avoid coupling). Distributed transactions are possible, but avoidable due to following reasons:

- They can take much longer to converge and are more error-prone than transactions against a single database
- All microservices may not have a relational database—they pick what suits their use cases best

Event-driven architecture (**EDA**) promotes an architectural paradigm where behavior is composed by reacting to events. Here, events imply a significant change in state—for example, when a customer checks in their hotel, the state of that object changes from *booked* to *consumed*. This may trigger multiple reactions in the system, from reconciliation of payment with the Seller (hotel owner) to sending an email to the customer asking them to provide feedback.

A schematic of a typical web application that uses EDA is shown here:

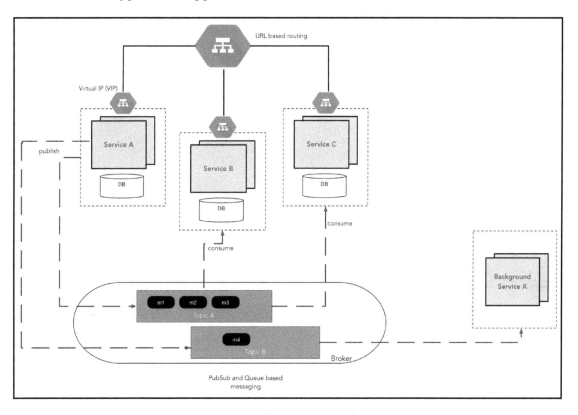

Here, the messaging bus serves as the event delivery mechanism. Services listen on Topics in the message queue, consume new messages, and then reacts to them. Messaging is covered in detail in Chapter 6, *Messaging*. The main advantage of this paradigm is that components are loosely coupled—they don't need to explicitly refer to each other. If the behavior needs to be extended so that new systems can react to events, the original plumbing and existing consuming components are unaffected.

Another application of this pattern is to prepare Materialized Views. The context here is the following—user-request fulfilment is enabled by multiple distributed services, however the system needs to present a view about the overall request. For example, in the hotel booking flow, the user would like to see their booking as it progresses through various states, such as INITIAL, PAYMENT_MADE, and BOOKING_CONFIRMED, along with ancillary details such as the check-in time at the hotel. All this data is not available with one service, thus to prepare the view, one naive approach might be to query all the services for the data and compose the data. This is not always optimal since the service usually models data in the format that it requires it, not this third-party requirement. The alternative is, in advance, to pre-populate the data for the view in a format best suited to the view. Here is an example:

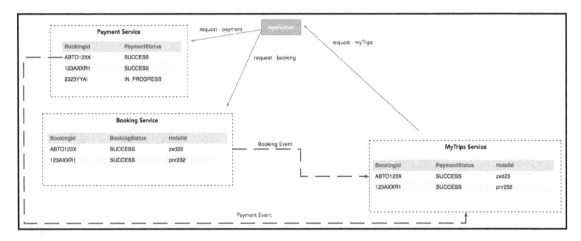

This pattern allows the decoupling promised by microservices, while still allowing the composition of rich cross-cutting views.

There are still things to consider there in terms of consistency—for example, what happens if the Booking Service updates the database, but before it can send out an event on the messaging bus it crashes? For the preceding materialized view use case, you can think of building reconciliation strategies, but the solution won't scale. The trick is to have an Event table in the local microservice database, which stores the intent to send a message. The update to the main table and this Event table can be atomic (using transactions). There is another background worker/thread that takes data from the Event table and actually fulfils the intent of sending the message:

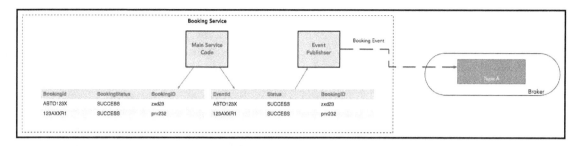

The preceding approach is generally called the event sourcing paradigm. The main philosophy behind the pattern is to model data operations as a sequence of events in an append-only log, rather than the absolute values. The current state is composed only when needed and is easy to do—just take the latest update, for example. Besides allowing for the efficient computation of varied goals, another key advantage of the event sourcing model is that, since it persists events rather than domain objects, it mostly avoids the object-relational impedance mismatch problem (`https://en.wikipedia.org/wiki/Object-relational_impedance_mismatch`).

In case the application cannot be rewritten to source events, an alternative approach is to mine the database updates as sources of events and then use the updates as triggers to generate messages.

 There is a tradeoff in terms of increased complexity with event sourcing.

The CQRS (Command and Query Responsibility Segregation) pattern needs to be followed. CQRS mean splitting application logic into two parts: the command side handles data updates, and the query side handles reads. The command side of the code does not care about the queries—it just sends the changes of the data as events. On the read side, these events are curated in the manner best suited for read (materialized views).

The consistency of different/distributed derived results is not guaranteed at all times. However, eventually, all derived results will be consistent. Thus, the applications should be able to handle eventual consistency (the BASE consistency model described in the *Consistency* subsection).

The Actor model

A specific variant of EDA is called the Actor model. Here, Actors refer to services that do the following:

- Abstract the level, which indicates a primitive unit of computation
- Encapsulate state

These Actors have mailboxes, where messages can be posted. The Actor sequentially takes each message from the mailbox and performs an action corresponding to the message. Each Actor has also some internal state that can affect the response to the messages.

Of course, there is more than one Actor and they communicate with each other asynchronously using messages. The overall system behavior is defined by these interactions and the processing by the Actors.

There are differences between this and the channel-goroutine semantics:

- Each Actor is uniquely identified by its mailbox. So, when someone is sending a message, it is intended to be processed by a specific Actor. In a contract, a channel is a generic pipe. More than one goroutine can listen on the pipe.
- The channels are in-memory. Mailboxes and generally cross-machine.

The actor model also follows the divide-and-conquer principle, and breaks up tasks until they are small enough to be handled by one sequential piece of code. The system can be reasoned about in terms of the messages exchanged. This is similar to OO programming, with the added powerful benefit that failure paths and actors can be different from the normal path. That way there is more freedom in handling unhappy paths. Another key advantage with other messaging systems is that both producers and consumers don't need to be alive at the same time, nor be operating at the same speed.

Generally, one actor assumes the role of a supervisor for a task and monitors the execution of the tasks in other actors. In case of risky or long-winded tasks, an Actor may spawn child Actors to do the sub-tasks and relegate itself to monitor the liveliness of the distributed computation among the children.

The Channel-Goroutine model is closer to the **Communicating Sequential Processes** (**CSP**), described by Hoare.

Erlang is the a famous example of languages that espouse this architecture style.

Stream processing

There are a few extensions to the EDA architecture paradigm for real-time processing. To evaluate and differentiate between them, let's consider a sample use case:

On our travel website, we want to know the number of visitors in the last 30 minutes and get a notification when this number crosses a threshold (say, 100,000 visitors). Let's assume that each visitor action causes an event.

The first (and most straightforward) application of the Distributed Computation model is to have Hadoop do the counts. However, the job needs to finish and restart within 30 minutes. With the Map-Reduce paradigm, such real-time requests can lead to brittle systems—they will break if the requirements change slightly, parallel jobs start executing, or when the size of the data exponentially grows. You can use Apache Spark to improve performance through in-memory computation.

However, these approaches don't scale, as their main focus is batching (and throughput optimization) rather than low-latency computation (which is needed to generate timely notifications in the preceding use case). Essentially, we want to process data as soon as it comes in, rather than batching events. This model is called stream processing.

The idea here is to create a graph of operators and then inject events into this processing graph. Processing can involve things such as event enrichment, group-by, custom processing, or event combination. Apache Storm is an example of a stream processing framework. A Storm program is defined in terms of two abstractions: Spouts and Bolts. A spout is a stream source (say, a Kafka Topic). A Bolt is a processing element (logic written by the programmer) that works on one or more spouts. A Storm program is essentially a graph of spouts and bolts, and is called a Topology.

Kafka streams is another framework that is built-in in the latest Kafka version (Kafka is discussed in detail in `Chapter 6`, *Messaging*) and allows per-event computation. It uses the Kafka partitioning model to partition data for processing it, enabled by an easy-to-use programming library. This library creates a set of stream tasks and assigns Kafka partitions to it for processing. Sadly, at the time of writing, this is not available for Go programs yet.

Apache Samza is another framework for stream processing and uses YARN to spawn processing tasks and Kafka to provide partitioned data for these tasks. Kasper (`https://github.com/movio/kasper`) is a processing library in Go, and is inspired by Apache Samza. It processes messages in small batches and uses centralized key-value stores, such as Redis, Cassandra, or Elasticsearch, for maintaining state during processing.

There are also **Complex Event Processing** (CEP) engines, which allow users to write SQL-like queries on a stream of events (say Kafka), with a key objective of millisecond response time. This pattern was developed initially for stock-market-related use cases. Though CEP and stream processing frameworks started with different requirements, over time, both technologies have started to share the same feature sets.

The following diagram summarizes the different stream processing techniques:

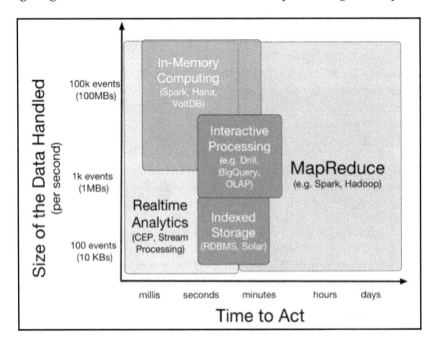

Summary

This chapter took a deep dive into distributed systems and their quirks. We looked at various aspects of consistency and consensus.

In the next chapter, we will look at messaging and integration patterns in more detail. We will deep-dive into a couple of commonly used messaging systems, and look at coding various patterns in Go using these messaging systems.

6
Messaging

In the previous chapter, we saw that messaging is a key enabler of communication in scalable systems. It offers reliable asynchronous communication with one-to-one communication (queuing) as well as one-to-many (Pub/Sub) models.

In this chapter, we will look at messaging in detail, starting with theoretical constructs and doing deep-dives into two widely-used systems. We will cover the following topics:

- Performance characterization
- Broker-based messaging
- Apache Kafka deep dive
- Brokerless messaging
- NSQ deep-dive
- Integration patterns

Performance characterization

A messaging system can be judged on its performance in four aspects—scalability, availability, latency, and throughput. These factors are often at odds with each other, and the architect often needs to figure what one aspect to compromise to improve the others:

- **Scalability:** This is how the system is able to handle increases in load without noticeable degradation of the other two factors, latency or availability. Here, load can mean things such as the number of topics, consumers, producers, messages/sec, or average message size.
- **Availability:** In a distributed system, a variety of problems can occur at a unit level (servers, disks, network, and so on). The system's availability is a measure of how resilient the system is to these failures so that it is available to end users.

- **Latency:** This is how much time it takes for a message to get to a consumer from a producer.
- **Throughput:** This is how many messages can be processed per second by the messaging system.

A classic tradeoff is between latency and throughput. To optimize throughput, we can batch messages and process them together. But this has a very negative effect on latency.

Broker-based messaging

A broker is a component that acts as the intermediary in a messaging system. Here, the clients connect to the broker and not to each other directly. Whenever clients want to send and receive messages, they need to specify a mailbox/topic/queue on the broker. Producers connect to the broker and send messages to a specific queue. Consumers connect to the broker and specify queue name from which they want to read messages. The broker has the following key responsibilities:

- **Maintaining the mapping of queues, producers, and consumers reliably**: This includes storing the messages in a durable format.
- **Handling message production**: This includes storing messages written by the producers.
- **Handling message consumption**: This means ensuring that consumers reliably get messages and providing constructs to avoid duplicate messages.
- **Routing and transformation**: Here, the message broker may transform or maintain multiple copies for each message to enable various topology models, which will be described in the following sections.

The queuing model

In the standard queuing model, there is a first-in, first-out durable buffer between a producer and a consumer, as shown in the following diagram:

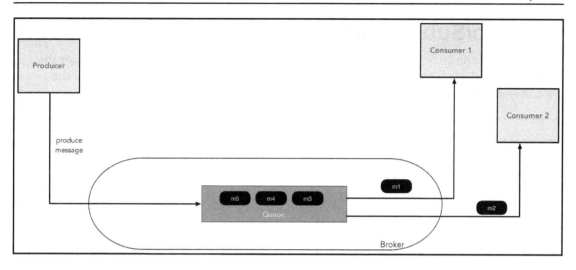

All producers and consumers connect to a **Broker** during initialization. consumers additionally express interest in certain queues by registering for consumption against them. Whenever a **Producer** sends a message to a **Queue**, the message is transported to the broker and stored in durable storage against the **Queue**. These messages are delivered to one or more consumers who have registered for the **Queue**. If more than one consumer is registered in the queuing model, each message is delivered to only one consumer, thereby enabling load-balancing semantics for message consumption and processing.

There are two ways in which consumers can get to the messages:

- **Pull mode:** The messaging client in the consumer periodically polls the broker to check for any new messages.
- **Push mode:** The consumers register an endpoint (say, an HTTPS URL) and produced messages are sent to the URL using protocols such as HTTPS POST.

The PULL mode is little wasteful, as there might not be messages at every pull. On the other hand, the PUSH mode requires consumers to have endpoints reachable by the broker, which is difficult to engineer through network firewalls.

The Pub/Sub model

The major difference between the queuing model and the Pub/Sub model is that, for the Pub/Sub model, each consumer gets a copy of the message, rather than just one of the consumers. This can be understood with the following diagram:

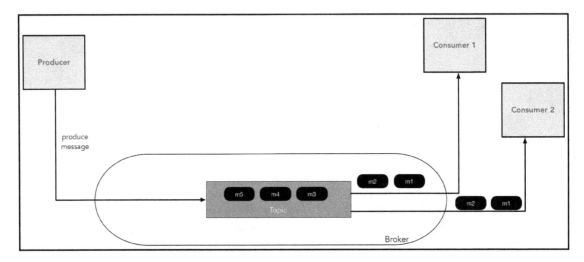

As you can see, **Consumer 1** and **Consumer 2** both get copies of the **m1** and **m2** messages.

This model is useful when you want a bunch of consumers to work on the same messages, which is usually the norm in **event-driven architecture** (**EDA**), which we saw previously.

One thought that might come to mind is, does this mean that load-balancing can't be done in a Pub/Sub setup? Won't it interfere with scalability?

Generally, messaging systems also provide load balancing semantics with **Topics** using something called **virtual topics** (a term used specifically by ActiveMQ, but it's a functionality that's available in most queuing systems). The scheme is shown in the following diagram:

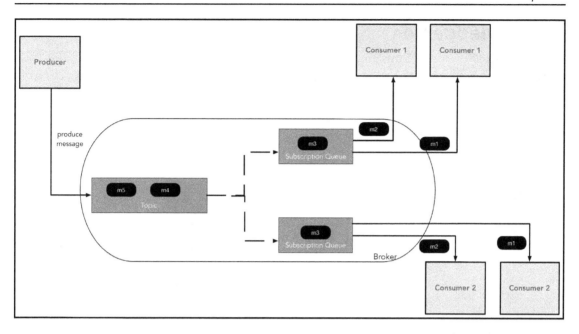

As you can see, the **Topic** still does Pub/Sub type message routing, but each consumer effectively gets a **Subscription Queue**. Multiple instances of the consumer can get different messages, thereby enabling scale-out and load-balancing for the consumer. It should be noted that the **Subscription Queue** is created automatically as part of consumers registering for consumption against a **Topic**; it doesn't need to be created manually.

Delivery semantics

When writing code that takes messages off a queue and performs some work, it is important to understand the semantics of message-delivery guarantees.

Acknowledgement

Consider this situation: a **Consumer** gets a message (**m1**) but before it can act on it, the message crashes (or restarts). Hence, **m1** is not fully consumed, but from the perspective of the **Broker**, it's already delivered. This can be better understood with the following diagram:

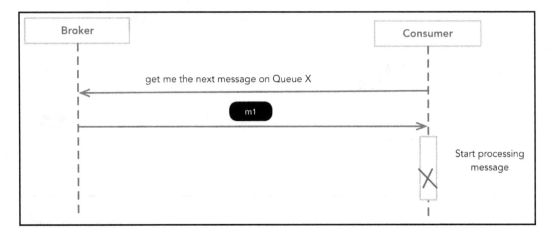

To handle such situations, **Broker** typically has facilities to allow consumers to acknowledge messages. Once a message is delivered, the **Broker** temporarily removes it from the queue and puts it in some other cold storage. The **Consumer** is supposed to send an acknowledgement for each message it consumes. When an acknowledgement for a message is received, it is removed from the cold storage by the **Broker**. Also, when sending a message to a **Consumer**, the Broker starts a timer for the acknowledgement deadline. If this time expires, the Broker assumes that the **Consumer** died while processing and moves the message from cold storage to the queue.

Does this enable reliable consumption? The acknowledgement model enables three types of reliable message delivery semantics, which we'll look at now.

At-least-once delivery

With the at-least-once delivery guarantee, the **Broker** ensures that it will deliver every required message at least once to the **Consumer**. Most of the time, a message will be received only once, but sometimes duplicates might arise. This scenario is described in the following diagram:

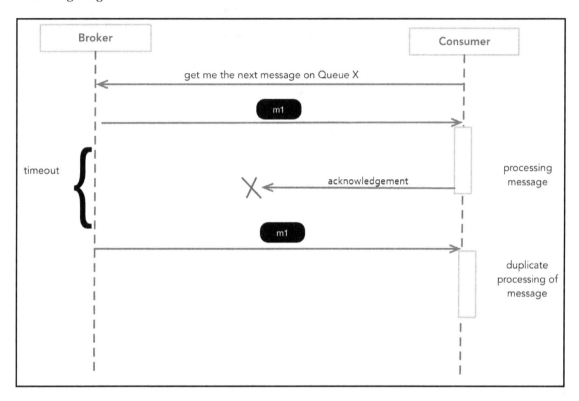

To avoid duplicate processing, the **Consumer** would need to deduplicate messages on its side. This is typically done by storing the message IDs in a database. When a message is about to be processed, this database is consulted to ensure that the message was not processed earlier. On the other hand, if the message-handling is idempotent, we can just ignore the duplicate processing.

At-most-once delivery

Sometimes it is essential to avoid sending duplicate messages, such as emails—you don't want to spam your customer. To enable this, the delivery semantics can be at-most-once. Not having **acknowledgement** is one way of enabling at-most-once delivery. However, since most messaging systems have acknowledgement, another way to achieve this is to acknowledge the message starting to process it, as shown in the following diagram:

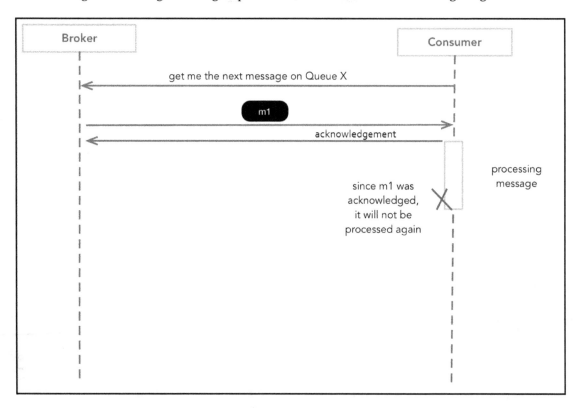

Exactly-once delivery

Exactly-once semantics is the most desirable guarantee, but is impossible to guarantee without some sort of cooperation between the broker and the consumer. If the broker uses acknowledgements to producers for publishing message, each message must have unique IDs for the broker to deduplicate retires.

On the consumer side, deduplication can be used to ensure that duplicate messages are not processed.

Some message systems, such as Kafka, allow atomic consume-from-one-and-publish-to-n semantics. This is extremely helpful for EDA architectures and we will look at these in the *Apache Kafka deep-dive* section.

Resilience

A lot of things can go wrong with the models described in this section:

- The broker can fail, which takes away any messages stored on it. To overcome this eventuality, generally brokers are deployed in a cluster of redundant instances. Every message is replicated on a set of machines as part of the write commit. If a message is replicated onto n brokers, that means the system can tolerate the failure of n-1 instances.
- The producer-to-broker communication can fail, which causes messages to be lost. This is generally solved by acknowledgements (as seen previously). Duplicate messages being produced can be avoided by having a sequence number for messages.
- The consumer-to-broker message communication can fail, which causes messages to be lost. Hence, messages should not be deleted from the Broker, unless there is an explicit acknowledgement from the consumer that the message has been processed. As we saw in the *Acknowledgement* section, when we do the acknowledgement, it can result in at-least-once or at-most-once semantics. Exactly-once delivery can be enabled by deduplication on the consumer side and cooperation between the broker and the consumer.

Many applications also need some atomicity guarantees in terms of *read from n queues and write to m queues*. Messaging systems such as Kafka provide transaction constructs to enable this. We shall see this in detail in the *Apache Kafka deep-dive* section.

AMQP

AMQP stands for **Asynchronous Message Queuing Protocol** and is an open standard for messaging systems. It was initially designed for financial systems (trading and banking) and as such, over indexes on reliability, scalability, and manageability.

The following are some of the constructs defined by the AMQP specification:

- It has a wire-level protocol that describes the packets (frames, in AMQP parlance) exchanged between brokers, producers, and consumers. There are nine types of frames defined by the spec, which are concerned with things such as connection setup/teardown and flow control.
- It has a self-describing encoding scheme to describe a range of data types. Also included are annotations that give entities additional meaning (for example, a string might be annotated to indicate that it's a URL).

In AMQP, messages are published to exchanges. The messages are then routed to different queues using rules called as bindings. Consumers fetch messages from queues:

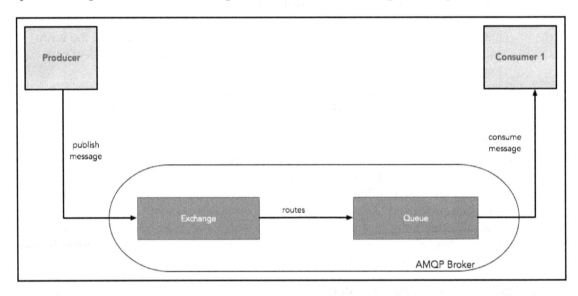

The network is considered unreliable and consumers may fail to process messages. Hence, the AMQP model has the concept of message acknowledgements: when a message is delivered to a consumer, the consumer sends an acknowledgement to the broker once it has consumed the message. This will be the trigger for the broker to remove the message from the queue. Acknowledgements are generally accompanied by timeouts; if a message is not acknowledged within a timeout, it is redelivered to the consumer.

The routing algorithm depends on the type of **Exchange**. Various recipes are available to enable queuing (one-to-one) or Pub/Sub (one-to-*n*) behavior. If, for some reason, a message cannot be routed, it is parked in a special queue called a *dead-letter queue*. RabbitMQ is an open source project using AMQP constructs.

The RabbitMQ management plugin provides an HTTP API, a browser-based UI, and a CLI for management and monitoring. It enables the definition of complex routing topologies with enterprise-grade security. The downside of the AMQP is that it's throughput is not as great as Kafka, complexity and extra resource utilization to maintain helper data structures for the routing metadata.

In terms of throughput, RabbitMQ provides a throughput of about 20,000 messages per second.

Apache Kafka deep dive

Apache Kafka is a streaming-messaging platform that was first built at LinkedIn but is now a first-class Apache project. It offers seamless durable distribution of messages over a cluster of brokers, and the distribution can scale with load. It is increasingly used in place of traditional message brokers, such as AMQP, because of its higher throughput, simpler architecture, load-balancing semantics, and integration options.

Concepts

In Kafka, **topic** is a formal name for queues where messages are published to and consumed from. Topics in Kafka offer the virtual topic queuing model described previously, that is, where there are multiple logical subscribers, each will get a copy of the message, but a logical subscriber can have multiple instances, and each instance of the subscriber will get a different message.

A topic is modeled as a partitioned log, as shown here:

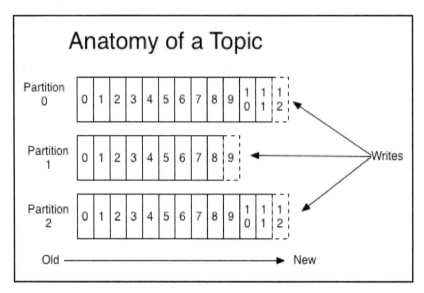

Source: http://kafka.apache.org/documentation.html#introduction

New messages are appended to a partition of a log. The log partition is an ordered, immutable list of messages. Each message in a topic partition is identified by an offset within the list. The partitions serve several purposes:

- A log (topic) can scale beyond the size of a single machine (node). Individual partitions need to fit on a single machine, but the overall topic can be spread across several machines.
- Topic partitions allow parallelism and scalability in consumers.

Kafka only guarantees the order of messages within a topic partition, and not across different partitions for the same topic. This is a key point to remember when designing applications.

Whenever a new message is produced, it is durably persisted on a set of broker instances designated for that topic partition—called **In-Sync Replicas** (**ISRs**). Each ISR has one node that acts as the leader and zero or more nodes that act as followers. The leader handles all read and write requests and replicates the state on the follower. There is periodic heart-beating between the leader and the followers, and if a leader is deemed to be failed, an election is held to elect a new leader. It should be noted that one node can be a leader for one topic partition while being a follower for other topic partitions. This allows for the load to be distributed evenly among the nodes of the cluster.

The messages remain on the brokers for a configurable retention time—which has no bearing on whether they have been consumed. For example, if the retention policy for a topic is set to one week, then for a week after the message is published, it's available for consumption. After this, the message is deleted (and the space reclaimed).

Unlike most other messaging systems, Kafka retains minimal information about consumer consumption. Clients can remember what offsets they have in each topic partition and attempt to find it randomly into the log.

Kafka also provides a facility of the brokers *remembering*, to the offsets for consumers—on explicit indication by them. This design reduces a lot of the complexity on the broker and allows for efficient support of multiple consumers with different speeds:

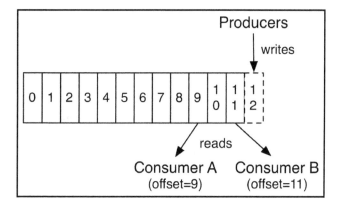

(Source: http://kafka.apache.org/documentation.html#introduction)

Consumer A can consume messages at its own speed, irrespective of how fast **Consumer B** is going.

Producers publish messages on specific topics. They can provide a partitioner of their choice—to pick a partition for each message—or they can choose a default (random/round-robin) partitioner. Generally, most Kafka clients batch messages at the producer side, so a write is just storing the message in a buffer. These messages are then periodically flushed to the brokers.

As described earlier in *The Pub/Sub model* section, the Kafka topic offers a Pub/Sub queuing model. So, there can be multiple logical consumers and each will get all of the messages. However, a logical consumer (say, a microservice) will have more than one instance, and ideally we would like to load-balance consumption and processing of messages across these consumer instances. Kafka allows this using a construct called **consumer groups**. Each time a consumer registers to a topic for messages, it sends a label (string) describing the logical consumer (say, service). The Kafka brokers treat each instance having the same group name to belong to the same logical consumer and each instance gets only a subset of the messages. Hence, messages will be effectively load-balanced over the consumer instances.

As described earlier, the topic partitions serve as a unit of parallelism for consumption of the messages. Let's look at how this happens. When a consumer instance registers for messages from a topic, it has two options:

- Manually register for specific partitions of that topic
- Have Kafka automatically distribute topic partitions among the consumer instances

The first option is simple, and there is a lot of control with the application on who processes what. However, the second option, called the group coordinator feature, is an awesome tool to enable scalability and resilience in distributed systems. Here, the consumers don't specify explicit partitions to consume from, rather the broker automatically assigns them to consumer instances:

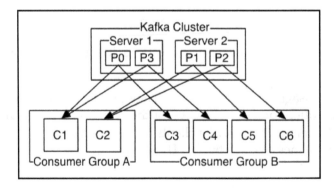

(Source: http://kafka.apache.org/documentation.html#introduction)

In the preceding diagram, the topic has four partitions spread over two servers. **Consumer Group A** has two instances, and each has two topic partitions assigned to it. On the other hand, **Consumer Group B** has four instances, and each is assigned a topic partition. The broker (group coordinator feature) is responsible for maintaining membership in the consumer groups through a heart-beating mechanism with the consumer group instances. As new consumer group instances come up, the topic partitions are reassigned automatically. If an instance dies, its partitions will be distributed among the remaining instances.

Publishing messages

Sarama (`https://github.com/Shopify/sarama`) is the most widely-used Go client library for Apache Kafka, written purely in Go. We will be using it to demonstrate various Kafka interactions.

Producing a message for Kafka involves multiple steps, including figuring out what partition of a topic the message must go to, finding the Leader for that topic partition, and transporting the message to that broker (leader) instance. In Sarama, the producer is based on the pipeline-concurrency pattern, where each message is processed by four structs. Each struct has a goroutine that implements a stage in the message-publish process, and these stages are connected by channels.

There are two options for the producer, as described in the following sections.

The AsyncProducer interface

As the name suggests, this is a non-blocking API that routes messages to the broker and provides signals about what happened to the message asynchronously through two output channels. Messages are ingested through an input channel. The `AsyncProducer` interface is documented in the following code:

```
type AsyncProducer interface {

    // AsyncClose triggers a shutdown of the producer. The shutdown has
completed
    // when both the Errors and Successes channels have been closed. When
calling
    // AsyncClose, you *must* continue to read from those channels in order
to
    // drain the results of any messages in flight.
    AsyncClose()
```

```
        // Close shuts down the producer and waits for any buffered messages to
be
        // flushed. You must call this function before a producer object passes
out of
        // scope, as it may otherwise leak memory. You must call this before
calling
        // Close on the underlying client.
        Close() error

        // Input is the input channel for the user to write messages to that
they
        // wish to send.
        Input() chan<- *ProducerMessage

        // Successes is the success output channel back to the user when
Return.Successes is
        // enabled. If Return.Successes is true, you MUST read from this
channel or the
        // Producer will deadlock. It is suggested that you send and read
messages
        // together in a single select statement.
        Successes() <-chan *ProducerMessage

        // Errors is the error output channel back to the user. You MUST read
from this
        // channel or the Producer will deadlock when the channel is full.
Alternatively,
        // you can set Producer.Return.Errors in your config to false, which
prevents
        // errors to be returned.
        Errors() <-chan *ProducerError
    }
```

The `Input()` method returns a write-only channel that accepts a pointer to a `ProducerMessage` struct. This is the main interface and clients write messages to this channel (encapsulated in the `ProducerMessage` struct). The client must read from the `Errors()` channel after publishing a message.

To reclaim the producer, we can call `Close()` or `AsyncClose()` on a producer to avoid leaks.

A sample usage of `AsyncProducer` using `select` on the various channels is given in the following code:

```
package main
import (
    "fmt"
```

```go
    "github.com/Shopify/sarama"
    "log"
    "os"
    "os/signal"
    "strconv"
    "time"
)

// Toy message that we want to send
type Message struct {
    Who          string
    TimeAsString string
}

func main() {

    // Create configuration
    config := sarama.NewConfig()
    // The setting below indicates the  level of  reliability needed
    //  Here we are saying we want all brokers in the ISR to ack
    config.Producer.RequiredAcks = sarama.WaitForAll
    // The total number of times to retry sending a message (default 3).
    config.Producer.Retry.Max = 5

    // you don't need to give a list of all the brokers, just few seeds which will
    // tell the client about other brokers in the cluster
    brokers := []string{"localhost:9092"}
    asyncProducer, err := sarama.NewAsyncProducer(brokers, config)
    if err != nil {
        // Could not connect
        panic(err)
    }

    defer func() {
        if err := asyncProducer.Close(); err != nil {
            log.Fatalln(err)
        }
    }()

    // Trap SIGINT to break from the loop and clean up.
    signals := make(chan os.Signal, 1)
    signal.Notify(signals, os.Interrupt)
    exitProgram := make(chan struct{})

    // Simple while(1) look to send current time.
    var nPublished, nErrors int
    go func() {
```

```
            for {
                    time.Sleep(5 * time.Second)

                    // construct a message
                    body := Message{
                            Who:            "aProcess",
                            TimeAsString: strconv.Itoa(int(time.Now().Unix())),
                    }

                    // marshall it
                    payload, _ := json.Marshal(body)

                    msg := &sarama.ProducerMessage{
                            Topic: "currentTime",
                            Key:    sarama.StringEncoder("aKey"),
                            Value: sarama.ByteEncoder(payload),
                    }
                    select {
                    case producer.Input() <- msg:
                            nPublished++
                            fmt.Println("Produce message")
                    case err := <-producer.Errors():
                            nErrors++
                            fmt.Println("Failed to produce message:", err)
                    case <-signals:
                            exitProgram <- struct{}{}
                    }

                    log.Printf("Published: %d; Errors: %d\n", nPublished,
        nErrors)

            }
        }()

        <-exitProgram // wait here till program gets killed

    }
```

You can also use separate goroutines to range over the `Errors` and `Success` channels, instead of using a `select` comprehension.

The Sync producer

Samara also has a blocking producer interface to wait until the message is reliably delivered. Its usage is similar to `AsyncProducer`, but instead of channels, there is a blocking `SendMessage()` method to be called.

The following code snippet illustrates the usage:

```
package main

import (
    "fmt"
    "github.com/Shopify/sarama"
)

func main() {

    // Config
    config := sarama.NewConfig()
    config.Producer.RequiredAcks = sarama.WaitForAll
    config.Producer.Retry.Max = 5
    config.Producer.Return.Errors = true  // For sync producer this needs to
be true
    config.Producer.Return.Success = true // For sync producer this needs to
be true

    // Connect to a Kafka broker running locally
    brokers := []string{"localhost:9092"}
    producer, err := sarama.NewSyncProducer(brokers, config)
    if err != nil {
        panic(err)
    }

    // cleanup
    defer func() {
        if err := producer.Close(); err != nil {
            panic(err)
        }
    }()

    msg := &sarama.ProducerMessage{
        Topic: "currentTime",
        Value: sarama.StringEncoder(strconv.Itoa(int(time.Now().Unix()))),
    }

    partition, offset, err := producer.SendMessage(msg)
    if err != nil {
        fmt.Printf("FAILED to publish message: %s\n", err)
    } else {
        fmt.Printf("message sent | partition(%d)/offset(%d)\n", partition,
offset)
    }
}
```

Consuming messages

Sarama provides a low-level message-consumption API, but there are higher-level libraries that provide the group coordination based on the load-balancing described in the *Apache Kafka deep-dive* section. The library is called Sarama (`https://github.com/bsm/sarama-cluster`).

 This library requires Kafka v0.9+ and follows the protocol described at `https://cwiki.apache.org/confluence/display/KAFKA/Kafka+0.9+Consumer+Rewrite+Design`.

The main interface is a channel on which messages are received.

A sample program is shown here:

```
package main
import (
    "fmt"
    cluster "github.com/bsm/sarama-cluster"
    "log"
    "os"
    "os/signal"
)

func main() {

    // setup config, enable errors and notifications
    config := cluster.NewConfig()
    config.Consumer.Return.Errors = true
    config.Group.Return.Notifications = true

    // specify Broker co-ordinates and topics of interest
    brokers := []string{"localhost:9092"}
    topics := []string{"topic_a", "topic_b"}

    // connect, and register specifying the consumer group name
    consumer, err := cluster.NewConsumer(brokers, "my-consumer-group",
topics, config)
    if err != nil {
        panic(err)
    }
    defer consumer.Close()

    // process errors
    go func() {
        for err := range consumer.Errors() {
```

```
                  log.Printf("Error: %s\n", err.Error())
            }
      }()

      // process notifications
      go func() {
            for ntf := range consumer.Notifications() {
                  log.Printf("Rebalanced: %+v\n", ntf)
            }
      }()

      // process messages
      for msg := range consumer.Messages() {
            fmt.Fprintf(os.Stdout, "%s-%d-%d-%s-%s\n",
                  msg.Topic,
                  msg.Partition,
                  msg.Offset,
                  msg.Key,
                  msg.Value) // <- Actually process message here

            consumer.MarkOffset(msg, "") // Commit offeset for this  message

      }
}
```

Most of the code before the `for` loop is setup code. The main consumption happens in the iteration over the channel returned by `consumer.Messages()`. Within this loop, whenever a new message is available, it will be delivered encapsulated by the `msg` object. After processing, the client can use the `consumer.MarkOffset()` call to commit the offset to Kafka—hence declaring that the consumer (group) has processed the message and, does not want to see it again. Typically, a handler function will be used to process the message and if the handler is successful, only then commit the message. For long-lived processing, we can ship the `msg` object itself to a handler function—and the message may be acknowledged later downstream. The second parameter to `consumer.MarkOffset()` indicates consumer state at the time of commit. This can be used as a checkpoint to restore consumption from a specific point.

Samara has tuneables to ensure that back-pressure can be applied so that consumers can process data at the rate they are comfortable with. Some of them are as follows:

- `Config.Consumer.MaxWaitTime`: This defines how long the consumer should wait before going to the Broker for more messages.
- `Config.ChannelBufferSize`: This defines the size of the buffered channels (input and output).
- `Config.Consumer.MaxProcessingTime`: This defines the time required for processing message at a consumer.

Stream processing

Goka (`https://github.com/lovoo/goka`) is a powerful Go stream-processing library that uses Apache Kafka. It can be used to build streaming patterns such as the CQRS and event sourcing architectures that we saw in `Chapter 5`, *Going Distributed*.

There are three main building blocks for a stream-processing application in Goka: emitters, processors, and views.

Emitters generate key-value messages into Kafka. For example, this could be a listener on a database change log and emit the change log as an event. A processor is a set of callback functions that consume and perform state transformations of messages. Processors are clustered in groups. As with the consumer group rebalancing feature of Kafka, Goka distributes topic partitions among processors in a processor group. Each processor group maintains state in something called agroup table. This is a partitioned key-value table stored in Kafka itself, with local caching. Views provide read-only access to the group tables.

The following diagram depicts the abstraction:

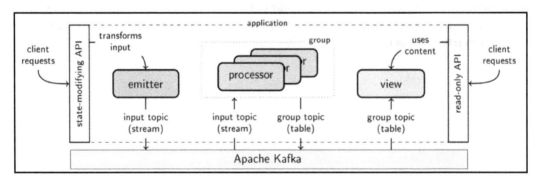

Source: https://github.com/lovoo/goka

This is an example of a processor that increments the number of messages seen:

```
func process(ctx goka.Context, msg interface{}) {
    var nMessages int
    if val := ctx.Value(); val != nil {
        nMessages = val.(int)
    }
    nMessages++
    ctx.SetValue(nMessages)
}
```

The `goka.Context` parameter passed is the most powerful construct, enabling the saving of the Group Table and sending messages to other Processors. More details can be found at `https://github.com/lovoo/goka` and you can see more examples at `https://github.com/lovoo/goka/tree/master/examples`.

Brokerless messaging

There are several advantages to the broker-based model:

- There is clear segregation between connected services. The only address a producer needs to know is that of the Broker.
- Producer and consumer lifetimes don't have to overlap. A Producer can send a message to a broker, die, and then much later a Consumer can come up and read the message.

There are, however, some drawbacks:

- The Broker can become a bottleneck, where all messages need to squeeze through. This can affect performance.
- There is no network I/O which is absolutely necessary.

For example, in a typical EDA architecture with a broker with four processors, we'll get a communication pattern such as this:

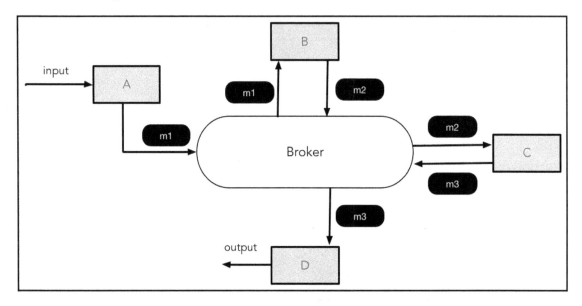

With a central broker, it cannot get more efficient than this. However, if the processors were allowed to talk to each other, we could have had much more efficient communication and lower end-to-end latency:

We can still retain some of the benefits of the brokered architecture (such as the isolation level) with the efficiency of the peer-to-peer architecture, if we let the Broker just act as a directory service, rather then a message forwarder.

NSQ is a messaging platform (incidentally written in Go), and it's described in the following section.

NSQ deep-dive

NSQ is a real-time distributed-messaging platform that encourages decentralized topologies as described in the *Brokerless messaging* section.

Concepts

An NSQ system consists of the following components:

- **The virtual topic construct**: Topics are the destination for messages being produced in NSQ. Each topic has one or more **Channels**, which are the queues for each consumer, thereby enabling Pub/Sub behavior. **Topics** and **Channels** are implicitly created on first use.

- **nsqd**: This is the main component; it receives, queues, and delivers messages to clients. It can run as a daemon or can be embedded inside a Go application. This can run standalone, but is normally configured in a cluster with nsqlookupd. These instances host multiple **Topics** (for all connected clients that produced messages) and **Channels** for all the **Topics**. The relationship between **Topics**, **Channels**, and nsqd is depicted in the following diagram:

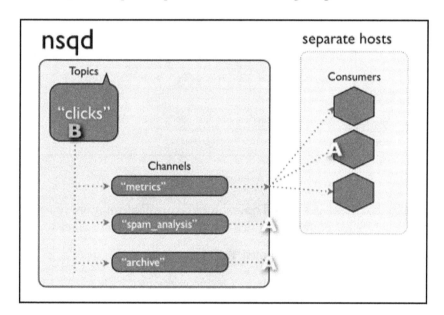

(Source: http://nsq.io/overview/design.html)

- **nsqlookupd**: This is the daemon that has the overall cluster picture and manages the topology. Clients query nsqlookupd instances to discover different nsqd instances that host messages (are the producers) for a specific topic. Its main job is to provide a directory service where clients (consumers) can look up the addresses of nsqd instances that host the **Topics** they are interested in consuming from.

Each nsqd instance has a long-lived TCP connection to nsqlookupd over which it pushes its state (such as health or topics). This is collated and then used by nsqlookupd to give the right set of nsqd instances to clients wishing to consume a specific topic. nsqd and nsqlookupd instances operate independently, without peer communication. For nsqlookupd, high availability is achieved by running multiple independent instances. Clients sum's poll all of their configured nsqlookupd instances and unit the responses.

Clients connect directly to **nsqd** instances, as shown here:

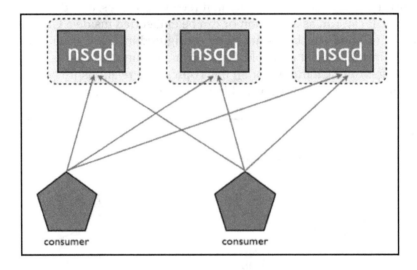

(Source: http://nsq.io/overview/design.html)

It should be noted that messages for a Topic might be available at more than one nsqd instances, and a client will connect to all nsqd instances hosting messages for a Topic.

When a client connects to an nsqd instance, the exchange is as follows:

1. The Client indicates it is ready to receive messages. Instead of a binary signal, the client sends a value, called RDY state, which indicates how many messages the client is ready to receive.
2. nsqd sends a message and temporarily moves the data to another local store (if retransmission is needed).
3. After consumption of the message, the client in the event of a re-queue client replies with a FIN (finish) packet and this message is then dropped by the producing nsqd instance's channel. If the client had an error, it can request the message again using a REQ (re-queue) packet.

4. nsqd runs a timeout after sending a message and, if there is no response, will automatically re-queue the message:

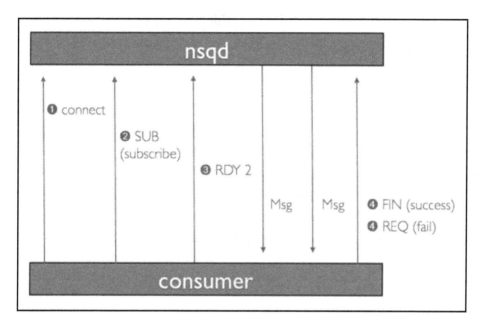

(Source: http://nsq.io/overview/design.html)

NSQ can store messages in memory and flush them to disk based on a configurable watermark. If durability for all messages is required, this configuration can be set so that messages are always written to disk. To achieve high availability, clients can write to more than one nsqd instance (this assumes that consumers are idempotent).

Publishing messages

Go-NSQ is the official Go client for NSQ. It's available at `https://github.com/nsqio/go-nsq`.

Here is the `NewProducer` function:

```
func NewProducer(addr string, config *Config) (*Producer, error)
```

It returns an instance of `Producer` for the specified nsqd address. There is a one-to-one mapping between an nsqd instance and a client Producer instance. The TCP connection is managed in a lazy manner (the connect will happen when publish is done).

Configuration contains a bunch of tuneables and is created through the `NewConfig()` method.

The `Producer` struct has two methods for publishing messages:

- Synchronous publish:

  ```
  func (w *Producer) Publish(topic string, body []byte) error
  ```

- Asynchronous publish:

  ```
  func (w *Producer) PublishAsync(topic string, body []byte, doneChan
  chan *ProducerTransaction, args...interface{}) error
  ```

This method sends the message asynchronously and returns instantly after calling. The `doneChan` channel gets an instance of `ProducerTransaction` with the `args` that were supplied and errors if there are any. The `args` are used mostly for housekeeping purposes.

The following code snippet demonstrates publishing a message:

```
package main

import (
    "fmt"
    "github.com/nsqio/go-nsq"
    "log"
)

func main() {

    // Connect
    pCfg := nsq.NewConfig()
    producer, err := nsq.NewProducer("127.0.0.1:4160", pCfg)
    if err != nil {
        log.Fatalf("failed creating producer %s", err)
    }

    // Publish Async
    destinationTopic := "my_topic"
    responseChan := make(chan *ProducerTransaction)
    err = producer.PublishAsync(destinationTopic, []byte("a_message"),
responseChan, "some_args")

    // Check for status
    // Done here  inline just for showcase
    status := <-responseChan
    if status.Error != nil {
        log.Printf("Error received %s \n", status.Error.Error())
```

```
    } else {
        log.Printf("Success Arg received : %s \n",
status.Args[0].(string)) // should be some_args
    }

}
```

Consuming messages

The `NewConsumer` method creates a new instance of NSQ consumer for a given `topic`. We need to specify the `channel` name and pass various tuneables as part of the configuration. The signature of the method is shown here:

```
func NewConsumer(topic string, channel string, config *Config) (*Consumer,
error)
```

The `Consumer` instance is supplied with a handler that will be executed concurrently through different goroutines. This handler will be given the messages consumed from the specified `topic/channel`. If configured, the `Consumer` instance will also poll nsqlookupd instances to discover and manage connections to nsqd instances. This is done by the `ConnectToNSQD()` method of the `Consumer` struct.

The following code snippet shows the basic usage:

```
package main

import (
    "github.com/nsqio/go-nsq"
    "log"
)

type MyMessageHandler struct {
    totalMessages int
}

func (h *MyMessageHandler) HandleMessage(message *Message) error {
    h.totalMessages++
    log.Printf("Message no %d received, body : %s \n", h.totalMessages,
string(message.Body))
}

func main() {
    config := NewConfig()

    topicName := "my_topic"
```

```
channelName := "my_chan"
cons, err := NewConsumer(topicName, channelName, config)
if err != nil {
        log.Fatal(err)
}

cons.AddHandler(&MyMessageHandler{})

// wait for a signal to quit
sigChan := make(chan os.Signal, 1)
signal.Notify(sigChan, syscall.SIGINT, syscall.SIGTERM)
<-sigChan

// Stop the consumer
cons.Stop()
<-cons.StopChan // wait for cleanup

}
```

You might be wondering how the acknowledgement of the messages happen. By default, the message is acknowledged when the handler returns. However, this auto-acknowledgement can be disabled by calling `DisableAutoResponse()` on the `Message` struct object in the handler. We can then call `Finish()` or `Requeue()` on the message object to acknowledge or request retransmission of a message. This is shown in the following code:

```
type MyMessageHandler struct {}

func (h *MyMessageHandler) HandleMessage(m *nsq.Message) error {
    m.DisableAutoResponse()
    delegateChannel <- m
    return nil
}

go func() {
    for m := range delegateChannel {
        err := doSomeWork(m) // some long winded tasks
        if err != nil {
            m.Requeue(-1)
            continue
        }
        m.Finish()
    }
}()

cfg := nsq.NewConfig()
cfg.MaxInFlight = 1000 //Maximum number of messages to allow in flight
```

```
(concurrency knob)
topicName := "my_topic"
channelName := "my_chan"
cons, err := nsq.NewConsumer(topicName, channelName, cfg)
if err != nil {
    log.Fatalf(err.Error())
}

// the method below is an alternative to AddHandler to enable concurrent
processing
// the second argument is the number of goroutines to spawn for processing
cons.AddConcurrentHandlers(&MyMessageHandler{}, 20)
```

Integration patterns

The messaging primitives we just looked at can be augmented with various functionalities to enable complex architectural patterns. In Chapter 5, *Going Distributed*, we took a look at the event-driven architecture paradigm. In this this section, we will have a more detailed look at various patterns of integrating components with messaging.

While these patterns can be implemented, in principle, through durable messaging (Kafka, NSQ, and so on), we will use use Golang channel primitives to demonstrate integration patterns.

The request-reply pattern

In this pattern, Service-A (requestor) wants some work from from Service-B (responder), and there is output expected out of the request. How does Service-B respond, considering that Service-B might be handling requests for a lot of other services?

The solution is to have the requestor mention the response topic (in this case, the channel) to the responder. This decouples the responder from requestor. A request message might look like this:

```
type Request struct {
    someArg string
    replyTo chan<- Response
}

type Response struct {
    reply string
}
```

Notice the `replyTo` channel that the requester is sending along with the message.

The requestor and responder code looks like the following:

```go
func responder(c <-chan Request) {
    for request := range c {
        var resp Response
        resp.reply = "reply-to-" + request.someArg
        request.replyTo <- resp
    }
}

func requestor(c chan<- Request) {
    myChannel := make(chan Response)
    for i := 0; i < 5; i++ {
        c <- Request{fmt.Sprintf("message%d", i), myChannel}
        resp := <-myChannel
        fmt.Printf("request %d, response %s\n", i, resp.reply)
    }

    // cleanup after my work is done
    close(myChannel)
}

func main() {

    requestChannel := make(chan Request)
    go responder(requestChannel)
    go requestor(requestChannel)

    time.Sleep(time.Second * 10)

}
```

The correlation identifier pattern

In an Event-Driven-Architecture setup, messages might flow through multiple services. In such an event, it is important that each message has a unique identifier to enable correlation and debugging in the service's code.

Golang has a variety of libraries that provide GUID-generation:

- Use time to enable entropy and to achieve time-clustering
- Fill the rest of the ID with random data
- Encode GUID as a URL-safe string in a way that allows lexicographic sorting

A summary of the various options is shown in the following table:

Package	Sample ID	Note
github.com/segmentio/ksuid	0pPKHjWprnVxGH7dEsAoXX2YQvU	4 bytes of time (seconds) + 16 random bytes.
github.com/rs/xid	b50vl5e54p1000fo3gh0	4 bytes of time (seconds) + 3 bytes of machine IDs + 2 bytes of process IDs + 3 random bytes.
github.com/kjk/betterguid	-Kmdih_fs4ZZccpx2H11	8 bytes of time (milliseconds) + 9 random bytes.
github.com/sony/sonyflake	20f8707d6000108	It's based on Twitter's design for generating IDs for tweets—simple but the least random. 6 bytes of time (10 ms) + 1 byte sequence + 2 bytes of machine ID.

To enable debugging, it is imperative to log these correlation IDs along with whatever the log needs to convey.

The pipes and filters pattern

In many requirements, a single event triggers a workflow (or a sequence of processing steps) as part of the required response to that event. For example, on a ticket payment, we might have to validate the payment, confirm the booking, and email an invoice. Each of the individual actions are independent and sometimes form part of multiple workflows. We need a way to stitch together these processors to enable different workflows.

The pipes and filters architectural pattern aims to provide a solution by dividing a workflow into a sequence of smaller, independent Processors (called filters). Filters are connected by messaging channels, called pipes.

Each filter has a very simple interface—it gets input messages from one inbound pipe and is supposed to write the output to an output pipe. It encapsulates the processing of the message internally, and can take more data as part of the context during initialization. The output pipe of one filter is connected to the inbound pipe of another filter to compose the workflow.

An example of a workflow that computes the $y = x^2 + c$ values is given in the following code.

The emitter filter is the start of the chain, and generates numbers from 0 to a given value. These numbers then flow to an `xSquare` filter that squares the value and outputs it to another pipe. This then goes as input to the `addC` filter, which does the last part of the equation processing:

```
func emitter(till int) <-chan int {
    out := make(chan int)
    go func() {
        for i := 0; i < till; i++ {
            out <- i
        }
        close(out)
    }()
    return out
}

func xSquare(in <-chan int) <-chan int {
    out := make(chan int)
    go func() {
        for x := range in {
            out <- x * x
        }
        close(out) // close forward
    }()
    return out
}

func addC(in <-chan int, c int) <-chan int {
    out := make(chan int)
    go func() {
        for x := range in {
            out <- x + c
        }
        close(out) // close forward
    }()
    return out
}

func main() {
```

```
// y = x*x + c
out := addC(
     xSquare(emitter(3)),
     5)

for y := range out {
     fmt.Println(y)
}
```

```
}
```

Once this is coded, it is easy to extend this to say $y = x^4 + c$—see the following code:

```
// y = x*x*x*x + c

out1 := addC(
     xSquare(xSquare(emitter(3))),
     5)

for y := range out1 {
     fmt.Println(y)
}
```

This will print the following:

```
5
6
21
```

The content-based router pattern

Often, in the pipes and filter pattern, we come across use cases where a message's destination is not always fixed but actually depends on the context in the message. For example, we might have different destination topics for with different hotels and flights processing (viewed) in a travel websites. The content-based router pattern examines the message content and routes the message based on the data/metadata contained in the message.

The routing function can be a brittle point of the system architecture and can be a placeholder for miscellaneous logic and frequent changes. One way to overcome this is to use a rules-based engine to decide on message routes. Govaluate (`https://github.com/Knetic/govaluate`) is a good rules-based evaluation framework that can be used to this end:

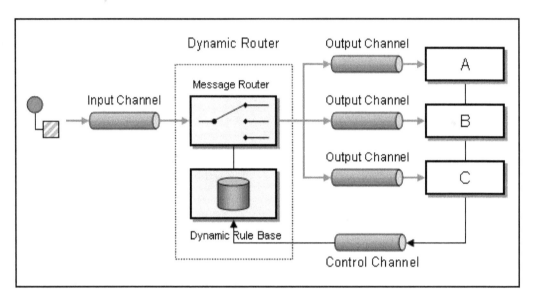

Source: http://camel.apache.org/dynamic-router.html

The fan-in pattern

There is a requirement to source messages from multiple sources and do some processing. It is not guaranteed which source will have a message ready at a given time. If we were to process all sources in a loop, the loop will block for a source that does not have a message. It is possible to check availability and add timeouts, but this causes extra complications in the code.

The ideal solution is to merge the messages into one `fanIn` channel, which can then be used for processing. The following code snippet demonstrates this pattern:

```
func main() {
    c := fanIn(emitter("Source1"), emitter("Source2"))

    for i := 0; i < 10; i++ {
        fmt.Println(<-c) // Display the output of the FanIn channel.
    }
```

```
}

// this combines the sources to a Fan-In channel
func fanIn(input1, input2 <-chan string) <-chan string {
   c := make(chan string) // The FanIn channel

   // to avoid blocking, listen to the input channels in separate
goroutines
   go func() {
         for {
               c <- <-input1 // Write the message to the FanIn channel,
Blocking Call.
         }
   }()

   go func() {
         for {
               c <- <-input2 // Write the message to the FanIn channel,
Blocking Call.
         }
   }()

   return c
}

// dummy function for a source
func emitter(name string) <-chan string {
   c := make(chan string)

   go func() {
         for i := 0; ; i++ {
               c <- fmt.Sprintf("[%s] says %d", name, i)
               time.Sleep(time.Duration(rand.Intn(100)) * time.Millisecond)
// Sleep for some time
         }
   }()

   return c
}
```

We could have also used the `select` keyword for doing the `fanIn` and, in fact, this is more **idiomatic Go**. The `fanIn` with `select` looks like this:

```
func fanInSelect(input1, input2 <-chan string) <-chan string {
   out := make(chan string)
   go func() {
         for {
               select {
```

```
                    case in := <-input1:
                            out <- in
                    case in := <-input2:
                            out <- in
                    }
            }
    }()
    return out
}
```

The `fanIn` pattern can be combined with the request-reply pattern to enable sequencing between the input of the `fanIn` channel. After sending a message, each source would block on its own Boolean channel, which is passed as part of the message to the `fanIn` channel. The Source is then effectively stalled until the `fanIn` processor unblocks it by signaling on the channel.

The fan-out pattern

Besides routing messages as a whole, a router can split messages and then give them to different components for processing. This is demonstrated by the following code snippet:

```
type Message struct {
    body string
    key  int
}

func main() {
    evenPipe, oddPipe := fanOut(emitter())
    sink("even", evenPipe)
    sink("odd", oddPipe)

    time.Sleep(10 * time.Second)

}

// this combines the sources to a Fan-In channel
func fanOut(input <-chan Message) (<-chan Message, <-chan Message) {
    even := make(chan Message) // The fan-out channels
    odd := make(chan Message)  // The fan-out channels

    // spawn the fan-out loop
    go func() {
            for {
                    msg := <-input
                    if msg.key%2 == 0 {
```

```
                        even <- msg
                } else {
                        odd <- msg
                }
        }
    }()

    return even, odd
}

// dummy function for a source
func emitter() <-chan Message {
    c := make(chan Message)

    go func() {
        for i := 0; ; i++ {
            c <- Message{fmt.Sprintf("Message[%d]", i), i}
            time.Sleep(time.Duration(rand.Intn(1000)) *
time.Millisecond) // Sleep for some time
        }
    }()

    return c
}

func sink(name string, in <-chan Message) {
    go func() {
        for {
            msg := <-in
            fmt.Printf("[%s] says %s\n", name, msg.body)
        }
    }()
}
```

The topology consists of an emitter that connects to a `fanOut` component, which multiplexes the output onto two output channels based on the key in the `Message` body (this snippet is also an example of the Content-Based Router pattern).

The background worker pattern

Sometimes a part of message processing doesn't need to produce any output that is immediately needed. For example, when a ticket is booked and the payment is made, it's OK to get **Ticket booked successfully!** to the user, while sending them a detailed itinerary through email; we don't need to block the client on the *book ticket* API until the email is sent.

The background worker pattern solves such situations by enabling a component to delegate work to other components that work in the background.

The `worker.go` and `worker_test.go` file (`https://github.com/cookingkode/worker`) is an example of a generic framework where woker goroutines accept work of the following type:

```
type Work struct {
    Key  string
    Args interface{}
}
```

The framework uses the key to distribute the `Work` messages to a set of background workers.

A background worker can be spawned off from a handler function, which takes the `work` object as a parameter:

```
func sampleHandler(work *Work) {
    fmt.Printf("Dummy Handler \t")
    fmt.Printf("Work :: %v : %v\n", work.Key, work.Args)
}
```

A driver program can then spawn workers and assign work:

```
func Driver () {
            // Create 4 workers of
    w := NewWorker(4, sampleHandler)
    w.StartWork()

            // give some work to the workers
    dumbWork := &Work{Key: "hi", Args: "there",}

    w.Push(dumbWork)
    w.Push(dumbWork)

    time.Sleep(6000 * time.Millisecond)
    // By this time sampleHandler should have printed twice

            // Stop
    w.StopWork()
}
```

Summary

In this chapter, we learned about some messaging theory and Apache Kafka and NSQ. Messaging plays a key role in building microservices. We also describeed various messaging patterns like request-reply, fanout, pipes-and-filters with working code.

In the next chapter, we will learn about building APIs.

7
Building APIs

Services rarely operate in isolation. They interact with one another over the network to enable macro behavior. Using a specific (often standardized) protocol, data is exchanged at specific endpoints. There are two forms to this communication:

- Using an **Application Programming Interface** (**API**)—a `Request/Response` model over a network protocol such as **Hypertext Transfer Protocol** (**HTTP**)
- Using messaging—where services exchange messages to exchange data

Messaging is covered in `Chapter 6`, *Messaging*. This chapter focuses on the first model of communication.

Endpoints

In the API model, whenever a service needs something, it makes a network call to a known endpoint with a request and gets a response back. The service making the call is frequently called the client, and the other is the server. It should be noted that a service can be (and is frequently) both a client and a server in the context of different interactions.

Networking basics

To enable communication over a network, a set of rules for data exchanges is imperative. Such rules are typically standardized through protocols and grouped into various layers—each layer of the communication stack dealing with a specific charter. The following diagram depicts the traditional networking layers and related protocols:

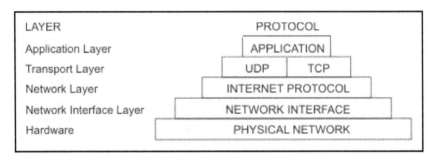

Most API network communication occurs over **Transmission Control Protocol** (**TCP**). Here, before the actual data exchange, the client needs to make a connection to the server. To do this, the client needs to know the following:

1. The IP address of the machine hosting the service.
2. The network port on which the service is listening to requests.
3. After the network connection is set up, the client will need some application layer specifics to perform the communication, including the following:
     - An application protocol specific endpoint (for example, a URL in the case of HTTP)
     - The data contract—what date is needed, the serialization format, and so on

Service discovery

The first step in performing communication is figuring out the endpoints. This process is called service discovery. This is complicated by the following facts:

- The endpoint addresses (for example, IP addresses) are generally dynamic and change frequently.
- Services are generally deployed in a cluster of redundant instances, so there is more than one instance (endpoint) that can service a request.
- The number of instances changes with time—autoscaling according to the load.

There are essentially two ways of doing the service discovery, which are as follows:

- Server-side service discovery
- Client-side service discovery

Server-side service discovery

As already described, services are deployed in clusters, and clients generally do not (and should not) care about which specific instance of the service is honoring the request. In a server-side service discovery architecture, such a cluster is fronted by a **Load Balancer** (**LB**), which takes a request and routes it to an appropriate service instance, as shown in the following diagram:

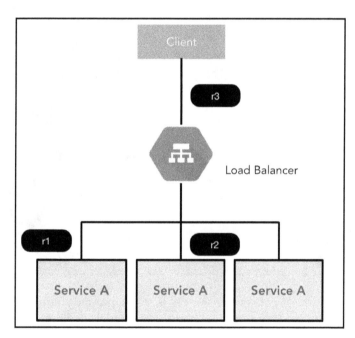

Generally the LB has a set of **Virtual IP Addresses** (**VIPs**), one for each service. This is a collective network (IP layer) endpoint for the service. There is a static list of **backend** instances against this VIP, and the LB multiplexes the requests from clients onto the set of the backend instances. Even though this list is static, there are various mechanisms to enable automatic reconfiguration, for example, when instances come up and go.

A popular open source LB is NGINX (`https://www.nginx.com/`). It is designed for high performance and extensibility. It consists of a limited set of worker processes (usually one per CPU core) that route requests using non-blocking event-driven I/O (using the non-blocking provisions of the native kernel such as `epoll` and `kqueue`). The following diagram depicts the architecture of a worker process, and more information can be found at `https://www.nginx.com/blog/inside-nginx-how-we-designed-for-performance-scale/`)

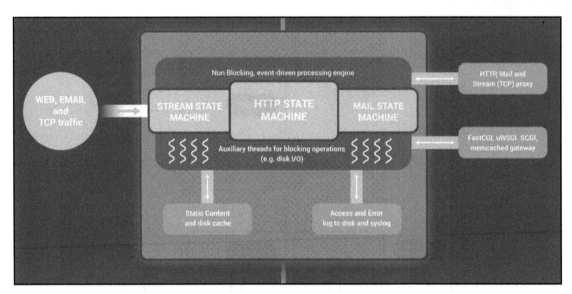

The NGINX configuration of backend instances is static, but a dynamic configuration can be built in using ancillary components, such as the Consul Template. Essentially, these solutions watch for events about new or dead instances, rewrite the NGINX configuration file, and gracefully restart the NGINX processes.

For connecting to a service, clients usually start with the advertised URL, which is then converted by a **Domain Name Service** (**DNS**) to the VIP of the service. Clients then use this VIP and the advertised service port to initiate the connection.

The LB also frequently hosts a health-check functionality, to figure out the right set of backend instances. Instances that don't periodically check-in are declared unhealthy and removed from the VIP's backend instance set.

 In some cases it might be necessary for a client to continue interactions with a specific service instance during the course of a user session. One of the reasons for doing this might be performance (the state needed for responding to requests might be cached at that instance). This feature is supported by most LBs using **sticky sessions**. Here, the clients pass in an identifier (frequently a cookie), which the LB uses for routing, instead of the default random routing method.

There are a few key advantages of server-side service discovery, including the following:

- Clients don't need to know about the service instances
- High availability and fault tolerance is easily enabled

There are few disadvantages:

- The LB can be a **Single Point of Failure** (**SPOF**) and needs engineering for resiliency
- The clients cannot choose a specific service instance, if for some reason they feel this will be better

Client-side service discovery

In client-side discovery, the client is responsible for determining the endpoints of available service instances and then routes requests to them. The client queries a service registry, which is a database of available service instances, and then routes requests to an instance that it feels is the best option. This could be as simple as a round-robin load balancing algorithm or a more complex one, which takes things like server instance network round-trip-time and so on. Every server instance connects to the service registry on startup. It also periodically updates its health status with the registry. The architecture is described in the following diagram:

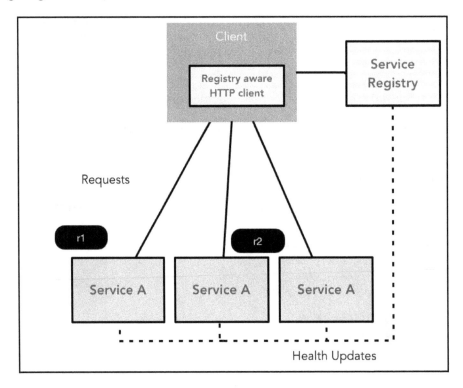

As you can see, we need a special registry-aware HTTP client, which can manage connections to multiple server instances and route requests.

Netflix Eureka is a service registry in the Netflix OSS stack, and Netflix Ribbon is an IPC client, written in Java, that works with Eureka to load balance requests across service instances. Non-Java apps can interact with Eureka using its REST API. In Golang, `https://github.com/hudl/fargo` is a client that does this. It can register an instance with Eureka, enable check instance health (using heartbeats), and also query Eureka for the set of instances for an application. The load balancing algorithm currently implemented is random. To connect to Eureka and get a list of apps and instances, use the following:

```
c = fargo.NewConn("http://127.0.0.1:8080/eureka/v2")
c.GetApps() // returns a map[String]fargo.Application
```

A service instance can register its help with Eureka using the following:

```
c.UpdateApp(&app)
```

Consul (`https://www.consul.io/`) is another open source service discovery platform. It organizes services in a service catalog and provides a DNS and HTTP API interface on top of it. It monitors registered service instances and manages a healthy set for each service. The `Catalog.Services` method (`https://godoc.org/github.com/hashicorp/consul/api#Catalog.Services`) can be used to query the instances for a service as described here: `https://www.consul.io/api/catalog.html`. The `QueryOption` parameter can be used to tweak the nodes the client is interested in, for example using `QueryOptions{Near: "_agent"}` will result in Consul returning the closest node to the client first (closed in terms of least network latency).

Data serialization

This section provides a quick primer on the three main data serialization options: XML, JSON, and Google **Protocol Buffers** (**Protobuf**). It also provides benchmarking on serialization/deserialization on these and other (less used) formats.

XML

Extensible Markup Language (**XML**) is a standard for defining a serializable format, which allows a producer to encode data in a text format, without having to define explicit contracts with all consumers. It is derived from **Standard Generalized Markup Language** (**SGML**), and is language-independent.

The following XML snippet describes a hotel object:

```
<?xml version="1.0" encoding="UTF-8"?>
<root>
   <city>New York</city>
   <name>Taj</name>
   <no_rooms>3</no_rooms>
</root>
```

An XML document can be hierarchical. The following snippet describes a hotel chain:

```
<?xml version="1.0" encoding="UTF-8"?>
<root>
   <chain>
      <element>
         <city>New York</city>
         <name>Taj</name>
         <no_rooms>3</no_rooms>
      </element>
      <element>
         <city>New Jersey</city>
         <name>Leela</name>
         <no_rooms>5</no_rooms>
      </element>
   </chain>
</root>
```

XML documents have a schema and there is a standard called **XML Schema Definition (XSD)** to describe it. This allows easy communication of contracts as well as validation of documents against a schema.

JSON

JavaScript Object Notation (JSON) is a lightweight data format that is based on how JavaScript represents objects. It is officially defined in RFC 4627.

An object is the simplest entity in JSON, and the following snippet is an example:

```
{
   "name": "Taj",
   "city": "New York",
         "no_rooms": 3
}
```

It has three fields with specific values. The field names are always strings, while the values can be of different types such as integer, float, string, and so on.

JSON also has the concept of arrays. So a hotel chain can be described as follows:

```
{ "chain": [{
        "name": "Taj",
        "city": "New York",
              "no_rooms": 3
        },
        {
        "name": "Leela",
        "city": "New Jersey",
              "no_rooms": 5
        }
    ]
}
```

Like XML, JSON is self-describing and hierarchical, and can be parsed into an object at runtime. There is a standard for schema definition called JSON Schema, but it is not as widely used as XSDs.

Protobuf

Protobuf (or Protocol Buffers) is a language-neutral serialization format invented at Google. Each protocol buffer message is a small logical record of information, containing a series of name-value pairs. Unlike XML or JSON, here you first define the schema in a .proto file. The following is a .proto file describing a hotel object:

```
message Hotel {
        required string name = 1;
        required string city = 2;
        optional int  no_rooms = 3;
}
```

Each message type is a list of numbered fields, and each field has a type and a name. After defining the .proto file, you run the protocol buffer compiler to generate code for the object (in the language of your choice), with get/set functions for the fields, as well as object serialization/deserialization functions.

Performance

Different serialization formats have different characteristics in terms of serialization/deserialization of objects. This can play an impactful role in overall performance of your system, especially in microservice architecture, where a single user request is handled by multiple services communicating to each over over APIs or messaging using serialized objects.

The `https://github.com/alecthomas/go_serialization_benchmarks` page is a good store for related benchmarks on various serialization formats. Generally, formats that generate code from schema files (such as Protobufs) perform better than generic schema such as JSON, which need to use reflection to figure out object layout (fields and type). These types of serialization formats are, however, slightly more difficult to debug. For example, you can't just do a simple curl request to get the data; you would need a decoder with the deserialization to make sense of the encoded data.

Representational State Transfer (REST)

We have seen how service discovery can be used to get the set of instances for a service, and how data can be serialized for transport between the client and the server. Let's now look at one of the most popular options of interaction between the client and any instance.

Concepts

REST, or **Representational State Transfer**, is an architectural style for API interactions over HTTP. It is an application-level standard for the communication between the client and the server and is characterized by statelessness and clear client-server separation of concerns.

The key abstraction in this style is that of resource, which can be anything: a document, a ticket, a user, a collection of other resources, and so on. In a RESTful service, the interface consists of a hierarchical set of resources and methods defined for each of them to enable state transfer. Each resource has an unique ID, which identifies it. The transfer can be from the server to the client (get information) or from the client to the server (set information). The GET HTTP verb is analogous to what happens when a person clicks a link on a website. The entire content at the URL, which describes that object, is transferred from the server to the client and rendered in the browser.

Nearly all RESTful APIs use HTTP as a transport layer. Each resource gets a **Uniform Resource Identifier** (**URI**). The HTTP verbs such as GET, POST, PUT, DELETE, and PATCH serve as methods on the resource.

For example, the following is a simplified API example for hotels:

URI	Verb	Meaning
/hotels	GET	Get a list of all hotels on the website. At a minimum, this would typically be a JSON array with a tuple for each hotel, including the URI of the hotel, a unique ID, and probably the display name.
/hotels	POST	Creates a new hotel. Will take all the attributes needed to create a new hotel.
/hotels/<id>	GET	Get information (all attributes) about a specific hotel, whose identifier is <id>.
/hotels/<id>	DELETE	Delete the hotel with the specified ID.
/hotels<id>	PUT	Updates the attributes of a hotel. Takes the same parameters as create (POST).

Constraints

The term REST was introduced and defined in 2000 by Roy Fielding in his doctoral dissertation. The major focus on that paper was a set of constraints on an API aspiring to be RESTful. The main constraints are described in the following sections.

Client-server model

This constraint indicates the separation of concerns between the client (the View/Display aspects) and the business logic part. By separating these two, the user interface becomes portable/replaceable and the backend gets simplified.

Stateless

This constraint mandates that each request from client to server must contain all of the information necessary to process it. The server cannot store context across requests. This also implies that the session state (required for stateful processing of user interactions) is kept entirely on the client side and transported to the server on each request.

Statelessness improves visibility, reliability, and scalability of the system. Visibility is improved because a monitoring system just has to look at a single request in isolation to understand the request. As we see in `Chapter 9`, *Anti-Fragile Systems*, reliability is improved because a single server going down does not lose information; the request can be retried. Scalability is improved because the server instances can be increased or decreased as per the load and that the client requests can be served by any of the instance.

Like most architectural choices, there is a trade-off here. Statelessness makes the communication between client and server carry repetitive information and is therefore possibly more chatty. This design choice also means that user behavior is controlled at the client side, thus multiple clients will have to code this consistently.

Cacheability

In order to overcome the network efficiency limitation described previously, the cache construct was added. Essentially, the server can label each response as either cacheable or non-cacheable. If a response is cacheable, then the client can cache and reuse the response for future requests. To avoid stale data, generally a **Time-To-Live** (**TTL**) is added to cached data, so that it can be invalidated after the specified time.

Uniform interface

The REST paradigm promotes a uniform interface for all interactions between the client and the server. As described earlier, the key abstraction is the resource. A resource is identified by a **unique hierarchical name**, and can have multiple representations.

The key advantage of such representation is that it provides representation generality for a wide variety of information without having to specify the implementation/type that might not add value (and complicate) the resource definition. This also allows late binding of the reference to a resource representation through content negotiation, thus one client can request a JSON representation of a resource, whereas another can request an XML version.

Richardson Maturity Model

The Richardson Maturity Model is a measure of how RESTful an API definition is. It defines four levels (0-3), where level 3 designates the most RESTful API.

Level 0 – swamp of POX

At level 0, the API uses the implementing protocol (normally HTTP, but it doesn't have to be) like a transport protocol. There is no effort to utilize the protocol to indicate state; it is just used to pass requests and responses back and forth. The system typically has one entry point (URI) and one method (normally POST in the case of HTTP). For the hotels API, this means that the URL would be /hotels and all APIs would be POST to that, with the payload carrying more information about the request type and related data. Examples include SOAP and XML-RPC

Level 1 – resources

Here, the API distinguishes between multiple resources using different URLs. However, there is still typically only one method (POST) of interaction. This is better than the previous level because now there is a hierarchical definition of resources. Instead of going through /hotels, now the API assigns IDs to each hotel and uses that to see which hotel the request is for, so the API will have URLs of the /hotels/<id> form.

Level 2 – HTTP verbs

This level indicates that the API uses protocol properties (namely, HTTP verbs) to define the nature of the API. Thus GET is used for a read, POST is used to create a new resource, PUT to update a resource, and DELETE to of course delete the resource. The API also uses standard responses code such as 200 (OK) and 202 (ACCEPTED) to describe the result of the request.

Generally, most REST API implementations are at this level.

Level 3 – hypermedia controls

Level 3, the highest level, uses **Hypertext As The Engine Of Application State (HATEOAS)** to allow clients to deal with discovering the resources and the identifiers. For example, let's say we get details about a hotel (xyz) using the following API request:

```
GET /hotels/xyz
```

The preceding request will return a response of the following type:

```
{
    "city": "Delhi",
    "display_name": "Hotel Xyz",
    "star_rating": 4,
    "links": [
        {
            "href": "xyz/book",
            "rel": "book",
            "type": "POST"
        },
        {
            "href": "xyz/rooms",
            "rel": "rooms",
            "type": "GET"
        }
    ]
}
```

The response, besides giving details about the hotel (as per level 2), also gives information to the client about which operations can be done against the resource and how they should be done. For example, GET on /hotels/xyz/rooms will get information about available rooms in the hotels. Thus the client does not need to hardcode every resource representation, but rather can infer new resources and operations through the resource hierarchy. This is a form of code-on-demand.

The rel attributes define the relation-type for the HATEOAS links. Some are predefined (and one should not change their behavior), while some can be application-defined. The following are related links:

- **IANA—link relation**: http://www.iana.org/assignments/link-relations/link-relations.xml
- **HTML5 specification—links**: http://www.w3.org/TR/html5/links.html
- **RFC 5988—web linking:** http://tools.ietf.org/html/rfc5988

Building a REST service using Gin

In this section, we will use the design patterns already described to build a REST API in Golang. It's relatively straightforward to set up a web server using the Golang `net/http` package in the standard library. A `hello world` program is described as follows:

```
package main

import (
    "fmt"
    "log"
    "net/http"
)

func main() {
    // setup router
    http.HandleFunc("/", func(w http.ResponseWriter, r *http.Request) {
        log.Println("path", r.URL.Path)
        fmt.Fprintf(w, "pong! on %sn", r.URL.Path)
    })

    // listen and serve
    err:= http.ListenAndServe(":9090", nil)
    if err != nil {
        log.Fatal("ListenAndServe: ", err)
    }
}
```

It sets up a handler at a specific URL path, which takes in the request pointer and a response writer.

The `ListenAndServe()` method does the following:

- Instantiates an Http server
- Calls `net.Listen("tcp", addr)` to listen on TCP for the defined port (here 9090)
- Starts a loop and accept requests in the loop body
- Starts a Goroutine for every request
- Reads the request data
- Searches for the handler for that URL, and executes the code there

The crux of any Go web application is the ability to serve each request as a separate Goroutine, as shown in the following diagram:

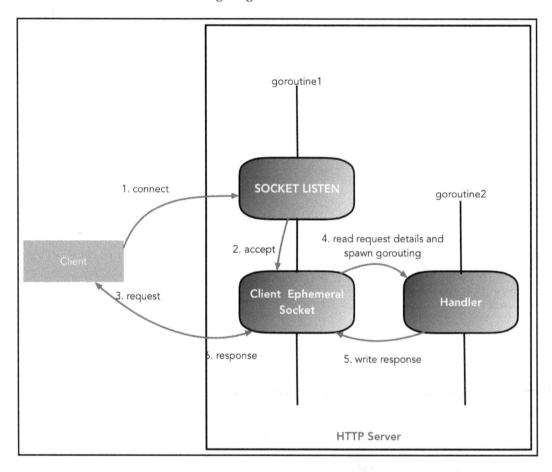

This ability increases the scalability and resource-efficiency of the server immensely.

Gin introduction

The Go `stdlib` library is powerful, but for real-world products, a lot of additional requirements in terms of middleware, routing, persistence, and so on crop up. It is advisable to use a suitable web framework as *guiding rails* for your API project. One popular framework is Gin. Some of its features are the following:

- Radix tree-based Go (Golang) routing
- Small memory footprint and predictable performance due to controlled engineering (in terms of memory allocations)
- Middleware framework where various middleware can be chained before the final handler
- Panic recovery during request handling
- Route grouping, with various middleware on different URL route hierarchies
- JSON validation
- Error management

Sample application

We will use the hotels API example described earlier and build a fully working version. To reiterate, the specific APIs would be as follows:

URI	Verb	Meaning
/hotels	GET	Get a list of all hotels on the website. At a minimum, this would typically be a JSON array with a tuple for each hotel, including the URI of the hotel, a unique ID, and probably the display name.
/hotels	POST	Creates a new hotel. Will take all the attributes needed to create a new hotel.
/hotels/<id>	GET	Get information (all attributes) about a specific hotel, whose identifier is <id>.
/hotels/<id>	DELETE	Delete the hotel with the specified ID.
/hotels<id>	PUT	Updates the attributes of a hotel. Takes the same parameters as create.

Generally, such a **Create Read Update Delete (CRUD)** app would use a database for persistence. But to keep things straightforward, we will use an in-memory Golang map. This will, of course, not work with more than one instance, but serves the purpose of describing the RESTful API.

The following code uses the `map` repository in a non-thread-safe manner. Maps should be protected with a Mutex for concurrent access in real-life code.

Router

The heart of the program is an API router, which multiplexes different URLs (and verbs) to specific handlers. Please see the next section (*Higher level patterns*) for more description of the router. This part looks like the following:

```go
package main

import (
    "fmt"
    "github.com/gin-gonic/gin"
    "net/http"
)

func main() {
    router:= gin.Default()
    v1:= router.Group("/v1/hotels")
    {
            v1.POST("/", createHotel)
            v1.GET("/", getAllHotels)
            v1.GET("/:id", getHotel)
            v1.PUT("/:id", updateHotel)
            v1.DELETE("/:id", deleteHotel)
    }
    router.Run()
}
```

As you can see, there is a **router group** called `v1`. This defines a specific API version and encompasses five routes. Versioning your API is always a good idea, as your contract will churn and not all your clients will move to the latest version at the same time.

The handlers use the HTTP verb-based method on the `RouterGroup` object returned by the `router.Group()` method and map a specific URL to a handler. Note that the URLs here are relative to the URL mentioned at the group level.

The `/:id` path indicates that `id` should be the path parameter; that is, any string will match at this place in the URL, and the specific string that matches will be available in the assigned handler. We shall see how to use this in the *Read* subsection.

Create

Before looking at what `createHotel` does, lets define a `Hotel` object. Again, using the example described previously, along with the HATEOAS links, our hotel type looks as follows:

```
type Hotel struct {
    Id          string `json:"id" binding:"required"`
    DisplayName string `json:"display_name" `
    StarRating  int    `json:"star_rating" `
    NoRooms     int    `json:"no_rooms" `
    Links       []Link `json:"links"`
}

// HATEOAS links
type Link struct {
    Href string `json:"href"`
    Rel  string `json:"rel"`
    Type string `json:"type"`
}
```

`Hotel` `struct` defines basic metadata about the hotel. `Links` `struct` defines the `HATEOAS` links.

We also define an in-memory repository to contain the hotels. As discussed earlier, this should really be a DB interface, but the map abstracts out the DB-related complexity to allow us to focus on the API aspects:

```
var (
    repository map[string]*Hotel
)

func init() {
    repository = make(map[string]*Hotel)
}
```

Now, on to `createHotels`:

```
func createHotel(c *gin.Context) {
    var hotel Hotel
    if err:= c.ShouldBindJSON(&hotel); err == nil {
        // add HATEOS links
        hotel.generateHateosLinks(c.Request.URL.String())
        // add hotel to repository
        repository[hotel.Id] = &hotel

        //return OK
```

```
            c.JSON(http.StatusAccepted, gin.H{"status": "created"})
    } else {
            // some params not correct
            c.JSON(http.StatusBadRequest, gin.H{"error": err.Error()})
    }
}
```

This uses the `ShouldBindJSON` method of the `Gin` request `Context` object to validate and parse/deserialize the request body to get a `Hotel` object. If there is an error, we return `http.StatusBadRequest`, which is `HTTP code 400`. This indicates that there was something wrong in the request (details in RFC 7231, 6.5.1). If we are able to get the `Hotel` object, then we just store it in the `map` repository and return `http.StatusAccepted` (HTTP code 202).

Not all the attributes of the `Hotel` object are required for creating the object, and specifically the HATEOAS links won't be present (the client won't know how they are formulated). The `generateHateosLinks()` method generates these links (for now just a *booking* link), as demonstrated by the following code:

```
func (h *Hotel) generateHateosLinks(url string) {
    // Book url
    postLink:= Link{
            Href: url + "book",
            Rel:  "book",
            Type: "POST",
    }

    h.Links = append(h.Links, postLink)
}
```

This takes the URL and appends `book` to allow HATEOS links of the following type:

```
"links": [
        {
            "href": "xyz/book",
            "rel": "book",
            "type": "POST"
        }]
```

To create a hotel, we can use a CURL request like so:

```
curl -d '{"id":"xyz", "display_name":"HotelXyz", "star_rating":4,
"no_rooms": 150}' -H "Content-Type: application/json" -X POST
127.0.0.1:8080/v1/hotels
```

Read

After creating, of course, the next step would be to retrieve the created hotels. There are two APIs here:

- GET /v1/hotels: Returns all the hotels that we have
- GET /v1/hotels/<id>: Returns data about a specific hotel

The getHotel() method retrieves information about a specific hotel, whose ID is given in the path parameter defined. The code is pretty straightforward:

```
func getHotel(c *gin.Context) {
    // get ID from path param
    hotelId:= c.Param("id")

    // get hotel object from repository
    hotel, found:= repository[hotelId]
    fmt.Println(hotel, found, hotelId)
    if !found {
        c.JSON(http.StatusNotFound, gin.H{"status": "hotel with id not
found"})
    } else {
        c.JSON(http.StatusOK, gin.H{"result": hotel})
    }

}
```

The Param() method of the Gin request Context object gives the path parameter named as :id. So for example, if the URL is /v1/hotels/abc, then the value of hotelId will be abc, since the getHotel() handler is defined for the /v1/hotels/:id path, where ID is the path parameter.

The rest of the code is pretty self-explanatory. If a hotel with the ID is not found then HTTP status code 404 (http.StatusNotFound) is returned. Otherwise, the Hotel object is serialized to JSON and sent to the client.

The API call looks like this:

```
curl 127.0.0.1:8080/v1/hotels/xyz
```

And the response is as follows:

```
{
    "result":{
        "xyz":{
            "id":"xyz",
            "display_name":"HotelXyz",
            "star_rating":4,
            "no_rooms":150,
            "links":[
                {
                    "href":"/v1/hotels/book",
                    "rel":"book",
                    "type":"POST"
                }
            ]
        }
    }
}
```

 Note the HATEOAS links that had been populated in the create handler.

Now, let's look at the `getAllHotels()` method. It just dumps the repository into a JSON map. The code for it is as follows:

```
func getAllHotels(c *gin.Context) {
    c.JSON(http.StatusOK, gin.H{"result": repository})
}
```

One can call this API as follows:

```
curl 127.0.0.1:8080/v1/hotels
```

This will return a JSON map of all hotels:

```
{
    "result":{
        "xyz":{
            "id":"xyz",
            "display_name":"HotelXyz",
            "star_rating":4,
            "no_rooms":150,
            "links":[
                {
                    "href":"/v1/hotels/book",
```

```
                    "rel":"book",
                    "type":"POST"
                }
            ]
        }
    }
}
```

Update

We are using the standard of having the PUT method perform an update for an object (well, some people may contest this). The updateHotel() handler is defined for the exact same path as GET for read, but for the PUT method. The code for the handler is as follows:

```
func updateHotel(c *gin.Context) {
    // get hotel object from repository
    hotelId:= c.Param("id")
    hotel, found:= repository[hotelId]
    if !found {
        c.JSON(http.StatusNotFound, gin.H{"status": "hotel with id not
found"})
    } else {
        //update
        if err:= c.ShouldBindJSON(&hotel); err == nil {
            repository[hotel.Id] = hotel

            //return OK
            c.JSON(http.StatusOK, gin.H{"status": "ok"})
        } else {
            // some params not correct
            c.JSON(http.StatusBadRequest, gin.H{"error": err.Error()})
        }
    }

}
```

If a hotel with the id is not found in the repository, the code bails out and returns HTTP status code 404 (http.StatusNotFound). Otherwise, we take the updates and store the modified object in the repository.

For example, we can make the following API call to update the star rating of the hotel we have created:

```
curl -d '{"id":"xyz",  "star_rating":5}' -H "Content-Type:
application/json"  -X PUT 127.0.0.1:8080/v1/hotels/xyz
```

Delete

The `delete` handler is also defined for the same paths as `read` and `update`. The code is pretty straightforward:

```
func deleteHotel(c *gin.Context) {
    hotelId:= c.Param("id")
    _, found:= repository[hotelId]
    if !found {
        c.JSON(http.StatusNotFound, gin.H{"status": "hotel with id not
found"})
    } else {
        delete(repository, hotelId)
        //return OK
        c.JSON(http.StatusOK, gin.H{"status": "ok"})
    }
}
```

If a hotel with the id is not found, then we return 404 (`http.StatusNotFound`), or else we delete it from the map and return `HTTP status code 200` (`http.StatusOK`).

GraphQL

The REST API paradigm is very elegant, and it is easy to model most real-world use cases with little difficulty. However, for the modern fast-paced web development needs, the rigid server-defined endpoints and schema can be a drag on developer productivity. Also, as discussed previously, the standard is not really network-efficient, especially if the client needs just a subset of the resource attributes. For example, let's say we are developing a mobile app, that has a search results page. Here, we don't want to get all the attributes of the hotels, since we may not have the screen real estate (or usability) to show all the data. To engineer this with a REST API, one needs to have a set URL and schema that gives all the hotels. However, if the app is deployed on a "tab", we may want to show slightly more information than on an app form factor. We can accomplish this by having another resource or having some query parameter to indicate form factor, but both are not necessarily clean. There still would be coupling of client needs and server code.

Schema

To get around the limitations described, Facebook developed a new way of doing APIs called GraphQL. It is an API whose style is more compatible with database query constructs, with schemas for different types and a runtime for executing queries and mutations.

GraphQL uses the **Schema Definition Language** (**SDL**) to define the schema of various types in the API, as follows:

```
type Hotel {
  id: String!
  displayName: String!
  city: String !
  noRooms: Int
  starRating: Int
}
```

This is the schema for a hotel. It has four fields: id, displayName, noRooms, and starRating, each with a description of its primitive type. The ! symbol indicates that the field is mandatory.

It is also possible to describe relationships between types. So we can have HotelChain, which has a set of hotels:

```
type HotelChain {
  name: String!
  hotels: [Hotel!]!
 }
```

Here the square bracket indicate an array.

Note that github.com/graphql-go/graphql provides support for graphql in Golang. The following code snippet shows how to define a Golang struct and an equivalent type in graphql:

```
type Hotel struct {
    Id          string `json:"id"`
    DisplayName string `json:"displayName"`
    City        string `json:"city"`
    NoRooms     int    `json:"noRooms"`
    StarRating  int    `json:"starRating"`
}

// define custom GraphQL ObjectType `hotelType` for our Golang struct
`Hotel`
```

```
// Note that
// - the fields  map with the json tags for the fields in our struct
// - the field types match the field type in our struct
var hotelType = graphql.NewObject(graphql.ObjectConfig{
    Name: "Hotel",
    Fields: graphql.Fields{
        "id": &graphql.Field{
            Type: graphql.String,
        },
        "displayName": &graphql.Field{
            Type: graphql.String,
        },
        "city": &graphql.Field{
            Type: graphql.String,
        },
        "noRooms": &graphql.Field{
            Type: graphql.Int,
        },
        "starRating": &graphql.Field{
            Type: graphql.Int,
        },
    },
})
```

Once we have the types, we can then define a schema, with root query and mutation structures:

```
// define schema, with our rootQuery and rootMutation
var schema, schemaErr = graphql.NewSchema(graphql.SchemaConfig{
    Query:    rootQuery,
    Mutation: rootMutation,
})
```

We shall see more details on the `rootQuery` and `rootMutation` structures later. This now defines the complete schema needed.

Endpoints

When working with REST APIs, each resource has a specific endpoint. This endpoint has multiple methods (verbs) which give/take data in a specific manner to enable behavior. However, the approach in GraphQL is the exact opposite. There is typically only a single endpoint. The structure of the data is not fixed; instead, the protocol is totally driven by the client. For example, in retrieving data, the client specifies exactly what it needs.

In Golang, we generally hook up the `graphql` endpoint as an HTTP handler, as follows:

```
http.HandleFunc("/graphql", func(w http.ResponseWriter, r *http.Request) {
        fmt.Println("[in handler]", r.URL.Query())
        result:= executeQuery(r.URL.Query()["query"][0], schema)
        json.NewEncoder(w).Encode(result)
    })

    fmt.Println("Graphql server is running on port 8080")
    http.ListenAndServe(":8080", nil)
```

Here `executeQuery()` is a helper function, which uses the `graphql-go.Do()` function to handle the `graphql` queries, using our preceding schema definition:

```
func executeQuery(query string, schema graphql.Schema) *graphql.Result {
    result:= graphql.Do(graphql.Params{
        Schema:        schema,
        RequestString: query,
    })
    if len(result.Errors) > 0 {
        fmt.Printf("wrong result, unexpected errors: %v", result.Errors)
    }
    return result
}
```

Queries

Lets, look at how retrieving data works in GraphQL. The following snippet is a sample query for all hotels in our systems, and moreover just the IDs of the hotels. This will be sent from the client to the server:

```
{
  allHotels {
    id
  }
}
```

The `allHotels` field in this query is called the **root field** of the query. Everything under the root field is the **payload** of the query.

The server will respond with a JSON detailing all the hotels, ids in the database, like so:

```
{
  "allHotels": [
    { "id": "xyz" },
    { "id": "abc" },
    { "id": "pqr" }
  ]
}
```

If the client needs the display name (or any other field), it has to ask for it explicitly in the query, like so:

```
{
  allHotels {
    Id
    displayName
  }
}
```

This exact specification of fields is possible even for nested fields. Thus, to get the name of the hotel chain and the display name of each hotel in the chain, the following query will work:

```
{
  allHotelsinChain {
    name
    hotels {
        displayName
    }
  }
}
```

Queries are explicitly specified by the `root` field name, and also can take arguments as follows:

```
{
  allHotels (city: Delhi) {
    id
    displayName
  }
}
```

The preceding is a query that takes the city name as an argument, and returns all the hotels in a specific city, and the ID and the display name for each hotel.

In `graphql-go`, the `rootQuery` structure that we defined previously handles all the queries. We create it using the `graphql.NewObject()` function. This creates a `graphql-go` terminology object that has fields, a name, and a resolver function, which describes what to do when such an object is invoked:

```
var rootQuery = graphql.NewObject(graphql.ObjectConfig{
    Name: "RootQuery",
    Fields: graphql.Fields{

        "hotel": &graphql.Field{
            Type:        hotelType,
            Description: "Get a hotel with this id",
            Args: graphql.FieldConfigArgument{
                "id": &graphql.ArgumentConfig{
                    Type: graphql.String,
                },
            },
            Resolve: func(params graphql.ResolveParams)
            (interface{}, error) {
                id, _:= params.Args["id"].(string)
                return hotels[id], nil
            },
        },
    },
})
```

Here we describe a query that takes in the hotel ID and gives the hotel object from an in-memory map called hotels. In real life, of course, one would use a database to store and retrieve entities, but the map serves the purpose of simplifying things and helping us to focus on the API semantics. Like the example in the REST API section, map is just a global variable:

```
// repository
var hotels map[string]Hotel

func init() {
    hotels = make(map[string]Hotel)
}
```

The following CURL request demonstrates how to query a hotel with a specific ID:

```
curl -g
'http://localhost:8080/graphql?query={hotel(id:"XVlBzgba"){displayName,city
,noRooms,starRating}}'
```

 See the following mutation example for actually creating hotel objects.

Mutations

Besides retrieving data, APIs also need to support changes or mutations to the data. There generally are three kinds of mutations:

- Creation of new data
- Update for existing data
- Deletion of data

Mutations follow the general structure of queries:

```
mutation {
  createHotel(name: "Taj", noRooms: 30) {
    id
  }
}
```

Here the mutation has a `createHotel` root field, and it identifies the mutation uniquely. We are giving it the `name` and `noRooms` parameters, with the `Taj` and `30` values respectively. Like a query, the payload here describes what we want in terms of the properties of the newly created object; here we are asking for the ID of the new person.

Continuing with our hotel example in `graphql-go`, the mutation root object defines all the various mutations (update, create, delete, and so on). For example, a simple create mutation is defined as follows:

```
// root mutation
var rootMutation = graphql.NewObject(graphql.ObjectConfig{
    Name: "RootMutation",
    Fields: graphql.Fields{
        "createHotel": &graphql.Field{
            Type:        hotelType,
            // the return type for this field
            Description: "Create new hotel",
```

```
Args: graphql.FieldConfigArgument{
        "displayName": &graphql.ArgumentConfig{
                Type: graphql.NewNonNull(graphql.String),
        },
        "city": &graphql.ArgumentConfig{
                Type: graphql.NewNonNull(graphql.String),
        },
        "noRooms": &graphql.ArgumentConfig{
                Type: graphql.NewNonNull(graphql.Int),
        },
        "starRating": &graphql.ArgumentConfig{
                Type: graphql.NewNonNull(graphql.Int),
        },
},
Resolve: func(params graphql.ResolveParams)
    (interface{}, error) {
        // marshall and cast the argument value
        displayName, _:=
          params.Args["displayName"].(string)
        city, _:= params.Args["city"].(string)
        noRooms, _:= params.Args["noRooms"].(int)
        starRating, _:= params.Args["starRating"].(int)

        // create in 'DB'
        newHotel:= Hotel{
                Id:          randomId(),
                DisplayName: displayName,
                City:        city,
                NoRooms:     noRooms,
                StarRating:  starRating,
        }
        hotels[newHotel.Id] = newHotel

        // return the new Hotel object
        return newHotel, nil
    },
        },
    },
})
```

Here we use the preceding map described to store the `hotel` object, after generating an ID for hotel. The ID is generated using the `randomId()` helper function:

```
// Random ID Generator
var letterRunes =
[]rune("abcdefghijklmnopqrstuvwxyzABCDEFGHIJKLMNOPQRSTUVWXYZ")

func randomId() string {
```

```
b:= make([]rune, 8)
for i:= range b {
        b[i] = letterRunes[rand.Intn(len(letterRunes))]
}
return string(b)
}
```

Note that this is not a good way of generating IDs—one big reason is the possibility of collisions. Generally when a DB is used, the ID is autogenerated as the primary key of the object.

The following CURL request shows how to create a hotel using the preceding definition:

```
curl -g
'http://localhost:8080/graphql?query=mutation+_{createHotel(displayName:"Ho
telX",city:"NY",noRooms:300,starRating:5){id}}'
```

Subscriptions

Using subscriptions, a client an can get updates on different events. The client holds a persistent connection to the server and the server streams data to the client.

For example, if we want to know of newly created hotels as a client, it can send a subscription like so:

```
subscription {
  newHotel {
    name
    id
  }
}
```

After this, a connection is opened between them. Then, whenever a new mutation is performed that creates a hotel, an event in the following form is streamed to the interested client:

```
{
  "newHotel": {
    "name": "Taj",
    "id": cdab123
  }
}
```

Higher-level patterns

Now that we have seen various API paradigms, let's discuss high-level patterns of API design. Some of these patterns deal with solving common concerns across a set of instances. Others describe a design pattern for structuring code in an API server.

Model-View-Controller (MVC)

The MVC design pattern is the most used pattern for designing API systems. The main idea behind MVC is separated presentation (`https://martinfowler.com/eaaDev/SeparatedPresentation.html`), where the architect endeavors to make a clear division between domain objects which model the real world and presentation objects which are the visual representation elements (or the GUI). This pattern defines clear responsibilities for each component:

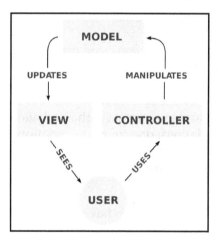

Let's have a look at each component in detail:

- **Model**:
    - Manages the application state and exposes data entities
    - Encapsulates business logic that governs that data, such as accessibility rules

- Responsible for persistence
- *Not* coupled with UI or presentation, and can be used with different user interfaces

- **View**:

  - Responsible for user interface
  - Handles rendering of information and user actions
  - Not stateful
  - Generally is very configurable with templates

- **Controller**:

  - Serves the role of the intermediary between the model and view components
  - Responsible for updating views on changes in the model
  - Responsible for orchestrating model updates based on user interactions
  - Generally hosts business logic around functionality

In traditional web applications, the view consisted mostly of templates that take some parameters, render something like a HTML page, and then send to a dumb client like a browser. However, with the advent of rich clients in modern applications, the view is increasingly embodied on the client side. It is either the mobile app or smart JavaScript code that renders UI elements and interacts with the backend using APIs. The UI code itself often follows MVC pattern variations: one common variation is the **Model-View-ViewModel** (**MVVM**) pattern, where the ViewModel is a semantic definition of the user interface, and the view is more concerned with actual GUI/ UX specifics/bindings to a specific UI form factor.

For designing backend APIs, most languages have support of web frameworks where the key feature is an HTTP router that essentially maps a request URL (or a prefix of the URL) to a handler function—the controller. We already saw how this works in the Gin framework. High performance routers like than in Gin or `httprouter` (another popular router in Golang) are based on Radix trees (compact prefix trees), and essentially the URL walks through the tree to figure out the handler.

 One might wonder why not to use a HashMap for the router; well, to allow for path parameter (for example, `/v1/hotels/:id/book`). Using the tree to navigate allows us to assign-and-jump URL segments with path parameters to get to the required handler. Generally there is a router instance for each method, for efficient representation of the router.

The controller generally defines logic to understand path/query parameters and interacts with the model. It hosts the main application business logic on how the API handling needs to be done. Generally, a web framework gives a specific format for the controller, so that the developer writing the controller for an API can access context such as the query parameters, the request body, and so on. Sometimes a set of handlers need to do similar things (for example, authorization), and such processing is generally done through middleware in the web framework. The applicable processing is done at the start or the end of each request processing for a specific handler.

The model components define the entities (typically structs) in Golang, the helper get/set methods, the persistence, and the business logic in terms of accessibility and so on. One way of enabling persistence is using **Object Relational Models** (**ORMs**), which help in mapping Golang structures into/from how the data is represented in the database. We shall look at ORMs and persistence in more detail in Chapter 8, *Modeling Data*.

Load balancing health checks

Services are generally deployed in clusters of redundant instances (for reliability and scalability, as described in Chapter 4, *Scaling Applications*, and Chapter 9, *Anti-Fragile Systems*). It is important for only clients to access health instances, to avoid service unavailability issues.

Health checks help in this regard. Generally, the pattern calls for each service instance to perform a deep health check (that is, check all subsystems) and tell the LB or the service registry about the instance health. Generally, the LB or the service registry has an agent which makes a call to each service backend instance and expects a response within a given time. To ensure good performance (low latency) for the health check API, one can make the actual deep health check asynchronous to the health URL API response.

API gateway

Typically in a microservice architecture, the granularity of APIs provided by individual microservices is often different than what a client needs. Also the set of microservices changes frequently. In such a scenario, clients don't want an overhead of coordinating and processing/consolidating API responses from multiple services. Also, modern applications have multiple user interfaces, with different requirements and network performances. For example, a desktop client (including a browser) will typically show a richer interface and have access to a stable network connection. On the other hand, mobile applications have limited screen real estate and also have to deal with slower/more finicky mobile networks.

The API gateway pattern provides a solution for this, by implementing a single entry point for all the backend services. At the least, it performs routing of specific URLs to a backend service, and provides common features such as authentication, throttling, and so on.

Some may also implement complex features such as aggregation (call multiple services and compose a consolidated response).

The pattern is depicted here:

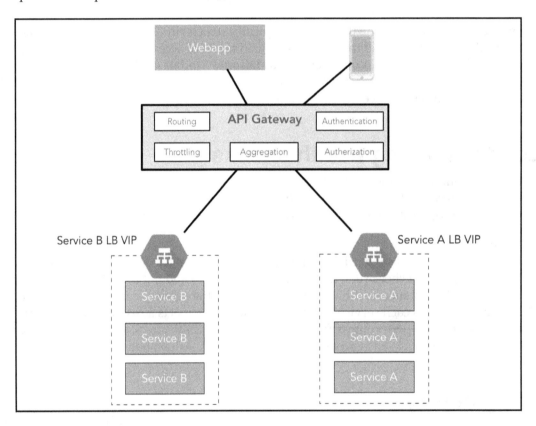

One problem that people saw with a single point of API aggregation is that different clients often have very different interaction models. The general-purpose API gateway becomes an anti-pattern, as there is no segregation of concerns. It also leads to development bottlenecks for rolling out new features, as now rollouts have to coordinate with this central team, and as all changes are made to the same artifact.

One solution to this problem is to have one API gateway for each frontend—what is called the **Backend For Frontend** (**BFF**) pattern. Each BFF is specific to a client (user experience) and will typically be maintained by the same team as the client. Thus you get both of the following advantages:

- A lot of the heavy lifting in terms of API calling and aggregation moves to the backend as in the API gateway pattern.
- There is no coupling of concerns in one monolithic code base.

The pattern is illustrated as follows:

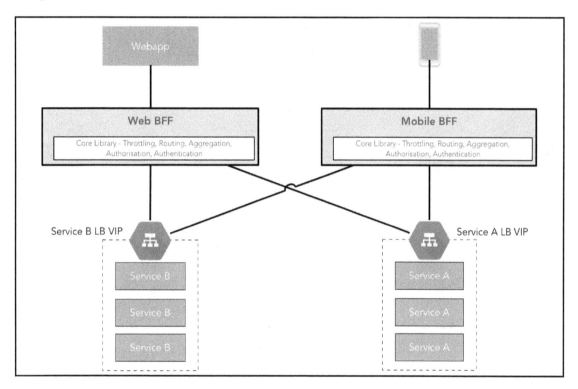

As you can see, there is often a shared library to host common code with only the client/UI specifics being different in each BFF service.

Sometimes, an aggregation can be very complex and have lots of use cases. In such a case, it's best to factor out a separate aggregation service. In our travel website example, search would be such a use case. In this case, the architecture would look as follows:

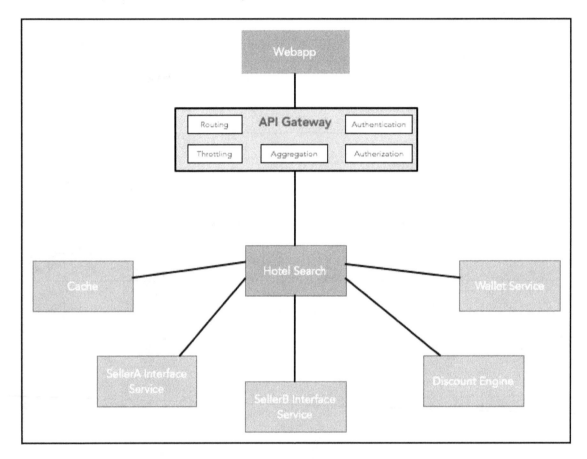

Go kit

In the Java/Scala ecosystem, there are a lot of frameworks that help in building API-based solutions. Examples include the Netflix OSS stack and the Twitter Finangle. Go kit (`https:/ /gokit.io/`) is a collection of packages that together give a slightly opinionated framework for quickly building a service-oriented architecture.

Go kit enforces separation of concerns through a decorator design pattern. It is organized in three main layers (with some sub-layers):

- Transport layer
- Endpoint layer
- Service layer

This is shown in the following diagram:

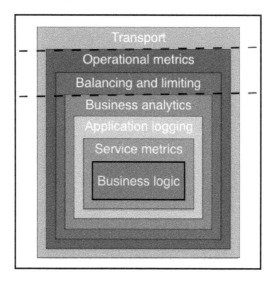

Reference: http://gokit.io/faq/#introduction-mdash-understanding-go-kit-key-concepts

The transport layer defines the bindings and implements protocol specifics of various transports such as HTTP and gRPC (Google RPC).

The innermost service layer is where the business logic is implemented in a transport-agnostic fashion. Reminiscent of the Java world, one defines an interface for the service and provides an implementation. This provides another layer of decoupling and ensures that contract and implementation are not muddled together and are clearly maintained separately. One can write service middleware to provide cross-cutting functionality, such as logging, analytics, instrumentation, and so on.

The middle endpoint layer is somewhat equivalent to the controller in the MVC pattern. It is the place where the service layer is hooked up, and the safety and anti-fragile logic is implemented.

Let's take an example of a service that counts vowels in a string. Let's start with our service implementation:

```
// CountVowels counts  vowels in  strings.
type VowelsService interface {
   Count(context.Context, string) int
}

// VowelsService is a concrete implementation of VowelsService
type VowelsServiceImpl struct{}

var vowels = map[rune]bool{
    'a': true,
    'e': true,
    'i': true,
    'o': true,
    'u': true,
}

func (VowelsServiceImpl) Count(_ context.Context, s string) int {
    count:= 0
    for _, c:= range s {
        if _, ok:= vowels[c]; ok {
            count++
        }
    }

    return count
}
```

The service has an interface that essentially takes a string and returns the number of vowels in it. The implementation uses a lookup dictionary and counts vowels in the string.

Next, we define the input and output response formats for our service:

```
// For each method, we define request and response structs
type countVowelsRequest struct {
   Input string `json:"input"`
}

type countVowelsResponse struct {
   Result int `json:"result"`
}
```

Using this, we can now define `Endpoint`:

```
// An endpoint represents a single RPC  in the service interface
func makeEndpoint(svc VowelsService) endpoint.Endpoint {
    return func(ctx context.Context, request interface{}) (interface{},
error) {
            req:= request.(countVowelsRequest)
            result:= svc.Count(ctx, req.Input)
            return countVowelsResponse{result}, nil
    }
}
```

 Till now, we have not defined how the data will reach or be available from the endpoint.

Finally, we hook up the endpoint using a transport of our choice. In the following example, we use HTTP as the transport:

```
func main() {
    svc:= VowelsServiceImpl{}

    countHandler:= httptransport.NewServer(
            makeEndpoint(svc),
            decodecountVowelsRequest,
            encodeResponse,
    )

    http.Handle("/count", countHandler)
    log.Fatal(http.ListenAndServe(":8080", nil))
}

func decodecountVowelsRequest(_ context.Context, r *http.Request)
(interface{}, error) {
    var request countVowelsRequest
    if err:= json.NewDecoder(r.Body).Decode(&request); err != nil {
            return nil, err
    }
    return request, nil
}

func encodeResponse(_ context.Context, w http.ResponseWriter, response
interface{}) error {
    return json.NewEncoder(w).Encode(response)
}
```

It uses JSON for the serialization format and uses the standard `net/http` package to define a `HTTP` server.

The preceding simple example was intended to give a minimal working example of Go kit. There are many more rich constructs such as middleware; for more details, please refer to `https://gokit.io/`.

Summary

In this chapter, we looked at REST and GraphQL API models in detail. We built real-life services using the principles and applicable constructs/libraries in Golang. We also looked at a popular *full-featured* API framework called Go kit.

In the next chapter, we will be introducing the entity-relationship, way of modeling data, describing various persistence stores. We will also take a deep dive into MySQL, Redis, and Cassandra.

8
Modeling Data

The most valuable asset in today's businesses is data, but data needs to be ingested and structured properly to be of maximum value. This chapter discusses how to model entities, their relationships, and repositories. We will also deep-dive into a few popular data stores, including using them in Golang to demonstrate the principles of data modeling.

In this chapter, we will cover the following topics:

- Entity-relationship modeling
- Engineering various consistency guarantees
- Relational data modeling and a hands-on deep-dive into MySQL
- Key value stores and a hands-on deep-dive into Redis
- Columnar stores and a hands-on deep-dive into Cassandra
- Patterns for scaling data stores

Entities and relationships

During requirements analysis, we identify key objects (things of interest) around which the system is designed. In database parlance, these are called **entities**. They are objects that are capable of independent existence and that can be uniquely identified. While in object-oriented design the focus is on modeling behavior, entity-relationship modeling is concerned more with attributes and the relationships of entities. In entity-relationship analysis, the relationships are derived from static attributes rather than behavior/interactions, as in the case of object-oriented analysis.

Entities can be usually identified from the nouns in the requirements. For example, in the travel website, a **Hotel** is a key entity. Requirement analysis gives us insights into the attributes of the entities. For example, the **Hotel** entity might have the following attributes:

A relationship defines how two entities are related to one another. They can usually be identified from the verbs, linking two or more nouns. For example, a **Hotel** can have more than one **Room**, each of which can be reserved at a specific date range—this implies the following relationships:

Diagrams such as the preceding one are called **entity-relationship** diagrams. It documents and helps to visualize how data is structured in the system.

The entities and the relationships are still at a conceptual level at early stages of requirement. However, as engineering progresses, these get crystallized into storage engine-specific databases, schemas, and other constructs. Also, as our understanding of the domain increases, the initial data design might undergo iterations, including the following:

- **Generalization**: Formation of entity hierarchies to delineate various related entities
- **Normalization**: Removing redundancy in the modeled entities (we'll learn about this in detail in the *Relational model* section)
- **Denormalization**: Figuring out that redundancy is required and can help in increasing performance in certain use cases (covered in much more detail in the *Scaling data* section)
- **Constraints/business rules**: Governance on what values entity attributes can take and the relationships between entities
- **Object relational mapper**: Mapping of objects in the computation space with the entities persisted in the storage system

Consistency guarantees

Besides modeling entities and their relationships, a key design choice in terms of consistency guarantees that the persistence layer (database) needs to give to the application. If a use case involves modifications of two or more entities, these guarantees from the storage system play a pivotal role in system architecture and SLAs. For example, consider the account transfer use case for a Banking application. After the transfer is done, the net debit/credit amounts should tally—no matter what happens in terms of infrastructure failure. Such logical units of work (debit from account x and credit to account y) are called **transactions**.

Let's look at some guarantees that databases (and storage systems in general) provide for transactions.

ACID (Atomicity, Consistency, Isolation, Durability)

ACID is a mnemonic for **Atomicity, Consistency, Isolation, Durability**. It represents one of the most widely supported (and needed!) set of guarantees from storage systems that involve transactions. An ACID-compliant database provides an environment where a high level of consistency can be engineered without complicating the application. This concept is standardized by the ISO (ISO/IEC 10026-1:1992 Section 4). Let's look at each guarantee in detail.

Atomicity

A transaction is atomic if it takes place entirely or doesn't happen at all. In no situation is the database left in a **half-modified** inconsistent state. The application code can issue read and write operations for a transaction within a session and either commit (make all the changes applicable and visible) or abort (none of the changes are made). Even if the applicable instance or the database instance that was performing the read/write crashes, the transaction stalls and is recovered later on, but never is the atomic constraint violated.

Let's see an example of atomicity. Consider the following simplistic pseudocode, which transfers $100 from account abc to xyz:

```
amountToTransfer:= 100
beginTransaction()
srcValue:= getAccountBalance('abc')
srcValue:= srcValue - amountToTransfer
dstValue:= getAccountBalance('xyz')
dstValue:= dstValue + amountToTransfer
commitTransaction()
```

If the balances in the abc and xyz accounts were $200 and $300, respectively, then after the transaction commits, the state will be $100 and $400, respectively. If there is a crash or the application encounters an error, the transaction will roll back and the balances will stay at the original amounts—$200 and $300, respectively.

Consistency

A storage systems enforces consistency on the transactions by ensuring that at the end of any transaction the system is in a valid state. If the transaction completes successfully, then all constraints defined in the storage system will stay applicable and the system will be in a valid state. If any error occurs in the transaction and there is a rollback, then the system is left in the original consistent state.

Again, as an example, let's take the account-transfer system. There is a constraint defined that there will be no overdraft—that is, the account balance will never be less than zero. If a transfer is initiated and in the preceding example, the abc account balance is $50, then the transaction will be aborted and rolled back because committing the transaction will leave the system in an inconsistent state—where the integrity or business constraints are violated.

Isolation

The isolation property guarantees that transactions do not contend with each other. Whenever there are parallel transactions working on shared entities, the systems exposes a consistent view of the system for all the transactions.

Let's start the discussion by analyzing the different effects of concurrent transactions:

- **Lost updates**: Consider two transactions that update an entity independently. In this case, one transaction will finish after another and the last transaction update will overwrite the previous one. For example, if an online editor modifies two transactions for the same document for two authors, then the last update will overwrite the updates of the original author—even though they might be working on totally different pages! To avoid this, the transaction could have locked the document as a whole so as to serialize access during modification.

- **Dirty reads**: If a transaction is allowed to read the modified (but not yet committed) value of some entities, then its logic is working with input that is still dirty, which means not committed. If the other transaction rolls back, then this transaction might leave the system in an undesirable state. Continuing with the example of the online editor, a second transaction (author) starts authoring the documentation that is being modified by a current transaction (author). The second transaction makes a copy of the modifications at that point in time and updates the second author's changes on top of it. Meanwhile, the first transaction rolls back (or changes some earlier data) and now the document that the second transaction will commit will be in a half-and-half state. This problem could be avoided if, when a read occurred, the transaction was blocked until the competing earlier transaction finished.

- **Non-repeatable reads**: Here, a transaction reads an entity more than once during its lifetime and each time the data returned is different—even though the transaction did not modify anything. This differs from dirty reads in that the changed data might be due to a committed transaction. Nevertheless, this phenomena might lead to erroneous computation. This type of problem can be avoided if all writers to an entity are blocked until concurrent transactions with readers of that entity are finished.

- **Phantom reads**: These occur when an entity that is being read in one transaction is deleted in another transaction. This can also occur when a transaction is working with a range of entities (documents by a specific author) and this range changes due to an insert. Again, this problem is solved by blocking transactions that modify an entity that is being currently read by other transactions.

ISO has defined different levels of isolation guarantees, and each specifies the degree to which one transaction must be isolated from other transactions. Here, isolation refers to the concurrency effects we just looked at. The levels and their implication on the concurrency effects are defined as follows:

Isolation level	Dirty reads	Non-repeatable reads	Phantom reads
Read uncommitted	Yes	Yes	Yes
Read committed	No	Yes	Yes
Repeatable	No	No	Yes
Snapshot	No	No	No
Serializable	No	No	No

Essentially, the isolation levels control the following:

- When, during a transaction (T1), a read occurs on entities that are being modified by another transaction (T2).
- The T2 read is blocked until the competing T2 transaction finishes (exclusive lock).
- The T1 read gets the value that was committed before T2 started.
- T1 reads the modified (but not yet committed) values by T2—there is no blocking.
- A more permissive isolation level increases the amount of concurrency in the system (thereby improving things such as throughput, responsiveness, and scalability) but there could be consistency issues, such as reading data that is not yet committed or writes that are lost (lost updates). On the other hand, a more restrictive (or higher) isolation level gives a much more stringent version of consistency but reduces the amount or concurrency (more blocking) and requires more system resources.
- Note that the serializable and snapshot isolation level provide the same isolation guarantee—but there is a difference in how it's achieved in full. In the serializable isolation level, there is an exclusive range lock on all the entities involved in the transaction. As opposed to this, with the snapshot isolation level, there is a copy (snapshot) of all the entities involved in the transaction, and read/writes work against these copies (version). During commit time, the storage system does the same consistency checks, but because competing transactions are not blocked, the snapshot isolation level gives a higher level of concurrency, albeit at the cost of more storage/resources.

Note that choosing a transaction isolation level does not affect the write locks that are acquired to perform data modifications. Here, the transaction always gets an exclusive lock on any data it modifies and holds that lock until the transaction completes—regardless of the isolation level.

Durability

A transaction is durable if, after it's committed, the changes to the storage systems are persistent, irrespective of hardware reboots. So, if the storage system maintained data in memory, this guarantee would not be met, since on restart the storage system would lose the data. Durability generally also involves keeping a **transaction log** so that even in the case of disk failures, the logs could be replayed to bring the system to a consistent state.

BASE (Basically Available, Soft state, Eventual consistency)

In 2000, Eric Brewer presented the CAP theorem to the world in his keynote speech at the ACM Symposium on the Principles of Distributed Computing. The theorem states that in the presence of a network partition, the system design can either provide availability or consistency. We shall dig deeper into the CAP theorem in `Chapter 5`, *Going Distributed*, but the immediate implications for storage systems are that for a distributed system providing ACID compliance is tough to engineer and does not scale well.

To overcome this, some modern storage systems offer an alternative model of consistency, called **BASE**—short for **Basically Available, Soft state, Eventual consistency**. Let's look at what this means:

- **Basically Available:** This system guarantees the availability that there will be a response to a request, but the response might not be consistent at all times.
- **Soft state:** The state of the system could change over time, even when there is no external input.
- **Eventual consistency:** The system will eventually become consistent. Generally, this happens when various concurrent operations are reconciled and a steady state is reached.

Relational model

The most common way of storing data is based on the notion of a relational model—an idea introduced by Dr. Edgar Codd in the early 1970s. Here, an entity is stored as a tuple (or row) of attributes (or columns). A database is simply a set of rows, all of which have the same set of columns (or schema). Tables are defined using a static data schema; relations between entities are modeled by foreign keys or relationship tables; rows from different tables can be referenced using foreign keys.

There are many ways of representing the conceptual data model presented earlier. However, not all representations are efficient for all use cases. To enable figuring out an optimal relational structure, Dr. Codd expressed a series of progressively more restrictive constraints on the structure of data. With each level of constraint/rules, the amount of redundancy in the representation will be reduced. This process of introducing constraints and refactoring the structure to reduce redundancy is called **normalization**, and each level is called a **normal form**. Let's look at the various forms.

The first normal form

A table is said to be in **1NF** (**first normal form**) if the following constraints hold:

- Each column must have a single value
- Columns must have unique names
- Each column must have attributes of the same data type
- No two rows can be identical

The constraint here is that every attribute (column) should be a single-valued attribute.

For example, the following hotel reservations table violates the first normal form because there is more than one phone number in the phone column:

Room ID	Hotel ID	Date	Hotel name	Hotel description	Phone	Star rating	Free to cancel	User ID
1	12321	01/01/2018	FairField Marriot SFO	Five-star hotel suitable for leisure and business travelers	+1-408-123123	5	No	abc

1	12321	01/02/2018	FairField Marriot SFO	Five-star hotel suitable for leisure and business travelers	+1-408-123123	5	No	pqr
2	12321	01/01/2018	FairField Marriot SFO	Five-star hotel suitable for leisure and business travelers	+1-408-123123	5	No	xyz
1	456	01/01/2018	Holiday Inn Menlo Park	Affordable business hotel	+1-408-123789 +1-408-123456	4	Yes	zzz

To be in the first normal form, the table would have to restructured as follows:

Room ID	HotelId	Date	HotelName	HotelDescription	Phone	Star rating	FreeCancel	Userid
1	12321	01/01/2018	FairField Marriot SFO	Five-star hotel suitable for leisure and business travelers	+1-408-123123	5	No	abc
1	12321	01/02/2018	FairField Marriot SFO	Five-star hotel suitable for leisure and business travelers	+1-408-123123	5	No	pqr
2	12321	01/01/2018	FairField Marriot SFO	Five-star hotel suitable for leisure and business travelers	+1-408-123123	5	No	xyz
1	456	01/01/2018	Holiday Inn Menlo Park	Affordable business hotel	+1-408-123456	4	Yes	zzz
1	456	01/01/2018	Holiday Inn Menlo Park	Affordable business hotel	+1-408-123789	4	Yes	zzz

The first normal form eliminates the phenomenon of repeating groups—it is a set of attributes that can take multiple values for a given occurrence of an entity type.

The second normal form

The primary key—a set of attributes that uniquely identity the row—for the hotel is `RoomId`, `HotelId`, and `Date`. In the preceding table, we can see that there is a lot of repetition of data. For example, `HotelDescription` only depends on `HotelId` and not on other attributes of the reservation. The problem with this repetition is that any mistake/change in the description would need to change in a lot of places.

To avoid this redundancy, Codd's second constraint states that, "Each attribute must be dependent on the entire primary key."

To enable this, the table must be refactored into two tables, as follows:

- **Reservations**:

Room Id	HotelId	Date	Userid
1	12321	01/01/2018	abc
1	12321	01/02/2018	pqr
2	12321	01/01/2018	xyz
1	456	01/01/2018	zzz

- **Hotels**:

HotelId	HotelName	HotelDescription	Phone	Star rating	FreeCancel
12321	FairField Marriot SFO	Five-star hotel suitable for leisure and business travelers	+1-408-123123	5	No
12321	FairField Marriot SFO	Five-star hotel suitable for leisure and business travelers	+1-408-123123	5	No
12321	FairField Marriot SFO	Five-star hotel suitable for leisure and business travelers	+1-408-123123	5	No
456	Holiday Inn Menlo Park	Affordable business hotel	+1-408-123456	4	Yes
456	Holiday Inn Menlo Park	Affordable business hotel	+1-408-123789	4	Yes

Now, with this schema, the reservations table has much less redundant information and all the non-key fields are dependent on the primary key.

The third normal form

A little bit of domain investigation reveals that the `FreeCancellation` column depends on the `StartRating` one—five-star hotels don't offer free cancellation, but others do. The fact that the free cancellation option is mentioned in the database as opposed to hardcoding in the code is good design—it makes changes to this policy easier, without touching/releasing code. However, the repetition of information does introduce redundancy. It can also lead to consistency issues—say that four-star hotels also stop offering free cancellations; it's much better to model this relationship separately.

Codd's third constraint states that, "Each attribute must be dependent only on the primary key." To enable this, we refactor the hotels table further, as follows:

- **Hotels:**

HotelId	HotelName	HotelDescription	Phone	Star rating
12321	FairField Marriot SFO	Five-star hotel suitable for leisure and business travelers	+1-408-123123	5
12321	FairField Marriot SFO	Five-star hotel suitable for leisure and business travelers	+1-408-123123	5
12321	FairField Marriot SFO	Five-star hotel suitable for leisure and business travelers	+1-408-123123	5
456	Holiday Inn Menlo Park	Affordable business hotel	+1-408-123456	4
456	Holiday Inn Menlo Park	Affordable business hotel	+1-408-123789	4

- **Cancellation policy:**

Star rating	FreeCancel
5	No
4	Yes
3	Yes
2	Yes
1	Yes

The Boyce-Codd normal form

So far, the forms we have discussed have focused on relationships between key and non-key attributes. We have reduced redundancy by ensuring that each attribute depends on the whole primary key and nothing else.

But it is possible in some cases that there might be dependencies within parts of a compound key. The next constraint states, "No part of the primary key may be dependent on another part of the primary key."

For example, say our flight reservation table had the following structure:

FlightNo	Airline	Date	UserId	Seat
AN-501	Emirates	01/01/2018	abc	5A
SQ-502	Singapore Airlines	01/01/2018	pqr	42B
SQ-502	Singapore Airlines	02/01/2018	xyz	5C
SQ-503	Singapore Airlines	03/01/2018	xyx	4C

Here, the primary key is defined as a compound key consisting of `FlightNo`, `Airline`, and `Date`. But it was seen that the airline's name can be inferred from `FlightNo`. Thus, part of the primary key is dependent on the other attributes. To enable BCNF, we refactor this table into two:

- **Reservations**:

FlightNo	Date	UserId	Seat
AN-501	01/01/2018	abc	5A
SQ-502	01/01/2018	pqr	42B
SQ-502	02/01/2018	xyz	5C
SQ-503	03/01/2018	xyx	4C

- **FlightDetails**:

FlightNo	Airline
AN-501	Emirates
SQ-502	Singapore Airlines
SQ-502	Singapore Airlines
SQ-503	Singapore Airlines

The fourth normal form

The first four forms (the first through third, and Boyce Codd) apply structural constraints that allow one to assert compliance. The fourth normal form, on the other hand, is a little more subtle.

To demonstrate, consider that we will be building a holidays feature on a travel website. Holidays mean a combination of activities and hotels. To model this, a table is created that defines all the destinations in which holidays are possible and the options that are available:

Destination	HotelId	ActivityId
Singapore	ABxx2	124
Singapore	ABxx2	567
Singapore	Psawe212	124
Dubai	sa0943	124
Dubai	we1321	124

This table documents all the possible activities/hotels options available at a destination.

The redundancy observed here is that there are multivalued dependencies. This is a type of dependency that exists between two attributes when, for each value of the first attribute, there is one or more associated values of the second attribute. For example, the fact that `activityid=124` (snorkeling) is available in Singapore is stored more than once.

The fourth constraint states, "There may be no independent sets of dependencies within a primary key." This leads to the fourth normal form. To move the model to the fourth normal form, the preceding table can be decomposed into two tables:

- `HolidayActivities`:

Destination	ActivityId
Singapore	124
Singapore	567
Dubai	124

- `HolidayHotels:`

Destination	HotelId
Singapore	`ABxx2`
Singapore	`Psawe212`
Dubai	`sa0943`
Dubai	`we1321`

SQL

Structured Query Language (**SQL**) has established itself as generic data definition, manipulation, and query language for relational data. It has been adopted by almost all relational database management systems. Besides constructs on inserting, updating, retrieving, and deleting data, the constructs also define transactional constructs to ensure ACID semantics and do joins (see the *Views* section).

A detailed description of SQL is outside the scope of this book. To learn more about SQL, try doing a quick Google search for SQL syntax and tutorials, or consult any of the many books on the subject.

Indices

The main goal of a database is to persist data on the disk. However, we do need to search and retrieve data efficiently from what we have stored. A database index is a data structure that helps in quickly locating data with specific attributes (keys). Most index implementations use balanced N-ary tree variants, such as the B+ tree to implement the index efficiently.

A B+ tree is an N-ary tree, like a B tree, but the difference is that the data structure contains only the keys—the values are stored externally. The primary value add of the B+ tree over a binary tree is the high fanout (pointers to child nodes) at each node. This allows for more efficient searches in the keyspace. This is crucial for databases, as more searches means more I/O operations (which are much more expensive than memory accesses). The reason for storing only keys (which is the difference between a B tree and a B+ tree) is that it allows much more search information to be packed into one disk block—thereby improving cache efficiency and reducing I/O operations on disks. The leaves of the B+ tree are often linked with one another to form a linked list; this enables efficient range queries or ordered iterations.

The following diagram shows a B+ tree with a maximum degree of 3, and 6 keys inserted:

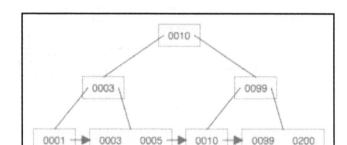

For more details, please refer to `http://www.cburch.com/cs/340/reading/btree/index.html`.

Views

Relational theory includes a construct for the combination of tables (relations) to arrive at a view of the data. A view is nothing but a relation that is assembled from others. Since this is derived data, the rules of normalization do not have to apply. Views are constructed using joins on a table.

The SQL JOIN clause is used to combine rows from two or more tables, based on a common column. Different type of joins produce different views. To demonstrate this, consider two normalized tables about reservations and customers:

- Reservations:

ReservationId	CustomerId	Date
123123	axy	01/02/2018
123124	axy	01/03/2018
123125	pqr	02/02/2018
123126	xyz	03/02/2018
123127	abc	03/02/2018

- Customers:

CustomerId	CustomerName	Phone
axy	Alex Hales	+1-408-123421
pqr	Chris Call	+1-408-723777
xyz	Stuart Broad	+1-408-888213
yyy	Chris Gayle	+1-408-666999

 The CustomerId column is shared between the two tables and serves as the common mapping column. To demonstrate different types of joins, there are deliberate discrepancies between the two tables.

Inner join

The inner join is a set intersection and is the default behavior. This join returns rows that have matching values in both tables:

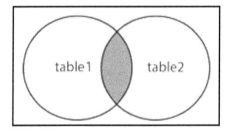

The following query does an inner join:

```
SELECT Reservations.ReservationId,
Customers.CustomerName,Reservations.Date
    FROM Orders
    INNER JOIN Customers
    ON Orders.CustomerID=Customers.CustomerID;
```

It produces the following result:

ReservationId	CustomerName	Date
123123	Alex Hales	01/02/2018
123124	Alex Hales	01/03/2018
123125	Chris Call	02/02/2018
123126	Stuart Broad	03/02/2018

 Only rows present in both tables are returned.

Left outer join

In this join, all the records from the table mentioned on the left are returned, along with matched records from the right table. Absent values are null:

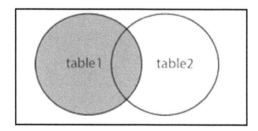

The follow query does a left join:

```
SELECT Reservations.ReservationId, Customers.CustomerName,Reservations.Date
FROM Orders
LEFT JOIN Customers
ON Orders.CustomerID=Customers.CustomerID;
```

It produces the following result:

ReservationId	CustomerName	Date
123123	Alex Hales	01/02/2018
123124	Alex Hales	01/03/2018
123125	Chris Call	02/02/2018
123126	Stuart Broad	03/02/2018
123127	NULL	03/02/2018

Right outer join

This is the counterpart to a left join—it returns all records from the right table and the matched records from the left table. The result is null from columns of the left table, when there is no match:

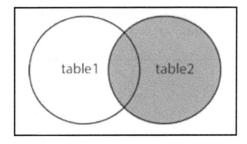

The follow query does a right join:

```
SELECT Reservations.ReservationId, Customers.CustomerName, Reservations.Date
FROM Orders
RIGHT JOIN Customers
ON Orders.CustomerID=Customers.CustomerID;
```

It produces the following result:

ReservationId	CustomerName	Date
123123	Alex Hales	01/02/2018
123125	Chris Call	02/02/2018
123126	Stuart Broad	03/02/2018
Null	Chris Gayle	NULL

Full outer join

This type of join does a set union on the two tables. It returns all rows where there is a match in either the left or the right table rows:

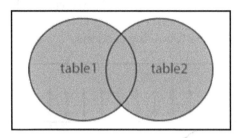

The follow query does a right join:

```
SELECT Reservations.ReservationId, Customers.CustomerName,Reservations.Date
FROM Orders
FULL OUTER JOIN Customers
ON Orders.CustomerID=Customers.CustomerID;
```

It produces the following result:

ReservationId	CustomerName	Date
123123	Alex Hales	01/02/2018
123125	Chris Call	02/02/2018
123126	Stuart Broad	03/02/2018
Null	Chris Gayle	Null
123127	Null	03/02/2018

MySQL deep-dive

MySQL is an open source relational database management system. Its unique design characteristic is the separation of query processing and other server tasks from the storage engine (which is responsible for data storage and retrieval). This separation of concerns lets you to trade off various features without changing your data model. The architecture is depicted here and described in the following sections:

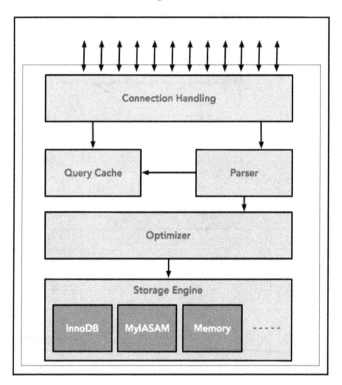

Connection management

Each client connection gets its own thread within the MySQL process. All the client queries are handled by that thread. The threads are pooled for efficiency. Authentication is based on the username and password. X.509 certificates can also be used across an SSL connection. Once a client has been authenticated, the server verifies whether the client has the right authorization for the query.

Query execution

After connection management, the next component involved is the query cache. This stores the result sets of read (SELECT) statements that have executed in the recent past. Before further processing, if there is a cache hit, results are returned from the cache itself.

MySQL parses queries to create an internal structure called the parse tree, and then performs query planning and optimization on it. These include rewrites, choosing indexes, choosing the order in which it will read tables, and so on. A pass hints to the optimizer through special keywords in the query.

The optimizer component is also responsible for the EXPLAIN feature, which helps developers in figuring out how a query is performing. Using EXPLAIN is as simple as prefixing the EXPLAIN keyword to the query:

```
EXPLAIN SELECT * FROM hotel_reservations LIMIT 10;
```

It produces the following output:

```
*********************** 1. row ***********************
id: 1
select_type: SIMPLE
table: hotel_reservations
type: ALL
possible_keys: NULL
key: NULL
key_len: NULL
ref: NULL
rows: 2
Extra:
1 row in set (0.00 sec)
```

There is a wealth of information in the output, the most important of which is described here:

- id: An identifier for each SELECT within the query. This is relevant for nested queries.
- select_type: The type of SELECT query. Possible values are as follows:
    - **Simple**: The query is a simple SELECT query without any subqueries or UNION
    - **Primary**: The SELECT is in the outermost query in a JOIN
    - **Derived**: The SELECT is part of a subquery within a FROM clause

- **Subquery**: It is the first SELECT in a subquery
- **Dependent subquery**: This is a subquery that is dependent upon on outer query
- **Uncachable subquery**: It is a subquery that is not cacheable (there are certain conditions for a query to be cacheable)
- **Union**: The SELECT is the second or later statement of a UNION
- **Dependent union**: The second or later SELECT of a UNION is dependent on an outer query
- **Union result**: The SELECT is a result of a UNION

- type: This is one of the most important fields and describes how MySQL plans to join the tables used. This can be used to infer missing indexes and/or whether the query needs redesign. Important values are as follows:
  - const: The table has only one matching row, which is indexed. This enables the fastest join since the value has to be read once, and can effectively be treated as a constant when joining other tables.
  - eq_ref: All parts of an index are used by the join, and the index is a PRIMARY KEY or UNIQUE NOT NULL. This is the next best possible execution plan for a query.
  - ref: All of the matching rows of an indexed column are read for each combination of rows from the previous table. This type of join appears for indexed columns compared using the = or <=> operators.
  - fulltext: The query uses a FULLTEXT search index—this is used for information retrieval in TEXT fields.
  - index_merge: The join uses a list of indexes to produce the result set. The key column of the EXPLAIN output will contain the keys used.
  - **unique_subquery**: An IN subquery returns only one result from the table and makes use of the primary key.
  - index_subquery: The same as unique_subquery, but returns more than one result row.
  - range: An index is used to find matching rows in a specific range, typically when the key column is compared to a constant using operators, such as BETWEEN, IN, >, and >=.
  - index: The entire index is scanned.

- `all`: The entire table is scanned. This is the worst join type and indicates a lack of appropriate indexes.
- `possible_keys`: Shows the keys that can be (but may not be used in the actual execution) used by MySQL to find rows from the table. If the column is NULL, it indicates that no relevant indexes could be found.
- `key`: Indicates the actual index used by MySQL. The optimizer always looks for an optimal key that can be used for the query, and sometimes it may figure out some other keys that are not listed in `possible_key` but are more optimal.
- `rows`: Lists the number of rows that were examined to execute the query. This is another important column worth focusing on for optimizing queries, especially for queries that use JOIN and subqueries.
- `Extra`: Contains additional information regarding the query execution plan. Values such as *using temporary* and *using filesort* in this column may indicate a troublesome query. For a complete list of possible values and their meanings, refer to the MySQL documentation (`https://dev.mysql.com/doc/refman/5.6/en/explain-output.html#explain-extra-information`).

To demonstrate how EXPLAIN can be used to help with debugging, consider the following query:

```
EXPLAIN SELECT * FROM
hotel_reservations r
INNER JOIN orders o ON r.reservationNumber = o.orderNumber
INNER JOIN customers c on c.id = o.customerId
WHERE o.orderNumber = PQR1111
```

This will produce the following output:

```
*********************** 1. row ********************
id: 1
select_type: SIMPLE
table: c
type: ALL
possible_keys: NULL
key: NULL
key_len: NULL
ref: NULL
rows: 70
Extra:
```

```
*********************** 2. row ********************
id: 1
select_type: SIMPLE
table: o
type: ALL
possible_keys: NULL
key: NULL
key_len: NULL
ref: NULL
rows: 210
Extra: Using join buffer
*********************** 3. row ********************
id: 1
select_type: SIMPLE
table: r
type: ALL
possible_keys: NULL
key: NULL
key_len: NULL
ref: NULL
rows: 3000
Extra: Using where; Using join buffer
3 rows in set (0.00 sec)
```

The preceding results indicate a bad query. The join type is shown as ALL (the worst) for all tables—this means that MySQL was unable to identify any indexes to help with join. The rows column shows that the DB had to scan all of the records of each table for query. This means that for executing the query, it will read *70 × 210 × 3,000 = 44,100,000* rows to find the matching results. This is very bad performance and will degrade as the data size grows. An obvious way to help this query is to add indices, like so:

```
ALTER TABLE customers
ADD PRIMARY KEY (id);
ALTER TABLE orders
ADD PRIMARY KEY (orderNumber),
ADD KEY (customerId);
ALTER TABLE hotel_reservations
ADD PRIMARY KEY (reservationNumber);
```

This will enable MySQL to utilize indices and avoid extended table reads.

Storage engines

MySQL stores each database as a subdirectory of the MySQL data directory in the filesystem. The MySQL architecture component responsible for this maintenance is called the **storage engine**. The ACID compliance is also primarily driven by this layer. It is a pluggable architecture that allows different plugins of different storage engines, as described in the following sections.

InnoDB

InnoDB is the default transactional storage engine for MySQL and the most important/widely used engine plugin. It's fully ACID-compliant with support for transactions. Its performance and automatic crash-recovery make it popular for non-transactional storage needs, too. You should use InnoDB for your tables unless you have a compelling reason to use a different engine.

InnoDB stores its data in a series of one or more data files that are collectively known as a **tablespace**. Each tablespace contains pages (blocks), extents, and segments. The InnoDB implementation includes a bunch of optimizations, including read-ahead for prefetching data from disk, an adaptive hash index that automatically builds hash indexes in memory for very fast lookups, and an insert buffer to speed up writes:

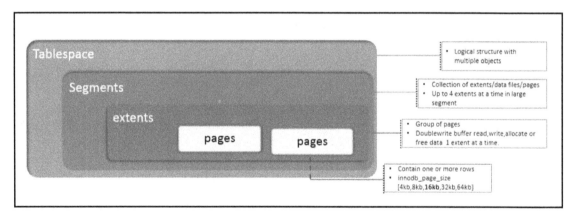

InnoDB defaults to the `REPEATABLE READ` isolation level, and uses **Multiversion Concurrency Control** (**MVCC**) to achieve high concurrency. For each row, the engine stores two additional/hidden fields that record when the row version and when it was deleted/expired. A system-wide number for each transaction is used to identify the version (rather than using timestamps). Thus, for `REPEATABLE READ` and the isolation level, the following apply to each operation:

- When a transaction starts, a new transaction ID is generated.
- **SELECT**: The engine examines each row to ensure that it meets two criteria:
    - InnoDB must find a version of the row that is less than or equal to the current transaction ID. This ensures that either the row existed before the transaction began, or the transaction created or altered the row.
    - The row's deletion version must be null or greater than the transaction's version. This ensures that the row was available (not deleted) when the the transaction started.
- **INSERT**: The transaction ID is stored in the version ID with the new row.
- **DELETE**: The transaction ID is stored as the row's deletion ID.
- **UPDATE**: InnoDB creates a new copy of the row, and uses the transaction ID as the version number for the new row.

The advantage of MVCC is the increased concurrency. The drawback is the additional storage and maintenance work.

MyISAM

This is the original, and oldest, storage engine included in MySQL. It does not support transactions. Its design is optimized more for speed and compact data storage, and is much simpler than that of InnoDB. The index structure is essentially a list of offsets within the data file. Inserts are just appends to the data file. However, deletes and updates are not so straightforward, since they can leave holes in, or fragment, the data file.

MyIASM does have some severe scalability limitations—the most important ones being the following:

- **Key cache**: Mutexes guard the key cache and serialize access to it.
- **Table locking**: Readers obtain read locks on all tables they need to read. Writers obtain exclusive (write) locks. Essentially, only one session is allowed to update a table at a time, forcing a huge serialization bottleneck for updates.

Thus, it's pretty ineffective for even moderate write loads.

Other plugins

MySQL has a variety of other storage engines either for experimental or specialized use cases. Some of them are listed here:

- **The archive engine**: Archive is not a transactional storage engine, but simply optimized for high-speed inserting and compressed storage. This supports only `INSERT` and `SELECT` queries, and it does not support indexes until MySQL 5.1. It's much more IO efficient compared to MyISAM. Archive tables are thus best for logging and data acquisition.
- **The CSV engine**: The CSV plugin can use **comma-separated values** (**CSV**) files as tables. However, indexes on the files are not supported. CSV tables are thus useful as a data interchange format, since the tables can be constructed from CSV files automatically, while also allowing access to the files from other programs.
- **The memory engine:** This plugin (formerly called `HEAP` tables) stores data in memory and thus is good when you need fast access to data, and durability after restart is not that important. They are useful as lookup/map tables, but generally it's advisable to use key-value stores for these use cases.

High availability/scalability

MySQL has a feature called partitioning, where data of a table is transparently split across multiple physical databases, called partitions/fragments. By default, the table's Primary Key MD5 hash is used for partitioning amount the fragments. If a transaction or query needs to access data from multiple fragments, then one of the nodes takes on the role of the transaction coordinator and coordinates work on the other nodes. This coordinator also combines results before forwarding to the application.

A typical high-availability configuration includes a master database that handles data write operations and is replicated to multiple slaves that handle all read operations. The master server continually pushes binlog events (which describe the changes) to connected slaves. In the event of master failure, a slave can be promoted to become the new master. The replication here is asynchronous.

MySQL Cluster is another alternative to the master-slave architecture and allows a set of nodes to serve both reads and writes. MySQL Cluster is implemented through the `NDB` or `NDBCLUSTER` storage engine (**NDB** stands for **Network Database**). There are some known limitations, described
here: `https://dev.mysql.com/doc/refman/5.6/en/mysql-cluster-limitations.html`.

Object Relational Mappers (ORMs)

While the application code can certainly interact with the database using SQL statements, you needs to be careful to ensure that the DB interactions are not strewn across the application layers. The **Data Access Layer** (**DAL**) is a layer that should be responsible for handling entities and their interactions with the database. The rest of the application is abstracted from the DB interaction details.

Objects Relational Mappers (**ORMs**) are a special form of DAL, which translate DB entities into objects. Generally this is done seamlessly behind the scenes via generic glue code.

GORM is the most popular Go ORM out there. To install it, we run the following command:

```
go get "github.com/jinzhu/gorm"
```

To use GORM, you must also specify the database to be used along with the drivers and dialect. Thus, the GORM import inside your application would be as follows:

```
import (
    _ "github.com/go-sql-driver/mysql"
    "github.com/jinzhu/gorm"
    _ "github.com/jinzhu/gorm/dialects/mysql"
)
```

To connect to the database, the code for `mysql` would be something similar to the following:

```
db, err:= gorm.Open("mysql",
"root:@tcp(127.0.0.1:3306)/users?charset=utf8&parseTime=True")
if err != nil {
    panic("failed to connect database")
}
```

Note the `parseTime` flag – this is used to enable `gorm` to translate MySQL `DateTime` fields to the Golang Time `struct`. Once connected the `db` handle can be used to perform operations.

Before looking at the operations, let's see what an entity that is managed by GORM looks like. It's a normal Go struct, which embedded the GORM `gorm.Model` struct. This base struct provides some standard fields, such as timestamps, as shown in the following example. Let's define a `User` entity/model:

```
type User struct {
    gorm.Model
    Name string
    Age  uint
}
```

GORM has a migration feature that allows the DB structure to be in sync with the entity definition. While this is cool in dev, generally it is not advisable to use this in production for fear of unchecked/unwanted DB changes, which can cause data loss. But since this is a dev example, we can initiate schema migration via the following code:

```
// Migrate the schema
db.AutoMigrate(&User{})
```

This will create a table called users, as follows:

```
+------------+-------------------+------+-----+---------+----------------+
| Field      | Type              | NULL | Key | Default | Extra          |
+------------+-------------------+------+-----+---------+----------------+
| id         | int(10) unsigned  | NO   | PRI | NULL    | auto_increment |
| created_at | timestamp         | YES  |     | NULL    |                |
| updated_at | timestamp         | YES  |     | NULL    |                |
| deleted_at | timestamp         | YES  | MUL | NULL    |                |
| name       | varchar(255)      | YES  |     | NULL    |                |
| age        | int(10) unsigned  | YES  |     | NULL    |                |
+------------+-------------------+------+-----+---------+----------------+
```

Note the `id`, `created_at`, `updated_at`, and `deleted_at` (for soft delete) timestamps. They are the additional fields inherited from `gorm.Model`. The name of the table is inferred from the struct name—it is the plural of the model name after translating the camel case to using underscore. For example, if the model name was `UserModel`, the table name would have been `user_models`.

Now that we have our database, we can create the following user:

```
// Create
db.Create(&User{Name: "James Bond", Age: 40})
```

This will insert a record in the database through a SQL query:

```
INSERT INTO users (name,age) VALUES ('James Bond',40);
```

We can query the database using various fields:

```
// Read
var user User
db.First(&user, 1) // find user with id 1
fmt.Println(user)

db.First(&user, "Name = ?", "James Bond") // find James Bond
fmt.Println(user)
```

This will translate to SQL queries:

```
SELECT * FROM users WHERE name='James Bond'  limit 1;
```

Entities can be updated as follows:

```
// Update - update Bond's age
db.Model(&user).Update("Age", 41)
```

This will update the entity as well as the database.

Deletion is somewhat quirky in GORM. The main API is straightforward:

```
// Delete - delete user
db.Delete(&user)
```

However, if the entity has the `deleted_at` field, then rather than deleting the entry, GORM will just set the `deleted_at` value to the current time. These records will be skipped for reads done via GORM. So, the preceding select query is really as follows:

```
SELECT * FROM users WHERE name='James Bond'  AND deleted_at IS NULL limit
1;
```

To actually delete from the database, you can use the `Unscoped` API:

```
db.Unscoped().Delete(&user)
```

The whole `hello world` program that writes, reads, and deletes is described as follows:

```
package main
import (
  "fmt"
  _ "github.com/go-sql-driver/mysql"
  "github.com/jinzhu/gorm"
  _ "github.com/jinzhu/gorm/dialects/mysql"
```

```
)
type User struct {
    gorm.Model
    Name string
    Age  uint
}
func main() {
    db, err:= gorm.Open("mysql",
"root:@tcp(127.0.0.1:3306)/users?charset=utf8&parseTime=True")
    if err != nil {
        panic("failed to connect database")
    }
    defer db.Close()
    // Migrate the schema
    db.AutoMigrate(&User{})
    // Create
    db.Create(&User{Name: "James Bond", Age: 40})
    // Read
    var user User
    db.First(&user, 1) // find user with id 1
    fmt.Println(user)
    db.First(&user, "Name = ?", "James Bond") // find James Bond
    fmt.Println(user)
    // Update - update Bond's age
    db.Model(&user).Update("Age", 41)
    fmt.Println(user)
    // Delete - delete user
    db.Delete(&user)
}
```

This program will not delete the James Bond entry, since `Delete()` is just a soft delete. After the program is run, the DB will have the following entry:

```
mysql>  SELECT * FROM users WHERE name='James Bond'   ;
+----+---------------------+---------------------+---------------------+---
----------+------+
| id | created_at          | updated_at          | deleted_at          |
name        | age |
+----+---------------------+---------------------+---------------------+---
----------+------+
|  5 | 2018-05-06 08:44:22 | 2018-05-06 08:44:22 | 2018-05-06 08:44:22 |
James Bond |    41 |
+----+---------------------+---------------------+---------------------+---
----------+------+
1 row in set (0.01 sec)
```

GORM has support for transactions. For example, the following code will either create both `userA` and `userB`, or will not create either user:

```
func createTwoUsers(db *gorm.DB) {
    userA:= User{Name: "UserA", Age: 20}
    userB:= User{Name: "UserB", Age: 20}

    tx:= db.Begin()
    if err:= tx.Create(&userA).Error; err != nil {
        tx.Rollback()
    }
    if err:= tx.Create(&userB).Error; err != nil {
        tx.Rollback()
    }

    //commit!
    tx.Commit()
}
```

GORM also has support for relationships, which translates object relationships onto the DB structure. Relationships can be belongs-to, one-to-one, one-to-many, and many-to-many. For example, the following program defines a belongs-to relationship between a hotel and a hotel chain:

```
package main

import (
    _ "fmt"
    _ "github.com/go-sql-driver/mysql"
    "github.com/jinzhu/gorm"
    _ "github.com/jinzhu/gorm/dialects/mysql"
)

type HotelChain struct {
    gorm.Model
    Name string
}

type Hotel struct {
    gorm.Model
    Name      string
    NoRooms   uint
    Chain     HotelChain `gorm:"foreignkey:ChainId"` // use ChainId as foreign
key
    ChainId   uint
}
```

```
func main() {
    db, err:= gorm.Open("mysql",
"root:@tcp(127.0.0.1:3306)/users?charset=utf8&parseTime=True")
    if err != nil {
        panic("failed to connect database")
    }
    defer db.Close()

    // Migrate the schema
    db.AutoMigrate(&HotelChain{})
    db.AutoMigrate(&Hotel{})
    db.Model(&Hotel{}).AddForeignKey("chain_id", "hotel_chains(id)",
"CASCADE", "CASCADE")
    // Create some entities and save
    taj:= HotelChain{Name: "Taj"}
    db.Save(&taj)
    vivanta:= Hotel{Name: "Vivanta by the sea", NoRooms: 400, Chain: taj}
    db.Save(&vivanta)
}
```

 AddForeignKey() is needed since the foreign key index and constraints are not set by GORM. It's an open issue.

Key/value stores

Modern systems demand a lot from the storage systems. There is a need to scale storage systems in terms of **queries per second** (**QPS**), the number of concurrent connections, the size of the data, and so on. Also, many applications need ultra-fast requests for a few use cases. While relational systems have, and continue to provide, a reliable persistence technology, the traditional scale-up approach, that is, using better hardware equipment, is not able to keep up with requirements. It is extremely difficult to provide ACID semantics in distributed systems, making scale-out for relational databases a difficult task. Note that there are mechanisms such as distributed transactions, but using them is very complex and they generally lead to very fragile systems. Joins are particularly inefficient in distributed databases. In single-instance databases, joins are efficiently handled using indices and data locality. In distributed nodes, joins will need movement of data across the network to execute the necessary comparison operations. These inefficiencies cause distributed joins to be a inefficient compared to single-node systems.

We will do a deep-dive on scaling data later in this chapter, but in this section we wil introduce a new class of storage systems, called key-value stores.

Concepts

The idea of key/value-based storage systems is similar to the concept of hash tables in programming languages. Like in the relational model, entities are stored as tuples, but with just one key that can uniquely identify the tuple. Relationships are not maintained at the storage level. The Value part of the tuple is pretty much opaque to the storage system.

The advantage with these reduced constraints is the scalability of the system. Using concepts such as distributed hash tables, the data space can now be sharded across multiple instances easily. Reads/writes need to go to only one shard (node) since there are no relationships that could affect other tuples. Scale-out can be easily handled by an efficient redistribution of tuples across new nodes. Another advantage of these systems is performance—they are generally a magnitude of times faster than relational systems. We will look at distributed hash tables in detail in the *Scaling data* section.

A variant of the key-value store is document stores. Here, the data has a structure—usually XML or JSON. However, these systems allow documents of varying schemas to be stored in the same database. This allows storage of things such as optional columns for entities. These values are referred to as documents, hence the name. Compared to key/value stores, document stores allow for more complex queries, and aggregations over documents.

In the next section, we will do a deep-dive into a very popular key-value store, called **Redis**.

Redis deep-dive

Redis is an open source key/value store that primarily stores data in-memory, but offers options for persistence. Besides plain key-value maps, Redis also offers advanced constructs, such as data structures and publish/subscribe message channels.

Architecture

The Redis server is a single-threaded program written in C, which uses `epoll/kqueue` to enable asynchronous IO. You might wonder whether a single-threaded system can scale, but oh boy does Redis scale! The key insight here is that for storage systems, the CPU is rarely the bottleneck—most of the time is spent in I/O (network or storage). Kernel constructs such as `epoll/kqueue` allow application programs to initiate I/O and not get blocked by the operation. This way, a single thread can multiplex a lot of I/O operations.

The single-threaded architecture also provides one key benefit—no race conditions. Since there aren't multiple threads, there is no need for synchronization. This means that there are no lock contentions or nasty deadlocks.

The performance of the architecture can be seen from the benchmark shared by Jak Sprats on the Redis group (http://nosql.mypopescu.com/post/1078083613/redis-a-concurrency-benchmark):

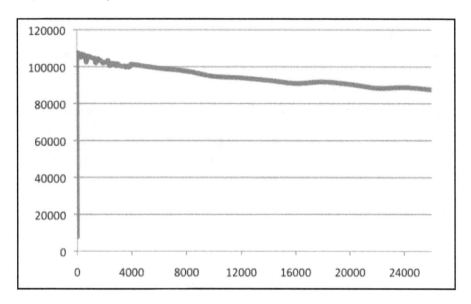

The x axis is the number of concurrent requests and the y axis is the performance in terms of QPS. The benchmark shows a performance of 90,000 QPS with 26,000 concurrent requests!

More benchmarks are detailed here: https://redis.io/topics/benchmarks.

Data structures

Redis has a wealth of data structures, but not maps. Here is a non-exhaustive list of the data structures:

- **Lists**: Essentially a linked lists of string elements with elements in the order of insertion (first in, first out).
- **Sets**: Collections of unique, unsorted string elements.

- **Sorted sets**: A data structure similar to sets, but where every string element is associated with a score—which is a floating number. The elements inside the sorted set can be accessed (iterator) in order of the score. This allows use cases of leader board, such as "Top-10 performing hotels."
- **Hashes**: These are maps with an additional level of fields and associated values. This allows a partial update of the value (just a field) and efficient retrieval (all the fields of the hash).
- **Bitmap**: Bit arrays with constructs to set/clear individual bits, count all bits set to 1, find the first set bit, and so on.
- **HyperLogLogs**: `HyperLogLog` is a probabilistic data structure that can efficiently estimate the cardinality of a set. We will look at probabilistic data structures in detail later in the chapter.
- **Pub/sub**: This construct allows clients to send (publish) messages to an abstract channel and other clients (subscribers) to consume messages from the channels. Details of this paradigm are captured in `Chapter 6`, *Messaging*. It should be noted that there is no storage of messages—only those subscribers who are currently listening get published messages.

For more details, refer to `https://redis.io/commands`.

Persistence

Persistence in Redis is achieved either using snapshots or by journaling.

Snapshotting means periodic writes of all objects in memory to disk to files, called RBD files. By default, the periodicity values are one of the following:

- 10,000 changes in 60 seconds
- 10 changes in 5 minutes
- 1 change in 15 minutes

When a *write to disk* is needed, Redis forks a child process for the save and this process is responsible for serializing all the data in memory, writing the serialized data to a temporary file, and renaming the temporary file to the actual one. While the fork may seem expensive, it's not due to the copy-on-write semantics offered by most operating systems. A page will be duplicated only when there are changes to it either in the parent or child process. When a fork happens, in many OSes, such as Linux, the kernel cannot predict the actual space needed, just the worst case that all pages will be duplicated. Some OSes, such as Linux, will, by default, fail the fork if there is not as much free RAM as all the parent memory pages. In Linux this can be turned off with the `overcommit_memory` setting, and this is necessary for Redis, which hogs a lot of memory.

The other approach—journaling—works by logging every write operation done by the server. The logins are done by appending to a file—which is very efficient. The log can be replayed at server startup to reconstruct the original dataset. This mode is called the **append-only file** (**AOF**) mode.

The AOF mode provides more reliability but at a performance cost, since now all writes must be logged to disk. The default `fsync` policy is flushed every one second—but this comes with the risk of losing data. If, to avoid this, the setting is changed to `fsync` at every write, the performance of writes will be significantly slower. Another disadvantage of AOF is that for use cases such as counters, the file can get big very fast with very little value (the old counter values are not needed!).

I generally recommend you don't enable persistence but rather use high-availability solutions (described in the *Clustering* section). Also, data that is a single source of truth should ideally not be stored in Redis.

 This is not the only persistence done by Redis. It includes a hand-coded virtual-memory manager, which works for the same use cases as OS virtual memory swap (move unused memory parts to the disk to free up memory). It's described here: `http://oldblog.antirez.com/post/redis-virtual-memory-story.html` by Salvatore Sanfilippo (the creator of Redis), with explanations on why the OS virtual memory management was not good enough for Redis.

Clustering

Redis supports master-slave replication. A single master Redis server can have multiple Redis servers as slaves. Sentinel is a tool that provides HA using this base replication construct. It has features for the following:

- **Monitoring**: Ensures all Redis instances are working as expected.
- **Notification**: Notes whether something is wrong with any of the Redis instances.
- **Automatic failover**: If a master is not working as expected, Sentinel can promote a slave to a master and reconfigure the other slaves to use the new master.
- **Configuration provider**: Sentinel acts as a source of authority for clients' service discovery; clients connect to Sentinels in order to ask for the address of the current Redis master.

For more information, check out the following resources:

- `https://redis.io/topics/sentinel`
- Go Redis client support for Sentinel: `https://github.com/mediocregopher/radix.v2/tree/master/sentinel`

Very recently, Redis has also launched Redis Cluster. Here, keys are distributed across a set of nodes, with automatic rebalancing as new nodes are added/removed. The distribution is achieved by partitioning the keyspace, which is split into 16,384 slots, where each slot can be hosted on one of the Redis nodes. Specialized clients are needed to connect to the cluster, and each client has a topology mapping of shard-to-Redis-node instances. High availability is achieved by replicating data on more than one shard node. There are some limitations with Redis Cluster. More information is available at `https://redis.io/topics/cluster-tutorial`.

Use cases

Redis can be used for multiple use cases; some are described here:

- **Session cache**: One of the most common use cases of Redis is to store sessions, generally as hashes. The reason for this is that user sessions generally have a lot of I/O, since every API request from the user needs the session and often results in some updates. Keeping the sessions in a database is an option, but the performance characteristics don't make for good API performance. Redis is perfect for this use case, since the session information, though important, is not absolutely important. Thus, durability is not that big of a concern.

- **Application cache**: Redis can serve as an external cache for data that is otherwise in a database. This allows applications to store/access frequently accessed or rarely changing data from the cache and not incur the performance penalty of the usually slower database.

- **Distributed lists**: If you want to maintain lists, such as like *newest items*, across multiple application instances, the list data structure of Redis is a perfect fit. LPUSH/RPUSH can be used to push items at the head or tail of the list, respectively. Other commands, such as LTRIM/RTRIM, can be used to prune the lists.

- **Keeping stats**: Redis offers easy engineering of distributed counters. The INCRBY command can be used to increment counters atomically, while others, such as GETSET, allow for clearing of counters.

- **Queues and Pub/Sub**: Redis queues and pub/sub channels can be used to exchange messages, enabling features such as background workers.

Golang usage

Taking a pause from the theory, let's look at how we can use Redis in Go. At the time of writing this book, there are two main Redis clients in Go:

- Redigo (https://github.com/garyburd/redigo) provides a print-like API for Redis commands. It also supports pipelining, publish/subscribe, connection pooling, and scripting. It's easy to use and the reference is located at https://godoc.org/github.com/garyburd/redigo/redis.

- Radix (https://github.com/mediocregopher/radix.v2) provides easy-to-use packages for most Redis commands, including pipelining, connection pooling, publish/subscribe, and scripting, but it also provides clustering support. The Radix.v2 package is broken into six sub-packages (cluster, pool, pubsub, Redis, sentinel, and util).

As an example, we will take a feature where we want to maintain likes about a hotel in Redis. The following struct defines the entity we want to model:

```
type Hotel struct {
    Id          string
    Name        string
    City        string
    StarRating  int
    Likes       int
}
```

Here, we will use the Radix client. To install it, use the following command:

```
go get github.com/mediocregopher/radix.v2
```

The first step is, of course, connecting. This can be done as follows:

```
conn, err:= redis.Dial("tcp", "localhost:6379")
if err != nil {
        panic(err)
}
defer conn.Close()
```

The code connects to localhost. Of course, in production code, you should take this value as a configuration item.

Next, let's look at how we can save a hotel entity in Redis. The following code takes a hotel and saves it in Redis:

```
func setHotel(conn *redis.Client, h *Hotel) error {
    resp:= conn.Cmd("HMSET",
            "hotels:"+h.Id,
            "name", h.Name,
            "city", h.City,
            "likes", h.Likes,
            "rating", h.StarRating)
    if resp.Err != nil {
            fmt.Println("save err", resp.Err)
            return resp.Err
    }

    return nil
}
```

As you can see, we are using the hashes data structure to store likes. This is because we know that the likes attribute will be independently incremented. HMSET is a multiple set for the hash object. Each hotel is identified by the string with the concatenation of "hotels" with the id of the hotel.

The following code gets a hotel with a specific hotel from Redis:

```
func getHotel(conn *redis.Client, id string) (*Hotel, error) {
    reply, err:= conn.Cmd("HGETALL", "hotels:"+id).Map()
    if err != nil {
            return nil, err
    }

    h:= new(Hotel)
    h.Id = id
```

```
        h.Name = reply["name"]
        h.City = reply["city"]
        if h.Likes, err = strconv.Atoi(reply["likes"]); err != nil {
                fmt.Println("likes err", err)
                return nil, err
        }
        if h.StarRating, err = strconv.Atoi(reply["rating"]); err != nil {
                fmt.Println("ratings err", err)
                return nil, err
        }

        return h, nil
}
```

Here, we are using the HGETALL command to get all of the fields of a hash. Then, we use the Map() method of the response object to obtain a map of field names to the values. We then construct a hotel object from the individual fields.

Now, coming to the likes, which is a key method that required is to increment counts of a hotel. Along with maintaining counts, we also have a requirement of determining the most-liked hotels. To enable the latter requirement, we use a sorted-set dataset. The first code snippet implements a like for a hotel:

```
unc incrementLikes(conn *redis.Client, id string) error {

        //  Sanity check to ensure that the hotel exists!
        exists, err:= conn.Cmd("EXISTS", "hotels:"+id).Int()
        if err != nil || exists == 0 {
                return errors.New("no such hotel")
        }

        // Use the MULTI command to inform Redis that we are starting a new
        // transaction.
        err = conn.Cmd("MULTI").Err
        if err != nil {
                return err
        }

        // Increment the number of likes  for the hotel. in the album hash by 1.
        // Because we have initiated a  MULTI command, this HINCRBY command is
queued NOT executed.
        // We still check the reply's Err field  to check if there was an error
for the queing
        err = conn.Cmd("HINCRBY", "hotels:"+id, "likes", 1).Err
        if err != nil {
                return err
        }
```

```
        // Now we increment the leaderboard sorted set
        err = conn.Cmd("ZINCRBY", "likes", 1, id).Err
        if err != nil {
            return err
        }

        // Execute both commands in our transaction atomically.
        // EXEC returns the replies from both commands as an array
        err = conn.Cmd("EXEC").Err
        if err != nil {
            return err
        }
        return nil
    }
```

This uses the `MULTI` option of `redis` to start a transaction and update both the likes for a hotel and the `likes` sorted set atomically.

The following code snippet gets the top-three liked hotels:

```
func top3LikedHotels(conn *redis.Client) ([]string, error) {
    // Use the ZREVRANGE command to fetch the hotels from likes sorted set
    // with  the highest score first
    // The start and stop values are zero-based indexes, so we use 0 and 2
    // respectively to limit the reply to the top three.

    reply, err:= conn.Cmd("ZREVRANGE", "likes", 0, 2).List()
    if err != nil {
        return nil, err
    }

    return reply, nil

}
```

The `ZREVRANGE` command returns the sorted set members in reverse order of rank. Since it returns an array response, we use the `List()` helper function to convert the response to `[]string`.

Wide column stores

Wide column stores, or column-oriented database systems, are storage systems that store data by columns rather than by rows. For example, consider the following simple table:

FirstName	LastName	Age
John	Smith	42
Bill	Cox	23
Jeff	Dean	35

In an RBDMS, the tuples would be stored row-wise, so the data on the disk would be stored as follows:

```
John,Smith,42|Bill,Cox,23|Jeff,Dean,35
```

In **online-transaction-processing (OLTP)** applications, the I/O pattern is mostly reading and writing all of the values for entire records. As a result, row-wise storage is optimal for OLTP databases.

In a columnar database however, all of the columns are stored together. So, the tuples would be stored as follows:

```
John,Bill,Jeff|Smith,Cox,Dean|42,23,35
```

The advantage here is that if we want to read values such as `FirstName`, reading one disk block reads a lot more information in the row-oriented case. Another advantage, since each block holds the similar type of data, is that we can use efficient compression for the block, further reducing disk space and I/O.

Such databases are useful in analytics explanations. Examples include Amazon Redshift and Vertica. The details are outside the scope of this book.

Column family stores

An increasing prevalent new family of stores are column family stores, which partition rows so that a table can stride across multiple machines. On each machine, the row data is structured as a multidimensional sorted map. The distribution helps in scaling the store to a large amount of data, while the sorted attribute helps in doing things such as range scans. This design was first promulgated by the Google BigTable team (`https://ai.google/research/pubs/pub27898`).

In the following sections, we will take a detailed look at an example: Cassandra.

Cassandra deep-dive

Apache Cassandra is an open source implementation of the BigTable idea, but with other constructs as well. For example, it also incorporates several design principles of Amazon's Dynamo for fault-tolerance and data replication. Cassandra was developed at Facebook, but has been released as open source.

The following sections describe the Cassandra internals, and then we will write Go code to use Cassandra.

Data distribution

One simple way of partitioning rows over a set of nodes is to use hashing. You can pick a hash function, and use something such as `hash(key_x) % n_nodes` to get the node that would store the data for `key_x`. The problem with this scheme is that adding/deleting nodes would mean that the `hash(key_x) % n_nodes` values would change for pretty much all the keys, and thus cluster scaling would mean moving around a lot of data.

To get around this, Cassandra uses a concept called **consistent hashing**. We had looked at consistent hashing in `Chapter 5`, *Going Distributed*. Here is a quick recap:

Consider a circle with values on it ranging from [0-1], that is, any point on the circle has a value between `0` and `1`. Next, we pick a favorite hashing function and also scale it from [0-1]. For example, if the hash function has a range from [0-X], we use the following function:

```
ringKey= hash(key) % X
```

Using this function, we can map machines (instances) and objects (using the keys) on the [0-1] range.

If we have three machines, we use the modified hash function to map each machine to a point on the circle:

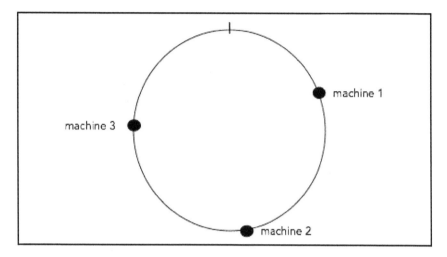

Now, we can see that the 0-1 range has been split into intervals among the machines. Suppose we have a key-value pair in the hash table. We need to do two things:

- Use the modified hash function to locate the key on the circle.
- Find the first machine that appears clockwise from that point and store the key there.

This is demonstrated in the following diagram:

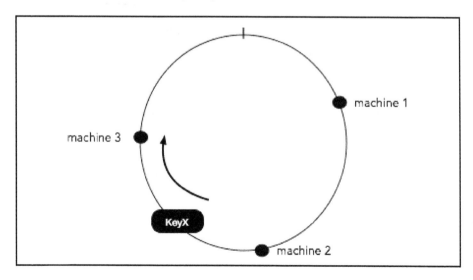

KeyX maps to a point and the machine closest from the clockwise side in **machine 3**. Hence, KeyX is assigned to `machine 3`.

From a programming perspective, *find closed machine clockwise* is easily achieved by storing the point values of the machines in a fashion that is easy to find *the next highest number after y*. One way is to use a linked list of machine hash values in a sorted order and to find the assignment. Just walk this list (or use binary search) to find the first machine with a hash value greater than, or equal to, the hash of the key. We can make this a circular list so that, if no machine with a "larger key" is found, the computation wraps around, and the first server in the list is assigned.

Now, let's say we add one more machine to the cluster, like so:

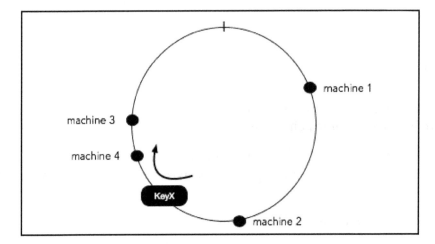

As you can see, most of the assignments are not affected by this change, which is in contrast to the naive hashing approach, where nearly every assignment changes. The only reassignment happens between the machine that originally was in the clockwise direction and the new one that was provisioned.

The partitioner in Cassandra is used to generate the token (equivalent to the hash in the preceding description) and thus is key to figuring out which node to go to for a given key. The default partitioner uses `MurmurHash` to compute hash values.

One issue with consistent hashing is that it is possible to have an unequal distribution of load – some machines might have more data or be busier than others. To overcome this, Cassandra (in v1.2) introduced the virtual nodes concept. The following diagram depicts this scheme:

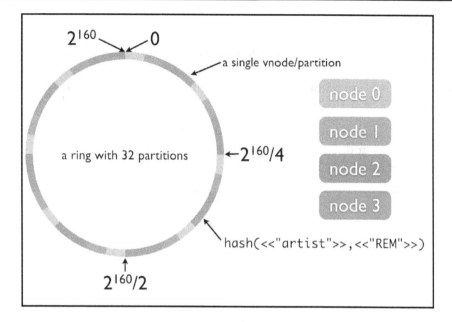

Here, instead of actual machines, a set of virtual nodes are assigned on the hash ring, and each machine gets an equal (but random) portion of vnodes.

Cassandra stores replicas on multiple nodes to ensure reliability and fault-tolerance. The number of actual copies is determined by the replication factor tuneable. How the replica nodes are chosen depends on the configured replication strategy. In the SimpleStrategy, once a node is found on the hash ring, the walk continues until the required number of replica nodes is found. More involved strategies consider rack, datacenter, and other properties of nodes, so that all replicas don't fall in to a single fault domain.

Whenever there is replication, there is a question of consistency. Cassandra delegates the consistency options to the clients via tunable consistency. Clients can select quorum levels for read/writes—choosing the right consistency value for each use case.

Write paths

Cassandra is masterless—there are no primary and secondary nodes/replicas. A client can connect with any node in the Cassandra cluster. Once connected, the node acts as the coordinator and drives the required interactions with the rest of the cluster on behalf of the client.

On a single node, Cassandra uses log-structured merge trees to store data. The life cycle of a write is as simple as updating an in-memory table of row/column values and writing to a commit log (so that durability is retained):

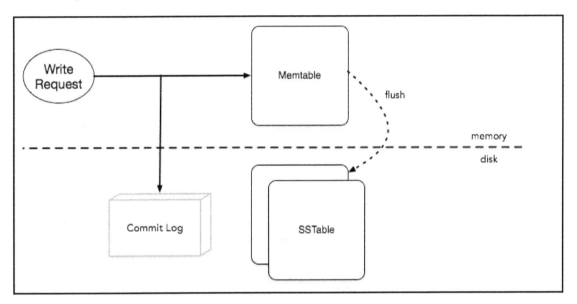

Periodically, the in-memory table (called **memtable**) is flushed to disk and the data is converted into SSTable format—where the keys are stored in sorted form. Obviously, this will lead to a large number of SSTables. To keep things sane, Cassandra does compaction, where multiple SSTables are merged into a single big one. Since each SSTable has keys in sorted order, the compaction operation is as efficient as a merge of multiple sorted lists. There are various algorithms for compaction—each to optimize for specific things, such as disk IO or read performance.

Read paths

The read path is not necessarily as efficient as the write path. To get the required columns for row, the read might need to get data from the memtable and various SSTables that might have different parts of the data. The read is effectively a merge across all these data structures:

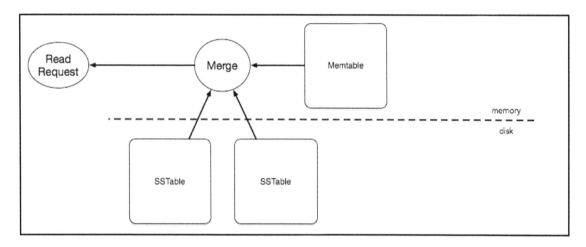

There are ancillary data structures, such as bloom filters, which help in figuring out whether an **SSTable** contains a given row, thereby avoiding reading (expensive disk I/O) for each **SSTable**. Compaction also helps read performance since the number of **SSTables** to be compared is reduced. The **SSTable** format includes an offset lookup, which helps in figuring out the offset within the **SSTable** file for a given key.

Golang usage

gocql (https://github.com/gocql/gocql) is a fast, popular Cassandra Go client that uses the native transport for communication with the Cassandra servers. Its various features are documented here: http://gocql.github.io/. We are going to use it to demonstrate Cassandra usage in Go. You can install it using the following command:

```
go get github.com/gocql/gocql
```

Let's continue with our employee example. We want to persist the following struct in Cassandra:

```
type User struct {
    Id        gocql.UUID
    FirstName string
    LastName  string
    Age       int
}
```

Here, ID is an UUID—each employee's unique ID in the system. The data type is borrowed from the `gocql` package.

To manage Cassandra, we use the `cqlsh` client. The first thing we do is create a keyspace in Cassandra. A keyspace is the equivalent of a database in the relational world. To do this, type the following at the cqlsh prompt:

```
CREATE KEYSPACE roster WITH replication = {'class': 'SimpleStrategy',
'replication_factor': 1};
```

 We can passing on tuneables about replication here.

Next, we create a table, called employees, in this keyspace:

```
create table employees (
id UUID,
firstname varchar,
lastname varchar,
age int,
PRIMARY KEY(id)
);
```

Now that Cassandra is prepped, let's write some Go code. The first thing to do is connect to the cassandra cluster. The following code accomplishes this:

```
// connect to the cluster
cluster:= gocql.NewCluster("127.0.0.1")
cluster.Keyspace = "roster"
session, _:= cluster.CreateSession()
defer session.Close()
```

The `gocql.NewCluster()` method takes the IP address(es) or hostname(s) of some of the nodes in the Cassandra clusters and lets the client discover the cluster topology. Next, using the cluster information, we create a session that will be used for doing the rest of the I/O.

Now, let's create a user and insert it into Cassandra:

```
// generate a unique id for the user
id:= gocql.TimeUUID()
// create the employee in memory
newEmployee:= User{
    Id:         id,
    FirstName:  "James",
    LastName:   "Bond",
    Age:        45,
}
// insert the employee
if err:= session.Query("INSERT INTO employees (id, firstname, lastname,
age ) VALUES (?, ?, ?, ?)",
    newEmployee.Id,
    newEmployee.FirstName,
    newEmployee.LastName,
    newEmployee.Age).Exec(); err != nil {
    fmt.Println("insert error")
    log.Fatal(err)
}
```

The `session.Query()` method takes a straight CQL string. The question marks (?) indicate positional parameters (as in standard SQL). These are substituted with the values given.

The following code shows the read and verifies that the employee was indeed inserted:

```
// Use select to get the employee we just entered
var userFromDB User

if err:= session.Query("SELECT id, firstname,  lastname, age FROM
employees WHERE id=?", id).Scan(&userFromDB.Id, &userFromDB.FirstName,
&userFromDB.LastName, &userFromDB.Age); err != nil {
    fmt.Println("select error")
    log.Fatal(err)
}
fmt.Println(userFromDB)
```

This should print the James Bond employee and show that the data was inserted correctly.

Next, we update the data:

```
// Update James's Bond's age
if err:= session.Query("UPDATE employees SET age = 46 WHERE id = ?",
id).Exec(); err != nil {
    fmt.Println("udpate error")
    log.Fatal(err)
}
```

We can see that James Bond is indeed grown a year older by doing a read:

```
var newAge int
// Select and show the change
iter:= session.Query("SELECT age FROM employees WHERE  id = ?", id).Iter()
for iter.Scan(&newAge) {
    fmt.Println(newAge)
}
if err:= iter.Close(); err != nil {
    log.Fatal(err)
}
```

This should print 46.

Finally, we delete James Bond from our employee roster:

```
// Delete the employe
if err:= session.Query("DELETE FROM employees WHERE id = ?", id).Exec();
err != nil {
    fmt.Println("delete error")
    log.Fatal(err)
}
```

Patterns for scaling data performance

So far, we have looked at various fundamental methods of modeling data. In some cases, we need to make a few tweaks to the canonical way of interacting with data to enable performance of a few use cases. This section talks about these types of patterns.

Sharding

A singleton database, however beefy, has limitations in terms of storage space and compute resources. A single server is also not great in terms of availability. Storage systems such as Cassandra distribute data by partitioning data opaquely. However, many systems (including most RDBMS systems) don't partition data internally.

The solution is sharding. This refers to dividing the data store into a set of horizontal partitions or shards. Each shard has the same schema, but holds its own distinct set of rows. Thus, each shard by itself is a database. The application (or driver) knows how to route requests for specific data onto certain shards. The benefits are as follows:

- The system can be scaled by adding additional shards/nodes
- Load is balanced across shards, thereby reducing contention for resources
- Intelligent placement strategies can be employed to locate data close to the computes that need it

In the cloud, shards can be located physically close to the users that'll access the data – this can improve scalability when storing and accessing large volumes of data.

Distributing data is not that tough. If specific affinity is not required, distribution can be done via a hash function. However, the challenge is in the redistribution of data when the topology changes, as described in the *Cassandra deep-dive* section. There are three main approaches to solve the lookup problem:

- **Consistent Hashing**: We covered this in the Cassandra cluster earlier.
- **Client-side Routing**: Clients have a lookup map to figure out which shard (node) hosts a particular key (hash). Whenever there is a topology change, the clients get updated maps. Redis Cluster does sharding in this way.
- **Brokered Routing**: There is a central service that takes IO requests and routes them to the appropriate shard based on a topology map. MongoDB sharding follows this approach.

Denormalization

The normalization process aims to remove redundancy in the modeled data. This leads to efficient updates, where writes don't need to update data at many places for overall consistency and data integrity.

However, there are limitations to this approach. One major limitation is performance: certain reads many need so many database operations (joins, scans, and so on) that they become computationally intractable. For example, let's say we have a use case of having resellers on the travel website. These people would take inventory and do bookings for customers as normal travel agents, in lieu of fees (paid at the end of every month) from the travel website. Let's say the bookings are modeled as follows:

- Bookings:
    - BookingId
    - Date
    - SKU
    - ResellerId
    - Amount
    - Fee
- Resellers:
    - ResellerId
    - Name
    - Address

Here, the `ResellerID` in the bookings table is a foreign key to the resellers table. Whenever a booking is done, the `ResellerId` and the applicable fees are populated by the booking DB transaction.

Now, there is a new requirement for an agent to figure out the total fees due to him in the current month. This can be engineered by doing a `GROUP BY ResellerID` on the bookings table, scanning for the required time range, and then doing a summation of the fees. However, this performance might not be acceptable and based on the isolation levels defined might cause bottlenecks in the write (business critical) path. One way to solve this problem is to maintain a count of fees due for the current month in the resellers table itself, like so:

- ResellerId
- Name
- Address
- Fees due

Every time a booking is made, the DB transaction adds the fees of the current booking to the fees due column; getting the current fees due is a matter of a simple table lookup. The trade-off we made, of course, is that the write path needs to do a bit more work in maintaining this aggregated data. In many cases, this trade-off is very much a sane choice.

 It is important that the update for the denormalized schema happens in a transaction.

Another reason we might want to do denormalization is to maintain history of the change. Normalized schema retain the *current state* of the system, and many times a use case calls for a *change log*. Denormalization helps here by maintaining the changes made in a separate model from the *current state* of data.

Materialized views

What happens when read performance is needed on many more *counters*, such as a fees due one? You can make the write transaction fatter by keeping the multiple denormalized tables updated, but at some point the overhead is going to be overbearing. Also, the counter or *view* needed of the data might have a business domain that is distinct from the one in which the event originally happened. Thus, trying to update all views might lead to a breach of the *separation of concerns* principle.

An alternative pattern to handle this situation is event sourcing and materialized views.

In event sourcing, the service doing the business transaction emits an event describing the change. In the case of the preceding Booking example, it can be a Booking Event. This event is sent out on a messaging Topic, thus employing a PubSub mechanism to broadcast the event to whoever is interested.

Materialized Views refers to utilizing the event and then constructing an aggregated/consolidated view, which is necessary to power a specific use case. To put it in another way, the data is *materialized* in a way best suited to a specific view. In the Booking example, another way to source the Fees due might be to have a separate service host the Fees Due API/view and construct the fees for each reseller based on the booking event. Let's say there are new requirements, say, *bookings done in the last 10 minutes*—then such a use case can be satisfied by a new API, which uses the same Booking event.

The trade-off in Materialized View versus denormalization is that one loses temporal consistency—the system eventually becomes consistent. The benefit is, of course, the extensibility of the solution.

Summary

In this chapter, we covered entity modeling, consistency guarantees, and looked at various database options. We did a deep-dive into MySQL, Cassandra, and Redis, and wrote Go code to get a hands-on perspective on how to use them to model data. We ended this chapter with a section on patterns to handle data performance when scaling.

In the next chapter, we will look at building highly reliable, fault-tolerant systems.

9
Anti-Fragile Systems

In *Nassim Taleb's* book *Antifragile*, he discusses behavior in complex systems and classifies them into three types:

- **Fragile**: These systems shatter when exposed to medium amounts of stress.
- **Robust/Resilient**: These systems are better than Fragile at handling stress, but are still vulnerable to low-probability failures.
- **Antifragile**: These systems have the thickest skin, and actually get stronger under stress. An example of this is the human body—when stressed at the right levels, muscles/bones get stronger:

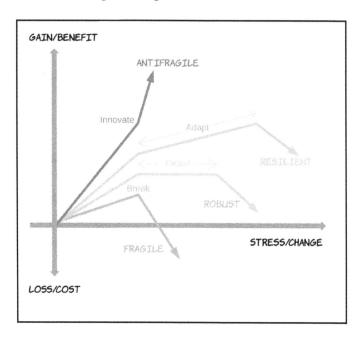

(Source: https://developers.redhat.com/blog/2016/07/20/from-fragile-to-antifragile-software/)

Software systems play a vital aspect in everyday life; consumers expect systems to be always on. A great deal of the architect's brain cycles is spent on ensuring reliability and fault-tolerance, which is the ability for a system to remain operational in the face of a few individual components failing. The cost of not meeting these expectations would be crippling to the business. Every minute of downtime translates to dollars in lost revenue, not to mention negative customer impressions.

Failures can crop up for various reasons; they manifest themselves not just due to coding bugs (such as memory leaks), but also due to infrastructure issues (such as disks failing). Modern software systems often end up depending on each other and external entities, so designing reliable systems gets even tougher.

Often, systems don't perform as expected, especially if stressed. This chapter explores architecting anti-fragile systems that thrive under stress; we will cover the following topics:

- Reliability metrics
- Engineering reliability—architecture patterns for ensuring high-availability
- Verification of reliability—ensuring that the system is tested for resiliency through unit tests, integration test, load tests, and chaos-testing
- Building resilience for dependencies
- Datacenter resilience

Let's begin our journey by taking a more formal look at what we mean by reliability. After that, we will look at what it means to make a service resilient, and then move on and look at a set of systems and dependents, and how we can engineer antifragility in the overall product.

Reliability metrics

IEEE defines software reliability as the probability of failure-free software operation for a specified period of time in a given environment. Building reliability into software first necessitates defining the metrics by which we will measure reliability, so that we know the current state and we can measure the effect of any changes. Different people have different viewpoints on what reliability in a software system means:

- Conforms to requirements
- Whether the system actually fulfils its purpose
- User satisfaction

It is useful to take all these perspectives into account when considering how reliable a system is and how it can get better. There are various metrics to measure the reliability of a software system, and they can be broadly classified as dynamic and static.

Dynamic metrics

Dynamic Metrics have the following characteristics:

- **Mean Time To Failure (MTTF)**: MTTF is defined as the time interval between the successive failures. An MTTF of 200 means that 1 failure can be expected every 200 time units.
- **Availability**: A measure of how long a service has been working without a fault. An availability of 0.995 means that in every, 1000 time units, the system is likely to be available for 995 of these. The percentage of time that a system is available for use, taking into account planned and unplanned downtime. If a system is down an average of 4 hours out of 100 hours of operation, then its availability is 96%.
- **Service-level agreements (SLA)**: These are definitions on how well the system is performing. An example of such a metric is API response latency; here clients expect a guarantee on the upper limit of the response time for various APIs.
- **Robustness**: The extent to the system tolerates unexpected inputs, scenarios, and problems.
- **Consistency and precision**: The extent to which software is consistent and gives results with precision.
- **Customer satisfaction/Net Promoter Score (NPS)**: This is the *most* important of all metrics and defines how well the system is serving its objective. Satisfaction with the overall reliability and quality of the system is usually obtained through various methods of customer survey on either a 5-point or 10-point scale.

Static metrics

These metrics typically measure the code quality and provide an indication of its reliability. Generally, metrics under static metrics include the following:

- **Cyclomatic complexity**: This is a quantitative measure of the complexity of a program. It is derived from the number of linearly independent paths through a program's source code. Generally, complex programs are much harder to engineer reliability into.
- **Defect amount and rate**: How many open defects are there against the production system? How many bugs are created with 100 lines of code?
- **Review/QC rejects**: This metric defines how many times a code check-in is rejected by code reviewers or QC. This is a good indicator of the quality of the code written by the developers.
- **Testability**: The amount of effort required to test the system and ensure that it performs its intended functions.
- **Maintainability**: The effort required to locate and fix an error during regular maintenance.

With this context, let's look at multiple facets of reliability in a modern microservices architecture.

Engineering reliability

As a quick recap from Chapter 5, *Going Distributed*, we saw that microservices interact with one another over the network using either APIs or Messaging. The basic idea is that, using a specific protocol, microservices will exchange data in a standardized format over the network to enable macro-behavior and fulfill the requirement. There are multiple places where things can go wrong here, as shown in the following diagram:

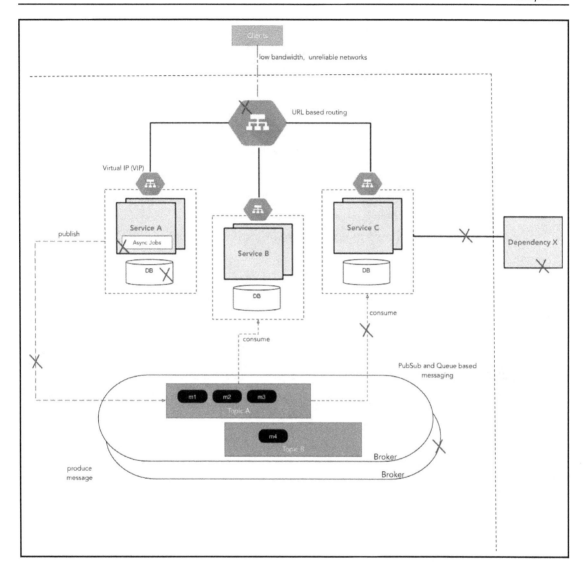

Preceding diagram is described as follows:

- A service may go down either during the service of a request from the client, or when it's idle. The service may go down because the machine went down (hardware/hypervisor errors) or because there was an uncaught exception in the code.

- A database hosting persistent data may go down. The durable storage might get corrupted. The DB can crash in the middle of a transaction!

- A service may spawn an in-memory job, respond with OK to the client, and then go down, removing any reference to the job.
- A service may consume a message from the broker but may crash just before acting on it.
- The network link between two services may go down or be slow.
- A dependent external service may start acting slow or start throwing errors.

Reliability in a system is engineered at multiple levels:

- Individual services are built as per the specification and work correctly
- Services are deployed in a high-availability setup so that a backup/alternate instance can take the place of an unhealthy one
- The architecture allows the composite of individual services to be fault-tolerant and rugged

We will look at dependency management in couple of the *Dependencies* and *Dependency resilience* section. For the rest, we will cover engineering reliability in the following subsections.

Rugged services

The building blocks of a resilient architecture are the services themselves. If they are not built to last, then all other aspects don't help much. Building resilient services involves two things:

- The service is built to the expected specs. This is covered in the *Reliability verification* section.
- The service does not have any local state.

As we saw in Chapter 4, *Scaling Applications*, having stateless computation is the key to scalability. Not having local state is also important in terms of building resilience in the system. A stateless app can be deployed in a cluster of redundant service instances, any request can be serviced by any of the available instances. On the other hand, if the service is designed to have local state, the failure one instance brings can cause outage at the system level (albeit to a subset of the customers). A common way in which local state crops up is when then is an it's in-memory store for cache or for user sessions. To enable resilience, such state should be externalized, say, in a store such as Redis (Redis resiliency is covered in detail in Chapter 8, *Modeling Data*).

With these expectations on individual services in place, the architect can have a system-wide lens to ensure that the system consists of multiple services, and the multiple instances of each service itself are resilient.

High availability

Would you go live with your service running on a single machine? Of course not! The machine going down, or a disk failing on the server, will bring down the entire service and affect customers. The machine becomes a **single point of failure (SPOF)**:

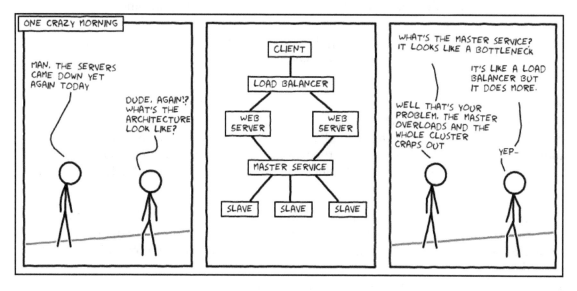

(Source: http://timkellogg.me/blog/2013/06/09/dist-sys-antipatterns)

Single points of failure can be removed by engineering redundancy—which means having multiple instances of the service/resource. Redundancy can be architected in two modes:

- **Active Mode:** If, as described in service-level reliability engineering, the service is stateless, redundancy is easily achieved by having multiple instances. If one fails, that load/traffic can be diverted to another healthy instance. We will see how this is done in the *Routing and health* section.
- **Standby Mode:** For stateful resources (such as databases), just having multiple instances is not sufficient. In this mode, when a resource fails, functionality is recovered on a secondary instance using a process called failover. This process will typically require some time, in order for the backup instance to gain state/content—but during this time, there will be unavailability. It is possible to minimize this time by having the secondary resource pre-launched but in a dormant state, and having state/context-sharing between the active and standby instance.

A system is said to be highly available when it can withstand the failure of an individual component (servers, disks, network links). Running multiple instances is not enough to build fault-tolerance. The key to the high availability of the system is that failures in individual instances don't bring down the whole system. This mandates reliable routing of requests to a healthy instance so that unhealthy instances don't get production traffic and compromise the health of the service as a whole.

To detect faults, you first need to find a measure of health. Health is relevant both at the host (or instance) level and the overall service level. A service is typically deployed with multiple instances behind a **virtual IP** (**VIP**) supported by a **load balancer** (**LB**). The LB should route requests to only those service instances that are healthy—but how does the LB know about instance health? Generally, there are periodic health check pings to a designated URL on the service (`/health`). If the instance responds with a normal response, we know it's healthy, otherwise it should be booted out of the pool maintained by the LB for that VIP. These checks run in the background periodically.

Many developers do engineer the `/health` URL, but hardcode a 200 OK response. This isn't a great idea. Ideally, the service instance should collect metrics about various operations and errors in the service and the health response handler should analyze these metrics to get a measure of the instance's health.

Network health is usually monitored and made resilient by the networking protocols such as IP and TCP. They figure out optimal routes across redundant links and handle faults such as dropped, out-of-order, or duplicate packets.

 This section assumes the server-side discovery of instances. As we saw in Chapter 5, *Going Distributed*, client-side service discovery is also possible. It comes with its own high-availability solutions, but these are outside the scope of this book.

Messaging

A reliable message delivery platform is the key to engineering a data pipeline in a microservices architecture. Once a message is received by a messaging solution (brokers), it should guarantee the following:

- The loss of a single broker instance does not affect the availability of the message for consumers.
- If producers and consumers experience outages/restarts, certain delivery semantics are honored. Generally, the semantics are as follows:
    - **At-least-once delivery:** The messaging system guarantees that a message is delivered at least once to a consumer. It is possible that duplicate messages are received, and the consumer is responsible for the deduplication of messages.
    - **At-most-once delivery:** The messaging solution guarantees that messages are delivered at most once. Some messages might get dropped.
    - **Exactly-once delivery:** A message is guaranteed to be delivered exactly once for each consumer. Generally, this guarantee is difficult to engineer without some sort of consumer-broker coordination.

To build reliability, a key messaging design pattern is called the competing consumers pattern. Multiple concurrent consumers can consume messages from the same topic, thereby enabling redundancy—as shown here:

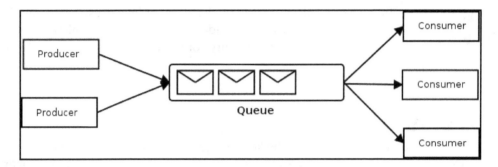

Besides the resiliency and availability benefit, such a pattern also enables the system to work at a higher throughput, and improves scalability (since the number of consumers can be increased/decreased on demand).

Another advantage of message-based interaction is the shock absorber behavior that queues bring in. With an API-based interaction, the consumer has to consume requests at the same rate at which the producer is making them. This impedance matching of all producers and consumers can be difficult to engineer in a non-trivial architecture. Message queues act as a buffer between the producer and the consumer, so that consumers can work at their own pace. The queues also smooth out intermittent heavy loads that otherwise could have caused failures.

Messaging architectures and related resiliency patterns are covered in detail in Chapter 6, *Messaging*.

The asynchronous computation pattern

Consider a typical sequence of an API flow:

1. Client calls service: POST/dosomework.
2. Service spawns a goroutine to handle the API request.
3. The API processing is involved and takes some time. The handler also needs to call an external dependency (DependencyI) to get the work done.
4. The client waits for the service to finish the work.

What can go wrong here? Well, multiple things! Consider the following:

- The client service interconnect network might experience a discontinuity. The client's socket will be closed and it will most likely retry. This is especially common if the communication is happening over the internet/WAN.
- If the client retry occurs, the Service might have already progressed in handling of /dosomework. Database entries might have been created, hotels booked, and so on. The service needs to ensure that such handling is idempotent!
- DependencyI might be down—or worse, take a long time to respond. In this case, if the client retries, DependencyI will also need to be idempotent.
- Since /dosomework takes some time, and the client is waiting for the response, the web service serving the request will need to exclusively assign resources while the operation is in progress.

Machines/networks can often go down. It is important that the software architecture is resilient to such failures and provides efficiency and consistency guarantees. One way to solve this issue is to have an async architecture. The service can just log (in durable storage) that such-and-such client requires /dosomework, and responds with a job ID. A bunch of background workers can then pick up this job and fulfill it. The client can gauge the progress of the job through a separate URL. This architecture pattern is depicted here:

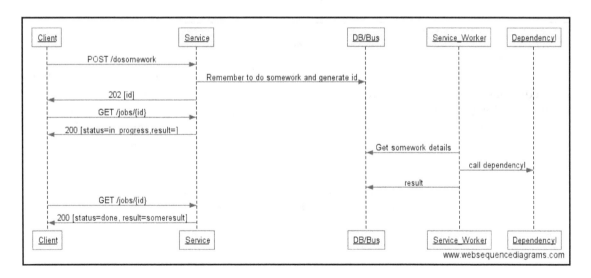

Messaging systems such as Kafka (covered in detail in Chapter 6, *Messaging*) lend themselves well to performing this log-a-job pattern.

A well-documented example of this architecture is the grep-the-web sample architecture for AWS, as described by Jeff Barr in his whitepaper (`https://aws.amazon.com/blogs/aws/white-paper-on/`):

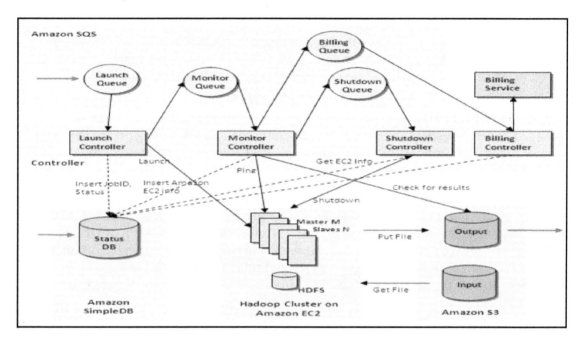

(Source: https://aws.amazon.com/blogs/aws/white-paper-on/)

This problem statement is to build a solution that runs a regular expression against millions of documents from the web and returns the results that match the query. The operation is meant to be long-running and involve multiple stages. Also, the deployment is assumed to be an elastic one in the cloud—where machines (**virtual machines (VMs)**) can do down without being noticed. As shown in the preceding diagram, the solution architecture consists of the following:

- **Launch Controller:** This service takes a grep job and spawns/monitors the rest of the services in the pipeline. The actual grep is done by MapReduce jobs using Hadoop.
- **Monitoring Controller:** It monitors the MapReduce job, updates the status in the **Status DB**, and writes the final output.
- **Status DB:** All services update the current stage, status, and metrics of the pipeline for each job in this DB.

- **Billing Controller:** Once a Job is scheduled, it's also provisioned for billing through the **Billing Queue** and the **Billing Controller**. This service has all the knowledge of how to bill the customer for each job.
- **Shutdown Controller:** Once a job is finished, the **Monitoring Controller** enqueues a message in the **Shutdown Queue**, and this triggers the **Shutdown Controller** to clean up after the job is down.

Here are some salient features of the architecture:

- The architecture follows the async design pattern.
- The system is tolerant of machine failures. A job stage carries on from the stage where the job failed.
- There is no coupling between the services (controllers). If needed, behavior can be extended by plugging in new queues and controllers, with a high level of confidence that the current processing won't break.
- Each stage (controller) of the job can be independently scaled.

The orchestrator pattern

The grep-the-web architecture is an implementation of the orchestrator pattern. This pattern is generally used for application workflows, which involve a number of steps, some of which are long-winded, or which might access remote services. The individual steps are generally independent of each other, but need to be orchestrated by some application logic.

The solution consists of the following roles:

- **Scheduler:** The orchestrator sets up the workflow graph of various steps to be performed and initiates the processing. This component is responsible for spawning Agents and passing on any parameters needed for each Agent.
- **Agent:** This is a container for running each step, and usually involves calling external services to perform the required step in the workflow. It generally employs the Hystrix pattern (see the *Dependency resilience* section) to ensure that it is insulated from the vagaries of the external service. There is typically one Agent spawned for each step.

- **Supervisor :** This monitors the status of the various steps being performed. It also ensures that the tasks run to completion and reconciles any failures that might occur. Periodically, this service also records the state of the workflow, such as *not yet started*, or *step X running*. It can also time individual steps to ensure that they finish within a certain budget. If it detects any agent to have timed out or failed, it arranges for a fallback action from that agent. Note that the actual fallback action has to be implemented by the agent; the supervisor just requests that the action be performed.

Generally, communication between these components happens through messaging queues. Often, the scheduler and supervisor roles are implemented in one orchestrator component.

The compensating-transaction pattern

A question arises in such a scenario, let's say the services want to have some sort of transactional semantics—either all the services finish successfully or none do. To keep things simple, let's assume that isolation (simultaneous operations not seeing intermediate state) is not required. This is a common use case for complex workflows (say, the fulfillment of booking on our travel website), where multiple actions need to happen with a possible modification of different data stores. In such scenarios, providing strong consistency semantics will not be scalable due to the distributed nature of the environment and contention due to the scale, and hence the architecture follows the async pattern. With this eventual consistency model, while these stages are being performed, the aggregate view of the system state might be inconsistent. However, when the stages are completed, all the services and data stores are consistent.

So, back to the original question—what happens if one service fails? How do the other services roll back their updates? A couple of immediate thoughts should spring into the mind of the astute architect:

- To honor the separation of concerns principle, the only component that can handle the undo is the service itself.
- The undo architecture should not add extra constraints to the scalable architecture. Therefore a central undo service won't be that great, since it would defeat the purpose of a distributed solution that can be composed of various stages.

The solution is for each service to implement compensating transactions. When performing this compensating transaction, the service rolls back the effects of the original operation. The rollbacks are typically also implemented through a queue, but here the messages are from the reverse direction. This pattern is similar to the one called *Sagas* by Clemens Vasters, in his blog (`http://vasters.com/clemensv/2012/09/01/Sagas.aspx`); it's depicted in the following diagram:

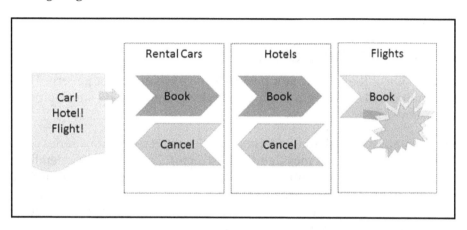

The compensation-transaction messages typically carry an identifier of the operation that needs to be rolled back, with the following expectations:

- The ID is common across all services.
- Each service knows what is to be done for undo, and maintains a database of job containing parameters for the undo.

It should be noted that the compensating-transaction logic cannot trivially replace the current state with the state at the time before the operation, since it might overwrite other operations that may have subsequently happened. For example, if a service is maintaining the number of requests in the grep-the-web example, it won't manage a DB, as follows:

Job ID	Count
job-id-123	44

Instead, here is a better way of storing parameters to enable the undo, which in this case can be the delta that the job did:

Job ID	Delta
job-id-123	+2

This is the crux of the compensation in the compensating-transactions pattern.

 This pattern assumes that the roll forward and rollback steps are idempotent. Messaging solutions generally implement at-least-once semantics and duplicate messages often crop up. The services utilizing this pattern should deduplicate messages before performing any operation.

The pipes and filter pattern

A simplified version of the orchestrator pattern is the pipes and filter pattern. This pattern extends the familiar Unix paradigm of simple-services-connected-by-smart-pipes to distributed systems.

This pattern decomposes a task that involves complex processing into a series of separate filters, which are connected by a messaging infrastructure, called *pipes*. Generally, each filter is a service with a specific contract—in terms on the expected input format. These filters can be reused so that more than one task can use the same filter to perform a specific action. This helps to avoid duplicating code, and makes it easy to handle changes in requirements by adding or removing filters from an org-wide set of the `filter` library. For more information, you can refer to https://docs.microsoft.com/en-us/azure/architecture/patterns/pipes-and-filters:

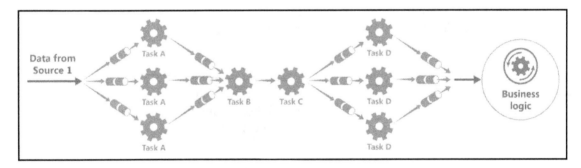

Hotspots

Every service has a breaking point—a maximum load for which it was designed. If the load exceeds this, the service can become unreliable. In a microservices architecture, requests are fulfilled by multiple services working in conjunction. This can cause hot spots on specific utility services, which are used by more than one service. A classic case is a **User Account Service**, which is the repository for all user-level data. For example, in the following diagram, the **User Account Service** is called by multiple services, for user-related information, and this service becomes a hotspot:

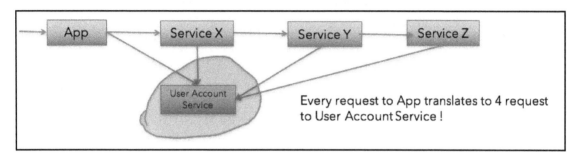

One solution to the problem is to carry the required data in every service call, like so:

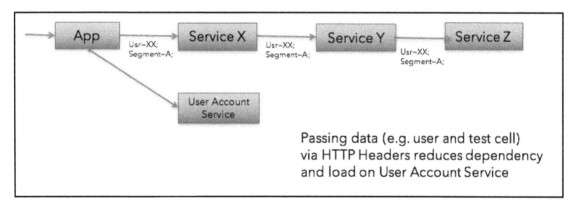

The tradeoff here is the increased amount of data that is carried in each microservice call.

The sidecar pattern

Many services need ancillary functionalities, such as monitoring, logging, or configuration. One choice is to implement these inside the main application code base, but then there are a few concerns:

- Our single-purpose principle is compromised. Changes will creep into the application for requirements that are not directly related to the responsibility of the service.
- Any bugs/crashes in any of the components will cause outages in the service.
- These components need to be built in the same language/runtime as the the main application. If there are readily available solutions, in different forms, they can't be directly reused.

The Sidecar pattern proposes an alternative—colocate these ancillary tasks with the main service, but host them inside in their own process or container, rather than in-process with the main application. The name comes from the similarity of how the sidecar services are deployed with the main application to how a sidecar is attached to a motorcycle.

The advantages of using a sidecar pattern include the following:

- Independence from its primary application in terms of runtime and programming language, thus enabling reuse
- **Locality**: Results in reduced communication latency as well as efficient sharing of resources, such as files
- **Resiliency**: Any sidecar that goes down does not bring down the main application

The sidecar pattern is often employed with container-based deployments, and these are usually referred to as sidecar/sidekick containers.

Throttling

The load on a service can vary over time (time of the day/year) as user behavior and the number of active users vary. Sometimes, there might be unexpected bursts or ramps in traffic. Every service is built and deployed with a specific load capacity in mind. If the processing requests exceed this capacity, the system will fail.

There are two options in terms of solving for a high load:

- When the load is genuine, we increase capacity (the number of servers, service instances, network capacity, DB nodes, and so on) to meet the increased traffic.
- When the load is not genuine/business critical, analyze and control the requests, that is, throttle the request.

Some throttling strategies include the following:

- Rejecting requests from an individual user whose crossed the assigned quota (say, making more than n requests/second to a specific API). This requires the system to meter the use of resources for each tenant per resource. A common way to implement throttling is to do it at the load-balancer level. For example, Nginx uses the Leaky Bucket algorithm for rate-limiting requests. Rate-limiting is configured with two main directives: `limit_req_zone` and `limit_req`. The first parameter defines what resource we are limiting and the throttle. The other directive is used in location blocks to actually implement the throttling. See `https://www.nginx.com/blog/rate-limiting-nginx/` for more details.

The objective of a leaky bucket algorithm is to smooth out a variable/burst rate of input to produce a steady output rate so that the capacity of the target resource is not exceeded. At a high level, implementation can be thought of a FIFO queue where the incoming requests are stored. At a set clock tick, n requests are dequeued and sent to the service for processing—here, n is the target output rate we are aiming for. We can add more intelligence to this basic concept by factoring things such as effort estimate for each request, rather than blindly taking in a set number of requests at each clock tick. The algorithm is described in the following diagram:

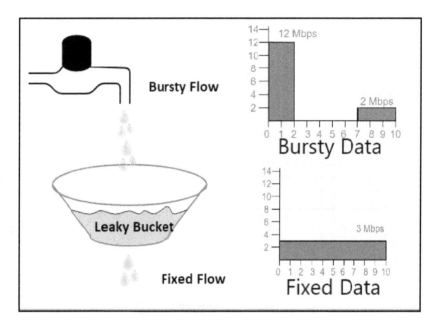

- Disabling or degrading a specific functionality so that instead of the whole service going down, a *graceful degrade* happens. For example, for a video streaming service, if the link is bad, a switch to a lower resolution can be made.
- Using message-based queues to stagger the load and make computation asynchronous (delayed).

Versioning

The last aspect of reliability is engineering for continuous evolvement of the microservices. Often, services have multiple clients and refactoring drives. During this course, the advertised contract (or spec) of the service changes. However, not all clients can move to the new version of the contract at the same time. Improper updates/deprecation of APIs/contracts is an often-ignored cause of instability and unreliability in microservice-based architectures.

The way to insulate your clients is through proper versioning of the APIs. Generally, this happens by adding a version number to the API URLs, like so:

```
/v1/hotels/add
/v1/hotels/search
/v1/hotels/<hotel_id>
/v1/hotels/<hotel_id>/book
..
```

When a new contract is needed to be deployed, we just upgrade the version and deploy the new routes effectively to the web servers and LBs. It is necessary for all the versions to be served from the same set of web server instances; the LB can route old versions to an older deployment so that the new code does not need to carry the baggage of old code.

In the next section, we will study reliability verification and the types of tests involved in it.

Reliability verification

As we saw in Chapter 1, *Building Big with Go*, a *contract* for a service is a definition of various operations that the service provides, with a clear definition of output for a set of expected input. This is also sometimes called the spec (short for specification). The spec might also include non-functional requirements, such as expected budgets for latencies of specific APIs and the expected throughput for which the service guarantees the response times.

The following diagram shows a relative graph of the costs of bugs at various stages of the software life cycle:

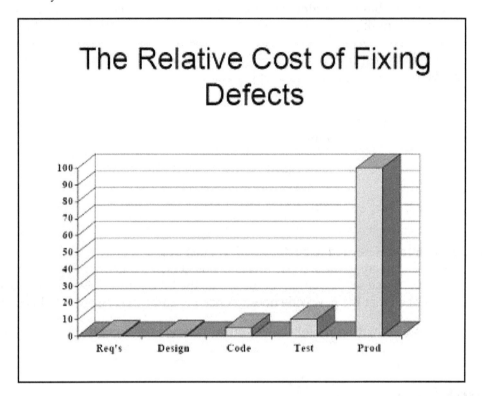

Source: http://jonkruger.com/blog/2008/11/20/the-relative-cost-of-fixing-defects/

As changes are made to the service, it must guarantee that the contract is always honored. Generally, the contracts flux, with an addition in functionality, but they should be backward compatible (ideally). A service designed in this manner will enable a robust architecture, while also allowing for the feature velocity that the business demands.

The goal of verifying service-level quality attributes is to first ensure that none of its advertised contracts (functional as well as non-functional) are broken. This validation is done via a regression test suite. This suite is best described by Mike Cohen's test pyramid diagram:

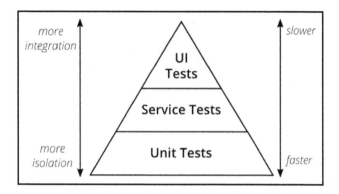

Source: https://www.mountaingoatsoftware.com/blog/the-forgotten-layer-of-the-test-automation-pyramid

The tests at the bottom of the pyramid focus more on code constructs; that is, making sure that individual modules are working as expected. The test higher up, and verifies the behavior from the user's perspective.

The key to finding bugs for a service early is having a regressions test suite that can be run early and often to ensure quality.

The constituents of a regression suite include the following:

- Unit tests
- Integration tests
- Performance tests

We will learn about each of these tests in detail in the following sections.

Unit tests

The scope of unit testing is to test individual modules (classes/functions) of the service. These are generally supported by a variety of frameworks (most of which are language-specific). Golang has a very powerful, in-built testing framework, as we saw in `Chapter 1`, *Building Big with Go*. Also, even though it is a strongly-typed language, packages such as reflect (`reflect.DeepEqual`) allow one to do a deep comparison of arbitrary data, such as expected versus got.

The units tests need two accompanying frameworks:

- **Mock/Stub:** When testing a specific module, we need other downstream-dependent components to fulfill behavior. Sometimes calling the live component may not be possible (sending an email via a live email service may not be an option, as we want to avoid annoying customers with spam). We should either mock or stub out the dependent modules so that we can exercise the code through various interesting paths. There is a subtle difference between mocks and stubs: mocks generally take a specification of what output to generate based on specific input. Stubs, on the other hand, are just canned answers. In the case of Golang, we saw in `Chapter 2`, *Packaging Code*, these can be done via service mocks or build flags. Another way to do it is using the go-mock package (`https://github.com/golang/mock_`). This package inspects source code and generates mock implementations for them.
- **Automation:** These should be automated so that they can be run on every commit, thereby solving bugs at the earliest possible stage. The Golang testing package (`https://golang.org/pkg/testing/`) provides comprehensive support for automated tests.

Your unit tests should run very fast. On normal developer machines, you can easily run thousands of unit tests within a few minutes. It is important to keep each test focused on small pieces of code, running in isolation.

Test-driven development (TDD) encourages taking this to the next level by writing unit tests even before writing code. The UTs guide the developer on what is missing during the development sprints.

A common issue with unit tests is they are tightly coupled to the implementation of the tested function that is implemented. This means that slight changes in the code need changes in the unit tests. The **behavior-driven development** (BDD) test tries to address this problem by focusing tests on behavior rather than implementation. BDD tests are written in a **domain-specific language** (DSL), which is more of the English prose style than other types of tests. GoConvey (`http://goconvey.co/`) is an excellent package for Go-based BDD tests. It builds on Go's native testing and coverage frameworks and adds a new layer of expressive DSL to write tests cases. It also has a UI for a better visualization of test results:

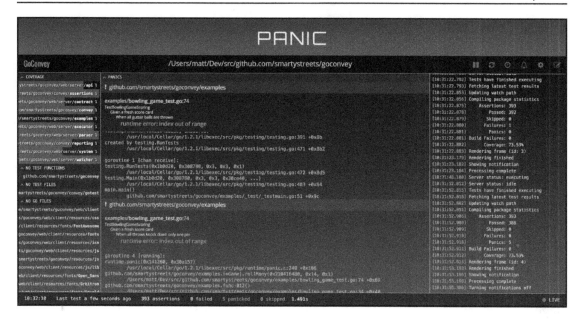

Integration tests

Once a service has been verified in isolation, it should be tested along with its dependents in a specific integration or stage environment. Services are rarely used in isolation, and these tests verify that the new build works in conjunction with other dependents. The test cases here should be at the system level and ensure that all the services work together to fulfill the desired behavior as per the requirements. This setup also typically uses production replicas of data stores. This is another place where bugs can be caught before going live.

The testing boundary here is generally the APIs that interact with the UI. The tests start with exercising the APIs at this Facade and validates end-to-end behavior.

Since these tests are higher up in the test pyramid, they focus on more business-related interactions. So, unit tests are more like this:

```
addTwo(x,y) should return 5, if x is 3 and y is 2
```

Integration tests are more like the following:

```
given user is logged in
and user clicks on a hotel search listing   item "x"
then the user should navigates to the    product details page of "x"
when user  clicks the  "book"   button
then price check should happen with   backend
then user should navigate to booking page
```

UI tests

Many applications have some sort of user interface, typically a web page or mobile app. These sets of tests validate the system as an end user would use it. In a way, these tests are related to integration tests, but are generally applicable for the facade-level services that directly interact with the clients (apps, web pages, and so on). The test cases are derived from the requirements (user stories) and try out all scenarios that the user would experience on the real app. These tests are generally run with the backend services in the stage environment.

There are many frameworks, such as Selenium, that help in automating these tests. We will not go into detail here as they are outside the scope of this book.

Performance tests

The goal of performance testing is to ensure that the non-functional performance requirements of the product are met. This generally translates to the following:

- **Latency:** The application should respond quickly, as described in the latency SLAs for various operations.
- **Scalability:** The application should handle the maximum prescribed user, **and yet** maintain the latency characteristics described previously.
- **Stability:** The application should be stable under varying load and load ramps.

There are various types of tests that ensures the preceding goals:

- **Load/Stress tests:** These check the application's ability to perform under various levels of loads (requests per second). The objective is to measure latency and the stability of the system under various conditions of load or stress.

- **Volume-testing:** Under Volume-testing, a large amount of data is populated in a database and the overall software system's behavior is monitored. The objective is to check the software application's performance under varying database volumes. These tests bring out issues with database modeling, such as an index not created on often-queried columns.

- **Scalability Tests:** The objective of scalability testing is to determine the software application's effectiveness in *scaling-up* to support an increase in the user load. It helps to plan addition to your software system. The tests aim to identify scaling bottlenecks and typically measure time to handle a request as a function of load, as depicted in the following diagram:

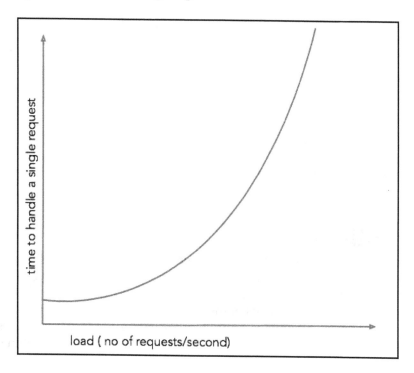

- **Endurance testing:** This test is performed to ensure that the software can handle the expected load over an extended period of time.

- **Spike testing:** It tests the software's behavior for sudden large spikes in the load. Generally, steep ramps in load can bring out issues that are different from endurance tests (constant load).

The following diagram illustrates the various tests we just discussed:

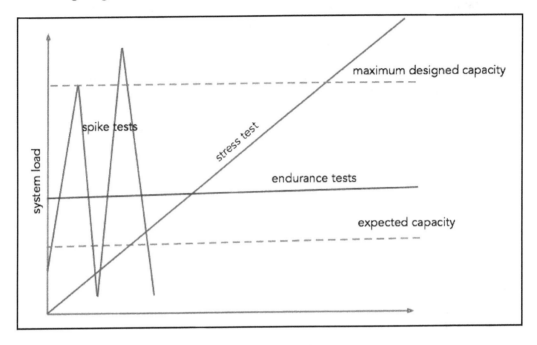

Chaos-engineering

Chaos-engineering is a technique that's used to evaluate systems for fragility and building constructs to help a system survive such chaos. Instead of waiting for things to break at the worst possible time, chaos-engineering believes in proactively injecting/crafting failures in order to gauge how the system behaves in these scenarios. Thus, disaster striking is not a once-in-a-blue-moon event- it happens every day! The aim is to identify weaknesses before they manifest in surprising aberrant behaviors. These weaknesses could be things such as the following:

- Improper fallback settings (see the *Dependency resilience* section)
- Retry thundering herds from incorrectly set timeouts
- Dependencies that are not resilient
- Single Points of Failure
- Cascading failures

Once identified, with proper telemetry in place, these weaknesses can be fixed before they bring customers in production. Having done a dry-run of actual disasters results in tremendous confidence in production systems.

Netflix is the pioneer in Chaos-Engineering and its Simian Army tool suite offers implementations to enable the required chaos. This facilitates the following Chaos-engineering process:

1. Define normal behavior via a set of metrics—these could be CPU/memory utilization, response time, or error rates.
2. Prepare a control group (no chaos) and an experimental group (where the Simian Army will reign). The hypothesis is that normal behavior will be observed in both groups.
3. Introduce chaos by simulating failure events, such as server crashes, disk malfunctions, or network partitions.
4. Verify the hypothesis that the control and experimental group both show normal behavior.

Some of the tools (*monkeys*) in the Simian Army are as follows:

- **Chaos Monkey:** Randomly disables production instances to make sure that redundancy and failure-tolerance are working as expected.
- **Latency Monkey:** Induces artificial delays and network partitions between client services and between services.
- **Conformity Monkey:** Finds instances that don't adhere to best practices and shuts them down.
- **Doctor Monkey:** Does the health checks that run on each instance and reclaims unhealthy instances.
- **Janitor Monkey:** Searches for unused resources and disposes them, thereby reducing clutter.
- **Security Monkey:** An extension of Conformity Monkey, it finds security violations or vulnerabilities (such as improperly-configured AWS security groups), and terminates the non-conforming instances. Another important role of this component is to ensure that all that SSL certificates are valid and do not need immediate renewal.
- **Chaos Gorilla:** Similar to Chaos Monkey, but simulates an outage of an entire Amazon availability zone, thereby verifying cross-geo high-availability.

For more details can be found here: `https://github.com/Netflix/SimianArmy/`.

Dependencies

Services are rarely exists in isolation; they have dependencies, both upstream and downstream. Every server will receive requests from clients (either UI or other services) that are counting on the service to honor the advertised contract and to live up to its SLAs. Each service also has a bunch of downstream dependencies (other services) that it depends on to get work done.

To understand the impact of dependencies on the overall system's, reliability, let's consider the Hotel Search service in the travel website we are building. Let's say we have built it to very high reliability levels (as described in the previous section) and we have an uptime requirement of four-nines (99.99% availability) to the clients. Now, the Hotel Search service depends on several other microservices, such as the Pricing Engine, Catalog Service, and Wallet, to display the hotel search results. When a request is received by the Hotel Search service, it makes calls to all these downstream dependencies to get the data needed to fulfill the request. Now, each of the dependent services may in turn have other dependencies and thus the dependency graph for services can get complicated very quickly.

In big software systems, such dependency graphs can get quite complicated, as shown here:

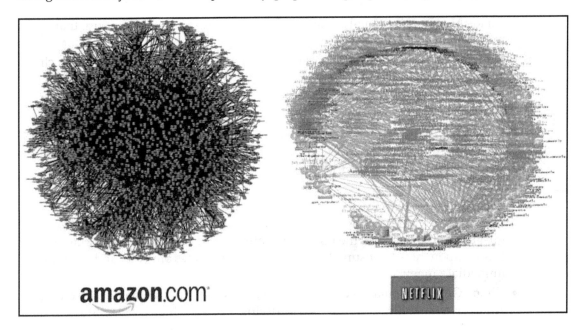

Image credit: Appcentrica

Building resilience in such systems means that we need to plan for dependency failures and mitigation plans so that we can mitigate protect against those failures.

Failure multiplication

Dependencies don't come for free. Even if all of the individual services are built to a very high quality, the reliability of the whole falls below the reliability of an individual service. For example, if the Hotel Search service is dependent on 5 other services (for simplicity, we will prune the dependency graph here), and it is built to 99.99%, availability, the actual availability of the overall Hotel Search feature is 99.99% which translates to about 99.94%. To consider the impact, lets see what 99.99% uptime means in terms of availability:

- **Daily:** 8.6 seconds
- **Weekly:** 1 minute 0.5 seconds
- **Monthly:** 4 minutes 23.0 seconds
- **Yearly:** 52 minutes 35.7 seconds

With 99.94%, the availability is as follows:

- **Daily:** 51.8 seconds
- **Weekly:** 6 minutes 2.9 seconds
- **Monthly:** 26 minutes 17.8 seconds
- **Yearly:** 5 hours 15 minutes 34.2 seconds

This means that with just five dependents, all of a high quality, the overall system degrades with an extra five hours of downtime per year.

With this impact in mind, let's look at mitigation strategies. But before that, there is another interesting issue that service dependencies bring out.

Cascading failures

Most software systems start simple. They are built as an all-in-one monolithic app, with modules packaging various code components. All packages are linked together in one big binary. Such a typical early version system is depicted in the following diagram:

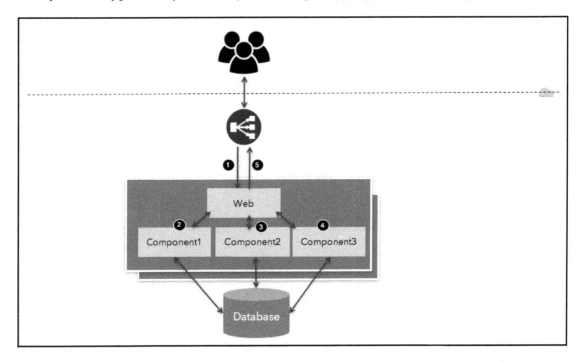

It takes requests and performs something of value using three components (modules/building blocks). These interactions are shown in the following diagram; the numbers describe the sequence of things that happen to fulfill a request.

However, as the system evolves and features get added in, there comes a time where we need to make calls to an external service (a dependent). Now, this external service can fail for multiple reasons that are outside our control, and obviously this will cause our application requests to fail:

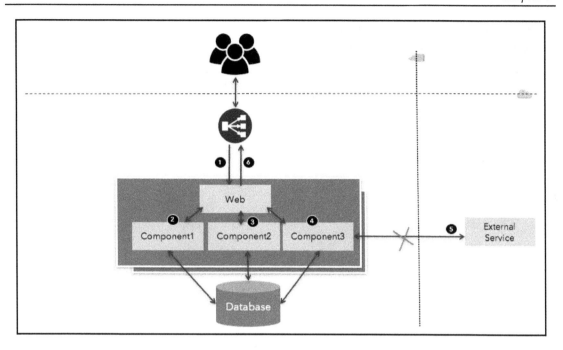

But consider what happens if the external service is just slow to respond. Here, the client and all resources in the original service are waiting for the request to complete, and this will impact on new requests, which may not even need the failing service. This is most evident in languages/runtimes such as Java or Tomcat, where each request effectively has a thread allocated, and if the client times out and retries for the slow request, we can very quickly degenerate to a situation such as this:

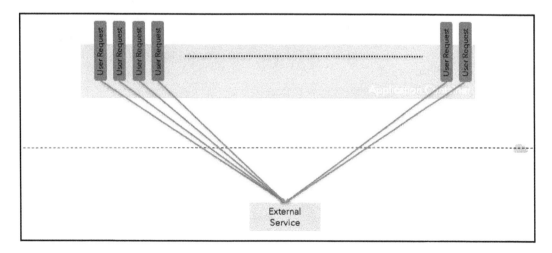

With increasing complexity and feature requests, the team decides to decompose the monolith into microservices. But this amplifies the problem! See the following diagram:

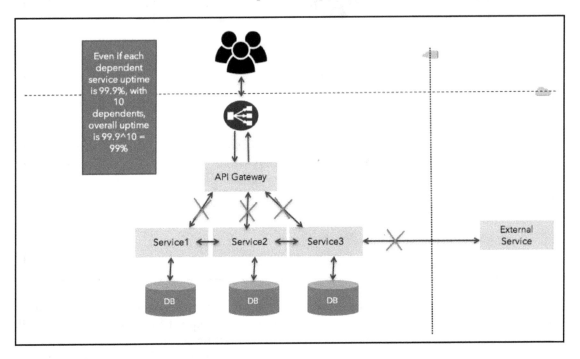

Today's systems are interconnected like never before, and with microservices, new services crop up at regular intervals of time. This means that the overall system will always be evolving—it is in a state of continuous change. In addition, in today's fast-paced development cycles, features will be added every day, and there are deployments multiple times in a day. This velocity, however, brings in greater risk of things going wrong and a fault in a specific service can cascade up to dependent services and bring multiple other parts of the systems down.

To guard against this catastrophe, and to build anti-fragile systems, the architect needs to apply specific design patterns when engineering such systems. The following section goes into detail on achieving resilience in such distributed systems.

Dependency resilience

The key to engineering resilience is to understand that there is no fault prevention—we should design to handle failures. Protecting the system's SLAs means building insulation to the faults that can happen to dependencies. In our design, we need to do the following:

- **Be nice to the broken service**: If the dependent service is down, we should not bombard it with more requests, thus allowing it time to recover.
- **Gracefully degrade**: Our clients should get a clear and timely error message
- **Provision monitoring/alerts**: We should be able to monitor the health of our dependents in the same way as we do monitoring of our own systems.

Though this sounds daunting, the good folks at Netflix have architected a comprehensive solution to enable applications to build such resilience. It's called Hystrix, and we will discuss it now.

An introduction to Hystrix

The problems just described were noticed at Netflix; the engineering team there developed a set of design patterns (and implementations in Java) called Hystrix to solve these problems.

The key idea is to wrap the dependency calls in command objects from Netflix. In Java, these commands are executed off the main request handling thread and delegated to a dependency-specific thread pool. This allows the Bulk heading of requests, that is, **Dependency X** down will only block all threads of the thread pool allocated to dependency-x. Other resources will be insulated and other requests that don't involve dependency-x can continue to be handled.

This is depicted in the following diagram:

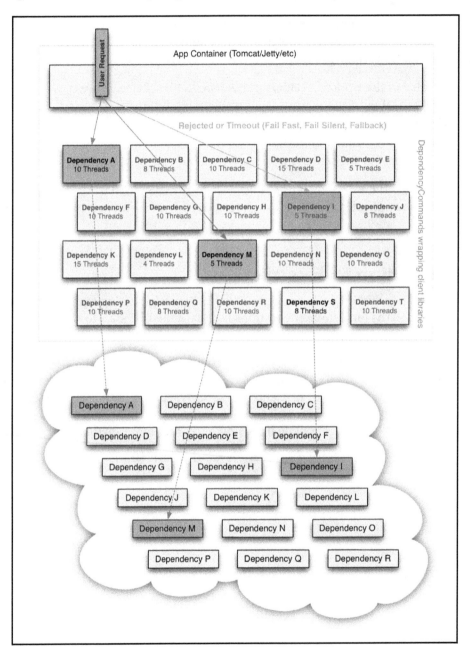

(Source: Netflix blog)

A dependency that responds slowly or with variable latencies is much worse than a service that fails fast, as the former causes resources to be hogged while waiting. To avoid this, the Hystrix set of patterns includes the Timeout concept. Each dependency is configured with a timeout (typically the 99.5 percentile of expected response latency) so that there is a worst-case time for which resources are blocked for a down service. If the timeout occurs before the service responds, then failure of the dependency is assumed.

The following sections cover Hystrix in detail.

Hystrix – fallback

A question that arises is what is to be done when a service is down (returns error or timeouts). Of course, the original required functionality cannot be executed. Hystrix recommends having a fallback configured for each dependency. What a fallback does, of course, varies from case to case and depends on the requirements. There are a few generic strategies, though:

- **Alternate Service:** If the main service endpoint is down, a backup service might be called. For example, if the Google search service is down, maybe we can call the Bing version.
- **Queue:** If the operation calls for the dependency to do some work, and the output of the work is not necessary for the request to be completed, then the request can be put in a durable queue for retry later. One example is sending an email for Booking. If the Email service is down, we can queue a request for the Email in something such as Kafka.
- **Cache:** If a response is needed from the dependent, another strategy is to cache data from previous responses. This type of caching is called *defensive caching*. The cache key generally includes the dependent service identifier, the API on that dependent service, and the parameters for that API. To keep the cache from exploding in terms of space requirements, strategies such as Least-Recently Used (LRU) can be employed. Here, when space budgets are breached, the least-recently-used item in the cache is reclaimed.

Hystrix – circuit breaker

Another important pattern in Hystrix is that of a circuit breaker. The key idea is for a service to fail fast if a dependent resource is not available, as opposed to waiting for a timeout/error for each service invocation during the period in which the dependent resource is down. The name comes from the familiar pattern of a circuit opening under a high load to protect internal resources. When requests start to fail for a dependent service, the `hystrix` library keeps count of the number of failures within a time window. If the failures are greater than a threshold (n number of failed requests within a given time or requests taking too long), the circuit for that dependency is moved to the Open state. In this state, all requests are failed. Periodically, after some configured amount of time, a single request is let through (Half-Open state). If the request fails, the circuit breaker returns to Open. If the request succeeds, the circuit breaker transitions to Closed and operations continue normally. To summarize, the states of the circuit can be in the following states:

- **Closed:** Operations that involve the dependency can happen normally.
- **Open:** Whenever a failure has been detected, the circuit *opens*, making sure that the service short-circuits requests involving the dependency and responds immediately.
- **Half-open:** Periodically, the circuit breaker lets a request pass through to gauge the health of the dependent service.

The circuit breaker workflow and fallback interactions are depicted here:

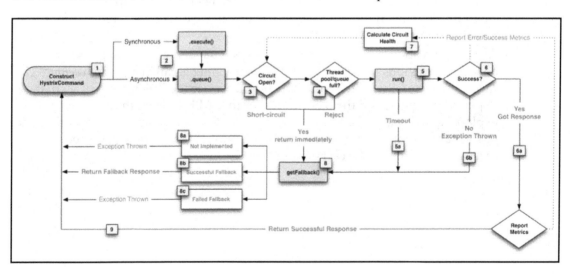

(Reference: Netflix blog)

Hystrix in Golang

In Go, the thread-hogging of requests of the Java/Tomcat world is not really a concern, since the web frameworks use goroutine(s) to service requests rather than dedicated threads. Goroutines are much more lightweight than threads, thus the problem solved by the Bulkhead Pattern is less of an issue. But, still the Hystrix solution is vital to enable fail-fast and circuit breaker behavior.

The most-used Golang library for Hystrix at the time of writing is `https://github.com/afex/hystrix-go/`. The following is the 'hello world' snippet of using the library:

```go
import "github.com/afex/hystrix-go/hystrix"

errors := hystrix.Go("a_command", func() error {
    // talk to other dependent services
    // return the error if one occurs
    return nil
}, func(err error) error {
    // do fallback action here
    return nil
})
```

Calling `hystrix.Go` is like launching a goroutine, and it returns a channel or error (errors) in the preceding snippet. Here, the first closure function is the Command Object, and this performs the actual interactions with the dependent service. If there is an error, the second closure function is called with the error code returned by the first command function.

Values can be returned from the Command using channels, like so:

```go
out := make(chan string, 1)
errors := hystrix.Go("a_command", func() error {
    // talk to other dependent services
    // return the error if one occurs
    output <- "a good response"
    return nil
}, func(err error) error {
    // do fallback action
    output <- "fallback here"
    return nil
})
```

Then, the client code can do a select comprehension over both the output and the errors, like so:

```
select {
    case ret := <-out:
    //   success
    //   process the return value
    case err := <-errors:
    //   failure
    //   handle failure
}
```

You can configure settings, such as timeout and maximum concurrent requests for each command, using a separate API, like so:

```
hystrix.ConfigureCommand("a_command",    hystrix.CommandConfig{
            Timeout:                    1000,
            MaxConcurrentRequests:      100,
            ErrorPercentThreshold:      25,
})
```

The CommandConfig struct is defined as follows:

```
type   CommandConfig struct {
        Timeout                 int `json:"timeout"`
        MaxConcurrentRequests   int `json:"max_concurrent_requests"`
        RequestVolumeThreshold  int `json:"request_volume_threshold"`
        SleepWindow             int `json:"sleep_window"`
        ErrorPercentThreshold   int `json:"error_percent_threshold"`
}
```

The various tuneables are as follows:

Tunables	Description
Timeout	How long to wait for a command to complete in milliseconds.
MaxConcurrentRequests	How many instances of this command can run at the same time.
RequestVolumeThreshold	The minimum number of requests that must happen before a circuit can be tripped due to health.
SleepWindow	The time to wait after a circuit opens before going to the half-open state (to test for recovery).
ErrorPercentThreshold	The percentage threshold of the number of errors to cause the circuit to open.

Hystrix monitoring

Hystrix has a comprehensive solution for aggregating streams of metrics from each service and monitoring and visualization of the stats thereof. There are companion projects such as Turbine, which enables event-stream aggregations and dashboards to monitor various commands in a single view, as shown in the following diagram:

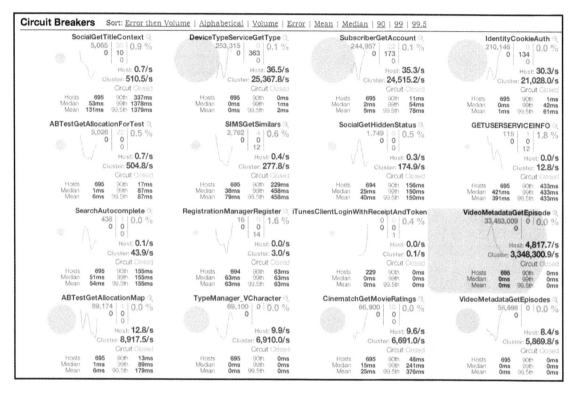

(Source: https://github.com/Netflix/turbine/wiki)

Turbine's architecture is depicted here:

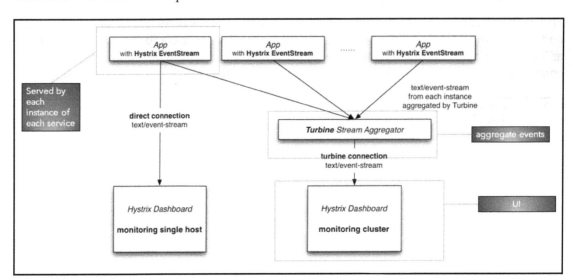

With hystrix-go, it is easy to set up the plumbing to send the streams of **server-sent event** (**SSE**) JSON that form the transport of the stats. All that you need to do is register the event-stream HTTP handler on a port and launch it in a goroutine. Then Turbine, needs to be configured to plug into this endpoint, and subsequently Hystrix Dashboard, to point to the Turbine instance. Once this is done, the graphs and stats, such as the one depicted in the preceding diagram will start showing. Here is the sample code to launch a stream handler:

```
hystrixStreamHandler   := hystrix.NewStreamHandler()
hystrixStreamHandler.Start()
go http.ListenAndServe(net.JoinHostPort("",   "81"), hystrixStreamHandler)
```

Database-level reliability

The system would be of little use if durable data is not stored in a resilient and consistent manner. There are various levels of consistency in databases. This topic is covered in detail in Chapter 8, *Modeling Data*.

Datacenter-level reliability

What happens if the entire datacenter goes down? To be prepared for this eventuality, you need to run your application cluster in more than one datacenter, and ensure that both deployments are in sync in terms of data. Building such architectures is typically under the purview of **business continuity planning (BCP)** and **disaster recovery (DR)**.

A common way to have DNS switch between deployments in two datacenters. A DNS name, such as www.mysite.com, resolves to a VIP of 4.4.4.4 with a specific **time-to-live (TTL)**. This layer can be made intelligent and, in the case of a datacenter outage, repoint the DNS name to a backup VIP, say 5.5.5.5. For doing this we need the deployments to happen in both datacenters and that the data is replicated (usually asynchronously) between the deployments. This scheme is described in the following diagram:

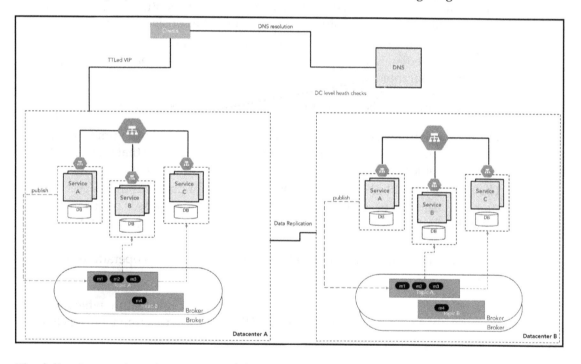

The following sections cover some of the attributes of these systems.

Consistency

There is no silver bullet for enabling consistency in such a distributed architecture. In fact, there are multiple flavors of consistencies:

- **Weak:** This is a best-effort consistency. There are no guarantees on the durability of the data. One example is cache stores—they are rarely replicated across datacenters. Applications that are well-suited to this model include video streaming and VOIP.
- **Eventual:** Here, the system eventually reaches a state of consistency. However, at a few given instances, each datacenter might have old data. DNS changes propagation, SMTP, and Amazon S3 are all examples of applications that use this mode. With this consistency model, there is no guarantee that a read immediately after a write will see the new value, but eventually all the deployments get the new value and reads would be consistent across.
- **Strong:** This is the highest level of consistency. All reads, irrespective of the location, immediately reflect a committed write. Transactional systems typically need these guarantees.

When designing a solution, we also need to consider three key design objectives:

- **The recovery-time objective (RTO):** The goal for the maximum time a restore operation should take after a disaster happens. It is the time that's acceptable in terms of business loss, for a specific feature system to be down.
- **The recovery-point objective (RPO):** The amount of data loss that is acceptable after a disaster has occurred. In most DR situations, data loss is not completely avoidable, but this metric for a feature indicates business impact of data loss for a feature.
- **Operation latency:** The acceptable latency times for various operations in a feature.

To consider the tradeoffs between these objectives, consider a simple feature where an API store updates to a User Profile in the DB. To enable DR resilience, this update needs to be replicated to the backup/other datacenter. There are few options here:

- Return OK to the client only when the write happens, both in the main datacenter as well as the remote datacenter. This brings about a strong consistent behavior, and minimizes the RPO. However, cross-datacenter writes can take a long time, and the Operation Latencies will significantly increase if we go down this route.

- Return OK when the write succeeds in the main datacenter. Ensure asynchronous replication to the remote datacenter, using mechanisms such as MySQL binary log replication. Here, the write finishes quickly, however it is possible that the datacenter goes down before the async write is made available in the remote datacenter.

- Instead of the two preceding extremes, the system can make a quick note in the remote datacenter about the write (and in a transaction log) and return OK to the client. Here, the operational latency is not compromised as much as in Option A, and the RPO guarantees are also good. But it might take more time for the system to come up and be primary as it replays the log to bring itself into a consistent state, thus increasing RTO.

Thus, each resource/feature/service needs to be looked in isolation and questions need to be asked to figure out the relative importance of RPO versus RTO versus Operation time. These questions could take the following forms:

- Is data from 10 minutes ago tolerable for customers?
- Is it OK for the service to be down for 5 minutes while we build consistency in the data?

Based on the answers, the design evolves toward improving performance or consistency.

Routing and cutover

When disaster does strike, we need traffic to be routed to the backup datacenter. The Service-Level Reliability pattern of having a load-balancer and multiple instances behind it with health checks will not work here. A more scalable option is to use the DNS-based failover. As a quick recap, DNS maps a URL to a VIP (for a load-balancer) through its records. It is possible, and normal, to have multiple VIPs against a URL, and typically strategies such as round-robin routing are used; the DNS name server will hand out a different VIP each time for a resolution request. This can be augmented so that the DNS service monitors the health of each datacenter VIP and, if the instance is deemed unhealthy, remove it from the set of records. This works particularly well if the system is deployed in a cloud environment, such as AWS, which has an in-built DNS server, such as Route 53. This can monitor health not just from /health endpoints, but also from logs and metrics from individual services.

We will look at deployment topologies in more detail in Chapter 11, *Planning for Deployment*.

Summary

In this chapter, we explored various facets of building resilient systems, from ruggedizing individual services to building high availability. All of these need to work together to enable systems that thrive under stress.

In the next chapter, we will look at a case study and build an end-to-end travel website!

Case Study – Travel Website

10

To perceive architecture, you need a big real-life system. Without this, there is a risk of readers getting lost in the details. They might understand how to employ specific techniques and Go constructs, but they may not have clarity in figuring out and analyzing coarser building blocks. To avoid this, we will use an online travel website as a *problem statement* so that we can employ multiple techniques we have learned so far and build a real-life product.

The product

We will be building parts of an e-commerce website that deals with travel. Examples of real world-related products include Booking.com and Expedia. The site will be a marketplace: the company will not own any inventory; rather, it is a place where travel-product sellers and buyers will connect. Let's start detailing the requirements by starting out with listing the actors involved.

Actors

The website will deal the following types of people:

- **Customers**: Those who want to consume travel-related items (flight tickets, hotels, cabs, and so on).
- **Sellers**: Those who bring inventory to the marketplace. For the case study, we will assume that the sellers give us an API to pull data off and do our bookings.

Requirements

As mentioned, we will be building a travel marketplace. It will connect the customers and the sellers. Both parties have varying requirements from the platform, and the marketplace needs to ensure that both are reasonably satisfied. This diagram describes the product at a high level:

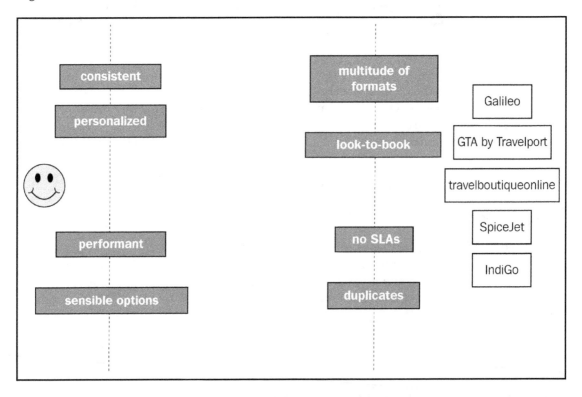

Let's look at the following points for more clarification between customers and sellers:

- Customers should be able to search for hotels and flights. Key functional requirements include the following:
    - The ability to show results from various sellers' sources.
    - Price consistency: Show prices that are close to what the customer would finally pay.
    - The ability to see discounts and promotions.

- Customers should be able to see personalized prices on the search results screen. These are essentially markdowns on the standard prices, and the discount is derived from a loyalty points-based rewards program. For example, if a hotel reservation is priced at $500, and if the customer's wallet has $100, then the price shown should be $400.
- Customers should be able to book hotels and flights. This involves handling payments and confirmation from the seller.
- Customers should be able to manage their booking, including cancellations.
- We should be able to onboard sellers quickly to the platform. It can be assumed that they give well-defined APIs for searching and booking.
- Customers should get an email invoice once they buy something.
- Customers should get an email if something goes wrong during booking.
- The search on the website needs to be fast. Customers should be able to see initial results within one second.
- Customers should be able to see prices that are close to what they would finally pay. This means we can't just cache data forever.
- Sellers do not offer high **Service-Level Agreements (SLAs)** to us, since we are just a fledgling startup. They do however offer good commissions.
- Sellers have a *look-to-book* ratio. They charge us if we do too many searches for too few bookings.

Data modeling

Before jumping into designing various features, as discussed previously, it is wise to think about various entities and their relationships. The following table gives an overview of this:

Entity Name	Description	Relationships
Customer	This is the most important user on the website. Every customer has a unique persistent entity that describes things such as the profile, history of bookings/interactions, payment preferences, and so on. When persisting, this entity has an unique customer ID, which can be used by other entities to refer to a specific customer.	Many other entities refer to a customer entity via the customer ID attribute (primary key).

Seller	Besides the customer, a seller is the next most important user on the platform. As mentioned, sellers can have varied characteristics. From a software perspective (of the limited requirements we have in the case study), the seller is effectively an API endpoint and a specific contract.	Many entities refer to a seller. In the database, these relationships take the form of a foreign key. But more interestingly, from the architecture perspective, we need to have a proxy for each seller, which also acts as an adaptor-interacting with the seller API on one side and the rest of the travel website platform on the other side. There will be more details on this in the following sections.
SKU	We need to have a unique ID for each item in our inventory. Although initially it looks as if the hotels and flights namespaces are distinct, a decision can be made to have a unique ID for each item across verticals. A **Stock-Keeping Unit** (**SKU**) is a standard term for such an ID. Having this unique ID across all product lines will future proof the design for future use cases such as Vacation (Flights + Hotels).	This will be part of the primary key for the most of the data stores. This should not be re-usable , as there might be requirements to audit past transactions. The SKUs form a hierarchical structure; specifically, some SKUs might have a parent SKU. For example, a hotel will have a SKU, and its parent SKU will be the ID of the city in which the hotel is located.
Date (check in/check out to/from hotel, for flights)	People want to search and book travel products on specific dates. The rates and availability will vary a lot according to the dates. RFC 3339 is the standard for describing dates. It has multiple formats, and we need to choose something that is easy to model in persist entities and API exchanges. This leads to a certain Golang specific complication, and the solution needs a wrapper over the standard `time. Time` data type. Please see booking section for details.	Dates are not very interesting relationship-wise. They are mostly attributes of other entities.

Booking	A booking describes an intent to make a reservation for a flight or a hotel. Doing the actual reservation can be a complicated, time-consuming process, and a booking-persistent entity instance encapsulates all status about the booking.	Has references to the customer, SKU, and dates.
Reservation	During the course of making a booking, a reservation needs to be completed by the seller. The reservation entity encapsulates this information.	A booking entity has references (owns) multiple reservation instances. For example, a return flight booking might have flights from two different sellers, and thus includes two different reservations.
Wallet	As described in the requirements, we want personalized prices driven by a loyalty-rewards program. Essentially, whenever a booking is made, certain points get credited. The customer can utilize these points in making future bookings. The wallet balance is used for marked down in the search results page.	This can be modeled as an amount per customer. Besides the scalar value, we should also store individual transactions, essentially a ledger of the debits and credits to a wallet account. Though the later is not strictly mandated by the requirements, doing so would allow us to perform audits easily and handle related future requirements.

High-level architecture

It is a microservices-based approach, with both messaging and API calls. As discussed in Chapter 8, *Modeling Data*, messaging systems allow scalability and resiliency. Service-to-service API calls are useful when a quick/in-line response is needed.

The high-level solution architecture is described in the following diagram:

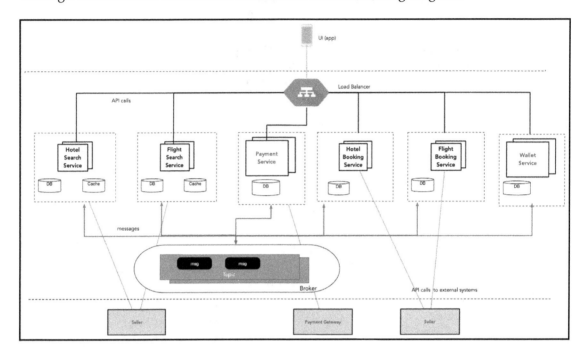

The following sections describe the search and booking services in detail.

Search

The search functionality is the first product feature that the customers will see. If the experience is not good, an immediate impact will be seen on the business. As described, the top key requirements of search are performance and personalization. Another requirement is to ensure that we don't incur high costs from the sellers, considering the look-to-book ratio. Let's look at how we can engineer the same.

In general, for the search, the inputs are going to be places and dates. Specifically for flights, the search inputs will be as follows:

- The onward date. The return date would be optional (only for return flights).
- The source and destination places (airports).

Whereas, for hotels the search parameters would include the following:

- The check-in and check-out date
- The city/country/hotel name where the room is desired

Generally, travel websites take the number of passengers as well. But since this does not affect the architecture drastically, it is ignored for the purpose of the solution engineering of this case study.

For both flights and hotels, the search response consists of the following:

- **A Static listing**: This is the elements of the *catalog* that match the query. The catalog is essentially a dictionary of items available. For flights, this is a cache of flight details (flight names, aircraft types, services offered, and so on) between any two airports. Here, the actual source of truth are the external sellers. Similarly, for hotels, the catalog contains content on the room types, images, ratings, and so on.
- **A dynamic part**: This is the prices for each element in the listing. Here, the prices vary based on the context (who's searching, when, whether there are discounts, and so on). You generally want the newest price available, so we need to cache prices less aggressively than the static listings. However, we also want to optimize look-to-book penalties, so our cache TTLs here have to be smart, as discussed in the following section.

Flights

As described previously, the search key for flights would be source and destination airports, along with the dates. These would be used by customers while searching.

To ensure that performance and cost (look-to-book ratio) requirements are met, we need to *ingest* data from the sellers into our system, rather than hit the Seller Search APIs indiscriminately on demand. As part of ingestion, we need to store data in the same format to enable efficient searches.

One of the main microservices inside flight search is the Flights Catalog. This is the repository of all static content about the flight (aircraft types, services available in-flight, logos, and so on). The high-level design for the same is shown in the following diagram:

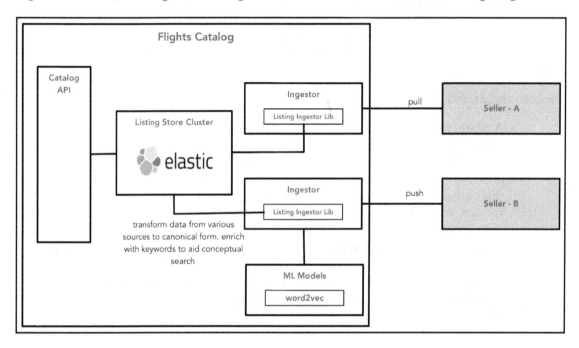

As you can see, there are multiple ingestors that take listing information from the external sellers and then do a transformation process on it before indexing the same in Elasticsearch. For example, a few sellers might be giving data in an XML-based API, while others might have a JSON-based API. Some sellers might have time mentioned in UTC, while others might be giving the time zone along with the time. We need to ensure that all such quirks are abstracted from the rest of the system. Some sellers offer a pull-based model; that is, we need to hit an API to get details. Other sellers offer systems which push data (for example, via webhooks) whenever there is a change in price or inventory. The pull-based model requires slightly more engineering, as we need to schedule refresh polls for various listings that are needed for the catalog.

Each seller has a specific ingestor dedicated to it. This code understands the specifics of the Seller API and transforms the data into the canonical format stored by the catalog and the rest of the travel website. This adaptor design pattern also helps us in onboarding new sellers to the platform in a fast and a reliable manner. You just needs to implement the travel website side contract using the new seller APIs and—voila!—the seller is integrated.

An important aspect to note in the Flights Catalog is that only the static data is ingested, not the prices. This is because of the following:

- The prices can be very volatile (see the following). They need a different storage/invalidation mechanism.
- The flight prices are generally available via a separate API with stringent throttling limits.

To simplify the processing of the keys, we can concatenate the source, destination, and dates into a string (a simple join of the string). This key is then used for ingesting listings (routes) and for the actual search. Such design choices help in keeping the rest of the code simple. You should take time to explore the entities in the domain and figure out such modeling constructs before jumping into implementation.

The transformations done by the ingestor. For the static content, include adding keywords to aid conceptual search. This is important since many places/things have multiple names that mean the same thing. For example, *NY* and *New York* mean the same place. One ML model that helps in a conceptual search is `word2vec`. It was developed at Google and essentially is a two-layer neural network that maps each word to a vector space (of a large number of dimensions) such that words that share context (for example, are found in similar phrases) are in closer proximity than others. The latter is called **word embedding** and is an efficient way to map words to vectors so that words that are conceptually similar are closer and have vectors which are close in the *n*-dimensional space of the word embedding. This is well depicted through the following diagram:

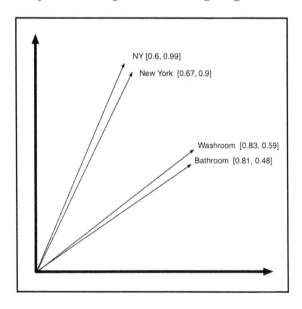

In a search, you might have multiple ML models to enrich the raw data in different ways. Also, at any point in time, you might be evaluating more than one version of a model. The key to abstracting the rest of the system from these specifics is to have a framework where your data scientists can iterate and deploy new models, while the rest of the ingestion pipeline remains the same.

After all the transformations, the data is stored into Elasticsearch. This essentially is a distributed collection of Lucene indices (each index is spread over multiple nodes (shards) in the cluster). The listings are converted to JSON documents before being ingested into Elasticsearch (`https://github.com/olivere/elastic`) is the most popular Elasticsearch client in Go.

Our main usecase here is n-gram-based queries of various attributes listed in the document using an inverted index . Along the search, we can rank documents that match using various pluggable similarity functions; one popular/simple one being **Term Frequency–Inverse Document Frequency** (**TF–IDF**). Here, TF is the number of times the query keyword is mentioned in a listing, while IDF is one the number of listings in which this keyword is mentioned. Specifically, the formula is this:

$$W_{t,d} = TF_{t,d} * log\ (\ N\ /\ DF_t)$$

Consider the following:

- $TF_{t,d}$ = number of occurrences of the term t in the document d
- DF_t = number of documents containing the term t
- N = total number of documents

The higher the $W_{t,d}$ score, the more relevant the listing is for the keyword. Elasticsearch provides a REST API for searching in the inverted index. The Catalog API provides a thin wrapper on top and performs ancillary tasks such as authentication.

As described, the flight prices need to be cached to avoid hitting the throttling limits of sellers. However, we need to scale the TTLs appropriately. To engineer a good solution, we need to understand the domain/business quirks. A search for a flight that is ahead in the future (say, three months) is unlikely to change in the next three days. However, a search for the same day or the next day is going to return prices that are very volatile. Thus, prices for the same/next days should be cached for a very short time. This intelligent scaling of TTLs helps us manage the price variability in the system.

Besides the regular prices, we also have requirements for the personalization of prices—this could be in terms of discount coupons, promotion campaigns, wallets, and so on. An important insight here is that we need not cache just prices; in fact, we should cache as much aggregated response as possible. If you look at the previous discussion, the only thing we cannot cache is the wallet markdown (since the amount in the wallet can be utilized in many places). Thus, we can cache the aggregated response with a smart TTL, and then on every search call the wallet service to get the amount available for a markdown.

We can use Redis for the key-value store. This is a very efficient way of doing TTL-based KV lookups. The reason for high-performance in Redis is that it stores data in memory. A question that might be asked is this: *Won't it be a risk to maintain data in memory?* As we saw in Chapter 8, *Modeling Data*, Redis can be clustered for high availability. Thus, we can survive single machine downtime. Besides, this store is just a cache and not the final source of truth; thus, it's OK to optimize for performance, at the price of not being totally durable.

As flights get booked, we need to invalidate the cache after a certain threshold so that the price/availability information is not stale. This will be driven by messages from the Booking Service, as described in the Reservation section.

The high-level search design is depicted in the following diagram:

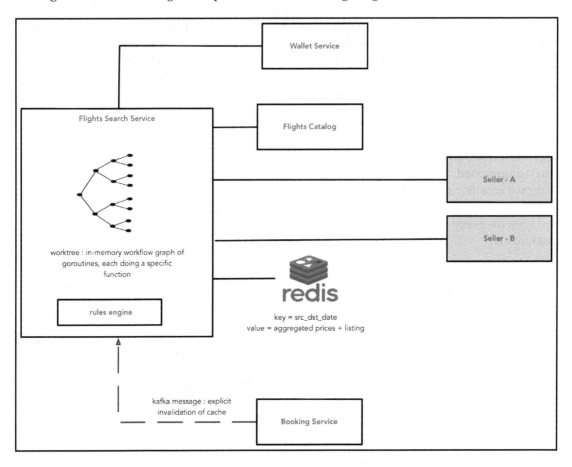

For the messaging (Kafka) part, please refer to the *Reservation* section.

The main component is the Flights Search service. It is responsible for making multiple computations/API calls, most of which are concurrent and can be parallelized. The parallel calls include other services such as Sellers, Wallet, Redis cache, and so on. Golang is perfect for modeling such concurrency:

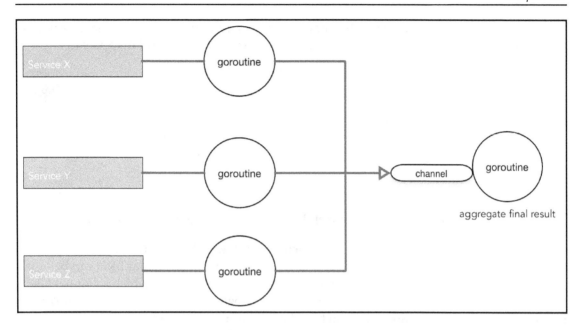

However, we need to develop a framework that allows developers not to worry about the the boilerplate code and just focus on the business logic.

An example generic framework, `CommandTree`, is described next (the code is at `https://github.com/cookingkode/worktree`). This framework allows the coding of such workflows in a MapReduce paradigm. The leaves of the tree are *mappers*, which kickstart the processing by producing some data (in this context, by making API) and transform the data into a generic format. The internal nodes are *reducers*, which run some sort of function on the data and then pass on the output upstream. Finally, the root of the tree has the aggregated final result.

The core of the library is the `CommandTree` data structure, which is based on the composite design pattern. It also leverages the fact that in Go, functions are first-class objects. The struct definition is given here:

```
type CommandTree struct {
    Reducer func(inp []interface{}) interface{}
    LeafFunctions []func(inp interface{}) interface{}
    LeafFunctionsInput []interface{}
    nChildren int
    LeafFunctionsOutput []interface{}
}
```

The Leaf entities are the *children* of the node, and are mapper functions, and the data that is needed for those functions. There is a method called `AddMapper` to add mappers to a `CommandTree` object, as defined in the following code snippet:

```
func (t *CommandTree) AddMapper(f func(inp interface{}) interface{}, input
interface{}) int {
    t.LeafFunctions = append(t.LeafFunctions, f)
    t.LeafFunctionsInput = append(t.LeafFunctionsInput, input)
    temp := t.nChildren
    t.nChildren += 1
    return temp
}
```

All `AddMapper()` clients add a multiple child mappers, it's functions, and the input data.

The reducer is essentially a reference to a function that takes all the output of the mapper functions and produces a final output for this `CommandTree`. A particular SKU can be available from more than one seller. In such a case, we should choose which seller to show the SKU from. A reducer is a place that can host such logic. The client of the `CommandTree` library can attach any function that matches the ' `func(inp []interface{}) interface{}`' signature using the following helper method:

```
func (t *CommandTree) AddReducer(f func(inp []interface{}) interface{}) {
    t.Reducer = f
}
```

You can kick out the processing (execution of mappers and the reducer) of the `CommandTree` through the `Run()` method. This spawns a goroutine for each mapper, aggregates the data over a channel, and then finally runs the reducer to give the final output. There is a fair bit of wrapper code to enable this:

```
// Wrapper struct for the results returned by the Mapper
type ResultFunction struct {
    Child int // The index into the LeafFunctions array, to identify the
Mapper
    Result interface{} // Generic result of the mapper function
}

// Wrapper function for the Mapper function so that it can be spawned as
goroutine
// It take reference to the result channel and send the Mapper function
output on
// the same channel after wrapping it with ResultFunction - to identify the
mapper // function
func wrap(c chan ResultFunction, child int, todo func(inp interface{})
interface{}, inp interface{}) {
```

```
        var result ResultFunction
        startTime := time.Now()
        result.Result = todo(inp)
        endTime := time.Now()
        log.Println("WRAP TOTAL ", endTime.Sub(startTime))
        result.Child = child
        c <- result
    }

func (t *CommandTree) Run(_ interface{}) interface{} {
    channel := make(chan ResultFunction, t.nChildren)
    defer close(channel)
    t.LeafFunctionsOutput = make([]interface{}, t.nChildren)
    for i, f := range t.LeafFunctions {
        go wrap(channel, i, f, t.LeafFunctionsInput[i])
    }

    remaining := t.nChildren
    for remaining > 0 {
        result := <-channel
        remaining -= 1
        t.LeafFunctionsOutput[result.Child] = result.Result
    }
    return t.Reducer(t.LeafFunctionsOutput)
}
```

The key to composition is the fact that the Run() method can itself be a mapper to another CommandTree object. This is the specific reason for the Run() signature to be as it is—the input of this function is just a dummy, and should be given as nil, as shown here:

```
// Since the input is a generic interface , one way of passing multiple
parameters
// is a compound structure
type TwoArgs struct {
    X int
    Y int
}

// A Mapper, which returns the Product of X and Y
func mult(i interface{}) interface{} {
    args := i.(TwoArgs)
    return args.X * args.Y
}

// A Mapper, which returns the Sum of X and Y
func sum(i interface{}) interface{} {
    args := i.(TwoArgs)
    return args.X + args.Y
```

```
    }

    // A Reducer which just sums the child mapper outputs
    func merge(results []interface{}) interface{} {
        var sum int
        for _, x := range results {
            sum += x.(int)
        }
        return sum
    }

    // Finally the usage of a two level work tree
    func main() {
        level2 := worktree.CommandTree{}
        level2.AddMapper(mult, TwoArgs{2, 3})
        level2.AddMapper(mult, TwoArgs{2, 2})
        level2.AddReducer(merge)
        level1 := worktree.CommandTree{}
        level1.AddMapper(level2.Run, nil) // ← when nesting use nil for Run
        level1.AddMapper(sum, TwoArgs{2, 2})
        level1.AddReducer(merge)
        fmt.Println(level1.Run(nil).(int)) // ← execute the whole tree}
    }
```

This framework allows the search service to reduce the amount of boilerplate code and, as we see next, this is re-usable, even in the hotels search.

We need an ability to isolate business rules and yet run them on every fresh ingestion of prices. This brings us to another interesting aspect of the design: the rules engine. This allows definition of various rules in text, such as format. The rules here can be used to augment code that calculates things such as Cache TTL and the amount of discount to be offered. `https://github.com/Knetic/govaluate` is a good option for the rules engine library. An example of rules is shown in the following code:

```
    bookingErrorsExpression, err :=
    govaluate.NewEvaluableExpression("(bookingErrors * totalNoBoookings / 100)
    >= 90");
    inputs := make(map[string]interface{})
    inputs["bookingErrors"] = 96;
    inputs["totalNoBoookings"] = 100;
    bookingErrorsCrossedThreshold, err :=
    bookingErrorsExpression.Evaluate(inputs);
    // bookingErrorsCrossedThreshold will now set to "true"
```

The low-level design needs to figure out exactly what part of the computation has to be structure via configurable expressions (rule engine) and what part is best done explicitly in code. A common design flaw is over-reliance on rules; trying to map each computation into a rule can be inefficient, and this can lead to complexity. You need to judiciously evaluate what computation needs to be generic/configurable and what is best written as simple, straightforward code.

On the website, the search box essentially will be as follows:

Enter the source city/airport:
Enter the destination city/airport:
Onward date:
Return date (optional for return ticket):
Number of passengers:

The search key is the concatenation of the source, destination, and date of travel. For return tickets, the source/destination values are exchanged, and the return date is used as the date to form the search key. This search key is then sent to the Flights Search API, which uses the `CommandTree` pattern discussed previously to build out the computation tree. The mappers here would be calls to the catalog service and Redis. If there is a cache missing, then calls need to go to the sellers for price/availability information. The Flights Search service will then return the reduced value at the root as the API response, after serializing to JSON.

 The aggregate response would have to be augmented with the response of the wallet service so that the final markdown price can be shown on the UI. The wallet service can never be cached; this is to avoid giving discounts that cannot be reconciled.

Hotels

Searching for a hotel is similar to searching for a flight. Customers will search for hotels in a specific city, or they can directly give the hotel name. Thus, we want to have a catalog that can serve hotels based on more than one keyword in the listings. Elasticsearch is able to handle this, and thus we can continue to use it as the key datastore for a hotel's static listing.

One of the main difference in a hotels search is the way the sellers structure prices. Hoteliers price each room on a specific day, and the customer query can be across a range of check-in and check-out dates. The naive search algorithm will just get the rates for dates between the check-in and check-out dates from the datastore and sum the rates to get the final value. However, in the case of a hotels search in a city, doing this for each hotel in the city being searched will not scale to the required performance numbers. Thus, while caching is needed, the caching solution has to be intelligent in a slightly different way than the flights one. The trick to good performance is pre-computing the total price for all *most frequently used* check-in/check-out day combinations. This has to be done at the time of ingestion of prices from the sellers. The astute reader may reason that the pre-computation will lead to a large number of writes amplification. Thus, we need a storage solution for the price store, which has good write performance.

Cassandra is just the right tool for the job. However, we need to model the data carefully. As we have seen, Cassandra is a partitioned data store, and the key to good read performance is to avoid scatter-gather for queries. In the hotel-search context, queries are for a specific city or hotel name. Thus, we can optimize the price store to serve for a whole city. The city becomes the partition key for our Cassandra column family. The data model looks like the following:

Field/Column	Meaning
SKU	Unique ID for a hotel or city. This is the partition key and is used to distribute the information between nodes of the Cassandra cluster.
CheckInDate	The check-in date. This is first part of the clustering/sorting of the table/column family. This allows efficient search for a given check-in date for a specific hotel or city.
CheckOutDate	The check-out date. This is second part of the clustering/sorting of the table/column-family. On a specific node, the data is first sorted on the check-in date and then on the check-out date. Thus, this allows an efficient search for a given check-in date for a specific hotel or city.
ParentSKU	For a hotel, this is the city. For a city, this is null.
RoomId	A unique identifier for a room. Elasticsearch will contain static information about a room including images and so on.
BasePrice	The base price of the room.
Taxes	The taxes on the room.

Thus, the primary key for the store will be (SKU, CheckInDate, CheckOutDate). As described, this compound key means that SKU will be the partition key while CheckInDate, and CheckOutDate will be the clustering keys.

 Microservices allow individual services to be polyglot in terms of the infrastructure. While this freedom is good, it is important to restrict the platform footprint to a few recipes for each infrastructure building block (DB, messaging, and so on). This helps in many ways, including allowing people to apply learning across teams and having holistic monitoring systems in production.

On the website, the search box essentially will display the following set of information:

- Enter name of city or hotel
- Check-in date
- Check-out date

Once the user enters the details, the frontend will make a call to the Hotel Search Service, which in turn will hit the catalog and the price store in parallel. The catalog will return static details about the entity (city or hotel), the details being things such as rooms, URLs for images, and so on. The price store, as described, returns pricing information. The search service merges both responses (this becomes efficient, as both the catalog and the price store will return data as a map keyed by RoomId) and present the combined information to the frontend (UI).

Since the price store caches only the most frequently used check-in/check-out day combination, it is possible that the query needs to be served by sourcing data from the seller itself. This of course would not be as performant as the results from the price store, but since we cannot efficiently store all possible combinations of check-in/check-out day, this tradeoff is necessary.

Besides this, as we discussed for the flights search, calls are made to the wallet service to get the applicable amount for price personalization.

The high-level hotel search architecture is summarized in the following diagram:

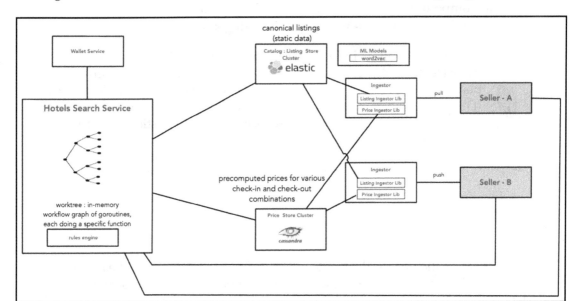

Booking

The booking flows have very different characteristics and requirements than Search. More than performance, reliability is the main requirement here. If the customer has made a payment, then they should get the reservation. The good thing, though, is that booking is always a fraction of your searches, so you do not have the stringent performance requirements that we saw for Search.

Additionally, there is a workflow associated with booking. Once the payment is made, the system needs to make a reservation with the seller, email the customer, and so on. We will be designing an **Event-Driven Architecture** (**EDA**) pattern to handle booking. The flow should be similar to flights and hotels, so we can deep-dive into the hotels' booking flow to glean insights.

The high-level architecture is depicted through the following diagram:

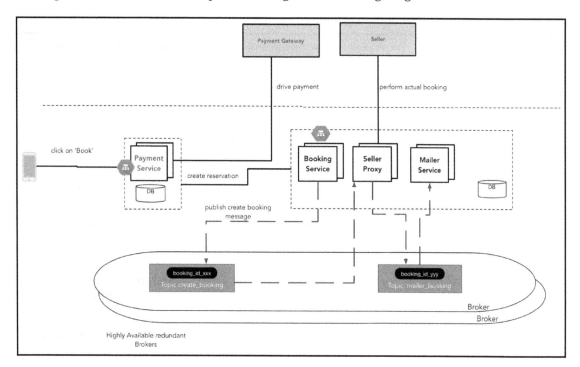

The backbone of the architecture is the messaging layer. In the example implementation here, we will be using Kafka. It is responsible for relaying messaging between various microservices that drive various stages of the booking process. The following sections will go into this in detail.

Payment

When the customer clicks on *Book* on the website, they first need to do the payment. This is a substantially complicated/cohesive task and is best done by a separate microservice **Payment Service**, in our case.

The following sequence diagram describes the flow involved in the common case of using a credit card for the payment:

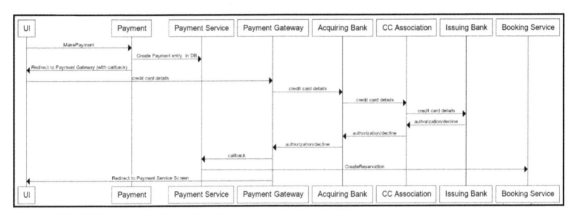

Let's look at the following steps:

1. When the customer clicks on the **Book** button on the search results page, the `MakePayment` API of the **Payment Service** (SKU) is called. The API parameters describes the SKU (which hotel, flight) and the amount.
2. The **Payment Service** makes a note of the in-flight Payment in its DB and then redirects the UI to the **Payment Gateway**, along with a callback URL. The **Payment Gateway** is very specialized software and is generally an external service.
3. The payment gateway converts the message to a standard format and then forwards the transaction information to the payment processor used by the travel website, the acquiring bank. This is the bank with which the website has made an account to handle payments.
4. The payment processor of the acquiring bank forwards the information to the card association (for example, Visa/MasterCard/American Express), and the card association in turn sends the transaction to the customer's card's issuing bank (the bank that issued the card to the customer).
5. The issuing bank receives the credit card information, verifies that the debit can be made, and then sends back an authorization or declines back to the credit card association.
6. The credit card association forwards the response to the acquiring bank, which in turn forwards it to the **Payment Gateway**.

7. The payment gateway receives the response, and then fires a callback that was given at the time of the initial redirection. This allows the payment service to know the payment status. If the Credit Card was authorized, then the payment service makes an API call to the booking service to create a reservation (see the Reservation section).

8. The UI is then redirected back to the payments page, and, subsequently, if the card was authorized, the customer is taken to the reservation screen. If there as a decline, the customer is given an appropriate error message.

Reservation

Once the payment callback is fired, we need to create a reservation entity in our booking database. The booking workflow will go through various stages, and this persistent entity will be responsible for maintaining the reservation status for all the microservices involved in the workflow.

The booking service is a REST API, and we will implement it using Gin (which we covered in Chapter 5, *Going Distributed*). The `createReservation` API, which is called during the Payment Callback, is defined in the following code:

```
func createReservation(c *gin.Context) {
    var (
        reservationDTO HotelReservationDTO
        err error
        )

    if err = c.ShouldBindJSON(&reservationDTO); err == nil {
        fmt.Printf("In createReservation : %+v\n", reservationDTO)
        err = persistReservation(&reservationDTO)
        sendMessageToPerformBooking(&reservationDTO)
        //return OK
        c.JSON(http.StatusAccepted, gin.H{"status": "created"})
    }

    if err != nil {
        // some inputs parameters are not correct
        c.JSON(http.StatusBadRequest, gin.H{"error": err.Error()})
    }
}
```

The `HotelReservationDTO` is a data-transfer object and represents an object that the client and server understand. It describes the details of the reservation:

```
type HotelReservationDTO struct {
    CustomerId uint `json:"customer_id" `
    PaymentIdentifier uint `json:"payment_identifier" `
    SKU uint `json:"entity_id" `
    RoomId uint `json:"room_id" `
    CheckIn ReservationTime `json:"check_in" gorm:"type:datetime"`
    CheckOut ReservationTime `json:"check_out" gorm:"type:datetime"`
}
```

You might be wondering why we used `ReservationTime` instead of the standard `time.Time`, well, `ReservationTime` is just a simple wrapper over `time.Time` and this is needed so that the encoding/JSON package can understand how exactly to serialize/deserialize the time. Currently, the package only accepts time in a specific format of RFC3339 (for example, `"2018-11-01T22:08:41+00:00"`), and this is unnecessarily inconvenient for us, where we want to give a date such as *2018-12-07*. The workaround in Golang is the wrapper struct, as shown here:

```
const reservationDateFormat = "2006-01-02"

type ReservationTime time.Time

func (t *ReservationTime) UnmarshalJSON(bytes []byte) error {
    rawT, err := time.Parse(reservationDateFormat, strings.Replace(
        string(bytes),
        "\"",
        "",
        -1,
    ))
    if err != nil {
        return err
    }
    *t = ReservationTime(rawT)
    return nil
}

func (t *ReservationTime) MarshalJSON() ([]byte, error) {
    buf := fmt.Sprintf("\"%s\"",
time.Time(*t).Format(reservationDateFormat))
    return []byte(buf), nil
}
```

From the preceding code, it functions as follows points:

- It creates the reservation entity in the database using `persistReservation()`.
- It then sends a Kafka message to the Seller Proxy to actually perform the booking using `sendMessageToPerformBooking()`.

For persistence, we will use MySQL as the relational database. To avoid boiler plate code, we will use an **Object Relational Mapper** (ORM), specifically **gorm** (https://github. com/jinzhu/gorm). The `persistReservation()` function is defined here:

```
func persistReservation(res *HotelReservationDTO) error {
    // Note the use of tx as the database handle once you are within a
transaction
    tx := db.Begin()
    defer func() {
       if r := recover(); r != nil {
         tx.Rollback()
       }
    }()

    if tx.Error != nil {
        return tx.Error
    }

    //TODO : Check that there is no overlapping reservation
    if err := tx.Create(&HotelReservation{
        CustomerId: res.CustomerId,
        PaymentIdentifier: res.PaymentIdentifier,
        SKU: res.SKU,
        RoomId: res.RoomId,
        CheckIn: time.Time(res.CheckIn),
        CheckOut: time.Time(res.CheckOut),
        Id: makeId(res),
        Status: Initial}).Error; err != nil {
            tx.Rollback()
            return err
    }

    fmt.Println("created hotel reservation..")

    // update the entry for availability threshold
    var threshold AvailabilityThreshold
    tx.Where("entity_id = ? AND room_id = ?", res.SKU,
res.RoomId).First(&threshold)

    fmt.Printf("\nthreshold = %+v\n", threshold)
    tx.Model(&threshold).Where("id = ?", threshold.ID)
```

```
        .Update("availability", threshold.Availability-1)

    // NOTE : availability is just a threshold for update here.
    // Even if availability is 0, reservation is forwarded to the Seller
    // And availability >0 in thresholds DB is not a guarantee of
reservation
    if threshold.Availability <= 1 {
        // we have reached threshold
        sendInvaliationMessageToPriceStore(threshold.SKU, threshold.RoomId)
    }
    return tx.Commit().Error
}
```

It kickstarts things by starting a transaction. This is important because we will be updating more than one table, and we need ACID semantics. The two main tables being updated are these:

Name	Utility	Schema

hotel_reservations	Details about a reservation, including the status.	<pre>+---------------------+--------------+------+-----+---------+-------+
		| Field | Type | Null | Key | Default | Extra |
		+---------------------+--------------+------+-----+---------+-------+
		| customer_id | int(11) | YES | | NULL | |
		| payment_identifier | int(11) | YES | | NULL | |
		| entity_id | int(11) | YES | | NULL | |
		| room_id | int(11) | YES | | NULL | |
		| check_in | datetime | YES | | NULL | |
		| check_out | datetime | YES | | NULL | |
		| status | int(10) | YES | | NULL | |
		| id | varchar(100) | NO | PRI | NULL | |
		+---------------------+--------------+------+-----+---------+-------+</pre>

availability_thresholds	Hold triggers—when the availability trigger is fired, the caches in the price store need to be invalidated, to avoid stable data.	<pre>+--------------+-----------------+------+-----+---------+----------------+
		| Field | Type | Null | Key | Default | Extra |
		+--------------+-----------------+------+-----+---------+----------------+
		| id | int(10) unsigned | NO | PRI | NULL | auto_increment |
		| created_at | timestamp | YES | | NULL | |
		| updated_at | timestamp | YES | | NULL | |
		| deleted_at | timestamp | YES | MUL | NULL | |
		| entity_id | int(10) unsigned | YES | | NULL | |
		| room_id | int(10) unsigned | YES | | NULL | |
		| availability | int(11) | YES | | NULL | |
		+--------------+-----------------+------+-----+---------+----------------+</pre>

The `availability_thresholds` table is one way to keep the price store caches fresh. After a few bookings are made, the booking service sends a message to the price store . The price store will then drop caches for which the availability threshold (the `availability` field) reached 0. Once fresh data is loaded, the price store service will send another message to the booking service, to update availability.

When the reservation is inserted, a key attribute is the status. In the preceding code, the status is in the initial state, but as the workflow progresses, then the status evolves. The status is modeled as an enum:

```
type Status int

const (
    Initial Status = 0
    BookingMade Status = 1
    EmailSent Status = 2
)
```

The sendMessageToPerformBooking() sends a Kafka message to create_booking topic, to enable the next stage of the workflow: the seller proxy. This is explained through the following code:

```
func sendMessageToPerformBooking(reservationDTO *HotelReservationDTO) {
    log.Println("sending message to kickstart booking for ",
reservationDTO)
    bytes, err := json.Marshal(reservationDTO)
    if err != nil {
        log.Println("error sending message to Kafka ", err)
        return
    }

    // We are not setting a message key, which means that all messages will
    // be distributed randomly over the different partitions.
    msg := &sarama.ProducerMessage{
    Topic: "create_booking",
        Value: sarama.ByteEncoder(bytes),
    }
    partition, offset, err := kafkaProducer.SendMessage(msg)
    if err != nil {
        fmt.Printf("FAILED to publish message: %s\n", err)
    } else {
        fmt.Printf("message sent | partition(%d)/offset(%d)\n", partition,
offset)
    }
}
```

The seller proxy microservice takes this message sent by the `sendMessageToPerformBooking()` and does the actual booking with the seller. The Seller Proxy code starts off by doing a few initializations, the main one being registering as a consumer on the `create_booking` topic.

We use the Sarama cluster (`https://github.com/bsm/sarama-cluster`) library to use the Kafka high level consumer API. The brokers heartbeat individual consumer instance and distribute partitions of the Kafka topic to healthy instances. The `init()` code is as follows:

```go
func init() {
    // setup config, enable errors and notifications
    config := cluster.NewConfig()
    config.Consumer.Return.Errors = true
    config.Group.Mode = cluster.ConsumerModePartitions
    config.Group.Return.Notifications = true

    // specify Broker co-ordinates and topics of interest
    // should be done from config
    brokers := []string{"localhost:9092"}
    topics := []string{"create_booking"}

    // trap SIGINT to trigger a shutdown.
    signals = make(chan os.Signal, 1)
    signal.Notify(signals, os.Interrupt)

    // connect, and register specifiying the consumer group name
    consumer, err := cluster.NewConsumer(brokers, "booking-service",
topics, config)
    if err != nil {
        panic(err)
    }

    // process errors
    go func() {
        for err := range consumer.Errors() {
            log.Printf("Error: %s\n", err.Error())
        }
    }()

    // process notifications
    go func() {
        for ntf := range consumer.Notifications() {
            log.Printf("Rebalanced: %+v\n", ntf)
        }
    }()

    //start the listener thread
```

```
        go handleCreateBookingMessage(consumer)
}
```

The actual work is done by the `handleCreateBookingMessage()` function, which is spawned as a go routine at the end:

```
func handleCreateBookingMessage(consumer *cluster.Consumer) {
    for {
        select {
            case partition, ok := <-consumer.Partitions():
            if !ok {
                panic("kafka consumer : error getting paritions..")
            }
            // start a separate goroutine to consume messages
            go func(pc cluster.PartitionConsumer) {
                for msg := range pc.Messages() {
                    var reservationDTO HotelReservationDTO
                    if err := json.Unmarshal(msg.Value, &reservationDTO);
err != nil {
                        fmt.Println("unmarshalling error", err)
                        // Commit even on error to avoid poison pills
                        consumer.MarkOffset(msg, "")
                        continue
                    }

                    // make actual booking with seller - here :)

                    // update status in DB
                    updateReservationStatus(&reservationDTO, BookingMade)
                    fmt.Printf("processed create booking message %s-%d-%d-
%s-%s\n",
                        msg.Topic,
                        msg.Partition,
                        msg.Offset,
                        msg.Key,
                        msg.Value) // <- Actually process message here
                consumer.MarkOffset(msg, "") // Commit offset for this
message
                }
            }(partition)

            case <-signals:
            fmt.Println("consumer killed..")
            return
        }
    }
}
```

It listens to incoming Kafka messages and when a message is received, and it does the following:

- De-serializes the payload
- Makes the actual reservation with the seller
- Updates the status in the `hotel_reservations` DB using `updateReservationStatus(&reservationDTO, BookingMade)`
- Marks the message as read

Although not shown, on a successful booking, it will also put a trigger message for the mailer service, which will notify the customer of the successful booking.

Summary

The Travel Search feature is slightly different for both flights and hotels. But by extracting common elements such as WorkTree and Listing Ingestor Lib, we can leverage coding done at one place in other places.

In the booking design, we saw how the EDA pattern helps us cleanly segregate various workflows. We use a persistent queue such as Kafka instead of channels, because we want resiliency of instances going down. The workflow can take a long time, and we don't want a bad customer experience, such as a missed booking, due to transient infrastructure blips.

In the next chapter, we will look at the deployment details of Golang applications.

11
Planning for Deployment

Now that your application is ready, you want to deploy it so that customers can access it. However, you don't do a deployment that is fragile or else the inevitable hardware/software glitches will affect customer experience. You want to be able to be able to reliably deploy new features and fix bugs in production, while minimizing the amount of time spent or mistakes made.

This chapter discusses deployment architectures that enable resilient architecture, scalability, and high-feature velocity. It starts by laying out the landscape of typical production setups, and then goes into the details of building continuous integration and deployment pipelines. We'll also look at the following:

- Deployment architecture for modern apps
- Continuous Integration/Continuous Delivery pipelines
- Monitoring solutions
- Cloud platforms
- Security considerations

Deployment architecture

A deployment architecture is a mapping of the system architecture to a physical environment. This environment consists of machines that run code, load balancers, databases, network elements, and so on. The mapping of a logical architecture and software artifacts to a deployment involves the following:

- Defining what infrastructure components are needed
- Defining the environments needed
- Sizing analysis for each environment: Estimating the number and characteristics of the resources needed for an efficient environment
- Management strategies: A pipeline that defines how new code gets deployed in an environment

This section discusses the typical components, configurations, and environments of production systems.

Components

A typical software system rarely consists of just the code. Engineering non-trivial systems means working with a wide variety of system components.

The following diagram describes typical components in a modern microservices architecture deployment:

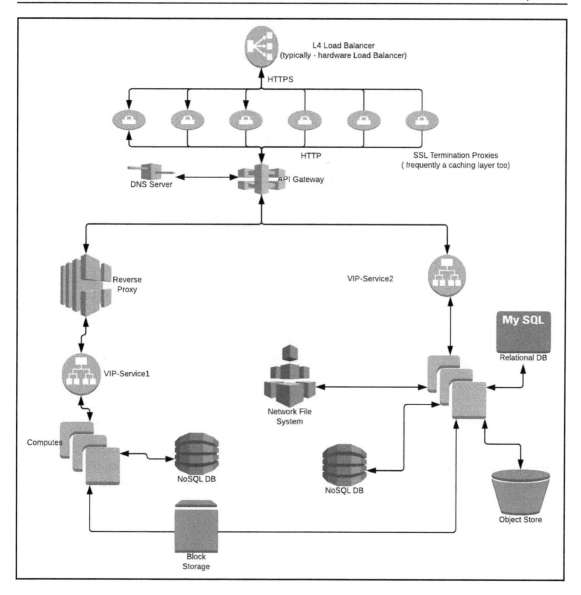

The following sections describe each component in more detail.

Computes

We need compute hardware (CPU and memory) to run the code. This section describes the various choices available for computes.

Physical Servers

Early architectures deployed code on physical servers. Each server was arranged in a rack with a switch and a storage array:

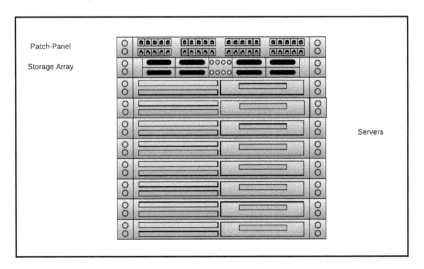

The components of a rack (server blades, network switches, and so on) are often classified in terms of their sizes or Rack Unit. This is a unit of measure used to describe the height of a device mounted in a 19-inch rack or a 23-inch rack and is approximately 44.45 mm (1.75 inches) high. Device form factors are often in terms of multiples of rack units (1U, 2U, and so on).

Physical servers provide the best performance for hardware, however, they are difficult to manage, are often unevenly utilized, and don't really have scalability (scaling here implies buying new hardware).

Virtual machines

Virtualization refers to technology that simulates hardware, such as CPU/memory on top of actual hardware, hence creating multiple *virtual machines* on top of actual hardware. The underlying hypervisor layer traps instructions that are privileged and/or go to shared state and simulate isolated environments for each virtual machine.

Virtualization enables multiple benefits, including the following:

- Better hardware resource utilization
- Allowing you to save/restore the state of a machine
- Easier maintenance, including features such as the migration of virtual machines from one physical host to another, allowing for easier maintenance of physical hardware
- Allowing applications that run on different operating systems to be deployed on standard hardware

There are many virtualization vendors including the following:

- Microsoft Hyper-V
- Linux Kernel Virtual Machine (KVM), Qemu, and related ecosystems such as Openstack
- Citrix Xenserver

Containers

Virtual machines work by packaging the application and the operating system. This makes the packages (referred to generally as images) pretty fat. It also is pretty inefficient since there are multiple operating systems running on top of the actual "host" OS.

Containers enable isolation at an OS level, using constructs such as the following:

- Quota allocation and the enforcement of resources, for example, CPU, memory, block I/O, and network
- Namespace isolation functionality that provides each container with an isolated view of the operating environment, including filesystem, process trees, user IDs, and so on

This isolation mechanism is much more efficient than the guest operating system concept in virtual machines. This enables the deployment of a lot of containers onto a single computer.

Containers initially lacked a standard packaging system. Docker solved this problem by providing a standard for packaging, a runtime (daemon), and tools (client) for packaging, managing and distributing containerized applications. The packaging format is called an image. It essentially is a template listing instructions for creating a container. Very often images are derived from another image and list specific customization from the base image.

For example, one can have an image that is based on a CentOS and installs Nginx and the application. Docker also has the concept of a registry, which is a repository of Docker images. Docker Hub and Docker Cloud are public registries that anyone can use, but one can also run their own private registry for images within an organization, as shown in the following diagram:

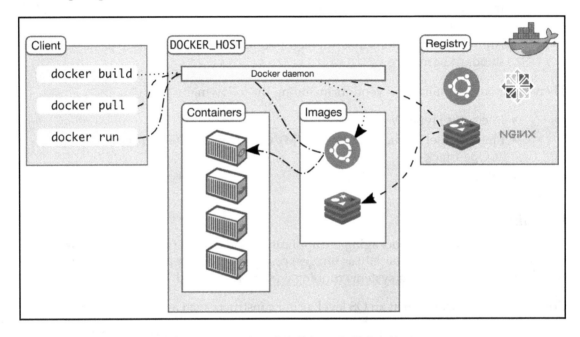

Reference: https://docs.docker.com/engine/docker-overview/#docker-architecture

While containers are cool, managing them at scale requires specialized solutions. There are many options for orchestrating containers. Kubernetes, Mesos, and Docker Swarm are some of the popular solutions.

Compute Attributes

As described previously, computes could be virtual machines or containers. The important attributes of compute instances include the following:

- Computing power: The number and speed of CPUs and cores
- The amount/configuration of RAM and cache
- The type and size of persistent storage (disks)
- Virtualized/physical machines or containers

Besides the hardware characteristics, we also need to define what other services need to run on the instance. These ancillary programs include the following:

- Process monitoring components such as supervisors
- Sidecar components, which allow connections to remove services via proxies
- Log ingestors, components that ship logs to centralized setups such as Splunk (see the *Monitoring* section)

Storage

Datacenter storage technology has three main flavors:

- **Direct Attached Storage (DAS):** This is the traditional storage solution, where disks are attached directly to servers. Access is generally arbitrated by an intelligent controller.
- **Network Attached Storage (NAS):** Here storage is essentially at a filesystem level and is shared between multiple servers using some sort of networking protocol. The remote filesystem is "mounted" at a specific location in the server operating system's filesystem tree. Two common NAS protocols are **NFS (Network File System)** and **CIFS (Common Internet File System)**. CIFS requires a dedicated separate storage server which all of the other servers to connect in order to access the data. Besides allowing for the sharing of data, the key advantages of NAS are as follows:
    - More efficient utilization of available storage capacity
    - Centralized management
- **Storage Area Networks (SAN):** Just like NAS, an SAN offers shared storage. However, SANs provide block-level access instead of sharing filesystems. This means file sharing is not possible, but the other advantage of efficient utilization is retained. SANs sometimes use specialized networking (such as Fibre Channel) in addition to the storage servers. The iSCSI protocol is a SAN solution that uses existing Ethernet devices and IP protocols, hence enabling a cost-effective SAN solution.

Networking

Networking design is a critical element of the data center architecture and hence the deployment architecture. Networking in data centers is generally based on a layered design, as shown in the following diagram:

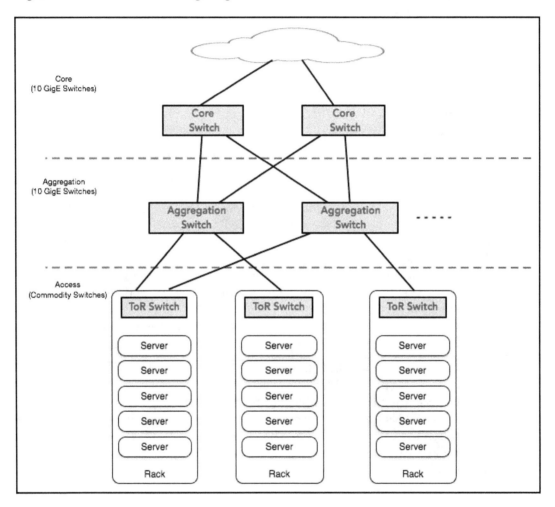

The **Core** layer provides a high-speed packet switching backplane for all flows going in and out of the data center. **Access** routers/switches, in addition to doing fault-tolerant routing, provide additional functionalities such as spanning tree processing, firewalls, intrusion detection, and SSL offload. The **Access** layer consists of **Top-of-the-Rack** (**ToR**) switches, which connect the actual servers to the networks. As you can see, there is a lot of redundancy in the wiring to avoid single points of failure. The routing protocols ensure that the redundant links are efficiently and correctly used.

Besides the hardware elements, there is a logical grouping of networking elements. Typically, in three-tier applications, the network is also segmented into three tiers (web, application, and database). This allows—among other things—restriction of network access across tiers. In today's environment, this logical architecture is implemented using **Virtual Networks** (**VLAN**), where multiple L2 isolation domains are implemented on top of the same physical networking infrastructure. Security Groups define which ports are allowed in and out of the network segments.

Load Balancers

A **Load Balancer** (**LB**) is a device which distributes incoming API requests to multiple computing resources (instances). It is able to do the following:

- Handle more work than what a single instance is capable of
- Increase reliability and availability through redundancy
- Gracefully upgrade code in instances with zero downtime

LBs can work either at the Transport or Application layers of the networking stacks. The different levels are as follows:

- **HTTP**: Here the LB routes HTTP requests to a set of backend instances. The routing logic is typically based on URLs but can also use other characteristics of the requests (User Agent, Headers, and so on). The LB typically sets some standard headers such as the X-Forwarded-For, X-Forwarded-Proto, and X-Forwarded-Port headers to give the backends information about the original request.

- **HTTPS**: HTTPS is very similar to HTTP, but the key difference is that, to be able to route requests on HTTP headers/components, SSL needs to be terminated. One the payload is decrypted and inspected for routing, the requests to the backend can either be encrypted through HTTPS or HTTP. This mandates that we must deploy an SSL/TLS certificate on the LB. The SSL and TLS protocols use X.509 certificates to authenticate both the client and the backend application. These certificates are a form of digital identity and are issued by a **certificate authority (CA)**. The certificates typically contain information such as a public key for encryption, a validity period, a serial number, and the digital signature of the issuer. Managing certificates becomes a key maintenance activity for the SSL termination.
- **TCP**: Traffic can also be routed at the TCP level. A typical example might be connecting to a set of redundant caches.
- **User Datagram Protocol (UDP)**: This is similar to TCP load balancing but more rarely used. Typical use cases might be protocols such as DNS and syslogd, which use UDP.

Depending on the level at which the LB is operating, different routing strategies are possible, including the following:

- **Direct routing**: Essentially just change the L2 network address and redirect the packet to the backend. This has huge performance benefits as the LB does very little work and the return traffic (from the backend to the client) can happen without the LB in between. This however requires the LB and backend servers to be on the same L2 network
- **Network Address Translation (NAT)**: Here the L3 address are rewritten and the LB stores a mapping so that the return traffic can be redirected to the correct client.
- **Terminate and Connect**: For most application-level load balancers, operating at the packet level is very difficult. So they terminate the TCP connection, read the data, store the payload across packets, and then, after enough information is available to make routing decisions, forwards the data to to a "backend" server via another set of sockets.

Each service (microservice) has a specific endpoint, typically a **fully qualified domain name (FQDN)**. A **Domain Name Server (DNS)** identifies the IP address for this instance. Typically this IP address is a **virtual IP address (VIP)** and identifies a set of instances (each having an actual IP address). The application level (L7) LB is the place where one provisions the VIP for each service.

Load balancers should only forward traffic to *healthy* backend servers. To gauge health, typically backend services are expected to expose an endpoint which the LB can query for instance health.

A typical production setup consists of a combination of L4 (TCP) and L7 (HTTP) load balancers with a layer of machines terminating SSL, as described in the previous diagram.

API Gateways

APIs are the lingua franca of modern applications. With a microservices-based architecture, there are multiple services whose aggregated whole is the API set of the application. An API Gateway is the "front door" to this set of APIs .

API gateway responsibilities include the following:

- Authorization and access control: Ensures that only authorized applications are accessing the APIs
- Quotas/throttling: Enables quotes and rate limits for specific APIs from specific clients
- Monitoring
- API version management
- Reducing chattiness in a microservices architecture: Enables clients to call one endpoint, which, internally, can orchestrate across multiple backend microservices

There is a feature overlap between LBs and API gateways. Generally, the former focus more on efficient routing and the latter are more feature rich. We already had an detailed look at an API gateway in Chapter 7, *Building APIs*. The following diagram provides a quick recap:

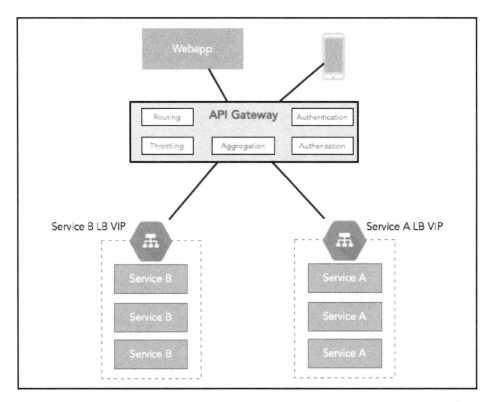

Reverse proxies

The major objective of reverse proxies is to put some functionality in between the request and the server/backend code. The functionality can be things such as SSL termination (HTTPS) or often caching.

Varnish is a HTTP proxy that is focused on caching. It gets the requests from clients and tries to answer them from its own cache. If Varnish cannot find a response from the cache, the request is forwarded to the backend server. Once the backend server responds, the answer can be cached before forwarding the same to the client. Varnish decides whether or not to cache the response based on the Cache-Control HTTP response header.

The performance benefit of Varnish can be quite dramatic, with response times often in microseconds.

Messaging brokers

As discussed in `Chapter 6`, *Messaging*, message exchange between services is a key building block for resilient, high-throughput architectures. Brokers are components that host the messages and perform the routing between producers and consumers. One example is Kafka message brokers.

When deploying brokers, it is essential to have a good estimate of the messages-per-second needed for each Topic. This enables us to compute configurations such as the CPU/memory requirements of the brokers and the storage needed for hosting messages.

Another common configuration is the replication factor, which defines the number of nodes on which the message is replicated on. This, in turn, defines how many node failures the Topic can survive and still be able to serve messages to consumers. However, to achieve such reliability, the nodes need to straddle different fault domains. Here, fault domain refers to a group of nodes, which share a common power source and network switch.

Some brokers such as Kafka contain complicated features, such as Group Co-ordinator, which enables highly available message consumption. However, in order to get this right, we need to define tuneables such as heartbeat timeouts (between the brokers and the consumers) correctly.

Environments

The individual components described previously combine together to form an "environment." The most important one is the production environment. This is the one that fulfills requests from the customers. However, there needs to be parallel environments for multiple development efforts.

A modern system goes through constant churn in terms of features/requirements and releases happen often. It is important to test the releases in a controlled environment before they get to production. This ensures that software bugs/regressions are not caught by customers first. This is known as a QA environment. Generally, the QA environment is much leaner than the production one. This is generally the first place multiple services integrate with each other, in order to fulfill a specific feature.

Sometimes the lean QA environment is not good enough to verify the non-functional requirements of the system. It is important to characterize performance of a specific release and ensure that new code has not caused performance regressions. This kind of testing generally involves a lot of load. Hence, it needs an environment close to production (or scaled appropriately so as to predict actual production performance). Hence, a performance test is generally performed in a separate environment. To save costs, this environment is generally virtual and decommissioned when not used.

There are many variations on this basic recipe of a deployment environment. One popular combination is called blue-green deployment. Here, two identical production environments (called Blue and Green) are maintained simultaneously. At any given time, only one of the environments (say Blue) takes live production traffic. New deployments go to the other cluster (say Green). Once the new deployment is vetted, the live/standby environments get flipped at the load balancer level. This technique has a couple of key benefits:

- Almost zero downtime as the new deployment happens on a totally different cluster
- If there is an issue in the current live environment, the last stable environment is available on hot-standby

The flipside of this strategy is the cost in maintaining two production-grade environments.

The following diagram depicts the Blue-Green deployment strategy:

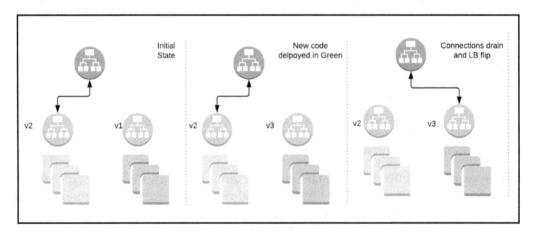

Capacity Planning and Sizing

Capacity planning (or sizing) of an environment is the process of determining the number and configurations of various components in an environment, so that the system requirements and business goals are satisfied with the required SLAs. This is not an exact science but rather its rough calculations with input from required SLAs, past design experience, domain knowledge, and applied creative thinking.

For computes, the main resources are CPUs and memory. The domain knowledge and system design indicate how much of these resources are needed for a single request:

- Is the API handling resource intensive? If yes, then more core CPUs might be needed.
- Is the API handling IO bound? If yes, then ancillary hardware like DMA will probably impact performance (rather than larger cores).
- If there is a lot of in-memory caching or recursion, then memory requirements might be large.

With these inputs one can characterize how much a single instance (of specified specifications) can serve in terms of requests per second. Once we know that each instance can handle x requests/sec and the SLA required from the service is y requests/sec, then the total number of instances can be easily found out using ceil(y/x).

As described in `Chapter 8`, *Modeling Data*, databases come in various forms and shapes. However, there are a few general considerations for production deployment:

- High availability: Ensure that no DB instance is a single point of failure.
- Storage configuration: The DB writes data to the disk. In most modern operating systems, this path is not as straightforward, and care needs to be taken to ensure that durability and performance goals are met. This includes various buffer/cache parameters in the filesystems.
- Backup: Most business-critical data is also backed up. This involves periodic snapshotting and shipping of this snapshot to a remote archive.
- CPU/memory requirements: Depending on the number of IO operations to be supported per second, appropriate CPU and memory needs to be provisioned for the the database instance.

- Compliance and access control: Production data needs to be appropriately secured such that only only a limited required set of users have read/write access to the databases. Some data might be needed to be kept encrypted (privacy concerns).
- Scripting of creation/modification of the database entities (tables, views, procedures, and so on) and having the scripts in source control.

Golang is much more resource efficient than other languages like Java. Thus, even if you have an existing system that you are migrating, the preceding exercise is fruitful.

Disaster recovery

As discussed in Chapter 9, *Anti-Fragile Systems*, disaster recovery implies ensuring business continuity and application availability in the event of a large failure like an entire data center going down. A failover deployment is kept in near sync with the main deployment via replication. Each component/service defines how important consistency in the failover site is. The tradeoff for consistency is the performance/efficiency drop in shipping data in real time to the failover side. The actual *flip* happens through DNS changes. The following diagram from Chapter 9, *Anti-Fragile Systems*, provides a quick recap:

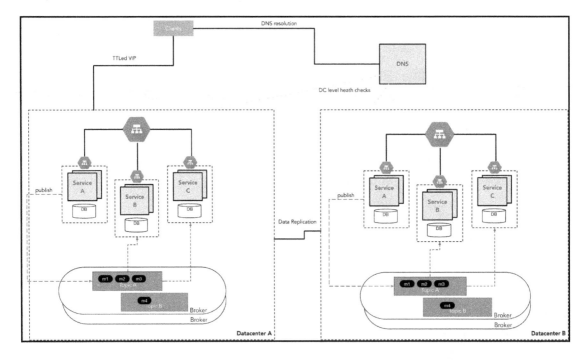

CICD

The **continuous integration, continuous delivery** (**CICD**) model was defined by Tim Fitz in his seminal book *Continuous Delivery: Reliable Software Releases through Build, Test, and Deployment Automation* in 2010. Essentially, it mandates an automated pipeline which can take new code, perform required checks/builds, and then deploy it in production. Such a system is a prerequisite for high-feature velocity development that is typical of most modern applications.

This section describes the concepts behind CICD. It describes a simple implementation and then deep dives into Go tooling which can aid in building CICD pipelines.

Overview

The CICD approach advocates the following:

- Continuous integration—continuous merging of code across developers, the automation of unit tests, code packaging, and integration with other systems of the product/organization
- Continuous testing of this integrated product across development milestones (not just at the end)
- Automated build promotion to higher-level environments based on predefined rules
- Continuous release, where promoted builds are deployed automatically to production environments

The CICD workflow or pipeline defines the various stages and gates for code to reach production from a `dev` environment, and offers tooling to automate this process. The trigger for the whole process is a webhook installed in the source control system (for example, GitHub). This hook triggers a *pipeline*, involving a set of processes which take the code, package it, test it, and deploy it, as show in the diagram:

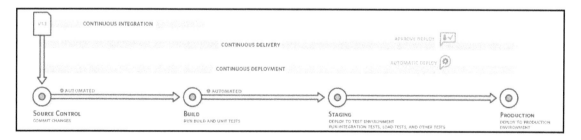

Jenkins

Jenkins is an open source automation server written in Java in 2004 by Kohsuke Kawaguchi. Jenkins can act as the end-to-end CICD orchestrator, which gets triggered from a commit and is able to build, generate documents, test, package, and, perform staging and deployment.

This section provides an overview of how to use Jenkins to set up a simple CICD pipeline for Go deployment with code hosted on GitHub. The Jenkins server will be deployed on a laptop (with macOS) and the deployment target will be an Ubuntu container.

Sample Code

In order to demonstrate an end-to-end CICD pipeline, one needs to have code to run! For this example pipeline, we will use a simple Gin-based HTTP serve. The sample code is shown here:

```go
package main

import (
    "fmt"
    "github.com/gin-gonic/gin"
)

func main() {
    fmt.Println("starting application..")
    // setup and route
    r := gin.Default()
    r.GET("/health", func(c *gin.Context) {
        c.JSON(200, gin.H{
            "status": "ok",
        })
    })

    // listen and serve on 0.0.0.0:9000
    r.Run(":9000")
}
```

We will trigger builds and deployments from this source directly (https://github.com/cookingkode/cisample).

Installing Jenkins

The official website for Jenkins is `https://jenkins.io/` and one can download Jenkins from there. Once downloaded, one can run it via the `java -jar Jenkins.war` command. Once you download and install Jenkins, you can access Jenkins through a web browser (`http://localhost:8080` by default). You should see a screen like the following:

Installing Docker

We need to have a target for deployment. In real life, this would be some sort of image of a VM/container, but here we will run a Docker container locally and deploy code on it. To run an Ubuntu container, use the following:

```
docker run -p 9000:9000 -p 32:22 -it ubuntu /bin/bash
```

This command will deploy an Ubuntu container and name it Ubuntu. It will also perform a couple of port mappings to allow for ssh and access to the HTTP server (which runs on port 9000).

We will be using SSH to transport artifacts onto the deployment target. Hence, we need to install the ssh server on the container. One can do this using the following commands:

```
apt-get update
apt-get install openssh-server
service ssh restart
```

After this, one needs to generate a key pair on the build server (in this case, the dev laptop):

```
ssh-keygen -t rsa
```

After this, we need to copy the public key (`~/.ssh/id_rsa.pub`) contents into `~/.ssh/authorized_keys` on the target server (which in this case is the Ubuntu container). Make sure your `.ssh dir` has `700` permissions and the `authorized_keys` file has `644` permissions.

Setting up Plugins

From here, we need to install some plugins to help with our CICD pipeline. Navigate to **Manage Jenkins | Manage Plugins** as we need to download the following:

SSH plugin This plugin executes shell commands remotely using SSH protocol.	2.5	Uninstall
PostBuildScript Plugin	2.5.0	Uninstall
Go Plugin Automatically installs and sets up the Go programming language (golang) tools for a build.	1.2	Uninstall
Infrastructure plugin for Publish Over X Send build artifacts somewhere.	0.21	Uninstall
Publish Over SSH Send build artifacts over SSH	1.18	Uninstall

These plugins will be used to compile Go code (Go plugin), execute custom scripts for building (**PostBuildScript Plugin**), and publish it to a remote server and execute the commands (the **Publish Over SSH** plugin). After the plugins finish downloading, we need to configure them globally. To do this, from the main Jenkins dashboard, navigate to **Manage Jenkins | Global Tool Configuration** and search for the **Go** section and set up the version:

The next step is to configure our SSH keys for deployment. From the main Jenkins dashboard, choose **Manage Jenkins | Configure System** and navigate to the **SSH** section and enter the following:

- Either the path of the key file or paste the private key content in the **Key** textbox
- The server details

In the following screenshot, the key is hidden:

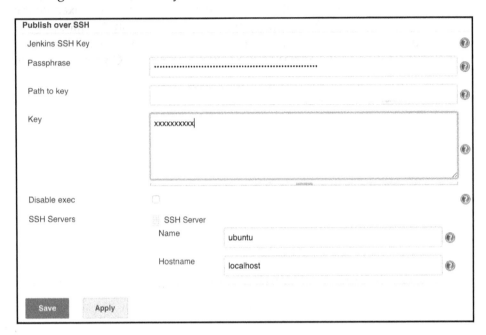

Here, since we have mapped port 32 to 22, make sure you go to **SSH Servers | Advanced** and set up the SSH **Port** as 32:

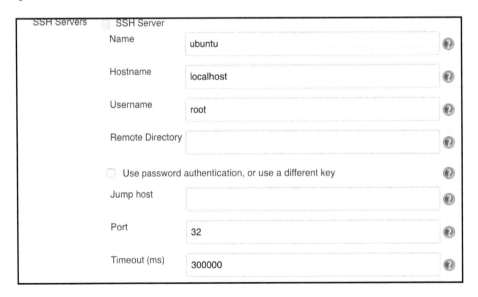

Once this is done, it is recommended to use the test connection button to ensure connectivity.

Creating a project

At this stage, we are all set to create a new project for our pipeline. Choose **New Item** from the main Jenkins dashboard, give it an appropriate name, and select **Freestyle Project**. This type allows us to set up our own workflow. The name is important as it will be the project binary that is built. After this, set up the Git (GitHub) URL of the sample project:

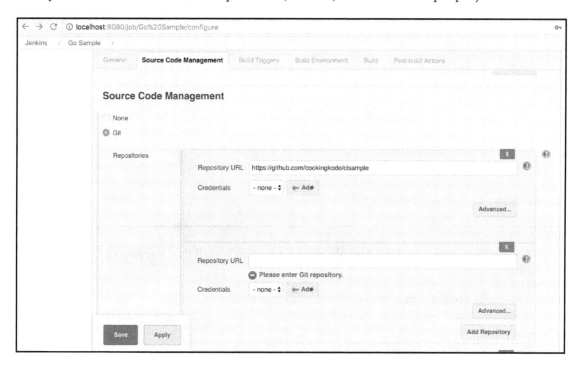

In this example, Jenkins is running on a laptop and the code is in GitHub, so we will be using build triggers rather than triggering the pipeline manually. You can leave the Build Triggers section empty.

We need to set up the Go version:

With this set, the workflow will download and you can install that version of Go prior to the builds.

Next, we configure the actual build. We can do this in discrete steps. In this example, we use just two steps—one to fetch Go and the other to do the build, as shown in the following screenshot:

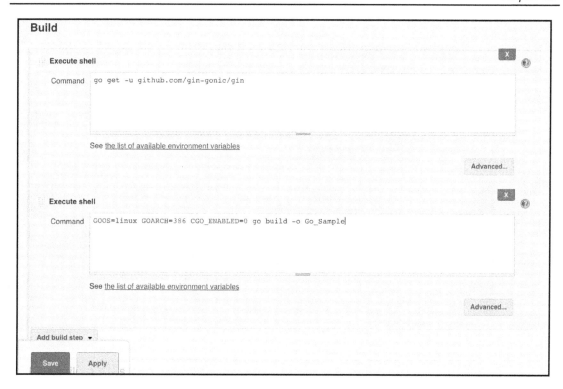

 Note that the GOOS=linux GOARCH=38 prefix is needed as my Jenkins server is on macOS, and I am going to the binary in Ubuntu in the container.

After setting up the **Build**, we need to set up the **Post-build Actions**. Here, we copy over the binary (built on the Jenkins build server) and then execute it on the target container:

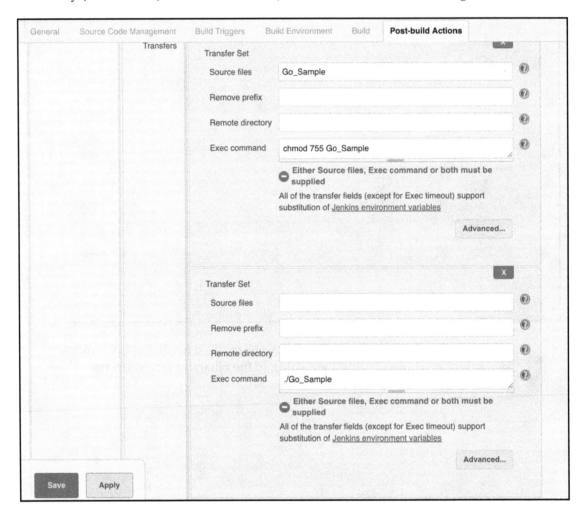

Finally our project is created.

Running the Build

Once the project is set up correctly, one can navigate to the main dashboard and fire up a build, as shown in the following screenshot:

Once the build is successful, one can test that the binary is deployed by navigating to `http://localhost:9000/health` and looking at the sample response we coded.

Target Configuration

In the sample, we set up a simple Docker container to host the binary. In real-world applications, one might need to tune few parameters to ensure correct behavior. This includes the following:

- `GOPATH` (which should be set to `$HOME/go` with GVM)
- `GOBIN` (which should be set to `$GOPATH/bin`)
- `GOMAXPROCS` (to the required number of cores/the parallelism required)

One also needs to ensure that the application process has enough privileges/limits to do its job. Most operating systems apply a wide variety of limits on various resources that a process can utilize. These include things like file descriptors, number of open files, and so on. In Linux, the ulimit tool can be used to check and manage these settings.

Finally, the Go process should be daemonized and set up as a service. For example, in an OS like Ubuntu this might mean setting up Upstart using a configuration like this one:

```
start on runlevel [2345]
stop on runlevel [!2345]
chdir /home/user/app
setgid app
setuid app
./app 1>>/var/logs/app.log 2>>/var/logs/apperr.log
```

Tooling

In the preceding sample, the CICD pipeline consisted of just doing a build (go get, and build) and deploy. However, building robust applications requires the CICD pipeline to perform lot more steps, including tests, code linters, and so on. The Go ecosystem really shines in this respect and has a plethora of tooling. The following is a brief list of Go tools which are useful in a CICD setup.

go fmt

The go fmt tool automatically formats Go source code. This includes tabs for indentation and blanks for alignment. For example, look at the following code snippet:

```
package main
import "fmt"
// sample code to demo
    // gofmt
        var b int=2;
func main(){
a := 1;
fmt.Println(" a,b : ");
        fmt.Println(a);
fmt.Println(b); }
```

It will be formatted to the following:

```
package main

import "fmt"

// sample code to demo
// gofmt
var b int = 2
func main() {
    a := 1
    fmt.Println(" a,b : ")
    fmt.Println(a)
    fmt.Println((b))
}
```

This happens thanks to Go `fmt`.

golint

The goal of the Lint tool is to make sure that the code respects the code style that is put forth in Effective Go and other public good-coding guidelines. This linter is not part of the Go tool suite so one needs to install it from `https://github.com/golang/lint`. The usage is fairly simple:

```
$golint -set_exit_status $(go list ./... )
```

The following are some issues that Go Lint catches. By default, `golint` only prints things on the console, so a CICD framework cannot easily figure out if there are any issues. The – `set_exit_status` option enables the `golint` return status to be non-zero and thus it infers errors in code. Some of the errors that `golint` flags are explored here:

- Variable names:

```
package errors

import fmt

var e = errors.New("error")

func main() {
    fmt.Println ("this program will give a golint error")
}
```

Here, `golint` would complain about the naming of variable e (`"error var e should have name of the form errFoo"`):

- Error returns:

```
package myapp

func fetchData() (error, string) {
    return nil, ""
}
```

- Last `else` in a function: Here, `golint` would complain that the error should be the last type when returning multiple items:

```
func IsGreaterThanZero(x int) int {
    if x > 0 {
        return 1
    } else {
        return 0
    }
}
```

Here `golint` would recommend that you have the last `return` outside of `else`.

Unit tests verify the functionality of the application. We have already covered how Go unit tests are written and the best practises for them. For each `.go` file, you need to have an associated `_test.go` containing the unit tests.

Clang has a detector for uninitialized reads called MemorySanitizer (described at `https://clang.llvm.org/docs/MemorySanitizer.html`). It can be used along with go test with the `-msan` flag. The CI framework should run the tests for all the packages with a command along the lines of this:

```
$go test -msan -short $(go list ./... )
```

Along with the status of the unit tests (whether there were any failures), a key metric of code reliability is code coverage. This indicates the amount of code that has been exercised by the unit tests. To calculate the code coverage ratio, we can use a script like this one:

```
$PKGS=$(go list ./... )
$for p in ${PKGS}; do
go test -covermode=count -coverprofile "cov/${package##*/}.cov" "$p" ;
done
$tail -q -n +2 cov/*.cov >> cov/total_coverage.cov
$go tool cover -func=cov/total_coverage.cov
```

go build

After we have ensured that the code meets the required quality gates, we need to compile it to make an binary. The Go team has put in special effort to make the builds fast and to enable cross compilation (as we demonstrated in the previous sample).

Footnote

It is essentially to spend time building a robust CICD pipeline. This allows for rapid deployments and feature velocity, while maintaining quality gates.

In the sample, we triggered the pipeline manually. However, as described earlier, we should configure web hooks to trigger the pipeline on code pushes. The GitHub steps for setting in this are are pretty straight forward. Navigate to the **Webhooks & Services** tab and choose **Configure Services**. Find the **Jenkins (GitHub plugin)** option and fill it with the URL to your Jenkins server, which should be something like `http://<Name of Jenkins server>:8080/github-webhook/`. Make sure to tick the `Active` checkbox and ensure things work by using the **Test Hook** button:

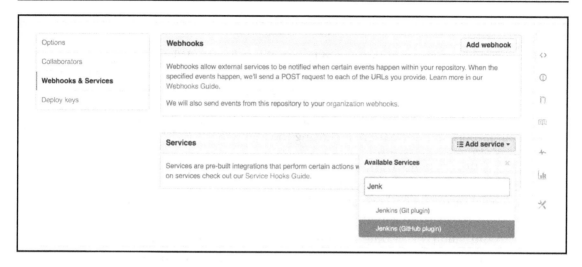

Monitoring

Once your code is deployed, you need to monitor what's going on. This requires upfront investment in figuring out the monitoring architecture and setting things up so that you are not blind once the application goes live. Without monitoring, when there are inevitable outages, your team will have limited insight into what's going on. This will hamper debuggability and ultimately impact the customer experience.

This is why proper monitoring is essential. There are five aspects to monitoring:

- Proper logging
- Proper emission of all relevant and important metrics from the application and infrastructure
- Well-designed dashboards that reflect the health of the application
- Actionable alerting system on the key metrics measured
- Having a production reliability team, which might include a **Site Reliability Engineering** (**SRE**) team and an efficient on-call rotation schedule for all developers in the team

We shall go into the details of each in the following sections.

Logs

Logging is the first thing to implement in terms of monitoring. When debugging problems in applications, developers are mostly involved in coming through the logs to put together an event chronology of what happened and where things went wrong.

To maximize the benefit of logging, it is important that the logs follow a specific structure and contain important information, including the following:

- A short, crisp description of the event that is being logged.
- Relevant data like request ID, user ID, and so on. Things like a username (email), social security numbers, and customer name should not be logged (or be masked) to avoid leaking private information about customer.
- A timestamp describing the time of occurrence of the event.
- An identifier for the thread and host for the instance of the service.
- File name, function name, line number.
- Important request and response details for all APIs.
- Tracing identifiers to identify service requests across microservices.

It is important to have a well thought out level for each log. Some information might be important in a debug environment, but in production, debug logs will become verbose and in certain situation create so much noise that the debuggability is hampered. Ideally there should be three levels:

- **Debug**: Verbose information, useful when analyzing programs in a non-production environment
- **Info**: Events that are useful for debugging in production
- **Fatal**: A critical failure that requires the program to exit

Go's standard library has a log package: `https://golang.org/pkg/log/` . It does not support leveled logging on its own but can be used to create different loggers for each level, like so:

```
Debug = log.New(os.Stdout, "DEBUG ", log.LstdFlags)
```

A common mistake is for the application to concern itself with managing log files. Instead, each process should write logs unbuffered (as an event stream), to `Stdout`. During development, the developer will view the logs in the terminal. In production, it's easy to redirect the same stream to a file `./my_service 2>> logfile` (the default logger in Go writes to `stderr` – 2).

If the standard log library is unsatisfactory, there are a wide variety of logger libraries which add functionalities like leveling on top of logs.

A quick note on logging inside packages when you want to ship to multiple developers. Here, creating a logger instance inside the package is not an good idea, since now the client application is coupled with the logger library that the package is using. Even worse, if the final application has many packages, each with a different logger with a different format, then browsing through the different logs will not be easy—not to mention the unnecessary bloat of logger libraries. In this case, it would be much more elegant to take a logger as input from the application (client) code, and the package can just use the logger to emit events. The client could specify the logger in an initialization function that the library provides.

Logs from each instance need to be aggregated and available at a central place. A common architecture for this is called the **Elasticsearch, Logstash, Kibana** (**ELK**) stack. Elasticsearch is an inverted-index database service that is based on the Apache Lucene search engine. Logstash is an ingestor tool that accepts input from various sources, transforms, and exports the result to multiple sinks, Elasticsearch in this case. Kibana is a visualization layer on top of Elasticsearch. Typically, Logstash takes logs from a file and ships them to Elasticsearch where they are indexed into different indices with the format `logstash-YYYY.MMM.DD`. One can use regex closure for search, `oo` to explore all of the log data from say June 2018, one could specify the index pattern `logstash-2018.06*`.

It's important to note that log files can get big very quickly. If they eat up the disk space then the application might get affected. Thus, it's important to rotate the logs to keep the most recent ones and discard the old logs. Ingestors like logstash have tuneables to rotate log files as part of the ingestion process.

Metrics

Key metrics need to be identified and monitored at each service, host, infrastructure, and support component (such as a database) level. All of these in total should provide necessary and sufficient information for describing the behavior and health of the system.

These raw metrics can be aggregated and processed to form higher-level metrics. They should be granular enough so that a developers can know the status of a metrics for a specific service on a specific host. It should also be possible to have the metrics aggregated so the metrics for the service are available across all hosts it runs on. For example, it should be possible to find out the CPU utilization of a service on a specific host and across all hosts that it is deployed on.

The following are some of the metrics that can be measured:

Infrastructure	CPU utilization Memory utilization Disk utilization IOPS of storage devices
Application (system level)	Number of goroutines Heap size Number of open file descriptors Number of database connections Kernel logs
Application (business level)	SLA performance for all API endpoints API success rates Business transactions Errors Crashes Application logs
Client	Real User Monitoring Client-side performance of all API endpoints Crashes Client Logs

The ELK stack also provides a component called **Metricsbeat**, which essentially ships Go metrics to Elasticsearch. For more details on tuning go apps with Kibana, you can visit `https://www.elastic.co/blog/monitor-and-optimize-golang-application-by-using-elastic-stack`.

Application Performance Monitoring/Dashboards

Dashboards (or APM tools) should provide a single-pane-of-glass view to the health of a system. This includes the hardware, the application, and related services. Well-designed dashboards give developers an easy, visual way to detect anomalies in system's health and behavior.

A popular application monitoring system is Newrelic. It has support for Go. The following screenshot showcases important metrics that can be gleaned in real time using the plugin:

Chapter 11

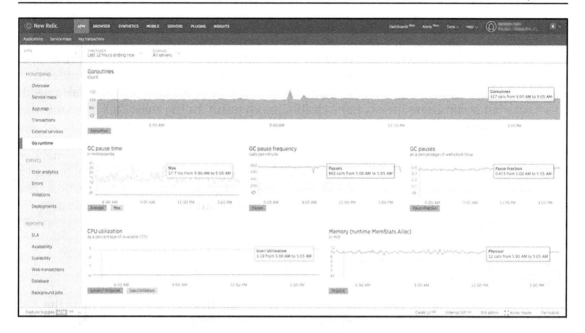

Reference: https://newrelic.com/golang

According to Newrelic, the Go agent has the following abilities:

- Viewing the datastore calls and external services your application is accessing
- Isolating operations that may be causing bottlenecks in responses
- Using deployment markers to view changes in app performance and runtime behavior between deploys
- Writing custom events and building custom dashboards with New Relic Insights

One important feature in dashboards is trend analysis. If we are seeing a graph of the response time of an API over the last few minutes, it is useful to have an overlay of the response time of the API—the same time last week for example. This enables developers to quickly grasp if there is a big anomaly currently for the API.

Most problems are caused by new deployments of code. To help developers quickly isolate problems in new code, it helps to include information about when a deployment occurred in the dashboard. The deployment times are shown as clear visual elements (for example, vertical red lines) in graphs of metrics (over time).

Alerts

Having dashboards is not enough; we cannot expect developers to constantly monitor dashboards 24/7. One needs real-time alerting. This means the ability to set thresholds on metrics and the identification of critical logs/events. As part of the alert setup, we also need to set up what is considered the communication mechanism for the alert. This mechanism can vary from a simple email to sophisticated solutions such as PagerDuty.

Breaching of these thresholds could lead to an outage, cause a spike in latency, or somehow affect customer experience, and hence a notification needs to go out to the relevant teams to set right the situation. Importantly, the thresholds should be set so that the notification goes out before a catastrophic situation occurs. There should be sufficient time for the team to debug and help correct the situation.

Team

There is no point in monitoring or alerts if there is nothing that is done to remediate the situation. Once an alert has been triggered, a team needs to triage, debug, and resolve each alert. There are two objectives here:

- Immediately bring the production environment to a stable state
- Collect all data necessary (if necessary, take out an instance from the production cluster) to enable effective root cause analysis

The first objective is of the topmost priority. Debugging a down system in production causes outage extension and inefficient debugging.

To help in production outages, there needs to be step-by-step instructions on how to debug various situations. This is typically called an on-call runbook. For each alert, the engineer can consult the runbook to identify known causes of deviations from the norm, how to correct the situation, and how to debug/collect more information. These runbooks are for both infrastructure as well as for each service.

Traditionally, organizations used to have an operations team, which used to do things by hand. The runbooks described here were more manual commands to run. However, with increased scale, complexity, and feature-velocity, people realized that such a process does not scale. Most organizations are moving to the Site Reliability Engineering (SRE) team, which was first set up by Google. An SRE team is a team of engineers who use software tooling to manage all the software and infrastructure of the application. Effectively, the runbooks are automated, so that actions previously done by hand happen automatically.

The SRE team is generally complimented by a set of "on-call" developers from the individual service teams. These on-call developers are responsible for their services in production, and do the detailed debugging and L2 support. They work very closely with the SRE team during production incidents.

While we described a quick introduction of how a DevOps team can be set up, there is still a lot of details to work out on. The details are, however, out of scope for this book.

Clouds

Cloud computing refers to the ability to provision computing infrastructure and higher-level services for an application from an external provider over the internet. Companies offering these multi-tenant computing services are called cloud providers and typically charge on a pay-per-use basis, thus enabling delivery of infrastructure and services in a utility model.

In the spirit of service-oriented architecture, cloud computing is packaged in three broad flavors, which are described next.

Infrastructure as a Service (IaaS)

Here, the cloud provider gives users direct access to computing resources such as servers, storage, and networking. Organizations use this and deploy their own technology stack of this infrastructure. Instead of purchasing hardware outright, users essentially rent hardware. The computing resources are scalable and one can control the type and number of instances. The following table gives a sampling of different types of compute instances in **Amazon Web Service** (**AWS**) and the IaaS offering (EC2) and showcases the rich variety available:

Type	Usage	Sample Cconfigurations
T2	Enables burst computing—essentially the user selects a baseline level of CPU performance with the capability to burst above the baseline. The ability to burst is controlled by CPU credits. Every T2 instance regularly gets CPU credits at an established rate that is based on the size of the instance. The credits are spent when the instance does actual CPU usage. These instances are suitable for workloads that do not require the full CPU consistently, such as developer environments.	t2.nano: 1 vCPU, 0.5G RAM, 3 CPU credits/hour t2.medium: 2 vCPU, 4G RAM, 24 CPU credits/hour t2.2xlarge 8 vCPU, 32G RAM, 81 CPU credits/hour
M4	M4 instances are general purpose instances based on custom Intel Xeon E5-2676 v3 Haswell processors (which are optimized specifically for AWS). These instances are also provided with enhanced networking, which increases the networking packet rate by up to four times while guaranteeing reliable latency. An example use case is mid-tier databases.	m4.large: 2 vCPU, 8G RAM m4.xlarge 4 vCPU, 16G RAM m4.16xlarge 64 vCPU, 256GRAM
C4/C5	C4 instances are compute-optimized instances, based on custom 2.9 GHz Intel Xeon E5-2666 v3 processors, with Intel Turbo Boost Technology enabled. These instances enable maximum performance at a given price. They are suitable for compute-bound applications such as media transcoding, gaming servers, and so on.	c4.2xlarge: 8 vCPU, 15G RAM c5.large: 2 vCPU, 4G RAM c5.4xlarge: 16 vCPU, 32G RAM c5d.large: 2 vCPU, 4G RAM, 1 x 50 NVMe SSD

X1/R4	These instances are best suited for large-scale, in-memory applications and offer the lowest price for a GB of RAM among AWS EC2 instances. They are intended for hosting in-memory databases and enterprise solutions such as SAP HANA and so on. These instances provide 1,952 GB of DDR4 based memory, eight times the memory provided by any of the AWS EC2 instances. R4 instances support enhanced networking. X1 instances provide SSD storage and are EBS-optimized by default.	r4.large: 2 vCPU, 15.25 G RAM r4.4xlarge: 16 vCPU, 122G RAM r4.16xlarge: 64 vCPU, 488G RAM X1.32xlarge: 28 vCPU, 1,952GRAm
G2	G2 instances are meant for applications which want to utilize GPUs, for example modeling, machine learning, rendering, transcoding jobs, and game streaming. These instances provide a high-performing NVIDIA GPU with 4 GB of video memory and 1,536 CUDA cores.	g3.8xlarge: 2 GPUs, 32 vCPUs, 244 G RAM
I2, H1	These are storage-optimized instances and offer fast SSD-backed instance storage. This is the best available storage option for random unput/output performance and provide maximum IOPS at a given lowest cost. H1 instances also offer enhanced networking and are best for use cases like MapReduce jobs, distributed filesystems such as HDFS, Apache Kafka, and so on. I2 instances are ideal for NoSQL solutions like MongoDB, Redis, and so on.	t3.4xlarge: 16 vCPU, 122 G RAM h1.2xlarge 8 vCPU, 32 G RAM

Platform as a Service (PaaS)

The **Platform as a Service** (**PaaS**) model is a higher-level offering than Iaas, where the cloud provider offers managed services for building blocks like databases, caches, and so on. This allows application developers to focus on business use cases without getting bogged down in infrastructure management. Compared to IaaS, the PaaS components are higher up in the software stack.

The advantage of PaaS should be immediately obvious. The software team can immediately get started with their development, spinning up utilitarian services as needed. Providers manage everything else, such as software versions, security, operating systems, and backups. Most of the services are very elastic and can be scaled vertically (for example, adding more IOPS) or horizontally (adding more numbers) on demand via a management console. The tradeoffs for PaaS services versus IaaS are listed here:

- Generally a higher cost than do-it-yourself solutions
- Vendor lock-in: If you code for a specific cloud service, it will be difficult to migrate the application onto another cloud stack
- Limited development setup: Developers generally share dev accounts on the cloud, because most PaaS services are not deployable on development machines

The following table offers insight into the vast array of AWS-managed services:

Databases	**Relational Database Service** (**RDS**) (`https://aws.amazon.com/rds/`)is a managed ACID-compliant relational **database-as-a-service** (**DBaaS**) where the database's resilience, scale, and maintenance are primarily handled by the platform. RDS offers familiar engines like MySQL, MariaDB, PostgreSQL, Oracle, Microsoft SQL Server, and also lately a new, MySQL-compatible internally developed engine called the `Amazon Aurora DB` engine. The storage type can be configured from magnetics disks to SSDs. One important feature that RDS provides is multi-availability zone high-availablity (replication across infrastructure fault domains). DynamoDB (`https://aws.amazon.com/dynamodb/`) is a multi-model NoSQL offering from AWS and can be used to model key values, documents, graphs, and columnar data. It is globally distributed, thus enabling high availability. Among other cool features, DynamoDB automatically scales capacity up or down, as the application requests volume increase or decrease. AWS Elasticache (`https://aws.amazon.com/elasticache/`) is a fully managed cache services which provides Redis and Memcached servers/clusters. Using these services absolves users of provisioning hardware and software for the cache solutions.

	AWS Redshift (`https://docs.aws.amazon.com/redshift/latest/mgmt/welcome.html`) is a fully managed elastic data warehouse. Its main objective is to act as a data lake where all business-relevant data is stored for long-term storage and enables multiple use cases like business intelligence and machine learning model training. Users can create clusters, where each cluster can host multiple databases. Each cluster comprises a leader node, and a set of compute nodes. The compute nodes actually host slices which are effectively shards of the data. The leader node receives queries and commands from client programs, parses them, and builds an execution plan for each compute node. The Leader creates compiled code and distributes it to the compute nodes (based on what data is a resident of each compute node). Once the Compute nodes processes the relevant code it passes on the results to the Leader node, which aggregates the result. Redshift stores the data in a columnar format. This, along with the **Massively Parallel Processing** (**MPP**) feature, makes it optimal for executing OLTP workloads. The compute node slices are databases based on PostgreSQL. Client applications can communicate with Redshift using standard open source PostgreSQL JDBC and ODBC drivers
Networking	AWS Virtual Private Cloud (`https://aws.amazon.com/vpc`) is an isolated, private network perimeter in the cloud. Once users get a VPC, they have control over their networking environment, including definition of IP ranges, route tables, subnets, and so on. Using a VPC, one usually creates a public internet-facing subnet for the web servers and another isolated subnet which has components like databases or application servers. The latter subnet does not have access to the internet. One can leverage multiple layers of security rules including security groups and network access control lists, to help control access to instances within subnets. The VPN gateway can be used to bridge external/current networks with the cloud VPCs. Sometimes the VPN connectivity does not offer the required bandwidth for interconnection of networks. AWS Direct Connect (`https://aws.amazon.com/directconnect/`) enables dedicated network connection from the current premises to AWS. AWS CloudFront (`https://aws.amazon.com/cloudfront`) is a **content delivery network** (**CDN**) service, which hosts content such as audio, video, applications, images, and even API responses close to where the clients are. This leverages the global AWS infrastructure files. CloudFront is also seamlessly integrated with other AWS infrastructure offerings like **Web Application Firewall** (**WAF**) and Shield Advanced to help protect applications from more threats, such as DDoS attacks.

API management	AWS Elastic Load Balancing (`https://aws.amazon.com/elasticloadbalancing/`) is a manager load balancer, which distributes incoming traffic across multiple backends, such as Amazon EC2 instances, containers, and IP addresses. It has L7 (application) and L4 (TCP) level load balancing features and can targets in a VPC. AWS API gateway (`https://aws.amazon.com/api-gateway`) is a hosted API gateway that enables features like traffic management, authorization and access control, monitoring, throttling, and version management. AWS Route 53 (`https://docs.aws.amazon.com/Route53/latest/DeveloperGuide/Welcome.html`) is a DNS service with additional features including the health monitoring of backend services.
Orchestration, management, and monitoring	AWS OpsWorks (`https://aws.amazon.com/opsworks/`) is a a managed Chef/Puppet which allows for CICD platforms and enables the automation of the configuration of the application/servers. AWS CloudWatch (`https://aws.amazon.com/cloudwatch/`) is a hosted service for monitoring cloud resources (like Amazon EC2 instances, Amazon DynamoDB tables, and Amazon RDS DB instances) , as well as application-level custom metrics and log files. One can also use Amazon CloudWatch to set alarms and automatically reacts to changes in these metrics. AWS X-Ray (`https://aws.amazon.com/xray/`) provides an end-to-end view of requests as they travel through different microservices/layers of an application. AWS Management Console is a unified console to manage all cloud infrastructure and services.

Software as a service (SaaS)

Software as a service (**SaaS**) provides you with a hosted product that is run and managed by a service provider. With a SaaS offering, you do not have to think about the infrastructure or even the tech stack of the service; you just need to know how to use it. An example of a SaaS application is web-based email where you can send and receive emails without having to install/manage an email server of your own.

Security

As applications become intertwined with human life and with more and more bad actors around, the need to secure your applications becomes imperative. A few of the common security threats are detailed here:

- **Sensitive data leakage**: Some of the data being passed over APIs and stored in databases can be incredibly sensitive (phone numbers, credit card numbers, and so on). Hackers might want to steal this data. Besides preventing such theft, there are often legal regulations on privacy to ensure that data is encrypted at rest and in transit. Companies can be liable for legal injunction if they allow theft from their platforms.

- **Denial of Service**: Denial of Service attacks attempt to make applications unavailable by overwhelming them with fake/spurious traffic. A particularly nasty form of such an attack is a **Distributed Denial of Service (DDos)** attack where the traffic is sourced from multiple sources to avoid detection of the traffic generation source.

- **Cross-Site Scripting (XSS)**: In these attacks, malicious scripts are injected into otherwise benign and trusted websites, such as in comments on a forum. When the user clicks on these links, the scripts are executed with the user authentication information cached in the browser and this can cause malicious behaviour.

- **Injection attacks**: Attacks such as SQL injection, LDAP injection, and CRLF injection involve an attacker sending some sort of script inside a form and when the script runs, it causes commands to execute without proper authorization. The script could be as destructive as dropping an entire database table.

- **Weak authentication**: Hackers get access to sensitive applications such as banking websites because the authentication mechanisms are not hardened enough. Simple authentication mechanisms like passwords can be easily stolen/inferred.

Some of the remediation strategies include the following:

- Authenticate and authorize all API requests: Authentication is used to reliably determine the identity of an end user. Authorization refers to the process of determining what resources only the identified user has access. For APIs, the authentication mechanism is often a temporal access token, which can be obtained/refreshed via an external mechanism. This token is sent with each API request. This token can be processed at the backend and can be used to reliably infer the identity of the user. Sometimes authorization information (like roles) are encoded in the token. There are many standards for authorization tokens, and JWT (JSON Web Tokens) is a popular one. It is based on an open standard (RFC 7519) for securely transmitting information between parties as a JSON object. This information can be verified and trusted because it is digitally signed, and thus tampering of the information in transit can be easily caught . JWTs can be signed using a secret (with the HMAC algorithm) or a public/private key pair. `https://github.com/dgrijalva/jwt-go` is an Golang library for JWT usage.

- For sensitive human-consumable applications like banking websites, **multi-factor authentication** (**MFA**) reduces the risk of compromised accounts. Here, besides a standard username/password authentication, an alternative authentication mechanism (such as sending a one-time code to a registered phone number) is used. Thus, even if the password is stolen, access is not granted to the hacker.

- Privacy concerns can be mitigated via the encryption of data. HTTPS is the de facto standard for secure messages and internally uses TLS/SSL to encrypt the payload. The standard Go library `net/http` package has `http.ListenAndServeTLS()`, which allows HTTPs to serve out of the box from a Go application. However, a more popular option is to use a sidecar, with a specialized HTTPS sink-like Caddy or Ngnix, which proxies a Go application. We already looked at Nginx earler; Caddy (`https://caddyserver.com/`) is an HTTPS reverse proxy, written entirely in Go. It has some cool features including :

  - **Modern ciphers** including AES-GCM, ChaCha, and ECC by default, balancing security and compatibility.
  - **Man-in-middle detection**: Caddy can detect when the client's TLS connection is likely being intercepted by a proxy, giving you the ability to act accordingly. Because it's written in Go, its not affected by memory-safety attacks like Heartbleed.
  - **Mutual authentication:** With TLS client authorization support in Caddy, you can allow only certain clients to connect to your service. PCI-compliant code.

- **Key rotation**: Caddy rotates TLS session ticket keys by default, thus helping preserve forward secrecy, as in visitor privacy. That said, at the time of writing, Nginx is still faster than Caddy. To see the performance comparison between the two, you can visit `https://ferdinand-muetsch.de/caddy-a-modern-web-server-vs-nginx.html`.

- **Quotas and throttling:** If a typical API has a profile of about two **requests per second** (**RPS**) per user, then a load of 10 RPS from a user can be deemed to be suspicious. Quotas can be used to ensure that specific users have a set limit, in terms of the number of requests per second for each API. Throttling also protects APIs from DOS attacks. Caddy has the `http.ratelimit` construct to rate-limit requests from a particular IP address. NginX has a more feature-rich rate limiter, allowing for the rate limiting of specific geos, headers, and so on (described in detail at `https://www.nginx.com/blog/rate-limiting-nginx/`). The NginX implementation uses the leaky bucket algorithm for rate limiting, where the leaky buckets represents a **first-in, first-out** (**FIFO**) scheduling algorithm.

- **Using security headers**: The HTTP headers have a variety of security-related headers. For example, the Allowed Hosts header provides a list of **fully qualified domain names** (**FQDN**) that are allowed to serve your site. This prevents attacks such as DNS cache poisoning .

This section was meant to provide a high level overview of different things to consider in securing applications. Security is a big area to cover and a detailed treatment is out of the scope of this book.

Summary

Planning for deployment is a much bigger effort than most people imagine it to be. If we don't give it enough thought and time, then we risk instability in production. This chapter introduced the common elements in production, and offered pointers on how to build a secure/robust code delivery pipeline.

So far in the book, we have covered various aspects of engineering systems in Go, ending with this chapter on deployments. In the following chapter , we will end the book by looking at various aspects of migrating non-Go application to Golang.

12
Migrating Applications

Go is a relatively new language, but it has quickly made a name for itself by being the most loved and most used language among developers. People love to code in it!

Here is a ranking of the most loved programming languages:

Language	Percentage
Rust	78.9%
Kotlin	75.1%
Python	68.0%
TypeScript	67.0%
Go	65.6%
Swift	65.1%
JavaScript	61.9%

Most wanted ranks can be seen in this illustration:

Python	25.1%
JavaScript	19.0%
Go	16.2%
Kotlin	12.4%
TypeScript	11.9%
Java	10.5%
C++	10.2%

Reference: https://insights.stackoverflow.com/survey/2018

Considering the excitement, a lot of programming work involves the migration of existing code. This chapter talks about some of the drivers for migration from other languages, such as Python and Java. We will cover a few gotchas for developers looking at Go from these backgrounds. Finally, we will also check out a process for orchestrating the migration (including strategies for handling generics).

Reasons for migration

In this section, we will look at concerns that people face in various languages and whether migration to Go can alleviate them.

Python

Python is an interpreted programming language known for its expressiveness and ability to support high-velocity product development. Its ecosystem also encompasses powerful frameworks, such as Django, that make building web applications extremely easy and error-proof. Many studies, such as the one in the following reference, have consistently shown that Python is more than twice as productive as Java:

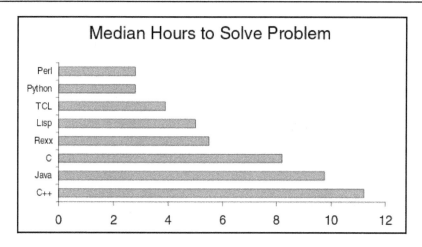

That said, Python is not without its quirks. The following list describes some of the challenges people face when developing with Python:

- **Performance:** Since Python in an interpreted language, computation performance is generally much slower than code that is compiled to native code, due to the extra level of indirection. There is also a lot of thread-serialization in Python programs due to something called the **global interpreter lock** (GIL). This is a lock (mutex) inside the Python interpreter and it is needed as the interpreter is not thread-safe. Without this lock, multiple threads executing inside the interpreter can cause severe consistency problems. For example, two threads can simultaneously increment the reference count of the same object, and, due to the race condition, the count could end up being incremented only once. To avoid such issues, Python code inside the interpreter is serialized by talking the GIL. The result is a pretty significant performance hit on multithreaded programs. The following table shows the performance benchmark results of Python versus Go:

Benchmark	Go execution time (seconds)	Python execution time (seconds)
Mandelbrot	5.48	279.68
spectral-norm	3.94	193.86
binary-trees	28.80	93.40
n-body	21.37	882.00
k-nucleotide	12.77	79.79

There are third-party packages, such as `gevent`, that tout concurrency, but the programming model is difficult and they rely on monkey-patching of other libraries, which may cause unexpected behavior.

- **Developer-induced complexity:** Python is a very dynamic language and sometimes the freedom causes developers to go overboard and write *cute* code. This code, over time, becomes very difficult to read, understand, and maintain. You cannot understand the code by just reading it; you need to run through multiple scenarios to get a feel for what's happening. One strange example is the following snippet, which changes the value to internal keyword `True`:

```
>>> True = False
>>> if True == False:
...     print "what "
...
what
```

- **Dynamic Typing:** The programming freedom offered by Python leads to another form of complexity: dynamic typing. Consider the following Python code:

```
ages = { "Abe" : 10, "Bob"   : 11,   "Chris" : 12}
def ambiguos_age(name):
    to_ret = "not found"
    try :
        to_ret = ages[name]
    finally:
        return to_ret
print ambiguos_age("Abe")
print ambiguos_age("Des")
```

Here, the `ambiguos_age()` function sometimes returns a string and sometimes an integer. This example might look contrived, but situations such as this can easily arise in production code where functions are deeply nested. This behavior can then cascade into external contracts (such as the JSON response of APIs). Now, if you have a typical Android app (written in Java, which is strongly typed), you will observe the strange behavior of the API sometimes breaking in deserialization.

There will also be a sense of familiarity for Python programmers. Go can alleviate many of the concerns here:

- The Go programming model epitomizes concurrency and parallelism. Python programmers immediately feel the freedom to model concurrency inherent in the problem they are solving.
- Go is strongly typed. The `ambiguos_age()` type of code errors are caught by the compiler! When I first ported Python code into Go, I was surprised by the amount of erroneous code that we had out there in production! While being statically typed, type inference in Go allows brevity, which is something Python programmers treasure.
- A lot of multithreaded code gets easier to read/maintain with channels. It might take some time to refactor all the mutex lock/unlock-based code into the pipes and filters model based on channels, but the long term maintenance benefit will more than pay off the initial cost of porting.
- One of the benefits of Python that I (and many other developers) like is the strong formatting guidelines—in particular, indentation. This allows consistency in program layout that enables, among other things, faster code reviews. Go is not as strict in enforcing indentation, although there's the need to start the bracket on the same line as the start of the block. The go fmt tool comes in handy to perform automated formatting (including indentation) and can be included in the Makefile to enforce consistent formatting.

> You might be wondering, *why are there brackets but no semicolons? And why can't I put the opening bracket on the next line?*
>
> Go uses brackets for statement grouping, a syntax familiar to programmers who have worked with any language in the C family. Semicolons, however, are for parsers, not for people, and we wanted to eliminate them as much as possible. To achieve this goal, Go borrows a trick from BCPL; the semicolons that separate statements are in the formal grammar but are injected automatically, without look ahead, by the laxer at the end of any line that could be the end of a statement. This works very well in practice but has the effect that it forces a bracket style. For example, the opening bracket of a function cannot appear on a line by itself (`https://golang.org/doc/faq#semicolons`).

There will be some gotchas during migration:

- Like most modern languages, Python has exception-handling as a key language construct. In fact, trying something out and catching an exception using the try-except construct is idiomatic Python. The Go error-handling is basically return of errors from the function and expecting the client to handle the error (which may mean passing it to its own caller). This leads to very verbose error-handling code. It also can be easy to write code that ignores errors in a function, which could lead to wrong behavior or even program crashes.

- Package-management is also something of a grey area in Go. The Python virtual environment concept (using `venv` and a `requirements.txt` requirements file) allows easy management of dependencies.

> There are upcoming standards, such as Dep and Govendor in the Go ecosystem, that aim to solve this. As we saw earlier, another easy way to manage dependencies is by using a vendor directory in your GitHub repository.

- Sometimes Go code is slower than Python. Yes, surprisingly so! A few years back, the Python simple JSON package was about 5x faster than encoding/JSON in decoding and about 2-3x faster than encoding/jSON in encoding. This was because the Python code actually utilized a C extension.

> JSON encoding/decoding has gotten faster, and there is a ticket to track this (`https://github.com/golang/go/issues/5683`). There are also many third-party JSON parsers that claim to be much faster (such as `https://github.com/valyala/fastjson`).

- Python programmers can get irritated initially that it takes longer to get to working code (working through all the compiler errors including things such as unused imports—which many developers feel is overkill as an error). But this is just an initial feeling, and they quickly understand the long term benefits of having better-quality code. There are also tools such as `goimports` (fork of gofmt), which you can plug into your editor to run as you save a file.

> Go marks unused imports as errors to enable build speed and program clarity. You can read more about this at `https://golang.org/doc/faq#unused_variables_and_imports`.

- **IDE**: Python has a variety of IDEs and Go initially did lack good support. Today, there are many plugins that allow things such as autocomplete. A comprehensive list of plugins can be found at `https://github.com/golang/go/wiki/IDEsAndTextEditorPlugins`. The most featureful is the GoLand IDE from JetBrains (`https://www.jetbrains.com/go/`).

Java

Java is a strongly typed interpreted programming language created by James Gosling. The first publicly available version of Java (Java 1.0) appeared in 1995, and since then it's been the mainstay of enterprise and web programming workloads. In 2006, Sun Microsystems started to make Java available under the GNU **General Public License** (**GPL**) and Oracle (which bought out Sun) continues this project under the name of OpenJDK.

There are a few reasons for Java's success:

- **Platform independence:** Java source code is compiled (transformed) into bytecode, which is a target-independent representation of the program. The bytecode consists of instructions that will be interpreted by the **Java virtual machine** (**JVM**)—JVM is an integral part of the Java platform. This mechanism makes programs very portable—packaged bytecode (JAR) can run unmodified on any platform where there is a supported JVM.
- **Object orientation:** Java provides programming constructs to enable object-oriented programming, including classes, inheritance, polymorphism, and generics. There is also support for advanced paradigms such as aspect-oriented programming.
- **Automatic memory management:** Unlike the other prevalent languages at that time (such as C++), the Java programmer does not need to manage dynamic memory manually. The JVM tracked memory allocation and freed objects that had no active pointers to them. This part of the JVM, called the garbage collector, has gone through multiple iterations to make dynamic memory allocation robust and minimally invasive.

- **Ecosystem:** The Java ecosystem has evolved to have incredible libraries that solve almost any generic problem you might have, including things such as database drivers, data structures, and threading support. There are sophisticated dependency management tools too—the most popular one being Maven. It is essentially a build framework—but not only does it describe how the Java program is to be built, it also lists its dependencies on other external modules and components. Besides the names of the dependencies, the versions are also mentioned. Maven then dynamically downloads Java libraries for these dependencies from one or more repositories, such as the Maven Central Repository, and stores them in a local cache. In case you are building a reusable library of your own, the Maven local can also be updated with JARs of such local projects. All this enables a comprehensive ecosystem of reusable components and dependency management.
- **Application frameworks:** The Java ecosystem has pioneered the frameworks around **Inversion of Control (IoC)** and **Dependency Injection (DI)**. These patterns allow the wiring of code dependencies without explicitly mentioning or instantiating specific implementations.

For example, consider the following snippet of code:

```
public class ContactsController {
    private ICache contactCache;
    public ContactsController() {
        this.contactCache = new    RedisCache();
    }
}
```

Here, `ContactsController` is an API provider for contacts, and to do its job, it uses a cache for the most frequently accessed contacts. The constructor explicitly instances a `RedisCache()` implementation for the `theCache` interface. This unfortunately defeats the purpose of the `ICache` abstraction since now `ContactsController` is coupled with a specific implementation.

One way to avoid this is for the client that instantiates the `ContactsController` class to provide the cache implementation:

```
public class ContactsController {
    private ICache contactCache;
    public ContactsController(ICache    theCache) {
        this.contactCache = theCache;
    }
}
```

At first glance, this solves the coupling problem. But, in reality, this transfers the burden to the client. In many cases, the client really does not care what type of cache you use.

The IOC/DI pattern allows the application framework to inject these dependencies, rather than the preceding two options. Spring is a popular example of such a Java application framework, and include, besides the DI, and other features such as transactions support, persistence frameworks, and messaging abstractions. The preceding code can be succinctly represented in Spring as follows:

```
public class ContactsController {
    @Autowired
    private ICache contactCache;
    public ContactsController() {
    }
}
```

Such powerful frameworks make writing large-scale code easy. Here, the `@Autowired` Spring annotation searches for a bean (object instance) that matches the definition and injects its reference into the object of `ContactsController` (which itself should be maintained by Spring).

- **Performance**: The JVM continues to be the subject of multiple optimizations to enable high performance. For example, it contains a Hotspot, **just-in-time** (**JIT**) compiler that translates frequently executed/performance-critical bytecode instructions into native code instructions. This avoids the slower interpretation that otherwise would have ensued.
- Awesome IDE support, including the open source Eclipse project and the *freemium* IntelliJ.

These types of features have made Java one of the predominant languages not just in backend systems but also in applications (Android).

One question you might have is regarding the name of the IoC pattern. You're probably wondering, *what exactly are we inverting?*

To answer the history behind the name, consider the early UI applications. They had a main program that initialized a bunch of components that drove individual UI elements. The main program would drive the whole program, plumbing data and control between the components. This was quite cumbersome coding. After a few years, UI frameworks were developed that encapsulated the main function, and you as an application developer provided event handlers for various UI elements.

This increased the productivity of developer as they were now focused on the business logic rather than coding the plumbing. Essentially, the program control went from the code that the developer wrote to the framework. This came to be known as IoC.

As with all good things in life, there is a flip side (although some points might be controversial). There are a few quirks with the Java ecosystem:

- **Verbosity:** Java code tends to be very verbose. Recent inclusions in the language specification, such as lambdas and related functional programming primitives, are targeted to alleviate this. But still Java code tends to be very verbose.
- **Opaqueness:** Powerful frameworks sometimes abstract out key aspects. For example, consider the new, shiny parallel stream feature in Java. It is one of the features that were added to reduce verbosity. But one gotcha here is that all parallel streams in the program use the same thread pool (ForkJoinPool.commonPool). This default causes a scalability bottleneck as all the parallel streams in the code contend for threads from the same pool!

There is a trick to solve this by defining a custom thread pool, like so:

```
final List<Integer>   input = Arrays.asList(1,2,3,4,5);
          ForkJoinPool newForkJoinPool   = new ForkJoinPool(5);
          Thread t2 = new Thread(() ->   newForkJoinPool.submit(() -> {
              input.parallelStream().forEach(n   -> {
                 try {
                     Thread.sleep(5);
                      System.out.println("In   : " +
Thread.currentThread());
                 } catch    (InterruptedException e) {
                 }
              });
          }).invoke());
```

- **Complexity/Over-Engineering:** Java's powerful constructs, including generics, can sometimes lead to *cute code*, which is unmanageable in the long run. This includes the definition of tall inheritance hierarchies that, besides making code difficult to read/understand, also make the system brittle due to the fragile base class problem. Frameworks such as Spring have become so complex that now the only way to use them reliably is to have a framework-over-the-framework such as Spring Boot (which gives a set of working libraries with sensible defaults for various tuneables). This creates a new set of threads to run the data computation of the stream, but interestingly the common-thread pool is also used along with the new thread pool.

- **Deployment Challenges:** The amount of resources needed by a Java process is not always clear. For example, Java developers define the Java heap size using the -Xmx and -Xms options (where mx is the maximum size of the heap and ms is the initial size). This heap is used for the allocation of objects within your Java code. Besides this, there is another heap that the Java process uses! Called the Native heap, this is the heap used by the JVM for its needs, which includes things such as JIT and NIO. So you need to carefully profile an application in a specific deployment context (basically dampening the platform-independence feature).
- **Developer Productivity:** Because of the verbose nature of Java and the need to deploy/test (the compiler rarely catches interesting bugs), a lot of developer time is spent orchestrating/waiting for the `dev/test` cycle. Frameworks such as Spring Boot have made things better, but still the productivity in no way in the league of Python or Go. You need active IDE support to have a chance of being productive.

The primary reasons people want to switch from Java to Go are resource efficiency, concurrent modeling, and developer productivity. There are many Java *purists* that still say Java is for web applications and Go is for system software, but in the world of microservices and API-driven development, this distinction is quickly disappearing.

As with Python, the journey from Java to Go will not be without its gotchas:

- **Pointers:** Java programmers generally are not used to dealing with pointers. They often make mistakes when using them—for example when deciding to passed a variable by reference or by value (in Java, everything is pass by reference).
- **Error handling:** Similar to Python, error-handling in Go and the lack of try-catch-finally can make the program verbose. It may also lead to the program working on the wrong data if errors are not caught for every function in a disciplined way.
- **Lack of generics:** Java programmers are so used to generics (at least using them, if not defining them) that it takes time to think in the Go way of doing things. There will be some time for which developers would feel inhibited.
- **Lack of Spring-like IoC frameworks:** Developers in Go typically define a main function that initializes and kicks off the computation in the program. You can engineer the distributed initialization using the `init()` function, but this generally leads to race conditions in big programs, so invariably you fall back to coding the main driver program.

- `new` and `make`: Though Golang touts simplicity/brevity, sometimes there are quirks. For example, the built-in `new()` function can be used to allocate zeroed storage of a type (new is common keyword in many languages). Go also has the `make()` function, which is a special built-in allocation function that is used to initialize slices, maps, and channels. A common, and deadly, mistake is to use new instead of make for something, such as a map, which later manifests as a panic when trying to access the uninitialized map.
- **Performance:** While Go is native and Java is mostly interpreted, there is still not a sizeable gap in the performance of the programs in both languages yet. This is because of the 20+ years of performance-engineering that has gone into the JVM and techniques such as the JIT compilation.

Migration strategy

In the previous section, we saw a few reasons why people might want to migrate to Go. This section talks about formulating a strategy for such a migration of existing code to Go.

Phase 1 – Learning Go

The first step is to ensure that all developers understand Go. In most projects, there will be at least a few developers who are not experienced Go programmers. By *understand*, I mean not just the theoretical part, but actually trying out various programming constructs to get a feel for the language. `https://tour.golang.org/` is a good start. Effective Go (`https://golang.org/doc/effective_go.html`) is another good resource for learning about the language. Besides an introduction, it also talks about best practices (package-naming convention, state-sharing, and so on).

In addition to learning your way around the language, it is also good to read some non-trivial Go code. You can find this on a lot of projects in GitHub, including the Docker source and the standard library. I find the `bytes/buffer.go` code (`https://golang.org/src/bytes/buffer.go`) is particularly well written/documented.

Installing Go on a laptop is easy for all standard distributions. But I recommend using **Go version manager** (**GVM**) to easily allow you to navigate `versions/GOROOTs/GOHOMEs`.

Phase 2 – Piloting a service

Once you understand Go, the next step would be to pilot migration on one of the services in your application. A common mistake is to take the simplest service as this defeats the purpose of learning anything from the pilot. You should pick something that clearly identifies the Go value proposition for your product.

The ideal service should be something that involves a lot of concurrency/orchestration, such as a web-facade API. They generally also have some persistence, allowing you to experience first-hand Go workings with DBs/ORMs. An API-based service also allows phased dial-up of traffic from the old to this new service—for example, in the travel website example, you can take traffic for hotels in a specific city on this new stack.

Phase 3 – Defining packages

Once you pick the service, the next step is to create the basic project layout and the packages for the Go port. This should not be too tough, particularly if the current code is well packaged. Keep an eye out for things such as circular imports. At the end, you should have a package structure that describes the main components of the service. This is also a good time to engineer the build harness, including writing the Makefile and architecting the dependency-management prerequisites.

Phase 4 – Porting main

Now you can port the main part of the service. You should delegate all the details to the packages, but the main program should spell out the control-flow in the program. For example, in a REST API service, the main would define the main router, a health check endpoint, and various router groups (like in Gin) for each resource, where each resource is inside its own package. Now, finally, you should be able to run your service.

This is also the time to write tests. Since most of the packages are mocked, it is expected that many tests will fail. This is the central tenet of test-driven development—write tests first and then code till the tests start passing.

Phase 5 – Porting packages

Phase 4 and *Phase 5* need to be done one after the other for each package.

Each package we've defined must now be ported from the original source to Go. This work can be distributed efficiently among multiple developers, with each team typically working off its own branch.

There might be a few decisions to make here, especially if the source includes things such as generics. We should list down the principles before starting coding. For example, for generics, the options for porting include the following:

- Check whether generic classes are really used or can be flattened out. Often, the generic code is just so that the earlier developer could try out a cool, new trick they had learned from a blog, rather than a real requirement in the code.
- Explode the generics into specific implementations. If the generics class is used for a few specific purposes, just bite the bullet and create two implementations. A real-life example can be found in the strings and bytes packages of the standard library: both have very similar APIs but different implementations.
- Engineer the generic nature using an interface. This involves the following:
  - Listing the set of operations that the generic algorithm or container needs
  - Defining an interface with these methods
  - Implementing the interface for each instantiation of the generic in the source
- Use `interface{}`, this allows us to store generic types in a reference. If the original generic does not care about the actual type of the data being stored, using an interface with a type assertion at the client can lead to generic Go code (https://github.com/cookingkode/worktree/blob/master/worktree.go). The downside of this technique is that we lose the compile-time type-checking and increase the risk of runtime type-related failures.
- Use a code generator, there are many tools, such as genny (https://github.com/cheekybits/genny), that take a template and then generate type-specific code. For example, the following code defines a template for a generic list type:

```
package list
import "github.com/cheekybits/genny/generic"
//go:generate genny -in=template.go -out=list-unit.go    gen "Element=uint"
type Element generic.Type

type ElementList struct {
        list []Element
```

```
}
func NewElementList() *ElementList {
        return &ElementList{list:    []Element{}}
}
func (l *ElementList) Add(v Element) {
        l.list = append(l.list, v)
}
func (l *ElementList) Get() Element {
        r := l.list[0]
        l.list = l.list[1:]
        return r
}
```

Here, Element is an identifier for the generic type. The Go generate comment causes Go generate to generate unit-specific code in a separate file, called `list-unit.go`. The generated code looks like this:

```
// This file was automatically generated   by genny.
// Any changes will be lost if this file   is regenerated.
// see   https://github.com/cheekybits/genny
package list
type UintList struct {
        list []uint
}
func NewUintList() *UintList {
        return &UintList{list:    []uint{}}
}
func (l *UintList) Add(v uint) {
        l.list = append(l.list, v)
}
func (l *UintList) Get() uint {
        r := l.list[0]
        l.list = l.list[1:]
        return r
}
```

The client can then use this `UintList` through a normal import. As seen, code generators such as this allow you to write effectively generic code.

Phase 6 – Improving computation

In the initial port, the concurrency might not be obvious. You need to carefully infer/reverse-engineer concurrency/simplification opportunities from the current code. For example, you might have coded a sequential list of functions that actually don't need to be executed in the given order, that is, they can be run concurrently. In other cases, you might have code (such as cleanup) that can be done after the function returns. This can be efficiently coded using the `defer()` keyword.

The tests that you wrote in *Phase 3* will help you avoid regressions and thus allow you to experiment with multiple levels of concurrency.

Having seen a strategy for migration, let's look at the final (but actually, the most important) part of migrating applications—building an awesome team to get the job done.

Building a team

When contemplating the migration of applications, one key concern for management is availability of talent/developers. Fortunately, Go is a very simple and easy-to-learn language, and if you have good engineers, they will pick it up quickly. The *Phase 1 – Learning Go* subsection of the *Migration strategy* section mentions some learning resources. In my experience, people get productive within a week of starting hands-on experiments.

 Another good resource is the Go Proverbs list (`https://go-proverbs.github.io/`). It provides a set of pithy recommendations; some of them, such as "the bigger the interface, the weaker the abstraction," are pretty profound.

The flip side is that there is high demand for Go programmers. So once you train them, remember to keep the developers energized and engaged. When interviewing developers for the team, what has worked for me is hiring developers who have great basic computer science skills and programming ability. A knowledge of multithreading, deadlocks, and synchronization primitives are also essential for non-trivial Go programs. On multiple occasions, I've found it easy to build a team of developers from non-Go backgrounds, teach them Go, and then get things done. The following plot shows median salary of developers using different languages and their programming experience:

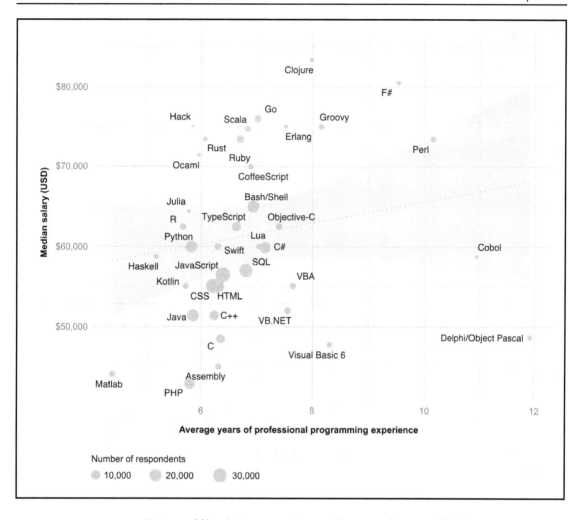

Reference: https://insights.stackoverflow.com/survey/2018

Summary

For the almost nine years since its inception, the popularity of Go keeps growing. The following Google Trends graph is another good indicator of the exponential growth in the interest of the language:

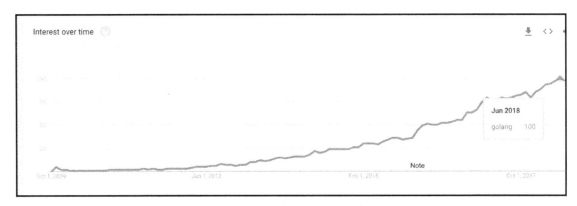

Reference: https://trends.google.com/trends/explore?date=2009-10-01%202018-07-30&q=golang&hl=en-US

In this chapter, we looked at how you can go about learning Go, building a team, and migrating applications to Go.

This is the last chapter in our study of Go. I hope you enjoyed reading, and at the very least got an alternative view of programming. As Alan Perlis said, in the dated-but-relevant *Epigrams of Programming* (`http://pu.inf.uni-tuebingen.de/users/klaeren/epigrams.html`), *"A language that doesn't affect the way you think about programming is not worth knowing."*

Other Books You May Enjoy

If you enjoyed this book, you may be interested in these other books by Packt:

Hands-On Serverless Applications with Go
Mohamed Labouardy

ISBN: 9781789134612

- Understand how AWS Lambda works and use it to create an application
- Understand how to scale up serverless applications
- Design a cost-effective serverless application in AWS
- Build a highly scalable and fault-tolerant CI/CD pipeline
- Understand how to troubleshoot and monitor serverless apps in AWS
- Discover the working of APIs and single page applications
- Build a production-ready serverless application in Go

Mastering Go
Mihalis Tsoukalos

ISBN: 9781788626545

- Understand the design choices of Golang syntax
- Know enough Go internals to be able to optimize Golang code
- Appreciate concurrency models available in Golang
- Understand the interplay of systems and networking code
- Write server-level code that plays well in all environments
- Understand the context and appropriate use of Go data types and data structures

Leave a review - let other readers know what you think

Please share your thoughts on this book with others by leaving a review on the site that you bought it from. If you purchased the book from Amazon, please leave us an honest review on this book's Amazon page. This is vital so that other potential readers can see and use your unbiased opinion to make purchasing decisions, we can understand what our customers think about our products, and our authors can see your feedback on the title that they have worked with Packt to create. It will only take a few minutes of your time, but is valuable to other potential customers, our authors, and Packt. Thank you!

Index

R

Radix
  reference 309
Raft 166
receiver 49
recovery-point objective (RPO) 370
recovery-time objective (RTO) 370
Red-Black Tree 114
Redigo
  reference 309
Redis
  about 304
  architecture 304, 305
  clustering 308
  data structures 305
  Golang usage 309, 310
  persistence 306, 307
  use cases 308, 309
Relational Database Service (RDS)
  reference 442
relational model 278
reliability metrics
  about 328
  dynamic metrics 329
  static metrics 330
reliability verification
  about 347, 348
  integration tests 351
  performance tests 352
  UI tests 352
  unit tests 349, 350
Representational State Transfer (REST)
  about 141, 238
  constraints 239
request-reply pattern 217
requests per second (RPS) 447
Resilient Distributed Dataset (RDD) 180
REST (Representational State Transfer) paradigm
  128
REST service
  building, Gin used 243
reverse proxies 414
RFC 5988
  reference 242
Richardson Maturity Model

about 240
  HTTP verbs 241
  hypermedia controls 241
  resources 241
  swamp of POX 241
round-trip-time (RTT) 123
router group 246

S

Sarama cluster library
  reference 400
Sarama
  reference 201
scalability bottlenecks
  about 118
  C10K problem 118
  Thundering Herd problem 120
scaling algorithms
  about 107
  complexity 107, 108, 109, 110
  distributed algorithms 111
scaling data performance
  denormalization 323, 324, 325
  materialized views 325
  patterns 322
  sharding 323
scaling systems
  about 129
  X-axis scaling 130
  Y-axis scaling 131
  Z-axis scaling 135
Schema Definition Language (SDL) 253
search functionality, travel website case study
  flights 379, 380, 381, 383, 384, 386, 389
  hotels 389, 390, 392
second normal form 279, 280
security threats
  about 445
  Cross-Site Scripting (XSS) 445
  Denial of Service 445
  injection attacks 445
  sensitive data leakage 445
  weak authentication 445
sensitive data leakage 445
server-side discovery 146

www.ingramcontent.com/pod-product-compliance
Lightning Source LLC
Chambersburg PA
CBHW060641060326
40690CB00020B/4474